CW00958042

Meme Wars

Meme Wars

*The Untold Story of the Online Battles Upending
Democracy in America*

Joan Donovan, Emily Dreyfuss, Brian Friedberg

BLOOMSBURY PUBLISHING

NEW YORK · LONDON · OXFORD · NEW DELHI · SYDNEY

BLOOMSBURY PUBLISHING
Bloomsbury Publishing Inc.
1385 Broadway, New York, NY 10018, USA

BLOOMSBURY, BLOOMSBURY PUBLISHING, and the Diana logo are
trademarks of Bloomsbury Publishing Plc

First published in the United States 2022

Copyright © Joan Donovan, Emily Dreyfuss, Brian Friedberg, 2022

All rights reserved. No part of this publication may be reproduced or transmitted in
any form or by any means, electronic or mechanical, including photocopying,
recording, or any information storage or retrieval system, without prior
permission in writing from the publishers.

Bloomsbury Publishing Plc does not have any control over, or responsibility for, any
third-party websites referred to or in this book. All internet addresses given in this
book were correct at the time of going to press. The author and publisher regret any
inconvenience caused if addresses have changed or sites have ceased to exist, but can
accept no responsibility for any such changes.

ISBN: HB: 978-1-63557-863-8; EBOOK: 978-1-63557-864-5

LIBRARY OF CONGRESS CATALOGING-IN-PUBLICATION DATA IS AVAILABLE

2 4 6 8 10 9 7 5 3 1

Typeset by Westchester Publishing Services
Printed and bound in the U.S.A.

To find out more about our authors and books visit www.bloomsbury.com and
sign up for our newsletters.

Bloomsbury books may be purchased for business or promotional use.
For information on bulk purchases please contact Macmillan Corporate and
Premium Sales Department at specialmarkets@macmillan.com.

CONTENTS

The story you are about to read describes information wars fought about the most controversial and disturbing topics in American culture in the twenty-first century—from heinous anti-Black racism to pedophilia to the "proper" role of women in society to the merits of democracy itself. To tell this story, we rely on direct quotes from the people involved in these wars. Often, these quotes contain offensive or graphic language. We do not present these quotes to horrify, but rather to accurately expose the tenor and content of the online subcultures that have influenced the United States over the last decade. To understand the power, allure, and danger of meme wars, it's imperative that these words be presented as close to verbatim as possible. However, we have redacted the most offensive language, specifically racial slurs, where we can. The information in this book is taken directly from the media output of the people fighting meme wars, including their online posts and video and audio interviews, as well as from journalist reports. But the internet is a problematic historical record because it is ephemeral. Things can be deleted from the internet, intentionally or accidentally. Some of the sources of this information have vanished since we began our research—either because the content was taken down by internet providers or platform companies, was deleted by its author, or because the website it was posted on is no longer online. Every day, more disappears. We have done our best to archive all source material. We hope that this book will serve as a lasting record of the past decade of meme wars online.

Introduction

Don't Tread on Me

"We're storming the Capitol! It's a revolution!" Elizabeth from Knoxville, Tennessee, told a reporter outside the U.S. Capitol on January 6, 2021. She had a blue Trump flag slung across her neck like a cape. As soon as she entered the Capitol, she tearfully related, police maced her in the face. As she cried into the camera, her fellow rioters walked into the frame carrying American flags, MAGA flags, Trump flags, and the familiar yellow flag with the coiled rattlesnake hissing the warning "Don't Tread on Me."

As soon as this video of Elizabeth hit Twitter, it went viral. Her melodic, plaintive tone, her earnest insistence that she was part of a revolution, even her strange piano-design scarf and flag cape made her memorable. People watching the insurrection unfold live shared video of her with glee. Millions watched the chaos happen in real time—on broadcast TV, social media, and video streams that the rioters themselves dutifully posted. A very real and coordinated attempt to thwart the democratic process of America was also a surreal media spectacle, and Elizabeth was one of the minor characters.

From Twitter to TikTok, Elizabeth became fodder for internet jokes. People remixed the video with autotune. Sleuths spun conspiracies when they noticed that she held a towel with something white and round in it that she rubbed on her red eyes. Was it an onion? some speculated. Maybe Elizabeth was a liar who hadn't really been maced, and perhaps the whole insurrection had been planned (it was, but not in the way these conspiracists meant) or was a hoax (it wasn't).

Elizabeth from Knoxville had been memed. No longer a person with a real identity, now Elizabeth from Knoxville was a character, a memorable piece of media that resonated with people for different reasons. The video clip of her was recontextualized, remixed, and redistributed, carrying all sorts of meaning. That's the definition of a meme, first coined by the biologist Richard Dawkins in his 1976 text *The Selfish Gene.* Supporters of the insurrection shared internet memes that focused on how Elizabeth had been treated badly by the police. People who thought the insurrection was a terrifying breach of democracy shared memes celebrating her macing, or mocking her impotent rage. These memes made clear what group the sharer was in, which is a key aspect of memes. Memes signify membership in an in-group. Sometimes they are such an inside joke that they are inscrutable to people on the outside. Yet even when they are popular and accessible, they contain a point of view and announce the positioning of the sharer. Elizabeth, in the memes, was an ally or an enemy, depending on where you stood.

She herself was clearly a member of a meme group, as her flag made clear: the MAGA tribe. And it was memes like MAGA that helped bring

Elizabeth to D.C. in the first place. Along with memes like "1776!," which people had been sharing as hashtags and chanting at rallies to indicate that this January day in 2021 was, as Elizabeth had said, a revolution. And memes like the Gadsden flag, that coiled timber rattlesnake on a yellow background, itself one of the oldest memes in American history, born to express the spirit of insurgency. The Gadsden is now associated with the right, but its first iteration was created by Benjamin Franklin in 1754 as a call to unite the colonies during the French and Indian War. The snake, native to America and dignified in its approach to violence because it always warns its prey with a rattle first, was meant to embody the American spirit. It was during the Revolutionary War that the flag turned into the familiar image you see on Twitter profile pictures, bumper stickers, and lawn signs today, designed by a South Carolina politician named Christopher Gadsden (hence the name), and it has over two centuries been adopted by everyone from the Ku Klux Klan to libertarians to women's rights activists. There's a twisted irony that a symbol of resistance to tyranny was used in an insurrection against the democratic government it was created to help form. But it makes sense that this flag would become a symbol for a homegrown insurgency; one hallmark of a lasting meme is its ability to be recontextualized, co-opted, and used against its creators.

Amid the chaos of that day, flags told the story. Insurgents plunged the flagstaff of Old Glory into the building's windows, piercing the glass, and with it the sense of security protecting the seat of government. Rioters paraded a Confederate flag solemnly through the halls, an act that hadn't even happened during the Civil War. Outside, they held up green Kekistan flags, which most people had never seen, proudly claiming the U.S. Congress for the esoteric denizens of a meme-made country that sprang from the bowels of the internet. Plain red or blue flags with two words on them dotted the congregation: TRUMP NATION. And everywhere, the Gadsden, poised to attack.

Many of the men and women holding these banners were dressed for war, in tactical militia uniforms bedazzled with a bricolage of badges and patches, and these too bore the memes that had brought them there. Some wore shirts emblazoned with the letter Q. Others wore patches that said "Veteran of the Meme Wars" or signaled their membership in various militias. All their shirts, patches, and flags marked different factions, from libertarians to white nationalists, symbols signaling different affiliations with common goals, but no centralized leadership. The boldest among them broke into the People's House, battling police, hurling racial epithets, taking selfies, smearing feces, and spilling blood along the way.

The memes played a significant role in mobilizing these troops and inciting the violence. The central idea animating the insurrection—that Trump had been denied his rightful victory in the election—was itself a memetic slogan, #StopTheSteal, a phrase hashtagged, printed on T-shirts, and adopted by politicians and millions of voters. In three short words, #StopTheSteal managed to convey the complicated idea that Joe Biden was an illegitimate president and Donald Trump had been wronged by a powerful system intent on subverting the will of the people, and it announced membership in the MAGA community. In the run-up to that day, memes were shared on Facebook, in chat rooms, and over encrypted messaging apps to drum up excitement and convince more people to head to D.C. In the charging documents from many of the people arrested for participating in January 6, the FBI often included internet memes shared by the insurrectionists as proof of ideology. Posting a meme with the Trump quote "Stand back and stand by" indicated that someone was part of the Proud Boys militia, whereas someone sharing a green Pepe the Frog meme in a post about the insurrection was possibly in the alt-right, that subfaction of extremely online far-right youths who made themselves famous in the 2016 election by "memeing the president into office."

Internet Subcultures in the Light of Day

These internet subcultures that had thrived in relative obscurity in the overlooked corners of the internet dramatically came into the light of day on January 6. Everyone watching CNN at home—which had its highest rating day ever during the insurrection—was suddenly seeing groups of people together in real life who had found each other and formed a community of like-mindedness online. These communities had been having a profound impact on American society for decades—mainstreaming fringe ideas through the sharing of memes, trolling celebrities and journalists and politicians, and generally getting up to all sorts of planned mayhem—but were largely unknown to most Americans until they emerged from the wires of the internet and showed up on the Capitol steps that day.

They came because they were summoned. And the person summoning them was himself a living, breathing meme: President Donald Trump. He embodied insurgency with every aspect of his behavior. He had embraced these communities during his first run. He retweeted them with gusto despite the press calling him out for it. He refused to disavow them. He said they were very nice people. He embodied their grievances even as he actually belonged to the wealthy elite. His face was already a popular meme on their message boards. He spoke their language and treated them with respect. Trump told these far-right fringe factions over and over, in tweets and speeches, to come to the Capitol that day to "fight like hell." It was a fight they had already been engaged in online, attacking Trump's enemies, spreading his lies, amplifying conspiracies that would help him reach his goal, believing theories like QAnon that existed solely to make him look all-powerful. When their meme general asked them to bring that war to Washington, D.C., they took buses, drove caravans, chartered private jets, and showed up.

Never before had all these factions been assembled in real life together. The closest they had come were Trump rallies during his campaign and presidency, or perhaps the 2017 Unite the Right rally in Charlottesville, which ended in a homicide, many arrests, and the destruction of the so-called alt-right coalition, as you will read in chapter 6. The horde who breached the Capitol were not the alt-right, though some alt-righters were there, nor were they GOP supporters, though some of them were there, too. They were not a homogeneous group of extremists but rather a collection of far-right and conspiratorial factions united by three things: extreme dissatisfaction with the status quo in America and their place in it; an aversion to or hatred of mainstream news and a corresponding preference for media that consisted of social networks and partisan outlets; and a loyalty to Trump. Aside from that, they disagreed on a lot. Some hated Jews, while others hated Jews a little but hated Black people more. Some hated women, some hated an imaginary evil cabal of

baby eaters. Some believed the Constitution gave them the right to be sovereign over themselves, some were anarchists, and some were even monarchists. Members of the Korean American cult the Moonies were even there.

But as you watched these insurrectionists swarm the Capitol, climb walls, and break into buildings with the barricades they had dismantled, as you watched them set up a gallows on the Capitol steps and chant "Hang Mike Pence," you would have been forgiven for not being able to tell the groups apart. Unless you'd been watching these subfactions closely for years—watching their YouTube channels, reading their forum conversations, following them on social media apps like Twitter and Gab, tuning into their podcasts, tracking their dramas—it would be extremely difficult to differentiate them.

From Ivory Tower to 4Chan

We were watching. We are a team of three researchers from the Harvard Shorenstein Center on Media, Politics and Public Policy, and by January 6 we had spent the past year together on the Technology and Social Change team monitoring these groups, and many previous years researching them. It's uncommon for a book to have three authors, but in this case it was essential, as we each bring to this text a specific research method and insight to answering this question: What led American culture to the point of insurrection?

Joan Donovan, PhD, is the research director at the Shorenstein Center and a sociologist who studies technology and social movements. Dr. Donovan wrote her doctoral thesis on the technology used by the Occupy Wall Street protesters and is well known for her pioneering research into how white supremacists used DNA testing to advocate for a white nation. She is the creator of the life-cycle model of media manipulation, which allows journalists and researchers to trace disinformation campaigns (as well as other manipulations). Dr. Donovan is also a former punk rocker and the co-inventor of the Beaver emoji. And she's technically Brian and Emily's boss, but for the purposes of this book, we're all just authors. You need to know this level of detail about us, because as you read this book you're likely going to ask yourself: What kind of crazy people would spend all this time watching these communities? Transcribing their hate speech? Learning their grievances and lingo? Watching their videos and tuning in to their podcasts? And how could anyone do such a thing without being members of these groups, or at least ideologically aligned?

The answer is, we three are all varying forms of extremely online weirdos, whose journeys to Harvard were by no means straight lines or foregone conclusions, and who have just the right amount of internet-induced brainworms, existential dread, and curiosity to be mostly immune to dogmatism—and dogmatism is a requirement for entry into many of the subcultures in this book. You have to believe. Even if the thing you believe is that nothing matters and you might as well burn the world down as you cackle with laughter, you have to believe. The belief we hold in common is that this work matters.

Brian Friedberg is an ethnographer, educated in anthropology and cultural studies, who has immersed himself in these subcultures for years, letting their words and images and feelings wash over him, getting his news from their sources. Ethnographers, documentarians of culture, are not there to participate, pass judgment, or misrepresent their subjects. They are there to witness, to understand, and to capture the ethos of a community. Brian was working as a professional musician when he first began digging deeply into lesser known but highly active groups online, and eventually he became a full-time internet researcher, working with Joan. Much of the primary source material for the early chapters of this book comes from fastidious notes he took each week as these events were unfolding.

When Emily Dreyfuss first began working with Joan and Brian in early 2020, she couldn't understand half the things they said. Meme war? Never met her. Emily is a technology journalist, best known for her tenure at *Wired* magazine, where she edited culture, political, and cyber-security stories and reported on the impact of technology on people's lives. In comparison with her two coauthors, she's also a normie—an extremely online normie, but a normie nonetheless. If you're unfamiliar with that label, it basically means someone who isn't steeped in internet subcultures. It used to mean anyone who wasn't online, but everyone is online now, so think of it like this: normies are on Instagram and Twitter, not the 4chan message boards where many of the events of this book took place. Emily spent most of the decade you will soon be reading about carefully avoiding caring about memes. Memes seemed to her to be inherently facile, dumb pictures of cats, jokes for jokesters, meant to alienate outsiders with their in-jokeyness and preach to the (dumb) choir with their humor. But when she was covering the 2016 presidential election for *Wired*, she began to realize her error. Memes, more than Hillary Clinton's emails, appeared to be deciding the fate of America. She began to pay much closer attention. If you're a normie, too, know that you have a companion on your journey through this book.

Together, the three authors will be your guide down the rabbit hole, as Virgil once guided Dante down to a figurative hell, only in this case that hell is real, an underworld composed of ones and zeros that change the foundation of the world, and rather than a Roman poet, your guides are three writers obsessed with media and politics.

While our individual pathways to this work give us different perspectives and political opinions, all three of us share a core belief that when people talk about politics, they are really talking about media about politics. And you can't talk about media without social media and the internet, which changed the way media is created, disseminated, and absorbed. It is for this reason that this book is filled with the alternative political media of our age—memes, and the artifacts and social media postings of the people who made them, shared them, and hypnotized others with them. This is a history book about a period that is still happening, which uses media—from news reports to forum posts and songs—to reveal the method behind so much of the current madness.

This book is a living history. It documents events you lived through and which impacted your life in large and small ways, but this isn't a story you are likely to know already. We will take you inside these subcultures whose wars raged below the surface of mainstream awareness. In these wars, the weapons were memes, slogans, ideas; the tactics were internet-enabled threats like swarms, doxes, brigades, disinformation, and media-manipulation campaigns; and the strategy of the warriors was to move their influence from the wires (the internet) to the weeds (the real world) by trading fringe ideas up the partisan media ecosystem and into mainstream culture. We'll explain what all of those things are in the pages to come. Much of this book will likely be new to you as these events transpired far, far down the rabbit hole where most people are lucky enough to never venture.

On January 6, pundits and people across America and the globe were shocked by what they saw. How could this be happening? How had we gotten to this point? What the hell was going on in American society? We were not shocked. For those who had been watching these communities—and we are far from alone; there is a wide community of internet researchers, journalists, and civil society organizations who watch these communities closely—the events of that day were entirely foreseeable. They were tragic. And sad. But they were not unexpected.

The simple reason for that is that the meme wars you are about to learn about have been tremendously successful, even as they largely ruined the lives of the people who directly engaged in them. The most powerful meme warriors now face indictment, prison, bankruptcy, and loss of family and identity, but their ideas, carried into the bloodstream of our society through memes, persist: Learn to code. It's about ethics in journalism. Race is real. It's OK to be white. Critical race theory. Let's go, Brandon. Blue Lives Matter. A deep state operates extralegally inside the U.S. government.

All of these are ideas born from meme wars.

Meme wars are culture wars, accelerated and intensified because of the infrastructure and incentives of the internet, which trades outrage and extremity as currency, rewards speed and scale, and flattens the experience of the world into a never-ending scroll of images and words, a morass capable of swallowing patience, kindness, and understanding.

But social media did not create culture wars, of course. They've been with us as long as we've had a nation. In his 1991 book *Culture Wars: The Struggle to Define America*, sociologist James Davison Hunter detailed how religious conflicts in America's diverse population evolved into the polarized, traditional-versus-progressive politic dichotomy of the time. While the now-ubiquitous term came from Hunter's analysis, it was popularized by Nixon-administration speechwriter and paleoconservative Pat Buchanan, who co-opted the phrase back in 1992 in a speech he delivered to the Republican National Committee. He shocked the room with his claims that there was a "religious war" raging in America, one as important as the Cold War itself, and that this spiritual enemy was liberalism. This idea was embraced and built upon by media operative and publisher Andrew Breitbart, who evangelized that politics was "downstream of culture," by which he meant that if you can shape the culture, you can shape the politics. Before social media, culture wars were spearheaded by evangelicals or radio personalities like Rush Limbaugh on the right, with progressive social movements like secularism and feminism positioned as their opponents on the left. They were amplified by TV pundits, and argued over on web forums and email chains and in mailers sent to your house. Social media did to the culture wars what spinach did to Popeye—it juiced them up.

Suddenly you didn't need a radio show to get your idea to millions of people. You just needed a viral tweet. You just needed to figure out the desires of a Facebook algorithm programmed to boost outrageous and emotionally stirring ideas, bury nuance far down your feed, and present information from your conspiracist grandmother and information from the *New York Times* in the exact same format, giving you the impression that they were basically the same. And more than that, the advancements of the internet in the twenty-first century and the advent of social media enabled culture warriors from across the country and globe to find each other and to gather together in communal spaces where their ideas could grow. No longer would an Ayn Rand–obsessed teenager in a small liberal town be isolated from other libertarians; now they could just log on and find their people.

Subcultures Against the Status Quo

All kinds found each other. Lovers of plushy toys as well as fans of Japanese manga comic books. Globalist-hating ultraconservatives as well as beatbox hobbyists. The internet is an incredible place to build community around a common interest, however odd or specific. The common interests of the factions of the far right who have reshaped our democracy are fairly simple: they do not trust the system or the establishment in any form. The media? Establishment. The government? Establishment, unless it is being actively run by an "outsider" like Trump, who they believe is himself antiestablishment. Universities, pundits, "officials" of any kind—all of these people who enjoy cultural power and influence—are not to be trusted. This lack of trust in the establishment necessitates the creation of an alternative ecosystem for media and for experts, since even antiestablishmentarians need news and information. Thus the necessity for a far-right media landscape to inform these communities, along with the elevation of far-right influencers on social media, who are positioned as outside the mainstream liberal culture and whose cultural cachet is therefore not a liability but an asset to the communities they cater to. Folks like Alex Jones, whose Infowars community grew out of public television, moved online, and has been encouraged by its leader to #StopTheSteal or harass the parents of murdered children in Sandy Hook, all while turning a tidy profit.

This community building quickly led to communal action, once the fringe cultures of the internet realized they could adopt the tried and true tactics of social movement building, bring them online, and deploy them to accelerate the pace of change. We start our book with the story of Occupy and the ways it inspired the far-right fringe, teaching people like Breitbart and Steve Bannon, his friend and predecessor at far-right alternative news site Breitbart News Network, how to use the participatory nature of the web and the free speech free-for-all of early social media companies to launch culture wars that drew blood. These people learned how to put their audience to work fighting their wars, urging them to share hashtags, pile on to comment sections, retweet, donate, and show up in the street, empowering them to help fight the ultimate battle against the establishment and demanding that they conscript others into this battle.

The meme warriors of the past decade were not initially fighting for a common goal like Stop the Steal. Their grievances were quite specific in most cases, though their solutions were not. Depending on their world-view, those summoned into the meme wars blamed varying enemies: the national banks, capitalism, immigrants coming to "take all our jobs," Communist liberals who wanted everyone to be gay and socialist, and so on. As the meme wars wore on, they became about replacement anxiety—white Americans' anxiety that immigrants and people of other races would displace their position at the top of the social hierarchy, and men's anxiety that women would displace them. Meme wars were also a way to push back against the general despair baked into late-stage capitalism, and the increased physical isolation that was also hastened by the internet. These warriors fought against the shifting definition of masculinity, cultural diversity, and the overreach of a perceived police state. There was no dearth of worries, both real and imagined, to justify these wars. Self-declared racists, sexists, and anarchists fought for what they thought was the best way to solve the perceived wrongs of the status quo. Often this status quo, their enemy, could be boiled down to the idea of neoliberal consensus, aka the mainstream culture, of which both the Republican and Democratic parties were a part, along with all major media outlets, Hollywood, the music industry, universities, and even the public school system.

The people who position themselves against the liberal consensus are insurgent against the presiding American culture, against multiracial liberal democracy and government involvement in social life.

It's essential to be able to talk about these insurgent groups on the right as a whole to discuss their impact, while also recognizing that within this umbrella of antiestablishmentarians there are very specific subfactions. In the book, we use the umbrella term "the red-pilled right" to refer to the collection of factions united by their opposition to the establishment. It is a label that encompasses the different groups of right-wing people online who have been using language, media, and tech-nology to fight a forever war. These are people with varying different political ideologies, all of which are reactionary, most of whose politics can be broadly categorized as libertarian, paleoconservative, or ethnona-tionalist. Subfactions of the red-pilled right include such groups as the alt-right, white nationalists, fascists, incels, men in the manosphere, trolls, red-pilled gamers, New World Order conspiracists, and militias. In mainstream coverage these groups are often discussed interchangeably due to their shared antagonism toward the establishment, which they most often express through hatred of the media. To the red-pilled right, the mainstream media is seen as a guardian and apologist of the establishment, and therefore the enemy.

The term *red pill*, like so many memes, comes from pop culture. Specifically it's from the film *The Matrix*, which was about a world that seemed normal but was actually a computer simulation. The main character is offered a choice between taking two pills: the blue one will allow him to go about in ignorance, enjoying his life, and the red pill will reveal the facade of his reality and the cruelty of his circumstances. He bravely chooses the red pill and can never go back.

The scene hit a nerve in the zeitgeist and this notion of the red pill was adopted by all sorts of different fringe groups simultaneously, who applied it to the specific issues they were passionate about. It first appeared in the Urban Dictionary in 2004, five years after *The Matrix* came out, with a straightforward definition: "'Red pill' became a popular phrase among cyberculture and signified a free-thinking attitude, and a waking up from a 'normal' life of sloth and ignorance." Over time, the term was taken up by right-wing millennials and Gen Xers to describe the ways they believed the media controlled how people get information and what stories even make the news. Now a red pill is anything that suddenly changes your mind about something fundamental to your worldview. For many in the past few years, COVID has become a red pill, for example, leading them to question their assumptions and beliefs about government or health care. Once you take a red pill, there is no going back. You've been "red-pilled." And now that you have awakened to the truth, you have a duty to red-pill others.

In the *Matrix* films, once a character is red-pilled, they are actively at war with the powers that be, who view their knowledge as dangerous in and of itself, since it could awaken all the humans who are living in ignorance and lead to a total uprising. The meme of the red pill has evolved so much that now there are not just red and blue pills but also black pills (which convince you to embrace nihilism) and white pills (which convince you to embrace optimism), and countless other variants.

The many factions of the red-pilled right have different names for the liberal institutions they are opposed to: Zionist Occupied Government, white genocide, the deep state, cultural Marxism, the New World Order, the cabal, the Cathedral, all of which we will explain. But no matter which term is deployed, the message is the same: American society is so steeped in the secular dogma of liberalism that it becomes the very substrate of culture, impossible to see because it's the air we breathe.

We chose the term "red-pilled right" carefully, because it does not ascribe any more commonality between these groups than they have. Many—possibly most—of the people who stormed the Capitol on January 6 had been red-pilled in some way or another. Certainly the rioters who played leading roles in the decade of meme wars before the insurrection had.

As we go through this book, we outline several meme wars that used red-pilled memes as a way to advance sexist, racist, and antisemitic agendas. Red pills often play on people's most deeply held beliefs and seek to draw out contradictions, especially in the liberal consensus. For example, young men's unemployment is explained by immigrants taking "American jobs." The "cancer" called feminism is to blame for lacking a girlfriend; genetic determinism is responsible for racial inequity. To be red-pilled is synonymous with being insurgent against the mainstream media, as the news is controlled by special—and often, in the red-pilleds' minds, Jewish—interests.

For a decade before 2021 this insurgency was expressed in minor online battles—against casting women in a Ghostbusters movie, say—or larger battles against legalizing gay marriage. In Trump the red-pilled insurgency found a political avatar who helped rally a digital army to meme himself into office. But then on January 6, the insurgency became a literal insurrection.

"Meme wars seem to favor insurgencies because, by their nature, they weaken monopolies on narrative and empower challenges to centralized authority," wrote Jacob Siegel for *Vice* in 2017. Meme warlords understand that if you control the narrative about politics, you control everything.

Breitbart was right: politics is downstream of culture. And with the connectivity of the internet, culture is now something that can be much more easily hacked.

Architecture of Subculture

The internet did not cause the insurrection. But it enabled it. The technology of any age in human history shapes the culture of that time. With the advent of agriculture and farming tools, humans developed stationary civilizations and abandoned thousands of years of itinerancy. The printing press made the written word accessible, heralding in the enlightenment. The telephone connected disparate communities, and the television ushered in an era of national culture, so that no longer did towns have little contact with the communities outside themselves; suddenly everyone in a country was watching the same show at night and laughing at the same jokes. A new generic "American accent" was born. Behavior and identity shifted.

So too did the design of the wires and tubes that make up the internet reshape our society and our behavior. The anonymity of the internet made people bold and free, and also able to distance themselves from the impacts of their words. Blogs democratized the publication of long-form words, while social media took the place of many in-person gatherings. Who needed a high school reunion when you had Facebook telling you who got fat and who got divorced? And it turned image-based memes and memetic slogans into a super powerful and efficient method for sharing ideas. Image macros, the most common form of internet meme, in which words are placed over a picture, require little skill to make and share, and are ubiquitous across the social web.

The internet could have been shaped differently. Social media "platforms" were not inevitable. Early social platforms like LiveJournal, BlackPlanet, Friendster, and Myspace were similar to telephone books with the added capacity to share posts, links, and comments. Similarly, today's biggest Silicon Valley tech companies began from modest intentions: a desire to connect people for specific reasons.

But then in 2006, Google's YouTube began to describe itself as a platform, a label that eventually took hold in the public lexicon to describe highly interactive websites with the capacity to upload user-generated content. Platforms wrap together a bunch of older communication technologies from radio, print, and television, alongside personalized content distribution and advertising. Their success is largely owed to a few mutually reinforcing coincidences: broadband, mobile phones, and wifi create a ubiquitous computing environment, where we are all jacked in to the matrix all day long.

There is no more "offline" to speak of. How did this happen? Concurrently with massive uprisings across the globe in 2011, Silicon Valley was still haunted by the specter of the dot-com bubble of the early 2000s, which bankrupted many online shopping companies who were spending far too much on television and print advertising in order to "get big fast" as a business strategy. The "get big fast" idea was simple; the sooner everyone knows your company exists, the more market share your company has early on, ergo market dominance later on. Though this had failed, tech investors didn't abandon the strategy; they adjusted the tactics.

With Web 2.0, social networking sites didn't sell anything, nor did they buy anything. Searching for profit drove design decisions about expanding the user base, remodeling advertising, and converting users into market value. Personal data was an artifact of time spent on these services. By leveraging people's networks and their content, a business plan began to emerge over the course of several years: turn the people into the product and sell their data. The digital economy converted every click, like, share, and mouse movement into "insights," an industry term for the ways marketers track user behavior. Shoshana Zuboff calls this data extraction process "surveillance capitalism," where users' online footprint becomes a valuable commodity. As digital marketing grew as an industry, there was an unmarked shift from social networking into social media. These sound the same, but they are different. The business model of social networking was to connect people to people and litter those pages with ads, but social media connected people to people and to ad-laden "content"—information, pictures, videos, articles, and entertainment—all in one place. The change resulted in a digital economy built on engagement, where content farms and clickbait mimicked the tone and style of news websites, but whose real intention was to make money off advertising. Clickbait ushered in an era of "fake news," which led us to the disinformation age of the 2020s, where it's so hard to tell truth from fact online that bad actors have figured out how to get what they want—be that money or power or something else—by spreading intentionally false information.

As personal data became a cash cow for social media companies, user experience could be tailored to meet the minutiae of user's interests to prolong their time on a site. The consequence was the development of personalized information ecosystems, where platforms centralized and formatted communication streams based on sets of user characteristics. No longer did everyone on the internet see the same information; algorithmic echo chambers shaped individual news feeds and timelines. It's now common for two people sitting side by side to receive very different online recommendations based on their past behaviors online. Political polarization was embedded into the back end of every tool we used to express ourselves, and into the ways we get our news.

But it's not simply that social media delivered content to users. It wasn't just some natural evolution of radio or television, or a means of independent broadcasting. It also became an opportunity for everyone to make money. In 2007 YouTube introduced a profit-sharing model that made average users into content producers. Over the next decade this created an influencer culture, where entrepreneurial creators cultivated networks of followers and subscribers and then monetized them through donations, subscriptions, or sponsored content. Creators, marketers, and activists understood social media as promotional spaces, where the convergence of professionals, hobbyists, and amateurs blended with corporate and grassroots approaches to cultural production and consumption. This mishmash of styles and powers and approaches made for an eclectic collection of personalities and content. In a word, the internet was "weird"—and, for some, profitable.

Some people are still making lots of money off the internet, but it isn't weird anymore. According to ancient internet parlance, the normies used to be the folks who weren't online. Now those people barely exist. The internet is where we do our banking and sign up for COVID tests. The internet itself is normie now. And it is this fact that makes it the perfect terrain for you to be drafted into a meme war. As you go about your day, reading the news, checking your feeds, googling around for businesses, and reading reviews, you might not realize you are walking through a minefield, but you are. Everywhere you traverse, a hole may be hiding—in the form of a hashtag, maybe, or a recommended video—into which you can fall, until you reach the lesser-known corners of the internet, the ones that are still fringe, the ones from which, if the memes are powerful and resonant enough, you may never emerge.

One of the key ways that meme warriors suck people down into these rabbit holes is through the artful use of red pills, which they scatter across the open internet, waiting for you. In this way, red pills are provocative ideas that challenge the status quo, and which meme warriors might send out in tweets, or drop into a comment section, or call in to a radio show to plug. The hope is that you might be driving your car and hear one of these ideas—which often take the form of memes—and your mind will be instantly changed, or at least you'll be curious enough about what you just heard to look into it, following the path into the rabbit hole that your research will lead you down.

The idea of a "rabbit hole" was first put into the popular imagination by author Lewis Carroll, who riffed on the long, winding tunnel systems that rabbits dug in his *Alice in Wonderland*, using it as a metaphor for a pathway to an unusual or unsettling environment. When applied to the internet, *rabbit hole* refers to a path that memes can entice you down as you follow them from website to website, particularly ones that are disturbing or taboo.

Rabbit holes are ultimately just a series of links clicked in succession, and are built into the design of social media. This design confers incredible power on people able to harness what we call the four Rs of media manipulation: repetition, redundancy, responsiveness, and reinforcement. These four Rs are integral to successful memes. *Repetition* is simply the act of posting, reposting, retweeting, linking, or sharing to circulate content to the widest possible audience instantaneously. Repeating something ad nauseam plays into our cognitive biases and gives the impression that the thing being repeated is important and legitimate, especially if the viewer sees the same or similar content with lots of engagement over the course of a few days. *Redundancy* occurs when content is shared across multiple platforms. Repetition and redundancy online can produce "connective action," which refers to the ability of a loosely affiliated group to take action together without knowing one another, as with hashtag movements. *Responsiveness* refers to the reactions that posts evoke, such as comments, likes, hearts, or retweets, which signal excitement about a particular topic. Social media is the only form of mass media where there is consistent interaction on a range of topics. This can be positive—or disastrous, leading to coordinated harassment or the recruitment of white supremacists and extremists. Responding brings communities together in replies, where more and more context and discussion occurs. Finally, *reinforcement* is conferred upon a topic by algorithms, which personalize experiences for users and promote similar types of content in recommendation and search returns. If you can game the algorithm such that it surfaces your ideas, as opposed to others', then you'll be more likely to win your meme war. The choices made by reinforcement algorithms are based on data collected about the users' interactions on the platform and across the web. Specific and unique keywords, like QAnon and #StopTheSteal, or names like Donald Trump, Rudy Giuliani, Steve Bannon, or Joe Biden, become turf wars where influencers, activists, governments, political operatives, journalists, and marketers battle it out for dominance in trending, recommendations, and search results.

While technology can help explain how people share media, it's culture that explains why. When analyzing memes, and in our research specifically memes about politics, messaging that resonates within and across different groups often encapsulates a history that resonates with their experience but is often wholly unrecognizable to most people in the outsider group. As the scholar Whitney Phillips explains, the collective resonance of memes takes hold when "something about a given image or phrase or video or whatever lines up with an already-established set of linguistic and cultural norms."

There may be no better example of the way the internet accelerates and enables the creation of subcultures, and the feeling of fun and chaos and creativity that this entails, than the community on 4chan called Politically Incorrect, or /pol/ for short. The site began in 2003 and has remained largely unchanged, a repository of internet history and a breeding ground for ideas, offenses, and counterculture. This book will reference the anonymous users on this active message board repeatedly as a kind of Greek chorus, giving a peek into the way extremely online fringe people viewed these events as they unfolded, and their notorious influence on public conversation via media stunts, pranks, and anonymous harassment campaigns.

From the Wires to the Weeds

All of this design baked into social media makes it a perfect mechanism for moving fringe ideas toward the mainstream over time. Political fringe ideas expressed online move from the internet into public space; and conversely, public events shape online coordination. We describe this as "going from the wires to the weeds," where interactions online (in the wires) impact behavior in the real world (the weeds).

There are two ways this can happen. The first is simple: someone makes an appeal online for people to show up and do something in real life (wires), and they do (weeds). Maybe it has an impact, maybe not. But it manifests in the physical world in some way, only to retreat back to the wires as the event ends, failing to have a broader and lasting impact in the world.

The other way is more complex. In this second way, someone makes an appeal online (wires) that leads to a real-life event (weeds), and at this event violence, conflict, or spectacle breaks out, which leads to media attention, which leads to conversation and action online (wires), which leads to a new event in the real world (weeds), which causes violence or spectacle, which leads to media attention, which leads to online discussion or planning (wires), which leads to another event in real life (weeds). This recursive cycle is a meme war.

Memetic warfare was an inevitable outcome of mixing propaganda with the velocity, novelty, and great rabbit hole of the internet. Before the internet, information control was considered one of the most important powers of any government. The 2016 election raised the alarm that social media had upended the government's ability to guard against informational attacks, as evidenced by the attention to Russia's memetic meddling in U.S. politics. But, perhaps much worse, the 2020 election illustrated that social media could be turned against U.S. democracy when wielded by domestic political actors.

To get from memes to meme wars requires political mobilization through community organizing, innovative uses of platforms to scale participation, and the ability to create immersive and subversive content. Meme wars are accelerated by the design of communication infrastructure that favors popularity over quality, a fractured media environment that thrives on sensationalism, and a low barrier to entry and few sanctions for participating.

This book is concerned with the insurgent use of meme wars to fight against the establishment and institutions. As you will see, many groups participate in meme wars. Governments use cyber troops to influence foreign affairs, corporations wage PR battles to sell products, activists launch memetic campaigns to change public opinion, extremists recruit using ironic memes, and conspiracy theorists piggyback their ideas into mainstream conversation with memes. When marketers use social media to grow audiences, it's praised as innovation. When activists rally thousands for public protest using platforms, their tactics are both cheered and criticized. When conspiracy theorists used social media to spread lies and dangerous speculation, this chatter was largely ignored—until Trump took office. In that way, Trump's election was the first social media candidacy that fully adopted meme wars as a campaign messaging strategy. With this strategy came red pills and rabbit holes, the pathway toward insurgency. Memes can convene armies and disarm enemies; they can also mobilize large groups of people when they are fed a steady stream of violence, aggression, and replacement anxiety.

It was a meme war that spilled into the streets of Washington, D.C., that day in January 2021. It was a decade of meme wars that radicalized people, that helped them forge their identities and find their communities, and it was a president and his political operatives who understand the power of meme wars who were able to send a tweet that drafted thousands into a battle against democracy itself. This book tells that story.

Chapter 1

We Are the 99 Percent

Entering the Era of Meme Wars: Occupy Wall Street

The Washington Monument swayed. It was August 23, 2011, and a severe
5.8-magnitude earthquake had just hit Virginia, destabilizing the bedrock
of Washington, D.C.—an unsettling metaphor in the nation's capital at
a time when the country was slowly recovering from the Great Recession
of 2008. Earthquakes were not meant to hit the East Coast. Geologists

called it historical and unprecedented. And yet, like the National Cathedral, damaged in the quake, America's housing market was also not meant to collapse. A Black man with an African father and a Muslim-sounding last name was not meant to be president. And yet here we were. Barack Obama was in the White House, the subprime lending market had decimated the U.S. economy, and tourists posing for selfies at the top of the spire grasped the shaking walls as debris fell on their heads.

The quake dominated the news cycle, but the papers of record took note of baseball scores (the Los Angeles Dodgers beat the St. Louis Cardinals 13 to 6) and box-office reports (the domestic race drama *The Help* was number one in the United States). Reporters covered the news that President Obama granted a temporary deportation reprieve for undocumented immigrants brought into the States as children, paving the way for what would become Deferred Action for Childhood Arrivals (DACA) the next year. But there was no mention in any press of another thing that happened that day: a cryptic video uploaded to YouTube threatening to change the world.

In the one minute and nine seconds of the video, a collage of protest and conflict footage flashed across the screen, overlaid with an illustrated mask modeled after British insurrectionist Guy Fawkes, whose failed plot to bomb the House of Lords in 1605, and his subsequent trial and execution, made him a folk legend. The mask became an icon in American pop culture when Guy Fawkes figured prominently in the 2006 blockbuster anarchist revolutionary drama *V for Vendetta*, itself an adaption of a 1982 graphic novel by Alan Moore.

In the late 2000s this Guy Fawkes mask became the symbol of revolution, and was adopted as something of an unofficial logo by hacker activist collective Anonymous. Sometimes referred to as "hacktivists," the Anonymous collective, composed of a global cadre of extremely online individuals, evolved from a group of scrappy pranksters into a protest collective that used the internet to force social change. In the months preceding August 23, 2011, Anonymous had pulled off high-profile pranks and hacks on Scientology, PayPal, Visa, and Mastercard, and were vocal supporters of the new whistleblower site WikiLeaks. In videos uploaded to YouTube and in memes spread around early social media, Anonymous members donned the Guy Fawkes mask, keeping their anonymity and building a visual brand—one of unlimited reach and total populist fury.

"Fellow citizens of the Internet," a computerized voice announced in this new video, "we are Anonymous. On September 17th, Anonymous will flood into lower Manhattan, set up tents, kitchens, peaceful barricades, and Occupy Wall Street for a few months. Once there, we shall incessantly repeat one simple demand in a plurality of voices. We want freedom. This is a nonviolent protest. We do not encourage violence in any way. The abuse and corruption of corporations, banks, and governments ends here. Join us. We are anonymous. We are legion. We do not forgive. We do not forget. Wall Street. Expect us."

The thing Anonymous wanted to be free from was "the system," the interlocking network of corporate greed and government corruption that screwed the normal people they claimed to be representing. Whoever posted that YouTube video didn't themselves invent Occupy, but they were part of a new media network that mobilized millions of people to join in the largest protest against global capitalism the world had ever seen.

Occupiers were motivated by the economic crises of the Bush and early Obama eras, and inspired by recent revolutionary movements in Northern Africa and Europe. From Tunisia to Egypt to Spain, social media was being used in unprecedented ways to organize mass social movements. These uprisings sought human rights and economic security and were emboldened by the promise posed by technology to create social change.

The Great Recession, the longest global market decline since the Great Depression of the 1930s, had been declared officially "over" in 2009 after newly elected Obama had signed a huge relief package into law, and many of the banks and insurance companies that had preyed on people's hopes and dreams for profit had been bailed out with taxpayer money. The money didn't go into the pockets of the people whose homes were lost. It went into the vaults of the banks that had sold the homes under false pretenses and then confiscated them when people couldn't pay their bills. The median household income in the country had declined for the fourth year in a row, to $50,054, and the average housing price in the country was $219,000. Wages were stagnating, and now, a decade into the twenty-first century, it appeared to many that America had gotten derailed somewhere along the way to greatness.

This feeling had been brewing. The media may have echoed the pronouncements from economists that the recession was over, but in real life, 2009 did not mark the end of the pain for people who lost their jobs, their homes, and their futures. What it did do was create a popular and powerful conservative movement to stymie Obama's planned tax hikes to pay for his stimulus proposal: the Tea Party—a movement born on television and operationalized by Republican professionals who saw in it the chance to create an alternate and powerful narrative about who was to blame for the problems in the country.

On February 19, 2009, CNBC aired footage of on-air editor Rick Santelli making an impassioned populist argument against Obama's tax hikes in a monologue from the floor of the Chicago Mercantile Exchange. "I tell you what, I have an idea, this administration is big on computers and technology, why don't you set up a website to have people vote on the internet as a referendum to see if we really want to subsidize the losers' mortgages." He was met with cheers from the crowd. "This is America! How many of you people want to pay for your neighbor's mortgage?" he demanded. "We're thinking of having a Chicago Tea Party in July. All you capitalists that want to show up to Lake Michigan, I'm going to start organizing."

The video went viral on YouTube immediately. This was a signal to national conservative leaders that Santelli's Tea Party idea was resonating out there with people. The next day, they got on the phone and came up with the Nationwide Tea Party Coalition. A week later, conservative groups around the country organized forty simultaneous Tea Party protests. This was big news, and the attention it got built momentum for a grassroots conservative movement from the edges of the right. On February 28, 2009, only nine days after Santelli first spoke the words "tea party," influential radio host Rush Limbaugh delivered a speech at the annual Conservative Political Action Conference, where Republicans iron out their agenda for the year. Limbaugh praised the Tea Party, saying of the bailouts, "After a while the people paying for it [will say] screw this. We're not putting up with it. And you're going to see—you're already starting to see evidence of these. All the tea parties that are starting to bubble up out there. Those are great. Fabulous." The GOP establishment knew a winning strategy when it saw one, and the Tea Party quickly went from scrappy to institutional.

Older conservatives were engaging in their first online activism, trained by touring Tea Party operatives who taught boomers how to drown out their liberal peers on Facebook through relentless posting, and by leaving negative reviews on liberal and left-wing materials on shopping and movie review sites. They were encouraged to make signs with shareable and shocking images decrying Obama and Beltway politics—what we now would call memes, though the term hadn't quite stuck back in 2009. Online organizing was becoming more important to the American right wing than ever before, and as older Americans moved

online, the web became an important terrain for the insurgent Tea Party Conservatives to occupy and finance.

By the midterms in 2010, the media reported that the Tea Party had completely remade the government—helping to take back the House from Democrats and stealing Senate seats, putting Obama's entire agenda, and potential legacy, in jeopardy. None of this seemed to help people in the country feel any more secure.

On the left, progressives spoke out against Obama's bailouts, drone strikes, and moderate social policy in progressive publications like the *Nation* and *In These Times*, but those articles, op-eds, and occasional TV appearances didn't really move the needle. Obama continued to cater to the middle, hoping for a compromise even after the Tea Party elections had delivered him a Congress prepared to obstruct his every step. By 2011 nothing like the Tea Party had emerged on the left because, well, the left was technically in power. But it wasn't successfully using that power to keep the middle or working class employed. The first *Time* cover of 2011 read "Where the Jobs Are," and went on to describe how some jobs were just never coming back. The *Time* cover for June was more direct: "What Recovery?" Unemployment nationwide was still 8.9 percent, homelessness was getting slightly better but was still pegged at 21 people per 10,000, and the majority of "people" getting handouts seemed to be corporations, who in 2010, with the *Citizens United* Supreme Court decision, now had the capacity to wield more political power than ordinary citizens.

Increasingly, it was clear that the economy wasn't working for a great many people—the financial crisis led to the start of a long decline in the wealth of American families, and widened the already large wealth gap between white households and Black and Hispanic households. As discontent rose across the American political spectrum, only a small percentage of the population saw any relief, benefit, or profit after the financial crises. All of these problems, all of this pain and suffering, all of these banking systems preying on people's vulnerability and politicians making promises they couldn't keep, all of this was happening to the vast majority of Americans, the ones whose lives were not enriched when the stock market rallied. While that elite, the 1 percent, got richer, everyone else just got angrier.

We Are the 99 Percent

This mass of the disenfranchised majority came to be known as the 99 percent, a meme with multiple origins. Anarchist academic David Graeber was using the phrase as a way to critique capitalism in his writing and organizing. Journalist David DeGraw, who ran the independent political news website Amped Status, used it as early as February 15, 2010. DeGraw published the first of a six-part series detailing the specter of financial terrorism, which opened with this proposal: "It's time for 99% of Americans to mobilize and aggressively move on common sense political reforms."

This pissed somebody off. Shortly after DeGraw published, his servers were attacked, taking his site down. He turned to Anonymous for help with both his site and the amplification of the message. They moved the 99 percent idea from indie media to social media.

The term made sense to people. It resonated across countries and even classes, because the pressure of the housing and jobs crisis didn't stop at borders. The phrase was understandable using context cues. And it demarcated a clear in-group and out-group—the 99 percent versus the 1 percent. Later, in the spring of 2011, *Vanity Fair* ran an article by economist Joseph Stiglitz entitled "Of the 1%, by the 1%, for the 1%." Stiglitz laid out the dire straits the vast majority of the country—including the middle class—were in, and argued that such deep income inequality was bad for everyone, even the richest people in the world.

Right around this time, DeGraw and Anonymous made the A99 platform, an independent protosocial network with an anarcho-libertarian political bent. On A99, activists shared information, organized, and remixed memetic propaganda about income inequality. They used the platform to plan what could be considered a dress rehearsal for the first real Occupy Wall Street gathering, called Operation Empire State Rebellion (#OpESR), set for June 14, 2011, using YouTube to spread the word.

It didn't amount to much. #OpESR's location was set for Zuccotti Park because of its proximity to Wall Street, and others were encouraged to hold concurrent protests in their home cities. Despite the online hype, only sixteen people showed up. And just four of them were prepared to camp. Stuck within a small alternative social media platform like A99, the buzz about the protest hadn't spread to more mainstream places like Twitter or Facebook yet.

In August, an amorphous coalition of left-wing activists created a blog called *We Are the 99 Percent* on the microblogging site Tumblr. At the time Tumblr was hugely popular with artists, activists, and other culture makers, because it supported different kinds of spreadable media, including text, video, and images. *We Are the 99 Percent* gave its readers very specific instructions for starting a protest movement, asking people to share photos of who they were and why they were part of the 99 percent. The point was for people to make their own media. People heeded the call.

The Tumblr admins reposted pictures submitted by real people who identified with the growing movement. The first was a selfie of a person in a Guy Fawkes mask, an allusion to Anonymous. Quickly a visual style on the blog emerged that involved a now-familiar format: a picture of someone holding up a piece of paper with writing on it. These words were demands, political statements, messages of support, and usually included some variation of "We are the 99 percent" or "I am the 99 percent." In a short time, thousands of people began taking selfies proclaiming their membership in the 99 percent and sharing them across Twitter, Facebook, Tumblr, and Reddit.

It was in this process of remixing and sharing that We Are the 99 Percent became a meme. It detached from its origin and got amplified by those who saw themselves in the new collective identity it represented. Activists remixed the selfie and turned the meme into a political tool. Authorless by design, the format was sticky and spreadable; individuals could share the blog's domain address, link to individual posts, or repost the images quickly. It also called for collective participation in a way that didn't network people to people, but people to content. Want to be a part of a movement? Take a selfie. You don't have to know each other; you can be united in this meme by your common struggle. That was the most important quality of this meme: the creation of a new identity for those who felt they had nothing left to lose. While others at this time were using social media to flaunt their conspicuous consumption or perfect-looking lives, Occupy made admitting to massive debt somehow cool.

Now that these activists had content to distribute, they needed more attention from the media to build a movement. "I sent [the Tumblr blog] on Twitter to different social media editors, to mainstream magazines. And the social media editor to the *Times* loved it and re-tweeted it and tweeted a little bit more about it. And then it just took off," said one of the Tumblr organizers, Priscilla Grim, in an interview in 2012. "It was really just using just a few different websites that were highly influential for what I was trying to push." She learned firsthand that nothing goes viral on its own; you need people power and attention to grow.

By the summer of 2011, the idea to occupy Wall Street had bubbled up within the 99 Percent coalition. They picked a place and time—again they chose Zuccotti Park in lower Manhattan, because it was close to Wall Street and technically open to the public, but privately owned and thus potentially easier to take over, since the city didn't have jurisdiction. Organizers called people away from their keyboards and into the streets with the memetic infrastructure of #OccupyWallStreet.

An iconic bit of early Occupy propaganda came from the print magazine *Adbusters*, which put together a poster for its July print issue of a horde of hooded anarchists rushing toward a ballerina dancing atop the iconic bull statue that stands on Wall Street. The copy read "What is

our one demand? #OccupyWallStreet September 17th. Bring tent."

Adbusters had been exploring this idea since the events in Tahrir Square, where hundreds of thousands of Egyptians had protested for weeks against the regime of then-president Hosni Mubarak. In June, the magazine had tweeted, "America needs its own Tahrir acampada. Imagine 20,000 people taking over Wall Street indefinitely." The *Adbusters* poster contained no contact information or logo, making it seem authorless and allowing people to define participation on their terms. The only specifics were a date and a hashtag: #OccupyWallStreet. If you wanted to learn what the hell #OccupyWallStreet was, well, you needed to look up the hashtag. The hashtag was also a way for people within the movement to communicate with each other.

The newspaper the *Guardian* coined the term "hashtag activism" to refer to Occupy and other Twitter-based revolutionary movements, noting that the hashtag was used to organize, evangelize, support, and track such movements. The hashtag had been a part of Twitter since 2007, but Occupy activists were trendsetters in using it to build a movement. Hashtags were easy, and they were free. They moved information faster and further than traditional media or advertising, allowing new ideas to reach far bigger audiences quickly and without a ton of legwork. Eventually press outlets, politicians, and influencers would use hashtags, too, but as with many other uses of technology, it started with activists.

As Occupy came together online and in the streets, it remained open-source like the international movements it was inspired by: anyone could volunteer to help organize, offer up ideas to the group, contribute. There was no leader. The first Occupy organizers were a commission of activists who self-sorted into teams. When September 17 rolled around, people actually came. A few hundred people meandered into and out of the park that day, and more came every day after for two weeks, to check out the meme they saw online. For this to turn into an occupation that provoked and challenged state power, though, more people would need to start camping overnight. The movement needed a catalyst to bring in new folks if it was going to have staying power.

So, naturally, a supporter went rogue to create a spectacle—or more specifically, a social media hoax. On September 19, twelve days after the protest began, the movement's "arts and culture team" received an email from a real-looking Gmail account. It made a remarkable offer: Radiohead, perhaps the biggest band in the world at the time, had heard about the protest and wanted to come to Zuccotti and play a free show in solidarity. Now this, Occupy organizers knew, would get people's attention. The very next day they announced at a press conference that Radiohead would be playing a show that night at the camp.

Perhaps no one was more shocked at hearing the confirmation that Radiohead was coming than the guy who sent the fraudulent email. From the comfort of his apartment nearby, twenty-three-year-old Occupy supporter Malcolm Harris couldn't believe it when a friend called to say, "They just confirmed it. Officially. It is confirmed." Harris watched in bemusement as the local media ran with the story, and social media blew up with excitement over the rumor he had planted. Radiohead trended on Twitter. Throngs of fans in the New York area began to flock to Zuccotti. Celebs tweeted about it, some blogs covered it, amplifying the rumor. Social media proved to be a handy tool for attracting attention and circumventing gatekeepers. Harris had exploited the openness of the movement, using imperson-ation to his advantage.

Radiohead had to issue a statement saying, uh, no, they weren't coming. Anonymous tweeted that the concert wasn't happening. But it was too late. Throngs of college-aged social media users went down to Zuccotti that night. Some left annoyed. Others stayed and joined the burgeoning crowd.

In the camp were millennials, Gen Xers, and boomers. There were college students, drug addicts, and union reps. There were the homeless people who moved into the encampments to make use of the food and facilities and ended up being some of the movement's most dedicated protesters. Union members dropped by at lunch to feed the crowds and preach about labor organizing.

Citizen journalists from both the left and right went down to the Occupy encampment and livestreamed what they saw. For many who showed up to the camps, their cell phones quickly turned into political tools. All of this surviving footage—media artifacts, testimony, documentaries, indie media accounts, and on-the-ground reporting—tells the story of an unlikely coalition of people fed up with the status quo, seeking a better world, while at the same time experimenting with technology in ways its inventors never imagined.

These citizen journalists were capturing intimate moments in the camps and spreading them through hashtags at a breakneck speed, creating buzz on social media, distributing livestream links and photos from the ground, and leaving legacy media scrambling to keep up. In fact, mainstream media eventually began to license footage from amateur Occupiers for their broadcasts, paving the way for filming protests live to become a profession.

The movement next got widespread attention on October 1, when thousands of Occupy supporters thronged over the Brooklyn Bridge, and the NYPD arrested seven hundred people. This display of state violence attracted more media, making talk of Occupy go national. Throughout September, October, and November 2011, the movement grew as a cycle of violence from police kept the Occupy protesters beaten, bloodied, and battle-worn—perfect fodder for mainstream and alternative media. When a University of California, Davis, campus police officer pepper-sprayed a small group of protesters at a November nineteenth student protest, witnesses captured footage of the incident from several angles and uploaded it to YouTube. Activist networks shared the videos online, and they promptly went viral, forcing mainstream media to begin covering the protests. Occupiers quickly realized they could set media agendas if they had recorded evidence to offer. Shortly after the pepper spray incident, Anonymous posted a YouTube video containing the name, home address, and phone number of the officer who perpetrated the act, an act of retaliation now referred to as "doxing."

Within weeks, there were over fifteen hundred groups organizing under the #Occupy hashtag across the globe. Occupy and We Are the

99 Percent became viral memes. Encampments sprouted in every continent except Antarctica, from London to Athens, Buenos Aires to Manila, from red states to blue, small towns to big cities. By November, when Occupy was in full swing, *Time* magazine wondered, "Can you still move up in America?" To the people drawn to the Occupy movement, the answer was clearly no.

The process of popularizing ideas has always required creating unlikely alliances, backdoor deals, and a high degree of coordination to find and engage new audiences. While few rose up to defend the 1 percent, the 99 percent clearly had found its people. By using the digital means available, We Are the 99 Percent supporters pushed their meme into popular culture. Celebrities endorsed the movement, politicians incorporated it into speeches, rich people hated it, bands wrote songs about it, and the media, depending on the outlet, loved or hated it. This use of technology to bring together a social movement was a watershed for technopolitical organizing. It presaged everything from #BLM to the #MeToo movement to the insurrection at the Capitol in 2021.

As a meme, We Are the 99 Percent worked to create an in-group and an out-group, and convey a sense that some force was at work on the majority of the population. But in terms of a policy position? It didn't do much. When Occupiers chanted "We are the ninety-nine percent," it wasn't at all clear what they hoped anyone would do about that. This pretty much summed up the overwhelming critique of Occupy, which was that the protesters' grievances were clear, but their demands were unspecific.

The media struggled to cover the Occupy movement because of this vagueness, as well as its vast network of participants and leaderless design. Everyone's voice was just as valid as anyone else's, which left Occupy open to co-option and misrepresentation, both purposefully and accidentally, as the media sought out stories to tell. For example, on September 25, a user of the Occupy Wall Street online message board posted a list of demands. Fox News covered it as if it were a collective statement on behalf of the movement. Later a disclaimer was placed on the post, saying that there was no list of demands. Media pundit Bill Maher called the whole situation "militantly vague."

Slavoj Žižek, a provocative philosopher who gave an impassioned speech at an Occupy camp at the height of the movement, wrote later that Occupy's "fatal weakness" was that "they express an authentic rage which is not able to transform itself into a minimal positive program of socio-political change. They express a spirit of revolt without revolution." Which is to say, it was true that Occupiers could not say what the movement wanted exactly, not only because the ideas were too voluminous but also because the frenetic structure of social media was so chaotic. What was consistent was that the people were going to take up space until someone in power made their lives better or forced them to leave.

And that's what happened. Through cycles of violence, press attention, outrage, in-person events, and hashtags, Occupy moved from the wires to the weeds from city to city until finally the institutions that the Occupiers were demonstrating against had enough. They'd had enough of the chanting, enough of the trash, enough of the tents, enough of the marching, enough of the accounts of belligerence and even violence in the camps, enough of the lines of people getting a hot meal in the middle of the camp or playing music, enough of all of it. By the end of December, mayors across the United States coordinated a massive crackdown on the encampments, with nearly eight thousand arrests. Protesters couldn't get reorganized in city parks. Instead, they retreated back online, using Tumblr and the #Occupy hashtag on Twitter and Facebook to try to make sense of what had just happened and figure out what should happen next.

Two powerful memes were left behind—Occupy itself, a tactic more potent than simply protesting, and We Are the 99 Percent, which highlighted the resentment against elites bubbling up in America's youth—as were two insights for the press and organizers. The media learned how difficult it would be to cover, and keep up with, protest movements in the internet era. And activists now understood that organizing tactics could be spread alongside memes.

End the Fed

Though Occupy is remembered now as a left-wing movement, the coalition wasn't politically monolithic, nor was it supported by the Democratic Party in any institutional way. Even with the culture wars of the era—the fight over gay marriage, for instance—the United States was a less polarized place than it was when Occupy was founded. People could still come together in the streets and yet vote for different candidates. Occupiers were outsiders, of many kinds. Theirs was an open movement, designed to include everyone's voice. This openness was both its greatest strength and its biggest weakness, leaving it vulnerable to partisans seeking to inject their own agendas into the movement.

At many of the Occupy camps, in the early days especially, you could find a popular meme whose origins were decidedly not of the left: the viral slogan "End the Fed." This was a phrase chanted in Zuccotti Park by a faction of Occupiers who loved U.S. congressman Ron Paul. Paulites, as they had come to be known, were passionate libertarians and antiestablishmentarians who had supported Paul's campaign for president in 2008 and now held out hope that Paul might actually win the nomination in the upcoming 2012 election. This was a very long shot.

Paul, a physician turned politician, had served three tenures as a representative from Texas between the years 1976 and 2013. He published many books, including bestsellers *End the Fed* and *Revolution*, and in 1988 briefly abandoned the Republican Party to attempt a run for president as a Libertarian. By the time of Occupy Wall Street he was the most prominent Libertarian in the country, despite never achieving household recognition for most Americans. The campaigns that emerged to support his bids for the highest office in the land were bottom-up, organic, and led by unwaveringly loyal devotees to his ideas. These folks had largely met online.

"I have never seen such a diverse coalition rallying to a single banner," Paul wrote of his supporters. "Republicans, Democrats, Independents, Greens, constitutionalists, whites, blacks, Hispanics, Asian-Americans, antiwar activists, homeschoolers, religious conservatives, freethinkers—all were not only involved, but enthusiastically so. And despite their philosophical differences in some areas, these folks typically found, to their surprise, that they rather liked each other."

Paul and his supporters did not believe in sweeping social reform but rather that the gold standard was sacred, and any government currency inflation unconstitutional. He was obsessed with the failures of the global

Ron Paul REVOLUTION banking system. Because Occupy had no stated goals other than to somehow disrupt the financial system, it was accepting of radical deregulatory positions, such as Paul's belief that if you ended the Federal Reserve, you would save America. Paul spoke to the growing unrest and recognition of wealth inequality among the general public, and identified those in power he held responsible. The physician turned politician wasn't an Occupy supporter per se, but he was sympathetic to the cause, calling it a "very healthy movement." Occupiers and Paulites were both outsiders and had fundamental issues with the system, but as time went on and Occupy's character became very left anarchist, many right libertarians left. But the movements continued to have much in common, and their use of technology would be imitated in the coming meme wars. Most significantly, both movements were outside the mainstream, distrustful of traditional media, and relied on new, alternative media to get word out.

"The internet will provide the alternative to the government/media complex that controls the news and most political propaganda," Ron Paul said in his 2012 farewell to Congress. Internet support was at the core of Paul's 2008 and 2012 campaigns. Paulites were pioneers of using the internet to meet, collaborate, and create alternative media when the mainstream media was, in their opinion, ignoring their candidate. Paulites blamed print and cable news networks like MSNBC and Fox for misinforming Americans and accused these outlets of not taking Paul's policy positions or campaigns seriously. Somewhat ironically, in order to overcome the media they so hated, they had to become the media themselves.

"The online enthusiasm for Paul completely outmatches the rest of the field. Paul's main site, his YouTube channel, his grassroots fan sites and the small hubs of support on left-wing, anti-war sites rattle with extra traffic whenever he appears on TV or in a debate," David Weigel wrote for libertarian magazine *Reason* at the time of Paul's first run.

People found Paul through indie documentaries like Aaron Russo's 2006 *America: Freedom to Fascism*, supporter-created websites, and search results. Supporters wrote the slogan "Google Ron Paul" in chalk on college campuses, printed it on signs, and even flew it on an enormous

blimp. This was meant to be an entrance to a rabbit hole. Before folks could support Ron Paul, they'd need to learn who he was, right? Well, googling "Ron Paul" would lead you to thousands of websites devoted to the presidential hopeful, dwarfing the web presence of any other Republican in the race. These sites were made by passionate acolytes and not associated with the Paul campaign. "The community of websites that was created by the Ron Paul movement is like its own world," one supporter said of the vast network of blogs, websites, forums, Myspace pages, YouTube videos, and the communities on Reddit, Digg, and online gaming spaces that helped spread the campaign's message. Young anti-establishment folks loved him. And so did people his own age. A group called the Granny Warriors used sites like Meetup to connect with other Paul supporters for rallies and campaigns.

"Traditionally in politics you developed your logo and you stay uniformed and everybody does this and you put this on every piece of literature and your TV, bumper stickers, everything else," Paul said in the 2009 film *For Liberty*. "I kept remarking the characteristic of our campaign was there was no characteristic, you know, it was miscella-neous, spontaneous, homemade and all shapes and sizes and colors. And it turned out that it was not uniform and everybody knew it, but it didn't seem to hurt us." Paul supporters weren't as connected in "real life" as they were online, so they had to make their actions count and, ideally, generate press coverage. Instead of using the internet to distribute information and call for community volunteering in a top-down model, which was popular with other politicians, Paul's community was self-organizing from the bottom up.

Along with making their own media, Paulites also turned to alternative media far outside the mainstream. Paul had a strong ally in one of alternative media's most entrenched and infamous broadcasters: Alex Jones. Jones and his Infowarriors praised Paul's commitment to a free and uncensored internet, but Paul's support from the online fringe went well beyond Jones. He was also beloved by some of the internet's most unsavory communities, such as 4chan. This was another glimpse into the future and its potential pitfalls for candidates who dallied with the fringe but who also needed mainstream support.

No website at the time better embodied a truly unrestrained vision of online speech than 4chan. Founded in 2003 by a fifteen-year-old named Christopher Poole, screen name Moot, 4chan mimicked a Japanese imageboard that allowed users to post controversial or copyrighted images accompanied by text on topical boards that would then auto-delete. On 4chan, every user was named Anonymous. In fact, it was on 4chan that the hacktivist collective Anonymous first took shape. The structure of the site was simple but specific: post threads tied together on boards devoted to specific topics, with new threads always beginning with an image post. The design paired with the anonymity of the site accelerated the formation of insular cultures on specific boards, and the site overall. Users were free to post what they wanted in an "anything legal goes" environment, and Poole legally held no responsibility for what was posted beyond that.

The site was moderated for illegal content, but was still littered with pornography, gore, torture, defamation, bombastic screeds, and lots of memes, organized around topics like literature, fitness, anime, and porn. While the majority of 4chan's message boards were intended for entertainment and hobbies, the intentional lack of consistent content moderation attracted many trolls and white nationalists to the site. They saw it as a place to speak approvingly but consequence-free about race and gender-based violence. One board in particular—/new/, their breaking news board—was a hotbed of this sort of increasingly Naziesque rhetoric, much to site owner Poole's concern.

In many ways, 4chan was the precursor to modern platforms like Facebook, Twitter, and Reddit, an infrastructure for interaction between people, though 4chan did not have an algorithm for sorting or recommending content or connections. It drew a large and loyal fan base of daily users and was a nearly perfect platform for making memes and fostering intense conversations along themes and within specific communities. Because it rode the edge of free speech, it quickly developed a reputation as a place where bad things were found, which pushed most people away, but drew others in. During the 2008 campaign, many 4chan posters were drawn to Paul and his libertarian ethos. They posted their support all over the site, including the popular board /new/, which would later be replaced by the Politically Incorrect board, /pol/, and got other anons excited about Paul, who in turn joined the Paul forums. This dynamic helped drive Paul's intense online fan base, and eventually cemented Paul as a hero of this era of 4chan, a meme in his own right.

Paulites on the Ron Paul forums noticed support from 4chan growing. One poster encouraged fellow Paulites to tolerate the site, but warned that it was "the bottom of the internet," and not for the "faint of heart/stomach." Topics in old Paul forums, where the moderators kept everyone focused on Paul, were far more positive than the violent sexual chaos of 4chan. In sloganeering threads, Paulites workshopped new unofficial campaign taglines and images. They may not have known it, but they were trying to meme Paul into the presidency just as anons on /pol/ would for Donald Trump in 2015.

As with Trump, Paul's ascent troubled the conservative establishment. In early January 2008, reporter James Kirchick published an exposé titled "Angry White Man" in the *New Republic*, resurfacing Paul newsletters that contained bigotry and conspiracism, which despite not being written by Paul himself, were nonetheless published under Paul's brand. Paul didn't shy away from the controversy. As Trump would a few years later, Paul saw cable news interviews as a political opportunity and went on CNN to defend his name. "The answer is no. I'm not a racist," he retorted. "This is a bit of a witch hunt. Maybe this is part of the anti–Ron Paul deal." Antimedia sentiment led to alternative media and community building that came together over shared goals and enemies.

It was a dynamic that would go on to be essential in the meme wars to come—even if, as in Paul's case, it didn't achieve its goals.

In February 2012, *GQ* published an article about how steeped in analogies from the film *The Matrix* Paul's libertarianism was. The Paul campaigns had awakened a lot of people who were disengaged from electoral politics, and his philosophies made their way into the Tea Party. "It's kind of like the rabbit hole," one supporter told *GQ*. "Once you do a little bit of research and you listen, it just leads to more and more and more information."

But if Paul had inspired elements of the fringe to create a vibrant grassroots movement, it wasn't enough to break him into the prime time of the Republican nomination. Still, his followers were passionately devoted to him. And they had modeled an internet campaign that showed how otherwise fringe voices could finesse a movement from the wires to the weeds. The whole deal was rich with memes, from End the Fed to the image macro portraying Paul as elder wizard Gandalf from *The Lord of the Rings*, pure in spirit and conviction and in possession of esoteric knowledge and power. The suite of memes the Paulites brainstormed, workshopped, and disseminated were fun, grabbed eyeballs, and helped solidify their movement and community. But by 2012, it was clear to most people—including a growing number of anons on 4chan—that

Paul's campaign was doomed. These anons believed that the Paulites of 2012 were deranged in their optimism.

This idea was encapsulated by the final viral meme of Paul's 2012 campaign: an image of Paul in the final Republican debate, hands raised in the air to wave at the supporters cheering for him despite his dismissal by the moderator and the more established candidates on the stage. It's Happening!, as this meme would come to be called, expressed both his supporters' disappointment that Paul wasn't going to win, and their critics' belief that their hope had been misplaced all along.

It's Happening! had a sense of mockery: the awkward wave, the earnest smile, the over-the-top colors were all meant to make Paul look foolish and Paulites even more foolish for believing he would ever be president. They'd been claiming that if Paul wasn't elected, America was done for. *Well*, this meme told them, *your worst-case scenario is happening.* The words were also a nod to 4chan, where threads to coordinate operations were labeled "Happening." For anons on /pol/, it was *never* happening, and perhaps never could without an approach that embraced the hate that libertarianism was struggling to distance itself from. The It's Happening! meme spread over the new months, a sign that the online energy of 2008 was never coming back. Steeped in the irony and dark humor of the chans, it was a glimpse into the future of meme warfare.

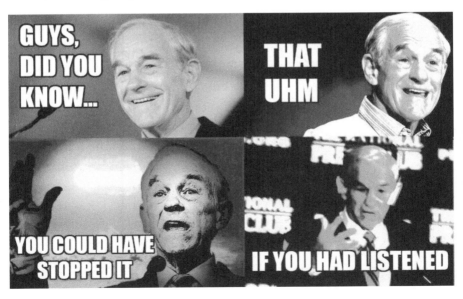

Once Paul gave up, a new reaction meme featuring his dejected face went viral among his supporters and anons. This became known as Doom Paul, and it was an admission that his libertarian utopia was never going to happen, and a suggestion that nothing good or radically different from the status quo was possible.

The Right Occupies Occupy

Doom Paul became an expression of a kind of nihilism that thrived on /pol/, a total loss of faith that the political establishment could ever change. This nihilism would itself go on to fuel many of the events in American politics in the next decade.

But right-wing operatives like Alex Jones and Andrew Breitbart didn't buy into this nihilism. They still felt that change was possible, and that media money could be made along the way. As publishers and broadcasters, they were interested in what the online network and community building of Occupy and the Paul campaigns could teach the right—and specifically media creators on the right—about how to build a movement.

Jones saw the momentum from Occupy as an opportunity to inject his particular kind of conspiratorial antiglobalism into the discourse. Jones has said that two events served as red pills in his own life: the disastrous siege of the Branch Davidian compound in Waco, Texas, by federal agencies in April 1993, which left eighty-two Davidians and four federal agents dead, and Timothy McVeigh's bombing of a federal building in Oklahoma City, which he said was revenge for Waco. "I learned that there was an agenda, there was manipulation, there was deception," Jones told *Texas Monthly* in 2010. "I didn't know what the full agenda was, but I wanted to find out." This spurred him to create a public access show on which he told his audience in July 2001 that "[Bin Laden is] the boogeyman they need in this Orwellian, phony system." He urged them to call the White House and say "we know the government is planning terrorism." Two months later, in the wake of 9/11, he burst into national infamy for having "predicted" that the government would stage a terror attack against the United States.

During Occupy, Jones played on leftist critiques of "globalization" in an attempt to hijack the movement's energy to focus on his obsession with "globalists." He staged two protests of his own piggybacking off the movement—Occupy San Antonio, in front of the state's Federal Reserve building, and Occupy Bilderberg, outside the 2012 gathering of the Bilderberg Group, a gathering of world leaders who meet once a year and were a constant target of his antisemitic conspiracies. To Jones, and the hundreds of years of American conspiratorial thought he represented, the 1 percent were composed of ancient bloodlines and cabalistic groups that used global capitalism to hide their "true" agenda—mass psychological and spiritual control carried out through occult rituals and genocidal social programs. Though this idea was not part of Occupy, in an open-source movement networked through social media, there was no way to guard the 99 percent against opportunists like Jones, looking to make a buck or ignite a fire on a specific issue.

Breitbart shared with Jones the belief that Occupy could be a blue-print for a more lasting cultural upheaval, one that used social media, memes, and physical presence to foment social change. Occupy's media spectacle expanded the ways in which American social movements could distribute their ideas, garner support, grab attention, and use blogs and social media to influence mainstream news. It also showed a whole new way to reach people who were not normally politically engaged and turn them into true believers. Occupy was truly a global phenomenon.

When Occupy ended, Fox News gloated that it had achieved nothing politically—no elected officials, no policy changes. But the movement did make income inequality a top priority for many Democrats. It also taught a new generation of activists how to organize using social media, outside of the confines of political parties and media gatekeepers. Anyone with an internet connection could participate and define their own goals.

Because the media had struggled so much to describe Occupy, after it ended there was still a chance for someone else to define it for history. Breitbart took up the task, seeing Occupy as a chance to establish that the left was a boogeyman.

Breitbart was hardly on the fringe of society, as a longtime collabo-rator on the extremely popular *Drudge Report*, cofounder of the *Huffington Post*, and founder of Breitbart News. But he was antiestablishment and a huge advocate for new media, which he saw as a way to move culture and set political agendas. In an interview with the Associated Press in 2010, he said he was "committed to the destruction of the old media guard," and in 2011 he told *GQ*, "My goal is to take down the institutional left." His targets were Democratic politics, lefty activism, mainstream journalism, and Hollywood, and his tactics seemed to be any means necessary. Destroying the legacy of Occupy would be a great way to hurt them all. He spent the last months of his life doing just that, creating a film called *Occupy Unmasked*, which was released in the fall of 2012, just before the presidential election, and six months after Breitbart's death. Narrated by Breitbart and produced with the help of friend and collaborator Stephen Bannon, it retold the story of Occupy. In this documentary, you can see both what the right learned from the movement, and how the right was prepared to villainize those who were a part of it. It was also a preview of the disinformation campaigns to come.

"The battle for the soul of America took an interesting turn in September of 2011," Breitbart says directly to the camera at the opening of the film.

Occupy Unmasked painted the Radiohead hoax as the instigating moment for the entire Occupy Wall Street movement. Portraying it that way served a strategic purpose, implying that Occupy was hollow from the beginning, an idea with a hoax at its heart, and a clear example of the left-wing politics of the mainstream media. Occupy, they argued, was a violent insurgency based on nothing but lies and craven, attention-seeking idiots who didn't even know what they were fighting for. If there was anything real about it, the film argued, it was that the movement was a secret campaign to reelect Obama.

Reviewing the film for the *Nation*, journalist Michael Tracey called it a "documentary" in name only, "just total fantasy: a deranged hodge-podge of bizarre memes, wild dot-connecting and unadulterated fury. Its central thesis holds that the movement was founded as—and remains—an elaborate front for the Obama reelection effort, having been surreptitiously organized by actors ranging from the SEIU, Rachel Maddow and 'professional anarchists' to Amy Goodman, Hamas, *Russia Today*, Matt Taibbi and the Anonymous hacktivist collective."

With images of upside-down flags and hypodermic needles, hippies on unicycles and banging in drum circles, Breitbart painted the picture of an absurd and dangerous carnival of radicals who defecated on the streets and wanted to burn the system down and dance on its grave. Footage of protesters inside Occupy camps was interspersed with images of snake charmers appearing to hypnotize dancing cobras, casting the young protesters as the snakes, being mesmerized by some greater power.

That greater power, the film argued, was the union-organized left. "Community organizers are radicals, anarchists, public sector unions who are hell-bent on a nihilistic destruction of everything this country stands for. These people hate this country," said Pam Key, a producer for Glenn Beck's Blaze TV network. "I was there with them getting fed poached salmon in a tent with anarchists on shrooms discussing whether or not they were going to assassinate people and when that might happen."

The film emphasized that the protesters would not even protect each other from violence, pointing to real accusations of sexual assaults at some encampments. "There's raping and there's pillaging and there's pooping!" Breitbart exclaimed.

The film shows Breitbart himself at Occupy L.A., in the city where he lived, walking with a camera crew among the protesters, challenging them to prove their intellectual and ideological bona fides on camera. No one in the final cut can give a straight answer as to what Occupy is or stands for. The closest they can get is that they want the end of capitalism, which, Breitbart and the film suggest, proves both that they are naive and that they hate the fundamental building blocks of American greatness.

Occupy stood for nothing on purpose, Breitbart argued, in order to bring in more people. If they had a coherent ideology, they would have alienated a lot of people who disagreed with them, but by carefully committing to nothing specific, they were able to create a larger a movement with their protests. The whole point of Occupy, Breitbart said, was to summon a progressive horde that could overthrow America.

As President Obama was battling for reelection, *Occupy Unmasked* told conservatives that the left was an enemy worth fearing and fighting. *Remember that silly Occupy movement last year?* it suggested. *No one should be laughing.* The film was a way to cleave the antiestablishment right from the antiestablishment left, and remind everyone that they were supposed to be enemies. Every trope and deranged meme, as Tracey had put it, lobbed at Occupy activists in the film would later be redeployed by Bannon and the Breitbart media empire to fight culture and meme wars in the decade to come. If Occupy represented a moment when people fed up with the system could come together despite partisan differences, *Occupy Unmasked* mapped the divergent paths those factions would soon walk.

Chapter 2

A Safe Space for Hate

The Last Rhodesian

When Dylann Storm Roof entered a South Carolina AME church in 2015 and killed nine Black parishioners, he had found his way there via the internet. As Roof detailed in his manifesto, "The Last Rhodesian," a horrific case study in how the rabbit hole works, his descent into white supremacy began in 2012.

It started when Roof wanted, he said, to learn more about Trayvon Martin's death. The media was covering the case, celebrities were posting about it, athletes were wearing hoodies to raise awareness, but Roof didn't think any of them were convincingly explaining why George Zimmerman had done anything wrong when he killed Martin one February day in 2012. "This prompted me to type in the words 'black on White crime' into Google," Roof wrote, "and I have never been the same since that day. The first website I came to was the Council of Conservative Citizens. There were pages upon pages of these brutal black on White murders. I was in disbelief. At this moment I realized that something was very wrong. How could the news be blowing up the Trayvon Martin case while hundreds of these black on White murders got ignored?"

The death of Trayvon Martin was a flash point for race relations in the United States, red-pilling a swath of extremist, far-right, and center-right conservatives that would later be lumped together by the press, and by influencers with an agenda, under the term *alt-right*. The many factions of the alt-right were actually far from united. They held varying beliefs and political stances, gathered on an assortment of websites, and used their own particular slang and jargons. What they had in common was an obsession with race, which they saw as an important and determining human characteristic. Some of these factions had been around for years; others, like the community on /pol/, were just coming into their own.

Roof, in his quest to understand Black-on-white crime, came into contact with many of these online white nationalist groups.

Black-on-white crime is a frequent topic of discussion on white supremacist sites—and is a term that to this day will lead you via search engine to the white supremacist internet. The information Roof stumbled upon on white supremacist forums is an example of "hate facts," misrepresented crime statistics or bits of racist pseudoscience repackaged as forbidden knowledge. These hate facts particularly revolved around recorded instances of violent crime committed by Black people. Often based on contested or out-of-date law enforcement data or academic studies, Black crime memes were red pills, scattered like traps across the internet to pull people down into the rabbit hole. In Roof's case, the results were fatal.

The Council of Conservative Citizens (CCC), whose web page Roof found in his first search, has been labeled by the Southern Poverty Law Center (SPLC) as a hate group. CCC's page is teeming with race-related content, with a heavy focus on the predicament of white farmers in South Africa. The man running it at the time of Roof's killing spree, a white supremacist computer programmer named Kyle Rogers, wrote frequently about Black-on-white crime. Rogers lived about twenty miles from Roof and had a business selling "patriotic flags." Lurking on message boards frequented by other white supremacists, he hawked Nazi, Confederate, and pro-apartheid flags, which Roof wore as badges in his Facebook profile photos. Their nearness is a stunning coincidence, and one that points out the shallow nature of community in these spaces; Roof had written about being lonely, but there is no evidence that Roof and Rogers ever actually met in real life or developed a friendship. Roof was not in any real way a member of Rogers's community, but just an unknown member of his audience.

The same month Roof crafted "The Last Rhodesian," he joined Stormfront, the oldest and biggest white supremacist website online, which had tens of thousands of registered users by 2015. Stormfront featured (and continues to feature) a message board and a web radio show hosted by former KKK leader David Duke. Stormfront was where most white supremacists hung out through the 1990s and early 2000s. They called themselves Stormers and they developed their own internal culture and slang. Under the name LilAryan, Roof posted a few times about wanting to meet up with others in the area. It's not clear that he followed through. What Roof found on the site was a mix of shock humor and violent racism that had its roots in Nazi zines and comics.

One popular meme on Stormfront in the early 2000s was an illustration of a bearded man in a yarmulke with a hooked nose, gleefully rubbing his hands together, who would later be known as the "Happy Merchant." Next to him was a crude caricature of a man with dark skin, exaggerated lips and nose, and African hair, raising a clenched fist. Below them were two animals—a rat for the Jew, a roach for the Black person. "Let's face it!" the text read. "A World Without [Jews] and [Blacks] Would Be Like a World Without [Rats] and [Roaches]." The image was credited to "A

Wyatt Mann," the alias of grindcore filmmaker and underground cartoonist Nick Bougas.

The character of the Black man in this foundational racist cartoon of the twenty-first century is often left out of later reproductions of the Happy Merchant, but would resurface in the online turmoil during the 2016 presidential race and beyond. This sort of anti-Black cartooning has a long American history but, like antisemitic memes, festered in siloed forums and little-known web pages till the advent of social media.

In the early Obama years, Stormfront membership surged. Membership in militias and hate groups exploded. While violent militias like the Patriot movement were wary of openly organizing on the internet because of government surveillance, white nationalists and racist trolls embraced the networking of the web, using fake personas to operate without accountability.

When Obama was reelected, new hateful sites were born, including the Daily Stormer, created by white supremacist Andrew Anglin in 2013 to appeal to millennial racists like Roof. Anglin is a millennial himself, born in 1984, and grew up, according to his own account, "spoon fed" liberal

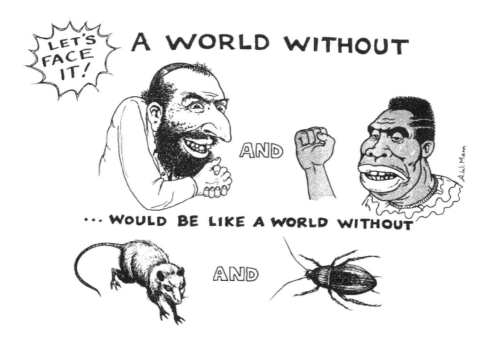

consensus politics. He rebelled by developing a critique of American empire through a mix of influences from leftist theorists like Noam Chomsky to conspiracy mavens like Alex Jones. "When I was 17," he said, "9/11 happened, and you know, the edgy material on the internet at that time was all edgy 9/11 type stuff." He'd spend nearly ten years in various truther movements, running his own website on which he posted tediously long-winded essays on Nazism, fascism, and alternative history. In manifestos like "Hail Victory: Brutal Extremism Is the Way Forward," Anglin riffed on Hitler's musings on a strongman capturing the will of a nation:

Where they preach materialism, we shall preach spirituality.

Where they preach multiculturalism, we shall preach nationalism rooted in blood and heritage.

Where they push abortion, pornography, homosexuality and promiscuity, we shall force the sexual morality of our ancestors.

Where they teach feminism, we shall teach that a woman has her place at home.

And he loved 4chan. It was during the period of Anglin's fascist awakening that the 4chan board /pol/, which Poole had created specifically to contain the white supremacists who were infiltrating his site, began to turn even more intensely toward racialized hatred.

In the past, the board had had a libertarian focus, with a side of racialized hatred. Everyone from traditional to radical to anarcho-capitalist anons were ready to discuss the principle of nonaggression on a moment's notice. Misogynists and bigots sought out /pol/ for its more structured political debate unencumbered by political correctness. It also attracted die-hard white nationalists—an increasing number of them, by site owner Poole's own estimation.

By the second Obama term, several years of sustained brigading (that is, targeted messaging in short bursts) and psychological manipulation by white nationalists from Stormfront had overwhelmed 4chan's libertarian streak. "Ironic" racist jokes gave way to genocidal fantasies. Hitler

jokes turned into a sincere interest in fascism. Today /pol/ is known as the go-to place for racist posting, workshopping white nationalist media manipulation campaigns, and crowdsourcing research about breaking news events.

Anglin created the Daily Stormer to establish a bridge between the white nationalist establishment and 4chan-style internet culture, embracing a new visual language that spoke to the youth. Named for *Der Stürmer*, Hitler's favorite conspiracy-laden antisemitic propaganda rag, which served as the tabloid of the Nazi Party, the website was basically /pol/ rants in essay form, steeped in conspiratorial and inflammatory rhetoric. Anglin aggregates the worst of real and fake news relating to Black crime, immigration, and intersectional feminism, putting a manic, bloodthirsty spin on it, all leading the reader back to the threat of a "white genocide," a meme he constantly repeats.

Anglin has his own theory of memetic warfare. "If you read this site with any regularity, you are aware that I focus on continually pressing certain memes, over and over and over again. This is a method by which, through repetition, you are able to give a person a lens through which they view reality. They then spread these memes both through various different internet outlets as well as in the real world. This exponential

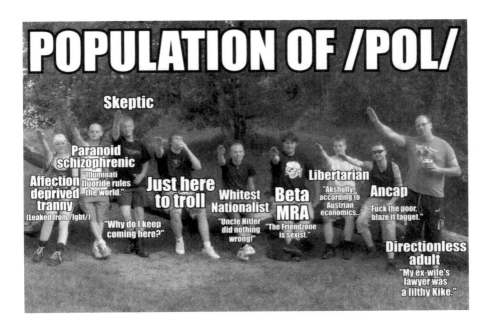

dissemination of simple and yet very powerful ideas, as it builds momentum, can continue to expand indefinitely." Hyperaware of memetic theory and the left-wing messaging tactics of his youth, Anglin was explicit about how he used them to build his troll armies.

"I had always been into 4chan, as I am at heart a troll," he wrote. "This is about the time [the now-defunct 4chan board] /new/ was going full-Nazi, and so I got into Hitler, and realized that through this type of nationalist system, alienation could be replaced with community in a real sense, while the authoritarianism would allow for technology to develop in a direction that was beneficial rather than destructive to the people."

Anglin changed the Daily Stormer's aesthetic to match visual trends in 4chan's meme culture. He kept up with the news. He would also repost articles from older white nationalist movement leaders like David Duke, and occasionally (and reluctantly) from right-wing organizations and outlets like the Council of Conservative Citizens and Breitbart News. But he would turn on any of these conservatives immediately if he felt they were being too "Jewish." Like many emerging hard-right figures at the time, he viewed conservatism as weak, ineffective, and a roadblock to total Aryan victory.

The infamous hacktivist weev joined the Daily Stormer team after his stint in prison and his time at Occupy. This shouldn't have been a surprise, considering the overt anti-Blackness and antisemitism that he had sprinkled into earlier interviews. Combining the ironic meme-heavy style of 4chan with a genocidal vitriol that put the ancient Stormfront forums to shame, the Daily Stormer proudly established itself as the edge—the end of the line, and the hardest right one could articulate in words before descending into a full-time genocidal obsession.

According to BuzzFeed and the SPLC, Dylann Roof was on the Daily Stormer forums under the screen name AryanBlood1488, posting comments that mirrored excerpts of his manifesto, as early as September 2014. Following his arrest, Roof's Facebook profile picture circulated across social media, showing an awkward and angry-looking young white man with a bowl haircut and ill-fitting clothes. He had eighty-eight "friends" on Facebook, a nod to the neo-Nazi dog whistle for "Heil Hitler," because *H* is the eighth letter of the alphabet. He took eighty-eight bullets with him to the church that horrible day. The "14" was shorthand for another infamous white nationalist slogan, the so-called Fourteen Words of white nationalist David Lane: "We must secure the existence of our people and a future for white children."

The Last Rhodesian, Roof's web page, had a simple black background with an oversize screenshot of a bloodied skinhead lying on the ground. He had registered the site four months before his rampage. Apparently Roof was nostalgic for a place he never experienced. Rhodesia is the name that white people living in modern-day Zimbabwe gave to the nation they hoped to form to avoid being ruled by a majority Black government. It is the stuff of legends on white-power websites.

On the Daily Stormer Roof clashed with Anglin when Anglin posted disparaging comments about CCC, a site that Roof felt loyalty to because it "woke him up to black on white crime in the beginning." If Roof had been searching for a community on these sites, he did not seem to find it.

What he and others did find was a safe space for their racist rants, political discussions, and memetic content. The sites were moderated to remove extremely violent calls to action that might draw the attention of law enforcement, but moderators also flagged and removed content from anti-racist activists, who would raid the forums from time to time to spread counternarratives or bait racists into impossible-to-win arguments.

After getting red-pilled on race, Roof concluded that he needed to be the catalyst to inspire other white men to take action. He finished his manifesto with a call to arms: "We have no skinheads, no real KKK, no one doing anything but talking on the internet. Well someone has to have the bravery to take it to the real world, and I guess that has to be me."

Killing people to bring attention to a manifesto was a well-known tactic in the white-power movement, especially after Anders Behring Breivik slaughtered seventy people in Norway in 2011. Roof targeted the people he had first been red-pilled on: Black Americans. He was wary of Jewish people as well, because they passed for white and held on to their identity, but his fantasies about them were less violent. In a strange twist in the manifesto, he speculated, "If we could somehow turn every jew blue for 24 hours, I think there would be a mass awakening, because people would be able to see plainly what is going on." While Roof reviled Jewish people, Hispanics, and East Asians, he ultimately targeted Black people because he feared race mixing and believed white women needed to "be saved." This fear of the sexualized Black male endangering the purity of white females is a hallmark of white supremacy.

After Roof murdered Sharonda Coleman-Singleton, Cynthia Hurd, Susie Jackson, Ethel Lance, DePayne Middleton-Doctor, Clementa Pinckney, Tywanza Sanders, Daniel Simmons, and Myra Thompson, the national reaction was despair, shock, and outrage. People took to social media to call out the connections between Roof's crimes and the day-to-day racism and vitriol Black people experienced in the United States. Academics and journalists pointed to the pattern of violence exhibited by white supremacists in online communities, and to Google's role in indexing Stormfront and CCC's content and leading Roof directly into white supremacist online forums.

Anons on 4chan's /pol/ reacted predictably, with celebratory memes making fun of Dylann's middle name (Storm) and calling the event a false flag, deployed by Obama and the Jews to cover up something else. They encouraged aggressive behavior, and some swarmed Facebook and started the page "Justice for Dylann Roof" to antagonize Black people and white liberal allies, while encouraging others on /pol/ to make a donation site for Roof, and to troll associated hashtags on Twitter. When Obama condemned Roof's actions, /pol/ pushed harder, using Roof's name and image to derail discussions about Trayvon Martin and race across mainstream platforms.

Roof's radicalization and manifesto captured a moment in web history when white-power groups—who used to hide in the shadows—learned how to cause a scene on social media by trolling, harassing, and creating their own media. Irony became a tool to hide one's true beliefs behind a veneer of jokes, which also served to weed out those who had little tolerance for racist humor. Roof wasn't joking about his racism, which is why he became a catalyst for so many who felt that the time for hiding behind irony was coming to an end.

Obama's America

Roof had said that it was Trayvon Martin's killing that sent him down the white supremacist rabbit hole. He was not alone. The response to Martin's death and the arrest of George Zimmerman, his killer, laid the groundwork for the identity-based meme wars to come.

Martin was seventeen, walking home within his father's gated Florida community, when self-appointed community watchman George Zimmerman pursued him in his car and then shot him.

Zimmerman's actions were initially justified as self-defense within the provisions of Florida's "stand your ground" law. In Zimmerman, half of America saw a killer, and the other a victim. When the 911 call that Zimmerman made moments before shooting Martin, during which he was advised not to follow Martin, was made public, it became a Rorschach test for liberals and right-wingers. Liberals heard the proof of a racially inspired killing; right-wingers heard a man defending himself from the threat posed by the presence of a young Black man. "He looks black," said Zimmerman on the call with the 911 operator that night. Depending on your interpretation, either Martin was being racially profiled, or Zimmerman was just giving a description (Zimmerman claimed it was not Martin's race but his hoodie, which the teen was reportedly wearing up on his head, that made him seem suspicious). If not for the media attention generated by the Martin family's attorney, Ben Crumps, and the subsequent surge of online activism, Zimmerman might never have even come to trial.

Martin's death and the opposing reactions to it embodied the Janus face of the United States itself. On one side was the aspirational America represented by Obama and on the other was the reality of racism and violence that Black people experienced in America.

Many white people, like Roof, found their nostalgic view of America threatened by the multiracial democracy of Obama's presidency. No one threatened the standing of whites more obviously than Obama, whose mainstream popularity raised the hackles of those who feared being replaced by people who looked like him. This backlash began the day the first Black president took office, as his experience, his legitimacy, his intelligence, and his country of birth were all questioned. From the beginning, the anti-Black trolls unleashed their worst on him, reaching a low mark in the infamous remix of Shepard Fairey's "Hope" poster as a lynching.

The attacks increased even more during Obama's 2012 reelection campaign, spear-headed by none other than Donald Trump. Trump positioned himself as one of Obama's most vocal critics. He was a primary amplifier of the "birther" theory that Obama was actually born in Kenya, or the love child of a man who was not his legal father. This theory, and related attacks on Obama's patriotism, had followed his political career from his Senate run in 2004 through his first presidential campaign in 2008, and ramped up as the 2012 primary season began. In media appearances, Trump pushed the birther theory on everything from *Good Morning America* to the *National Inquirer*, as well as on the Twitter account he was using more and more frequently.

Even though the recycled theory was absurd, it gained enough traction with right-wing media and GOP politicians that while running for his second term, Obama ended up releasing his long-form birth certificate to prove he was indeed American. That wasn't enough for Trump, who tried to bait Obama into releasing his college degree after questioning his ability to get into Harvard, based on rumors he'd heard that Obama was a "terrible student."

Obama's reelection for a second term was a nightmare for racists on the right, spurring them to fight back harder against the winds of racial "progress." Despite the optimists who declared the beginning of his term to be the end of racism, Obama presented a complication for race relations in the United States, where many questioned if he was truly Black because of his mixed family history. The whole issue was so fraught that he rarely spoke about race during his years in the White House. He had given one seminal speech on the subject when he ran for office the first time, but only after significant pressure from his party to respond to claims that his affiliation with Black firebrand Jeremiah Wright was disqualifying. There was a disastrous moment when he hosted the much-mocked "Beer Summit," in which he invited Black Harvard professor Henry Louis Gates to drink a beer at the White House with the white police officer who had arrested him for entering his own home. After he left office, a majority of people polled by CNN said race relations had "worsened under Obama."

Martin's death was something of a turning point for Obama. He spoke out about Martin's death in 2012, remarking that Martin could have been his son. In 2013, when Zimmerman was acquitted, Obama spoke out again. This time he did not simply extend thoughts and prayers, but made a bold statement about the everyday indignities he had experienced as a Black man walking around in a white world. Finally the country had a president who not only acknowledged the toll that racism takes on Black people but admitted he was not free from racial stigma himself, even as the nation's president.

At the same time that Obama was being both celebrated as the first Black president and condemned by those who questioned his right to office, everyone seemed to be expressing their opinions online about him on a relatively new social networking site called Twitter. Black activists, academics, technologists, politicians, and pop culture fans converged on "Black Twitter," a new and thriving online community, to discuss everything from the sacred to the mundane, religion, politics, and entertainment alike.

Writing for *Wired* in 2021, journalist Jason Parham described Black Twitter as a force "capable of creating, shaping, and remixing popular culture at light speed, it remains the incubator of nearly every meme (Crying Jordan, This You?), hashtag (#IfTheyGunnedMeDown, #OscarsSoWhite, #YouOKSis), and social justice cause (Me Too, Black Lives Matter) worth knowing about. It is both news and analysis, call and response, judge and jury—a comedy showcase, therapy session, and family cookout all in one."

Black Twitter was noticed by the mainstream. Admiring non-Black social media users reappropriated much of its slang and memes, often monetizing them without credit. Quick-witted Black reaction memes became ubiquitous during Obama's presidency. #ByeFelicia, #YouKnowYou'reBlackWhen, and #SaltBae all grew on Black Twitter, as did social justice campaigns and cultural critiques such as #OscarsSoWhite. Someone made a subreddit devoted to the best of Black Twitter. After it got inundated with trolls, admins locked the community to keep it a safe space.

To be Black in the United States was to be born into a diaspora, domestically and internationally. Now Black and Indigenous people used new forms of social media as a tool, creating a networked pan-Africanism for a better and more just society. Celebrities, journalists, activists, and even President Obama all joined in a chorus calling for justice for Martin, sparking a long and difficult discussion about race and stereotyping in the nation. Martin's killing was a catalyst, especially for many young people, including activists in New York City who were still connected online via the Occupy networks. It's also important to remember that there was a vibrant police accountability and abolitionist movement in the United States going back decades, which held numerous marches and vigils in memorial. The fact that Martin's killer did not immediately face charges allowed time for an intergenerational and multiracial coalition of thousands to come together, all calling for Zimmerman to be arrested.

In March 2012, hundreds of Occupy social media accounts and thousands of individuals began to post about Martin's death. The movement had been in a state of "obeyance," having retreated back into the wires after the camps were cleared a few months earlier, but now they sprang into action again. Organizers repurposed Occupy's conference-calling infrastructure to support the nascent #MillionHoodies movement, which grew into the Black Lives Matter movement. Street actions swelled to include thousands of participants across Los Angeles, Oakland, Boston, and beyond. Activists shut down highways to raise awareness. Journalists, in turn, asked questions that pressured politicians to investigate further. This cycle was nothing new. Since the civil rights movement, organizers had set media agendas by drawing large crowds, rallying speakers, gaining press coverage, and using the internet to organize. Now the internet took networked organizing to a new level.

The petition site Change.org collected digital signatures demanding Zimmerman's arrest, in what would become the site's largest campaign to date. In an echo of the We Are the 99 Percent campaign, celebrities, doctors, lawyers, and politicians wore hoodies and posted selfies to social media in support of #MillionHoodiesMarch and #Justice4Trayvon. When Fox News host Geraldo Rivera claimed that "the hoodie is as much responsible for Trayvon Martin's death as George Zimmerman was," the comment provoked widespread backlash online, showing right-wing agitators how inflammatory rhetoric would be rewarded with center and left-wing media coverage.

A digital discourse was emerging across the political spectrum in response to Black civil rights organizers' and intellectuals' use of social media. Right-wing blogs and alternative media like Breitbart News and the Daily Caller competed with one another to provide a coherent narrative that exposed liberal media as complicit in creating what they believed to be an manufactured racial divide in the United States. The implicit and explicit anti-Blackness in right-wing news was a more mainstream expression of the organized racism growing online.

An Internet Hate Machine

The rise of Black Twitter and a joyful Black technoculture didn't go unnoticed by the white supremacist internet, which at the time was vast and unrestrained. This was true especially of 4chan's /pol/, which had become by this time the internet's premier destination of racist humor, a meme factory pumping out content mocking liberals, media, activists, and anything else it could get a reaction to daily. Anons and other right-wing trolls launched harassment campaigns against popular Black Twitter users, assailed the media, and infiltrated Black Twitter hashtags to antagonize and annoy other users.

The pro-Trayvon #MillionHoodies meme elicited a grim response from some young men and organized online racists: a meme dubbed "Trayvoning," in which people posted pictures of themselves lying facedown in gray hoodies with a bottle of Arizona Iced Tea and Skittles, re-creating a photo of Martin's dead body. Photo reenactments had been hugely popular with teens in 2010 and 2011, inspired by pictures of popular athletes in unusual positions, such as rugby player David Williams lying stiff as a board on the field, and Tim Tebow kneeling in prayer. Trayvoning was a horrifying evolution of the format. (In 2020 a similar photo meme went around after a police officer murdered Minnesota resident George Floyd, with people kneeling on each other's necks in a cruel meme-ification of Floyd's death.)

Much of the mainstream white coverage of this internet trend focused on its connection to those other photo fads, barely tackling the racial implications at all—but Black journalists and bloggers saw the meme for what it was. Black journalists like Brande Victorian were some of the first to notice in May 2012 that Trayvoning was going viral, jumping from 4chan to the open web. Victorian reported on how organized Facebook groups were popping up, soliciting more and more original Trayvoning images from their growing lists of followers. White supremacist narratives were tagged into the discourse, with some participants in these groups claiming that the meme wasn't just a cruel, offensive joke—it was actually combating "racism against whites." Trayvoning, in their logic, was a way to fight back, given that "white people are becoming more and more oppressed"—an idea straight out of the white supremacist sloganeering playbook.

/Pol/ was watching the Zimmerman trial as closely as the rest of the nation, with more specific intent—to disrupt and troll any public conversations they could. Early in the trial, when a witness calling in remotely on his computer made the critical mistake of revealing his screen name, anons were able to Skype-bomb his testimony. They passed around his handle, relentlessly calling to interrupt him while he attempted to answer the prosecutor's questions. On July 11, when a new photo of Martin's body was released on MSNBC to much public backlash, /pol/ rejoiced: a new image of a dead Black boy to use for red-pill memes. The media was mostly using photos of a more boyish Trayvon from a few years earlier to represent him during the trial coverage. /Pol/ was one of the only places that compiled his more recent pictures, from when he was a teenager, which they claimed made him look like a fully grown thug and criminal.

Historically, U.S. media has made gruesome spectacles of Black criminality and death on television, radio, and print. The KKK made Black death a mainstay of their macabre events, which they documented in postcards depicting lynching. The meme-ification of Black death was not new here. What was new was the means by which Black death through photos was digitized and distributed to new audiences, particularly ones who were not necessarily seeking it out.

Liberal media struggled to keep up with the pace and fervor of online discourse. There was not much they could say that hadn't already been said over and over online. Media norms, which at the time dictated that calling racist actions "racist" was rarely done, pressed up against pressure from activists who urged the media to adopt an evolving vocabulary workshopped online. The mainstream media's every utterance was critiqued, as well as every silence and omission.

For right-wing outlets, reactions to Martin's killing became a different kind of media spectacle. Breitbart's long-standing mission to dig into liberal media contradictions made Zimmerman's case into contentious clickbait. Breitbart could amplify leftist criticism of mainstream media while also driving a wedge between Black and Latinx communities. The first Breitbart article about Trayvon, "Media Labels Hispanic Man White in Shooting of Black Teen," was published on March 9, 2012. Subsequent articles minimized the growing BLM movement and attacked the mainstream media, or MSM, as a co-conspirator: "Zimmerman Case: How CNN Disgraced Itself More Than Any Other Outlet," "Some More Things the MSM Never Told You About George Zimmerman," and "'Justice for Trayvon' Protests Draw Small Crowds; Nation Moves On."

In coverage of Obama's comments on Martin, Breitbart columnist Ben Shapiro focused on the media calling Zimmerman a "white hispanic." Shapiro has since gone on to found the Daily Wire, a popular conservative news website, and host his own YouTube show and podcast. His early coverage of the Zimmerman trial critically shaped how the right understood the role race played in Martin's death.

Any article on Martin and Zimmerman became a potential minefield. Battles were waged in the comments sections on Twitter and on Facebook, where many white Americans' comments revealed that they were unable to grasp that Zimmerman could be both white and Latino. Mainstream conservative media and anonymous online racists who frequented white supremacist message boards and /pol/ were united by anti-Black animus, but expressed it differently; hiding behind pseudonyms, the latter could be more inflammatory and explicit in their racism, using popular meme formats of the time to both praise Zimmerman for killing a Black teenager and question whether he counted as white.

Soon, a smear campaign about Martin's death began to overwhelm social media. On March 25, 2013, *Wagist* ran a piece titled "Was Trayvon Martin a Drug Dealer?," which became an influential early post in the emerging right-wing narrative. "The media narrative being sold is quite clear," the author wrote. "Trayvon Martin is the innocent victim here and George Zimmerman is a horrible bigot who attacked the young man for doing nothing more than buying skittles while being black." The article collated screenshots of Martin's social media content, attempting to label him a violent drug-dealing adult. "Hopefully this info paints a somewhat different picture of Trayvon than the one the media has been forcing down our throats for the last several weeks."

More than just a criticism of the media, the popularity of this post showed an appetite for alternative media, especially stories that criticized both the media and the teenager. This article was followed up on March 26 by the Daily Caller, which published all of Martin's tweets. A reporter for tech news start-up *Business Insider* found an image on Stormfront (the neo-Nazi blog that Dylann Roof had famously posted on) that was purportedly of Martin, and he published it in an article. The photo was a misidentification—it wasn't of Martin at all, and *Business Insider* had to run a correction. *Good Morning America* then used the same image and had to walk it back. Then, on March 27, Adrian Chen reported at Gawker that Trayvon's Yahoo email, Myspace, and Twitter accounts had been hacked and leaked to Stormfront and 4chan's /pol/ board by a white supremacist who went by Klanklannon. All of these incidents were just the tip of an iceberg of slander and misrepresentation of Martin that the right pushed to justify Zimmerman's shooting throughout the trial. Zimmerman's defense also made a big deal of this issue, and outlets like the *Daily Mail* published the images of Trayvon smoking weed and giving the middle finger, pushing a criminal narrative similar to what had developed in the community of /pol/.

The convergence of far-right and conservative backlash online against Martin and Black Lives Matter as a whole divided America by race in ways that were more pronounced than any time in recent history, funneled new users into places like /pol/, and foreshadowed the rise of the alt-right a few years later.

On July 13, 2013, the verdict came in on Zimmerman. He was acquitted of all charges, based on Florida's stand-your-ground law. Anons on /pol/ were elated. "2013 /pol/ was fuckin amazing," an anon remembered fondly in 2021. "Peak times around these parts. I remember we made the #Trayvoning hashtag go viral with teens taking pics lying on the floor next to a bag of skittles and Arizona iced tea. Good times." Black deaths weren't just something for the anons to gloat about; they were seen as opportunities to spread the anti-Democratic, anti-Black ideology that brought the anons together.

Human Biodiversity

Many extremely online right-wingers marked Martin's death as their "red-pill moment"—the point they "realized" that racial differences were real, as they put it, scientific; that Black people were inherently violent and criminal due to biology; and that they'd been lied to by liberal social institutions and the mainstream media. Once this red pill had been swallowed, no facts could change their view. With the expansion of this mindset, appetite for racialized content online grew. Mainstream conservative media, still in the grips of the Tea Party, wasn't about to start pushing anti-Black racism to the top of their coverage, so new media stepped up to fill the void. Websites like VDARE and online publications like *Taki's Magazine* (informally known as *Takimag*) provided an alt-right media, one that openly challenged the liberal consensus around American interventionism, domestic social policy, and racial equality.

Despite their racialist perspective, this alternative right yearned for something more energized, palatable, and intellectual than Stormfront and the last generation of white nationalism. Former Ron Paul supporters like future alt-right influencer Richard Spencer brought their antiwar politics and critiques of American economics. Suit-and-tie racists like Jared Taylor, who runs a white supremacist think tank called New Century Foundation, replete with academic degrees and decades of publishing, emerged from their low-profile research institutes. Anons on /pol/ added skilled meme production and chaos. What the skinhead subculture did for the 1990s racist movement the alternative right did now through their own websites, media, and memes. They were helped along by the embrace of a central racist tenet that they could disguise as science: the concept of human biodiversity, which they shortened to the acronym HBD. HBD signified the belief that "race is real," scientifically provable to be determinative of everything from criminal propensity to intelligence.

This pseudoscientific idea has deep roots in the racism-riven history of biomedicine in Europe and the United States, from phrenology in the eighteenth century to eugenics, mass sterilization, and the use of nonwhite subjects as guinea pigs for medical research in the twentieth.

By early 2010 most of these racist beliefs had fallen out of the scientific canon and been relegated to the fringe, but Stormfront resurrected debunked research on "human difference" to draw in new members. Of particular interest was any data regarding race and IQ, placing much importance on debunked or debated studies on the flawed intelligence measurement standard. Newcomers to Stormfront felt as though they were being told the truth about race and biology for the first time. "Have the facts to support your statements no matter what the argument is about. Use reasoning and logic, not emotions because that wouldn't get you very far," one Stormer wrote in 2004 in a lengthy thread titled "Bad Scientific Arguments Used by White Nationalists."

Threads like these were critical for workshopping modernized white nationalist talking points, where Stormers discussed ways to move past the stigma of association with Hitler and the KKK. Stormers had been trying to influence the public conversation around race for decades, but felt the Nazi association was impeding their efforts. They were too *obviously* white supremacists, tied to the language and symbols of past

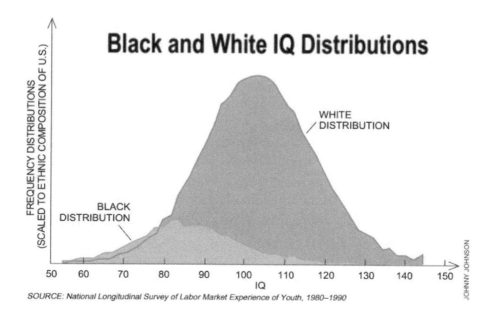

SOURCE: National Longitudinal Survey of Labor Market Experience of Youth, 1980–1990

movements like George Lincoln Rockwell's American Nazi Party and the Aryan Nation. If they were going to convince white America to join their race war, they needed a way to talk about their race beliefs without being immediately dismissed as Nazis.

In the late 2000s, when Stormfront began pushing race science, they reopened discussion of racial determinism and human differences in new ways and in new communities. This new racial "inquiry" went by many names—racialism, race realism—before, between 2007 and 2014, its proponents settled on the term HBD, turning it into a meme that radicalized a new generation of white men raised in the "colorblind" era of George W. Bush's "compassionate conservatism." Like many memes, this one had been hijacked. HBD had been hijacked from an anthropologist named Jonathan Marks.

Marks had this to say about his role in popularizing the term: "It is rare for a professor to birth a meme. . . . For me, it increasingly seems as though my lasting contribution will be to have coined the phrase 'human biodiversity' in my 1994 book of that name. Unfortunately it has come to mean the opposite of what I meant, due to the distortions of internet racists." HBD, he continued, "was intended as an alternative way of talking about human variation without the overarching assumption that our species sorts out into fairly discrete, fairly homogeneous races—as was assumed by scientists a century ago. But in the late 1990s, racists began to coopt the phrase as a more genteel and sciencey way to simply say 'race' in a way that sounded fresh and academic. In other words, they began to synonymize what should be antonyms."

Down the HBD rabbit hole newcomers would find Stormfront, /pol/, the Daily Stormer, and CCC, but also a proliferating number of other, less race-focused, groups, including factions of extremely online thinkers, known as rationalists and skeptics, who thrived on debate. A taboo like HBD was catnip for these communities to dissect.

These so-called rationalists were inspired by academics and atheists like psychologist Steven Pinker and Richard Dawkins. These writers and influencers liked to debate big ideas on blogs, at conferences, and on podcasts and YouTube. The skeptics, initially more focused on debating the existence of God than on Western philosophy, soon moved on to challenge other grand social assumptions. In the overwhelmingly white male space of the rationalist and skeptic movements, no topic was too taboo to consider. Evolutionary biology, the science of human difference, and the question of whether IQ was determined by biology (the subject of conservative political scientist Charles Murray's infamous *Bell Curve*) and therefore race and gender became a favorite intellectual exercise, since it was seen elsewhere as too hot-button to even mention. HBD gave these heterodox communities the vocabulary to discuss race on their own "intellectual" terms without feeling "racist"—though they still occasionally got labeled racist, such as when meme godfather Dawkins left a comment on a blog post about sexual harassment that many within the skeptic community interpreted as racist and sexist.

HBD's adoption within these communities gave it a sheen of intellectualism, allowing the meme to spread as a red pill far beyond the bounds of Stormfront.

Take the Red Pill

It was an influential critic of these rationalists who first popularized the term *red pill* as it is now understood, alongside a loose affiliation of reactionary writers pushing the limits of acceptable political theory. This new movement, "neoreaction"—or, as its adherents refer to it, NRx—challenged the idea that democracy and social equality were good for society, and that conservatism and skepticism were just as responsible for social decay as liberalism. These questions first came from Silicon Valley software engineer Curtis Yarvin, who in 2007 began publishing under the pseudonym Mencius Moldbug on a blog called *Unqualified Reservations.*

"Have you ever considered the possibility that democracy is bunk?" he asked at the beginning of his 2007 essay "The Case Against Democracy: Ten Red Pills." Though *The Matrix* was already popular, this is considered the first time a right-wing writer used the term *red pill* like this, presenting the reader with a series of "heretical theses" meant to provoke them to second-guess aspects of liberal democracy. Once these questions were asked, Yarvin explained, and you realized that the answer wasn't what you thought, you'd "taken the red pill." From that moment you couldn't help but be at war with what he called "the Cathedral," which became its own kind of meme.

The Cathedral was a right-wing flip of the one percent—singling out academics, journalists, celebrities, political leaders from both parties, lobbyists, and activists who pushed left and liberal ideologies that were "harmful" to a white majority as the gatekeepers of the "liberal consensus." Calling this consortium of people the Cathedral drove home the idea that modern liberalism in America is like a religion, a godless cult, a secular faith. The Cathedral has come to mean both the gatekeepers of the liberal consensus and that consensus itself, and is a synonym for the "establishment" and more esoteric ideas like the New World Order.

In Yarvin's work, once you took the red pill, you'd wake up enraged about the realities of the Cathedral. The term became popular with other NRx thinkers, too, and adapted to different scenarios. You got red-pilled *about* an issue. Partially this usage was likely due to where exactly the phrase became popular: Reddit, a collection of internet forums organized around specific topics. For many, Reddit was a cross-over point, a first stop on the journey from the mainstream internet to fringe spaces like 4chan. Home to users of every political persuasion, it was in its early days a bastion of near limitless free speech. Users had to sign in and make accounts, but those accounts could be pseudonymous. Everything up to the line of illegality was permitted, including "jailbait" pictures of teenage girls, horrific deaths caught on camera, and highly organized anti-Black racism. Red-pilling first took off in subreddits organized around misogyny after being normalized by NRx writers. On r/TheRedPill, Reddit's pickup artist community red-pilled men about women, claiming to be able to teach other men how to understand them so they could control and manipulate them. The manosphere, aka the communities of men's rights groups who gathered online (and in real life at conferences and retreats), red-pilled men about how women were not worth worrying about. That subgroup later led to the incel phenomenon, which red-pilled young men into believing that their "involuntary celibacy" was the fault of women and society.

But once the term caught on, it was used for all sorts of fringe topics beyond misogyny. Atheists on Reddit red-pilled each other about God. Conspiracy theorists red-pilled each other about, well, any kind of conspiracy. Most importantly, "red-pilling" became shorthand for a new kind of mass communication strategy. Videos of people confessing when they first took the red pill racked up views on YouTube. Being red-pilled carried an evangelical component. Once you were red-pilled, the dogma went, you should share what you learned and convert others. Red-pilling became an essential recruiting process. White nationalists coming from Stormfront would create dedicated "daily red pill" 4chan threads on /pol/ and elsewhere, with the express goal of shoving scientific racism, gender essentialism, and—inevitably—organized antisemitism down the throats of larger and larger audiences.

The HBD meme was gaining traction on Reddit, particularly in the rampant anti-Black subreddits that were being allowed to thrive there. One of the most influential of the early racist subs, r/niggers, was populated with a lot of the same materials and ideas from the old anti-Black forums and hate sites of the pre-social-media age, but now they were collected in a vast information ecosystem where millions of people came for their news.

Journalist Bridget Todd took Reddit to task in 2013 with a devastating critical writeup of r/niggers. After the outcry that followed, Reddit removed the sub from the site—but soon the hydra grew another head to take its place. This replacement subreddit was slightly more coded, with the name r/GreatApes. After a self-described period of explosive growth, a whole network of anti-Black subreddits emerged in July 2014 under the name the Chimpire. Their creator went by the handle Jewish_Neocon2 and described the purpose of the network as such: "Want to read people's experiences with n–ggers? There now is an affiliated subreddit for it. Want to watch chimp nature documentaries? We got it. N–gger hate facts? IT'S THERE."

A little over a week after the Chimpire was created, on July 17, 2014, police in New York city killed Eric Garner, an unarmed Black man, whom they held in a chokehold for allegedly committing the crime of selling loose cigarettes. A month after his death, police shot and killed a Black teenager, this time a young man named Michael Brown in

Ferguson, Missouri. Brown's killing inflamed the city, with protesters and counterprotesters taking to the streets for days at a time over the course of many months. It was on the streets of Ferguson that the movement against police violence took on the name Black Lives Matter. Organizers across the United States began to use #BlackLivesMatter to organize national protests. As with Occupy, Justice4Trayvon, and #MillionHoodies, journalists and other culture makers caught on quickly. The two deaths so close together highlighted that these killings of Black men were not isolated but a pattern in a system. The Black Lives Matter movement began to stand for them all.

During the Ferguson protests, the Chimpire subreddits did their best to disrupt liberal social media and news subreddits, spreading red pills and anti-Black memes ported over from /pol/. GreatApes had its own internal conflicts; it was starting to attract full-blown Nazis. These subfactions began to fight among themselves, the ideologues who believed HBD was a gateway to white nationalism versus the bigots who just hated all Black people. A new subreddit, r/CoonTown, catered to those with a fully red-pilled worldview, attracting some of the highest-profile trolls of the far right before Reddit finally banned it in August 2015, because users praised Roof's manifesto.

For those steeped in HBD and now considering white nationalism to be a solution to America's "racial problems," traditional conservative news and radio wasn't cutting it anymore. They needed edgier content, new broadcast personalities that shared their ideology. Enter the Right Stuff (TRS), a community that started in 2011 as a Facebook group and evolved into the preeminent white nationalist podcast network in America. Topics there generally revolved around HBD and its tangents, including attacks on demographic change and migrants, and Islamophobic rhetoric. TRS drew readers from the NRx space and fringe libertarian blogs that the TRS crew themselves also frequented. They used rationalist positions to debate, and enjoyed poking at the shibboleths of atheists, liberals, conservatives, and libertarians alike.

When some guys with technical talents in audio production joined the TRS crew, new possibilities for media making developed. On August 3, 2014, the first episode of their *Daily Shoah* podcast launched, just a few days before the Ferguson uprising began. It remains online to this day.

The title of the podcast was meant to be a parody of Jon Stewart's *Daily Show*, which was hugely popular at the time. The TRS guys were former fans of Stewart, the political comedian who defined progressive critique during the Bush presidency. They too hated Bush, to them the ultimate embodiment of emasculated neoconservatism. However, under Obama, they felt Stewart had lost his edge, and they grew to view him as an apparatus of the Democrats.

The *Daily Shoah* podcast gave TRS writers a chance to mimic their racist shock-jock icons like Greg "Opie" Hughes and Anthony Cumia of *Opie & Anthony*, cheered on by their growing audience as they further radicalized each other on air in real time. The description of the first *Daily Shoah* episode reads, "We discuss race, immigration, politics, religion and social life from our unique TRS perspective. Prepare your anuses and ear canals for the best social commentary on the internet."

What supposedly started as parody became sincere. The podcast moved on from jokes about HBD to an explicit endorsement of fascism. Over the years, there was a rotating supporting cast, with two main hosts, Mike Enoch and Seventh Son, soon joined by a "death panel," a rotating cast of cohosts with fake names from the TRS Facebook group and forums. Seventh Son, a professional musician and composer of many racist parody songs, brought an artistic flair to the program, while Enoch supplied the ideology. Before coming around to white nationalism, Enoch was first a liberal, then dabbled in leftism before moving into libertarian politics. In his posts and podcasts he recalls a youth spent reading Noam Chomsky and attending antiwar rallies, developing his politics in Bush's post-9/11 America. It was in the antiwar space that he first encountered right-wing anarchists, disciples of Austrian economist Ludwig von Mises who called their antistate, extreme free market radicalism "anarcho-capitalism."

The far right—particularly those with a history in the antiwar movement, like Enoch—has a much deeper understanding of the differences between leftism and liberalism than their conservative counterparts. Enoch says he saw the contradictions of liberalism firsthand from his upbringing, and was permanently ostracized from the left when he began to see Occupy as overwhelmed by identity politics that didn't favor white guys as lead characters. Unlike the scattered and disorganized leftists, shitlibs (liberals with shitty opinions) held the real power and needed to be undermined at every turn.

TRS would soon be forced to develop their own forum as their relentless Facebook trolling began to attract attention, and their accounts got "zucked"—their term for getting deplatformed by Facebook—for egregious TOS violations. As the forum culture developed, they became increasingly antisemitic, convinced that BLM activism was being controlled by a Jewish cabal. This connection between anti-Blackness and antisemitism was present in the earliest American white supremacist literature, and had long been a feature of their memes. The Happy Merchant was an early example; another was the Synagogue, a riff on Yarvin's Cathedral with a decidedly antisemitic twist. Many of the TRS guys had dabbled in NRx and the writings of Yarvin before moving on to harder white nationalist positions. Because Yarvin is Jewish, they distrusted his philosophy, but they were inspired by his many neologisms. TRS would continue to riff on these memes, for instance in the phrase "kosher sandwich," referring to Jewish control of both Democrats and Conservatives, with the goyim crushed between.

The far online right was beginning to unite under common terminology and an increasing reliance on the white supremacist canon, from texts like *Mein Kampf* that had animated white separatist groups in the past to the Zionist Occupied Government (ZOG) conspiracy popularized by the Aryan Nation in the 1970s and newer books like the antisemitic Culture of Critique series published between 1994 and 2004. Still, at this time TRS viewed themselves as above the fray, the only ones with the right answers; they showed a dislike for other viewpoints, especially those of boomer white nationalists who might want to use their forums to promote themselves.

TRS was a tight-knit crew, and many prolific racists who'd go on to make a name for themselves cut their teeth in the TRS community. One such was a Gen X poster, illustrative of his cohort, going by the name Spectre, who grew up with colorblind ideas about race in an almost exclusively white community. He said the shock of his contact with minorities outside his home area made him withdraw from urban life, and he spent his college years on 4chan and /pol/, where he became a self-described shitlord, a pejorative term for those who seek out marginalized people to troll online. Looking for a place to vent, he worked his way through Chimpout, Niggermania, and Stormfront, ultimately finding Reddit's CoonTown to be the best fit for his sensibilities. There he met guys in the TRS community who were using CoonTown as a battle-ground for trolling shitlibs and boosting racist subreddits, as Spectre put it on a podcast. After Roof's massacre, Reddit took CoonTown down, but Spectre had found friends who shared not just his anti-Black racism but also his growing interest in ethnonationalist solutions. Nazism and fascism were becoming a popular solution for the race problem set by TRS and the Daily Stormer.

"I find myself constantly engaging those around me on race-realism (race and IQ, r/K theory, HBD), feminism vs traditionalism, white geno-cide and the JQ [Jewish question]," Daily Stormer creator Anglin wrote in 2016. Groups like TRS and the Daily Stormer didn't think it was enough for them to feed the more "acceptable" anti-Black and misogy-nistic attitudes to Americans; they had to create an alternative media ecosystem, built upon revisionist history and pseudoscience, to attract new audiences and build political power.

The infrastructure of the internet, and the networked collection of these white supremacist and far-right sites, allowed memes containing these ideas to circulate further and faster than ever before. Roof had learned a false history on these sites, and decided on a grave goal: to spark a race war through murder. Though he didn't make friends with any of the anons or influencers in these networks before his crime, now they at least knew his name.

What we see in Roof's story, and the story of the HBD meme, is the way in which the rise of anti-racist movements provoked a reactionary backlash. The far right at this time began growing their online infra-structure so that they could better move their ideas—HBD—from the wires of the internet to the weeds of real life. Roof took it upon himself to enact these ideas on his own, but HBD's goal was not merely to incul-cate lone wolves—it intended to start a movement.

In November 2015, two young masked men uploaded video of themselves on their way to a BLM protest, armed and seemingly with violent intent. In this video, they shouted out /pol/ and instructed their audience to "stay white." Soon after, one would open fire on a crowd of protestors, injuring five. These men sent clear signals to their presumed audience on 4chan, their ominous video laced with meme references. Though an outlier, this event, like Roof, showed the real-world impact of the festering radicalism in the online right.

The left had the infrastructure for BLM in place through Occupy. The right, bristling under the Obama presidency, was increasingly receptive to not only racist dog whistles but the ideas of cryptofascists and white supremacists. The online infrastructure of the far right fostered and fed this growing white resentment, gave it form and function, and was a crucial precursor to the political battles to come.

Chapter 3

Gamers Rise Up

The Supreme Gentleman

As this white resentment grew, so too did a violent breed of male resentment, embodied horrifically in the meme "the Supreme Gentleman." The roots of this meme go back to May 23, 2014, when twenty-two-year-old Elliot Rodger murdered six people, injured over a dozen more, and then killed himself. The college dropout had been living in Isla Vista, a small community in Santa Barbara County densely populated with students from the University of California. Despite a privileged upbringing—his father was a Hollywood film director who had worked on the *Hunger Games* franchise—Rodger deeply resented women for denying him companionship, love, sex, and pleasure. After facing rejection in his teens, this resentment turned to uncontrollable rage. He hated women for dating other men, particularly men of color. Moments before his killing spree, he sent a maniacal manifesto titled "My Twisted World" to thirty-four people, including high school friends, his parents, and his therapist, detailing his life experiences and his gruesome plans for retribution. That night Rodger stabbed his three male roommates and then headed to a sorority house, outside of which he shot three women, killing two.

Unable to get entrance into the sorority house, Rodger got in his car and began firing out the window. He shot and killed a male student, and got into two shootouts with police, and struck people with his BMW before shooting himself. Along with his written manifesto, he had uploaded a final video to YouTube: "Elliot Rodger's Retribution," in which he referred to himself as "the supreme gentleman." This and other video diaries and his manifesto made Rodger into the patron saint of 4chan's incel haven /r9k/, memorialized in the Supreme Gentleman meme.

Prior to the rampage, Rodger's social life consisted mainly of online forums and playing *World of Warcraft*, a game where he could lose himself in the online world of combat and conquest. WoW has a rich online fandom community, but outside of gamer culture, WoW players are often stereotyped as lonely virgins, too damaged for a "real life." For Rodger, playing WoW with his friends was the happiest time in his life. But, he said, it couldn't make up for the rage he felt at being denied romantic love, as he put it. Explaining why he planned to murder women, Rodger wrote about feeling rage toward people in relationships, and how puberty affected his desires. In a macabre twist, he added that he wanted to kill his siblings, too, because they were having sexual relationships and he was not. He also spoke numerous times of his rage at seeing men of color dating white women, writing in his manifesto,

> I came across this Asian guy who was talking to a white girl. The sight of that filled me with rage. I always felt as if white girls thought less of me because I was half-Asian, but then I see this white girl at the party talking to a full-blooded Asian. I never had that kind of attention from a white girl! And white girls are the only girls I'm

attracted to, especially the blondes. How could an ugly Asian attract the attention of a white girl, while a beautiful Eurasian like myself never had any attention from them?

Only after he decided that he was going to kill his enemies and himself, Rodger said, did he feel relief and enjoy hiking and sunsets. For several months he plotted his "retribution." He began by making a video titled "Why Do Girls Hate Me So Much?" Shot from a fixed position in a parking lot drenched in the California sun, wearing a blue T-shirt and a blue plaid collared shirt, Rodger talked directly to the camera as if he was addressing all women. Girls had never given him a chance, he complained, despite him being "polite, sophisticated . . . the ultimate gentleman." At points in the video, he begins to pace and grows agitated as he talks about seeing other couples in love.

In his manifesto he outlined why he made this initial video: "It is my attempt to reason with the female gender, to ask them why they have mistreated me. *I was hoping I would get some sort of answer from girls.* In fact, a small part of me was even hoping that a girl would see the video and contact me to give me a chance to go on a date. That alone would have prevented the Day of Retribution, if one girl had just given me one chance. But no . . . As expected, I got absolutely no response from any girls. The only responses I got were from other men who called me names and made fun of me."

Elliot also participated in online forums like PUAhate.com (originally founded to satirize a subculture called pickup artists, or PUAs, but later a haven for misogyny) and posted on a bodybuilding forum, where he wrote, "Women have control over which men get sex and which men don't, thus having control over which men breed and which men don't. Feminism gave women the power over the future of the human species. Feminism is evil." In his manifesto, he admitted that the ultimate goal of his "retribution" was to induce terror, shooting and "splattering" everyone in Isla Vista; "I cannot kill every single female on earth, but I can deliver a devastating blow that will shake all of them to the core of their wicked hearts. I will attack the very girls who represent every-thing I hate in the female gender: The hottest sorority of UCSB."

With his posting history spread out across platforms, Rodger ensured that his menacing tirades would be found and reposted. In fact, attempts to remove these videos on YouTube have spawned a subculture of people who periodically reupload them. Anons on the /r9k/ board he was believed to have frequented tracked developments of his rampage in real time, picking through any info on the news and combing through his social media to learn more about this red-pilled killer.

In the days following the killings, more evidence of Rodger's misogyny was discovered by other online sleuths and eventually journalists. The hashtag #NotAllMen trended on Twitter as users debated the degree to which toxic masculinity, sexism, and rape culture had inspired Rodger's actions. Black cyberfeminist Shafiqah Hudson (@SassyCrass on Twitter) had originally used this phrase to poke fun at men interrupting women in the midst of recounting a trauma to explain that "not all men" are like that. Days later, a corresponding hashtag, #YesAllWomen, revived the online debate, making the point that even though not all men commit atrocities, women everywhere must remain on guard against misogynistic attacks because of the prevailing culture of sexism. This discussion was vitriolic and led to the harassment of journalists and feminists, but it hardly compared to what was happening in other online communities.

As the hype around Rodger built on /r9k/, and the discomfort of women grew hypervisible on Twitter, anons on /pol/ saw an ironic political hero. Rodger was biracial, sure, but a more acceptable type in the opinion of these HBD-bombarded anons on /pol/. They could join forces in memeing Elliot Rodger into the leader of the "beta uprising," a meme that indicated the rage some men felt at not fitting society's supposed "alpha male" standards. It also gave them a direct line into an ongoing conversation happening across 4chan about Rodger—his race. Perhaps his mixed-race status was to blame for his actions, his failures baked into his genetics. The HBD question, even comparing Rodger to biracial Obama, came up in memes as well.

Rodger's videos and manifesto embodied another meme that was already universally popular on 4chan, "that feeling when no girlfriend" (shorthanded as "tfw no gf"). Sometimes paired with "tfw no gf" was an image of Feels Guy, aka Wojak, a simple line drawing of a sad-looking face meant to convey empathy. In his "retribution" video, Rodger declared, "I'm the perfect guy, and yet you throw yourselves at all these

WE ALL KNOW THAT FEEL

obnoxious men, instead of me, the supreme gentleman. I will punish all of you for it." He followed this with a strange and eerie laugh. The phrase stuck out as embarrassingly awkward and was the kind of cringe that instantly became a 4chan favorite across all the boards.

Rodger's actions and internet footprint led the mainstream media to try to unpack an internet subculture they knew little about, the manosphere, a collection of forums, blogs, and websites devoted to men's rights activism, antiwoman, and antifeminist content. In response to the press about Rodger, a little-known Breitbart reporter named Milo Yiannopoulos published a piece explaining that Rodger wasn't animated by "everyday sexism," but rather that it was the video games that did it. He wrote, "So ignore the shoddy, opportunistic posturing from feminists about Rodger's crimes. It's the blurring of fantasy and reality in today's video game-obsessed young men that's the real enemy. If there's a cultural milieu that contributed to the creation of Elliot Rodger, it was that of nihilistic video games, not the myth of patriarchal oppression."

In a few months, Milo would become the most famous face of the red-pilled right, a one-name celebrity like Madonna. He self-described as a "shit-talking insurgent" and "virtuous troll," but he didn't look like a prototypical troll. He was tall, with an athletic build, and thick straight hair that he wore swept across his forehead. By the time he was at

Breitbart, he often bleached his brown hair blond or frosted the tips, and painted his nails. He was a classical British dandy who paid close attention to fashion and frequently wore suits with no tie, the shirt opened just a few buttons too many. He'd scowl over his signature dark sunglasses, exuding confidence and derision, with a look on his face as though everyone in the world were too stupid for him to deal with.

"I get paid to be me," he said. "I have the best job in the world. I get paid to ridicule and humiliate the worst people on the internet. The bullies, the abusers, the social justice lunatics who are most guilty of all of the things they preach against. They are the people who are the bigots, the bullies, the harassers, the people who make people's lives miserable for no good reason . . . the famed evil straight white male."

British born of Greek and Jewish descent, Milo Yiannopoulos was brought up Catholic, like his boss at Breitbart, Steve Bannon, but the most surprising thing about Yiannopoulos, given his religion and his politics, was that he was gay. At the time, being an openly gay conservative was far rarer than it is today. He briefly attended Manchester University and then Cambridge to study liberal arts before dropping out to enter the business of stirring up shit on the internet.

Yiannopoulos was an antagonist from the start. A prolific Twitter user, he used his quick wit to slay his enemies, parading his flamboyant lifestyle in an effort to deflect frequent accusations that he was a misogynist and homophobe. He had secured a unique Twitter handle—@Nero, like the infamously cruel Roman emperor—which helped him gain a large following. "He was really cool," he said of Nero. "The elites hated him but the people loved him. He was artistic, he was sadistic and hilarious." Like the emperor who was rumored to have started a fire that burned Rome, Yiannopoulos was there to watch feminism and social justice movements burn so he could "build his golden house" and define an entire generation of young conservatives.

Yiannopoulos worked up to his swagger. In his first journalism role as a writer for the *Catholic Herald*, Yiannopoulos made his first big media appearance, going on UK's Channel 4 for an awkward debate against gay marriage. It's painful viewing. The unpolished Yiannopoulos, pitted against the self-assured pop star Boy George, couldn't quite hold his own. He was nervous and didn't know where to look.

At his next gig, tech-writing for the *Daily Telegraph*, Yiannopoulos turned his internet fights with celebrities, particularly Stephen Fry, into viral stories. This seemed like a pretty good business model for tech journalism so in 2011, so he launched his own tech gossip blog, the *Kernel*, and appointed himself executive editor. The site got a lot of attention—including an early profile in the *Guardian* that referred to him as "the pit bull of tech media"—but ultimately ended in scandal after it came out that Yiannopoulos hadn't paid any of his contributors or employees, and had reportedly threatened some with blackmail if they published their complaints.

Yiannopoulos needed a new gig. Luckily for him, Bannon was on the hunt for fresh blood for Breitbart London, and was particularly keen to harness the energy of the extremely online crowd, which Yiannopoulos had demonstrated he could do. Yiannopoulos's hatred of the tech space grew as he made more and more enemies, and for a while on Twitter he teased a forthcoming book on the subject, titled *The Sociopaths of Silicon Valley*. He had a brief stint at *Business Insider* covering tech around this time as well, but it didn't last and neither did the book plans. The Breitbart gig slowly became his sole focus.

Yiannopoulos's first really popular Breitbart article was a glowing writeup of science reporter Nicholas Wade's controversial book *A Troublesome Inheritance: Genes, Race and Human History* in May 2014. Prominent evolutionary biologists accused Wade of drawing an "incomplete and inaccurate account" of race and natural selection. Yiannopoulos blamed the media for the controversy: "Journalists are often silent—or, worse, resort to name-calling—when they encounter research they find uncomfortable." His short article sparked over a thousand interactions in the comment section below, a debate that boiled down to two positions: Was race a product of culture, or was culture a product of race?

It's hard to say if Yiannopoulos had been exposed directly to HBD propaganda at this time, but his audience was clearly receptive to conversations about race science. His piece on blaming Rodger's mass murder on video games wasn't nearly as popular. In fact, he didn't have another viral hit until later that summer, when he began covering a brewing online meme war about video games and feminism, which became known as Gamergate. Seeing an opportunity to harness a passionate audience of gamers, he apologized for his early characterization of them as violent losers and began writing impassioned blog posts in their defense. "An army of sociopathic feminist programmers and campaigners, abetted by achingly politically correct American tech bloggers, are terrorizing the entire community," he wrote in his first Gamergate post. These stories made Yiannopoulos a must-read writer on the site. They also amplified the Gamergate meme war far and wide.

#Gamergate

Rodger's killing spree was the extreme violent expression of a feeling that women were to blame for his personal sorrow. It was a solitary act, randomly targeted at women who, he explained in his manifesto, he saw as stand-ins for an entire gender.

It was another misogynistic manifesto that sparked Gamergate. On August 16, 2014, the spurned ex-boyfriend of a video game developer and Tumblr blogger named Zoe Quinn posted a screed to his blog alleging that Quinn had cheated on him with five guys. One of those guys, he said, was a video game reviewer for the Gawker-owned game review site Kotaku. Quinn had just released an artsy indie game called

Depression Quest to the mainstream gaming platform Steam on August 11, and Kotaku and other niche gaming review outlets had given it positive coverage.

The vengeful post caught the attention of gamers, who read into it that Quinn had used her sexual relationships to get good press for *Depression Quest*. This idea snowballed into the claim that the wider video game industry was fundamentally biased and corrupt. Of course, the public display of such personal and intimate details of Quinn's life drew a lot of attention, but it also confirmed a deeper misogynistic belief—that women's success was rooted in their ability to wield sex as a weapon as a power over men.

Some gamers began harassing Quinn and the men she was alleged to have had relationships with. Eventually the harassment expanded to include other women who made video games or criticized the male-dominated culture of gamers or the stereotypes of women in many popular video games. The harassers' tactics were numerous. They doxed women and "swatted" them, calling fake bomb threats in at their addresses, causing law enforcement to show up to their houses. Reddit, 4chan, and other gaming forums lit up with the controversy; gamers coordinated about who to target; blog posts about the ways women were ruining gaming begat blog posts about how journalists were ruining gaming, too; the gaming press began covering it; the hashtag #Gamergate began to trend on Twitter—and a meme war was born.

This war pitted video game fans against video game critics, feminists against angry nerds, and the trolls of 4chan against the social justice advocates of Tumblr, a popular blogging platform known for lefty politics. The phrase "Actually, it's about ethics in gaming journalism" is perhaps the most enduring meme from the period. This refrain was used in earnest by supporters of the movement and dismissively by critics, who asserted it was really about getting women out of games. Yiannopoulos pushed the journalists versus gamers angle hard, positioning Gamergate as a fight between guys who loved video games and a video game tech press that had, as he put it, "sided with activists to pen soporific op-eds about the need for 'equality' in video games, while the people who actually play games just want to know if the latest instalment is good value for money." Gamergate pushers contended that the video game press had turned against its own audience, championing feminist theory and social justice norms at the expense of what gamers actually wanted, and in so doing painting gamers as bad people.

Fundamentally, Gamergate was an open-source reactionary movement, owing more to Occupy than traditional conservative movements of the past. It was loosely organized through a titular hashtag on Twitter. All you had to do was join in the hashtag, and you too were part of the movement. But that movement had many sides, most of them misogynistic and threatening. Using harassment, doxing, and coordinated media manipulation, Gamergate showed that even a loose, distributed coalition on the internet could cause real-world chaos if it had enough energy behind it. And it might do real damage if it could tap into the powerful ecosystem of right-wing news websites that thrived on anxiety and grievance and stood waiting to amplify reactionary narratives, whether they were racist, misogynist, or a bit of both. The idea with Gamergate was just to stir shit up. And it got results: Quinn and other women who were harassed fled their homes for fear of violence, and a conversation about video games and, most importantly, the power of gamers online was sparked. Gamergate proved famed game developer Gabe Newell's axiom: "No one is smarter than the internet."

The predominant interpretations of Gamergate are binary: it was animated either by genuine concern for journalistic ethics, or by misogyny. But for some people, Gamergate was about something else entirely: the tide of "social Marxism" and the infiltration of progressive radical social justice ideas into every walk of life, including gaming. This antimedia narrative resonated with a lot of right-wingers who weren't even gamers, who then adopted Gamergate as a political cause. Yiannopoulos was the flag bearer for this side of the movement, and it was these supporters who drew the through line to the alt-right and the coalition that came together to elect Donald Trump president shortly thereafter. Of course, it's easier to see this in hindsight. Gamergate coverage in 2014 was largely confined to tech publications. It was only when MAGA momentum began to build in late 2015 that the mainstream press reevaluated their understanding of Gamergate, looking back at what had happened and seeing in the tactics something like a set of drills before the Great Meme War of 2016.

Gamergate has been called a hate movement, a consumer revolt, or a great awakening, depending on who you ask. On one thing everyone can agree, though: after Gamergate, nothing was quite the same online. Here's how it went down.

Gamers Are Not Dead

"Gamers Are Dead," one headline read. On August 28, 2014, about a dozen articles from progressive tech writers at niche publications and more mainstream outlets like the *Daily Beast* and BuzzFeed condemned the burgeoning Gamergate movement. All, in their own ways, questioned what the gamer identity even meant anymore. For Gamergaters, the simultaneity of these articles was proof of a conspiracy. Their community and very identity, they believed, was under attack from social justice activists masquerading as industry insiders.

Gamers were some of the earliest users of the internet, and they remain one the most deeply entrenched groups of people online. Savvy and dedicated users of technology, they are quick to adopt new platforms and comfortable figuring out how to use tech in new ways. As a group, they're willing to shell out hundreds of dollars for upgraded gear, stand in lines for the latest games, and pay high monthly subscription fees for access to the proprietary gaming worlds. This makes them a powerful consumer force.

One thing gamers like to point out is that gaming is actually the highest-grossing entertainment industry in the world. It brings in more money than Hollywood, more money than the streaming video platforms, more money than sports. And yet the media often still treats gaming like a niche hobby for nerds or a dangerous on-ramp to degeneracy and violence. Both stereotypes have a long history, but though the image of a nerdy boy as the archetypal gamer wasn't so bad on its own, when paired with the idea that the nerdy gamer would go on to be a murderous psychopath, it became something gamers would get pretty defensive about.

In the late 1990s, as the internet was slowly dialing up and video game consoles were all the rage, a culture war erupted about whether games were ruining children's ability to make moral judgments. This was an evolution of a long-standing debate about violence and sexuality in popular entertainment. But because gaming was so interactive, and because by the late 1990s the consoles were getting better and better and the games more realistic, the argument that they posed a singular threat to kids—particularly boys, who played them more than girls—began to catch on. A lawyer named Jack Thompson led a campaign against the gaming industry, filing a series of lawsuits on behalf of the families of people murdered by teenage video gamers. He alleged in these suits (which were all dismissed) that the gaming industry was making "murder simulators," and that these games made children more violent and were therefore responsible for the killings. He singled out the game *Grand Theft Auto* in particular, after teenage murder defendants claimed it had inspired their crimes. The families of the children killed in Columbine filed a similar suit in 2003, as have many others over the years. Though none of these suits succeeded, Thompson's crusade to get video games out of the hands of children has had a major impact on the cultural understanding of gaming. You can see its influence, even, in the article that Yiannopoulos wrote about Elliot Rodger, which placed the blame for his violent worldview at the feet of "nihilistic video games."

The debate about the proper role of video games in society and whether they are toxic is still ongoing. This is part of what a subset of gamers use as justification for the idea that they are an oppressed group, who experience life as though they are a marginalized minority. The gamers who fought Gamergate fell into this category. They felt that women and the liberal consensus of this era were oppressing them *because* they were (mostly) white men with enough disposable income to play video games regularly. This is what scholars Kom Kunyosying and Carter Soles have called a "simulated ethnicity": "Geeks read their subcultural identity as a sign of markedness or as a put-upon status equivalent to the markedness of a marginalized identity such as that of a person of color."

These dynamics were intertwined with race, class, and the changing cultural status of "outsiders" and "victims." Geeks, of which gamers were a subset, were once portrayed as losers in comparison to the archetypal sexually active, athletic, gainfully employed white male, dubbed "Chads" by the resentful virginal nerds who lived at the fringes of the manosphere. They had access, in the minds of the emergent incels, to the highest-quality women, and as such, happier lives. The communities were influenced by the racial essentialism and replacement anxiety of the HBD blogosphere. They particularly vilified interracial relationships, especially white women dating outside their race, while fetishizing and envying any white Chad's sexual exploits. They saw these Chads as free to live a normie life, not subject to the relentless self-reinforcing negativity of incel culture, where being a loser was the norm.

For some gamers, whose identity was wrapped up in being an underdog, the way to maintain their status as an oppressed group was to fixate on how women and racial minorities were encroaching on what they saw as their territory. It was true that cultural criticism of video games was morphing into intersectional territory. A growing group of writers and public thinkers were pointing out that games lacked racial and gender diversity, and that when there were women or minority characters, they were presented hypersexually or stereotypically. Anita Sarkeesian, who would later become a major target of Gamergate, had launched a YouTube series called *Tropes vs. Women in Video Games*, in which she analyzed sexist stereotypes in popular video games. These critiques were similar to trends in other sectors like journalism and academia, and most were written by fans of gaming who were asking for more representation because of how much they loved the genre. But this presented an opportunity for male gamers to situate themselves as an identity under attack.

The Manosphere

Since the late aughts, a loose-knit group of communities had formed online centered on creating spaces for men to come together to air their grievances against women and liberal feminism in general. This collection of sites and the influencers who ran them came to be known as "the manosphere."

These digital spaces cropped up after years of culture war talk about "the war against boys," an idea popularized by the writer Christina Hoff Sommers in a book by that title that came out in 2000. The idea was that the dogma of modern feminism, along with economic changes, had displaced men's rightful position in society and now treated men as though they were all predators who needed to be "feminized." This, Sommers argued, ignored men's natural-born characteristics and left them to flounder and suffer. She laid the blame at the feet of feminists and academics who had, in her opinion, prioritized the needs of girls over boys.

Sommers's theories were in direct opposition to a decade or more of research that argued that men and boys were, indeed, in crisis—a crisis of what came to be popularly known as "toxic masculinity."

This idea of a "masculinity crisis" was amplified and argued over for the next decade and beyond, by journalists, academics, and even politicians, who fought back and forth about whether there was a crisis, what the crisis was, and what to do about it. The zenith of this kind of reporting came in 2010 with an article by Hanna Rosin in the *Atlantic* that declared "The End of Men." The article argued that society was now better suited to women, and that men's long reign at the top was over. This was upsetting to quite a few men.

They had plenty of places to air their feelings about it. By 2010 a network of various pro-men's groups had formed online, which "despite some conflicting agendas and tribalism, [were] united by an antagonism towards women, a vehement opposition to feminism, and the production of hyperbolic misogynist discourse involving the imagery of what Alex from *A Clockwork Orange* might call 'ultraviolence,'" wrote scholar Emma Jane in a journal article. These communities—which met on Reddit, 4chan, blogs, and forums—began to attract mainstream attention around 2012. They encompassed subgroups like men's rights activists (MRAs), pickup artists (PUAs), Men Going Their Own Way (MGTOW) and involuntary celibates (incels). Many of these sites and forums were outright misogynist and sexist, but others at least started more benign—as weight-lifting groups or places for men to get dating advice and life coaching. While not all who participated in these communities truly hated women, many came to misogynistic conclusions after stewing in pseudo-intellectual theories of female hypergamy and unfair advantages women supposedly used to oppress men sexually and socially.

Incels began to show themselves in desperate posts on 4chan, mainly on the /b/ and /r9k/ boards, in the late aughts. First expressing themselves as sad, angry, and sexually isolated, not yet taking on the name incel for themselves, they identified with the hikikomori, virginal Japanese male shut-ins. Like Rodger, incels believed that women held the power to give them sex but were intentionally withholding it from them.

The identity group of involuntary celibates actually dated back to the 1990s, and was originally a mixed-gender community that functioned like a support group. As communities grow, they often fracture, and the once pangender incel community took a dark turn when the forum love-shy.com became more welcoming to outright misogynists.

In 2008, the board r/MensRights appeared on Reddit. This board became a gathering place for the men's rights movement, which dated back to the late 1970s, and argued that society in the twenty-first century was discriminating against men. Men's rights activists often had specific policy recommendations they believed would improve men's lives. They held conferences and events. They wrote op-eds and filed lawsuits alleging gender discrimination, but failed to articulate much beyond reactionary antifeminism. As the SPLC puts it, MRAs existed "in a pseudo-academic, seemingly respectable bubble, using litigation to challenge female-only spaces or defend men accused of campus sexual assault though airing more disturbing ideas behind the scene."

Online, the truth was that MRAs didn't need to have anything to do with real policy recommendations. To be an MRA you just needed to hold the belief that gender, like race, conveyed inherent characteristics that dictated how men and women lived and was not, as the libs liked to say, a construct. The MRA red pill told men that they were aggressive and sex-obsessed by their very nature and that they needed to embrace that and force the rest of society to embrace it, as well. This was gender essentialism theory, similar to the HBD theory positing that race was a biologically essential characteristic.

The manosphere blog *Château Heartiste*, also launched in 2008, tied both biological theories together, promoting both the gender red pill and the race red pill. With posts like "The Sixteen Commandments of Poon," *Château Heartiste* sold itself as a mainly a pickup artist site at first, though it slowly began adopting HBD positions from 2010 on.

PUAs essentially believed the same thing, but rather than dream of a whole new society built around men's supremacy, they sold a vision of a quick fix for men. They attempted to break down gender interaction into a list of rules so that women could be outsmarted and gamed into submission. PUAs specialized in grifting off male anxiety, selling advice about how to make yourself more masculine and attractive to women.

In 2012, some PUAs split off from r/MensRights and joined r/TheRedPill. This subreddit billed itself as a place for "discussion of sexual strategy in a culture increasingly lacking a positive identity for men." The PUA red pill was that women could be dominated if you just knew the right way to deal with them. Psychological manipulation like negging—that is, insulting women to make them want to please you—could be learned and deployed if coached properly.

Mike Cernovich, a lawyer and internet troll most known for his support of Trump in 2016 and his pushing of conspiracy theories online, first made a name for himself in the PUA scene. He took up blogging in 2004 after graduating from law school, writing ostensibly about legal matters, but with a large focus on defending antifeminist ideas through a libertarian lens. A recurrent theme for him was the scourge of "false rape accusation." This was a personal interest, as Cernovich had been arrested for rape a year before he started his blog. A judge in the case dropped the charges but ordered Cernovich to do community service for domestic abuse. In the ensuing years, he got married and then divorced. He blamed the divorce on feminism brainwashing his wife.

Around the same time the "End of Men" article was flying around the internet, Cernovich started a new blog, *Danger and Play*, this time specifically focused on antifeminist ideas and advice on how men could get women to submit. He summed his PUA ideas up in a 2015 best-selling self-help book called *Gorilla Mindset*, in which he trained men to become "alpha males."

Cernovich made clear that the differences between PUAs and MRAs were mostly optics. Fully red-pilled about women, he attracted a following by making extreme statements and refusing to back down, using YouTube, Twitter, Facebook, and his blog to spread his message. "Date rape doesn't exist," he argued repeatedly, a charge that brough him liberal condemnation but hero status in the growing manosphere.

Another leading PUA, Daryush "Roosh" Valizadeh, used his manosphere persona to sell books, make TV appearances, and become a guru to troubled men. Valizadeh and Cernovich made bank off the manosphere, as did many others. They professionalized the manosphere, moving from a loose collection of ramblings on forums and obscure blogs to a big business.

By the time Rodger's manifesto was published online in 2014, incels had adopted many of the hate-filled ideas presented by Valizadeh and others, and some members of the community frequently advocated for rape. Rodger became a hero on incel sites. The photos of him standing alone, forlornly holding a gun, became a popular meme there.

Some in the manosphere went on to fight the Gamergate meme war, and helped build the movements' ranks and capacity. Yiannopoulos was not among the manosphere, but he'd been antifeminist from the get-go and was happy to promote the theory that straight white men were being oppressed. This brought him into alignment with people like Cernovich, who would go on to play a key role in Gamergate.

Cringe Watching

During Gamergate, the manosphere and reactionary gamers found they had some common enemies: namely feminists and social justice advocates. One of the most effective tactics for taking down your enemy online is to use their words against them. And to do that, you had to watch them closely. This is one of the reasons why antisemites will often have an encyclopedic knowledge of Judaism, or why anti-Black racists will be obsessed with the history of slavery. Online, to know your enemy meant to invade or at least lurk in their spaces, stalk their influential figures, and learn their memes and language. Sometimes called "hate-watching" now, "cringe-watching" around the eruption of Gamergate in 2014 was a favorite pastime of the manosphere, the racist right, and trolls everywhere.

They cringe-watched everything women did on the internet, from popular women tweeting with blue-checkmarked accounts to anonymous women posting on Tumblr. As they watched, they got angry. Gamergate took all this cringe material and turned it into a weapon to use against women.

A YouTuber known at that time as Internet Aristocrat was probably better than anyone else at weaponizing cringe. He made explainer videos for Gamergate, pulling all the threads together and evangelizing the idea that the whole problem with Quinn and the gaming press was really about censorship, and the social justice left was coming for everyone. This caught the attention of Yiannopoulos, who knew this animus could be parlayed into viral articles.

"And what is your real name?" Yiannopoulos asked Internet Aristocrat on his short-lived *Radio Milo* podcast. "Everybody wants to know who you are. You've been publishing these wonderful videos and nobody knows who you are."

"I'm a man who values his anonymity, but my first name is Jim, most people know me by Jim."

He went by many names. *Encyclopedia Dramatica*, a wiki-style archive of trolls and trolling events, describes the man as follows: "To some he's a Jerry Springer of the internet age; to others, a former Gamergater with a passion for clowns and furries. But most importantly, he's a 40 year old who does YouTube drama for a living." Jim was a hardcore gamer, an immaculate researcher, a smooth talker, and at times a prolific content creator. Like a lot of edgy extremely online guys, he employed racial slurs for their shock value. His real age was unknown, but he sounded to be somewhere between thirty and fifty, with a smooth, decidedly American voice with hints of a regional accent. He never showed his face, and it was disputed whether he'd been positively identified or doxed by the internet's most investigative trolls. He was an ever-shifting specter, and in the shitlord community, a living legend. Instead of just shocking you with racist jokes and sexist humor, Jim was here to hold your hand and walk you down all the many rabbit holes he'd been down before.

Jim's first Gamergate video, from August 18, 2014, was such an explainer. Gamergate posts kept getting removed from 4chan, so many Gamergaters migrated to the far more extreme alternative 8chan in frustration. Some people gathered in an internet relay chat to coordinate direct harassment of Quinn and dox her. When people in the industry came out to support Quinn, they got a target on their back; the Gamergaters leaped to harass them, too.

Jim did the research, but it took a celebrity to light the fuse. On August 27 actor Adam Baldwin (a distant relation to the far more famous Baldwin brothers) hashtagged the whole mess #Gamergate. Immediately, the hashtag went viral on Twitter, and Gamergate burst onto a more public radar. A self-described libertarian conservative, Baldwin had been a vocal conservative on Twitter for five years and was old friends with Andrew Breitbart. He shared Breitbart's distaste for Hollywood liberals, their pet projects, virtue signaling, and hypocritical contradictions, and the two bonded over their critiques of the industry.

The #Gamergate hashtag was immediately embraced both by the anons on 4chan and the content creators on YouTube. "Guys its happening" wrote an 4chan anon in response to Baldwin's formalizing of the movement. "How deep does this SJW [social justice warrior] money scamming shit in media go?" wrote another. Meanwhile, Internet Aristocrat kept making videos, and they kept going viral. He lived for the drama, and Gamergate was the perfect opportunity to make some.

Jokingly referred to as "an invincible god of the internet," Jim had been playing with fire for a long time. He was a member of an infamous trolling forum named *Metokur*, and a cocreator of *School Shooter: North American Tour 2012*, an unofficial modification for the game *Half-Life 2* in which players had to kill themselves before the police arrived after simulating a high school massacre. The game drew the attention of the FBI, much to Jim's delight, and he'd later adopt *Metokur* as an alias.

Never using his real name, or even one steady alias, Jim cycled through by his own estimation at least seventy YouTube accounts from the time he started making content in 2009. He mixed his desire to stir shit up with his curiosity to figure shit out—a classic troll combination—and was one of a kind at putting together a digital trail and showing the receipts. "I kind of like to know who runs the show," he said. "I like to know a little bit about the people behind the scenes, pull back the curtain, get a look at the wizard, if you know what I mean."

Behind the curtain, Jim saw a gathering coalition of forces—government, corporations, and academics—looking to crack down on the internet, specifically "free speech." This was the angle he pushed in Gamergate. "For two years before gamergate became a thing you have a lot of outlets writing articles that were shitting on their audience," he said about what caused Gamergate after the meme war had ended. "Gamers are terrible, gamers are toxic, trolls are terrible, nobody can play games anymore, we need more restrictions . . . look at where *Overwatch* is now, you make a joke and you're banned." He hated what he saw as the "sanitization online," the content moderation that aimed to silence people like him.

Summing up his views on censorship and free speech in a video from 2017 titled "Wake Up," he said, "You might say, Jim you're an asshole. I've looked at your videos, you say horrible things, I've heard you make racist and sexist comments, you made fun of people, you've trolled people. Why should anybody care what you have to say? Well, you should care because when my form of extreme speech is gone, yours becomes the extreme speech. It is on a downward spiral towards the lowest common denominator. They will find more and more things to be offended by, and they love to be offended. And these perpetually offended people are the ones that want to dictate to you what you can or

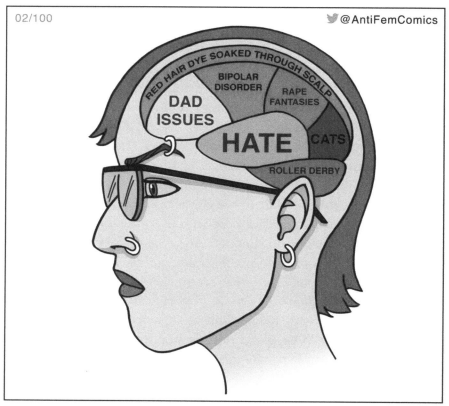

Inside the feminist mind

can't interact with, what is acceptable or unacceptable." These ideas are now a fixture of right and libertarian discourse ("free speech" itself has become a kind of meme), but at the time it was edgy stuff.

Before Gamergate, Jim made video essays criticizing what he saw as cultural degeneracy on the internet: out of control *My Little Pony* fandoms, zoophilia pride groups, furries with paraphilic sexual kinks. Certain of these communities would have influencers who'd get out of control, either through some kind of shocking admission or content of a sexual nature. That drama created smoke, and Jim knew where to find the fire. He'd watch more and more closely the infighting of these communities, their influencers. He and others like him used this research to fight a multiyear culture war—Tumblr for the left, 4chan for the right. Jim called 4chan home, and it was from Tumblr that he mined his cringeworthy content.

While 4chan and Tumblr both had left- and right-leaning communities, these weren't establishment political folks. Many people on both forums put more energy into cultural production than advocating for actual political policy. These were also both spaces where excess was indulged—and in these sites loosely coded as men's or women's, uninhibited personal and sexual expression thrived. Tumblr was seen as a feminist space, one grounded in intersectional politics that had far more allowance for the public expression of kink and sexuality alongside progressive politics like support for Black Lives Matter. Tumblr was also the place where the Occupy movement got its big boost through the *We Are the 99 Percent* blog.

For Jim, 4chan was the home of the raw male voice—a site where men were the default user, where women's positions were dismissively sidelined with the standard reply "tits or gtfo," which meant no one cares you are a woman here unless you tell us, in which case show us nudes and default to a male voice or exit the space. Within 4chan, the rhetoric of PUAs and other MRAs intermingled with the everyday stream of gore and pornography, and a reactionary chauvinistic politic of jokes was the norm.

Tumblr was a vast network of content to mine for 4chan's obsessive critique. Jim, and others like him, just sat and watched, plumbing Tumblr for new examples of outrageous feminist or queer aesthetics. They found lesbians with blue hair, disabled trans women, and fat academics. Tumblr was all about being real and finding yourself, which gave Jim and other shitlords a never-ending firehose of joke fodder. People on Tumblr showed their faces and names and signaled who they were with pictures and hashtags affirming their identity. They were there to find partners, allies, and friends in politics and sex, to share their photography, poetry, art, and music and to experiment with gender terminology in memes.

To Jim, the emergence of subcultures of the left was a degeneracy, a threat to the sacredness of the internet he called home. He considered feminists and zoophiles an equal threat. "Tumblr is a blizzard, it's full of snowflakes," he said. Jim considered himself the guide to taking "a swan dive into the deep end of the crazy pool."

In a video series called Tumblrisms, Jim would select a Tumblr on a specific topic and then use it as an example to explain the perverse ideology or identity it illustrated to his audience. He'd dig as deep as possible into the creators, trying to find some other link to them on social media or some real-world presence. It wasn't enough to see the degeneracy—Jim had to introduce people to the degenerate.

Based Mom

In mid-September, Gamergate got a new surge of energy and attention. First, Christina Hoff Sommers, whose criticism of the "war against boys" had been an early inspiration for the manosphere, endorsed Gamergate. Her involvement lent legitimacy to the movement's grievances and proved that it could be intergenerational and powerful beyond the extremely online set. It was also just great optics that a respected academic *woman* was willing to stand behind Gamergate. Sommers went on to be spokesperson for the movement in media, appearing on the likes of Ronan Farrow's MSNBC show. Gamegaters loved it and turned her into a meme, calling her "Based Mom."

One of Gamergate's most enduring memetic legacies is the co-optation of the word *based*, which would go on to become a foundational meme for right-wing insurgent movements. It all goes back to Brandon McCartney, a rapper from Oakland, California, at the turn of the decade, before Occupy or BLM.

Recording and performing under the stage name Lil B, McCartney was prolific, turning out free digital releases that were steeped in an abstract net aesthetic. Taking on the character of a benevolent, earnest prankster, his Lil B was deeply entrenched in the burgeoning meme communities of the early 2010s. Lil B was a hardcore gamer, social media powerhouse, and prolific troll.

Lil B smashed the mass media stereotypes of a rapper at that time, too. He'd wear pastel colors and dresses for photo shoots, and even named a mixtape "I'm Gay." Among his many provocative nicknames, Lil B began calling himself the BasedGod in 2010. In interviews, Lil B describes "based" as "being yourself. Not being scared of what people think about you. Not being afraid to do what you wanna do. Being positive." He would explain that he embraced the word as a radical act of reappropriation, that growing up he'd heard "based" used as a pejorative to refer to heavy drug users and their slowed-down lifestyle, a "basehead." Lil B remixed this old stereotype into a meme that would soon gain much wider circulation.

His rabid online fan base used his hashtags, made memes of him, sent him pictures of their feet with his name written on them in marker, and fully embraced "based." McCartney was hyperaware of how this new information ecosystem was changing how an artist made their mark. "Being the first artist to meme. TYBG, 'Thank You Based God,' is the first meme of music," he told Complex in 2021. He was the first of an emerging cadre of musical artists finding great success in online fan bases, changing how rappers dealt with the internet.

Based crossing over into generalized internet slang is but one of many examples of the appropriation of African American Vernacular English (AAVE) in geek culture, starting with the viral "Soulja Boy Tell' em" YouTube video from 2007. Long before the internet, white youth had been appreciating, observing, and co-opting AAVE and Black culture. Norman Mailer identified "the white negro" as the emergent archetype of the hipster back in 1957: white youth with cultural access who became imprinted with the desire to mimic Black culture, and the illusive quality of "cool" ascribed to Black jazz musicians. Before the internet, you had to hunt for this sort of music and style. Now music bloggers and major publications alike were scouring MySpace, SoundCloud, and Twitter to find the next big thing.

As rap artists like Lil B found a home online and flourished alongside the technoculture of Black Twitter, it didn't require as much work for white youth to find new slang and memes to add to their vocabulary. Despite an increased attention to the dynamics of cultural appropriation during the social justice era, called out by activists on Twitter and independent media, no one could stop words like Lil B's *based* from taking on deep reactionary meaning when put in the wrong hands.

From 2010 on, after being popularized by Lil B, *based* became intertwined with 4chan and gamer speak. It took on a new meaning: if you have a controversial opinion, and aren't afraid to share it, that's based.

Based roughly meant "good" for the in-group it was signaling to, akin to the fluidity of the word *cool*. For /pol/, though, *based* started to mean something more specific—being unafraid to speak your mind about how racist or sexist you were, and how confident you were in being an unapologetic white man.

For /pol/, anti-Blackness was based, and after Zimmerman's acquittal in 2013, anons on /pol/ started describing Zimmerman as "so based" for getting off scot-free after Trayvon Martin's killing. Hitler was also based, as was Chilean dictator Augusto Pinochet. Any minorities who seemed to share their reactionary worldview were also deemed based. Gamers who saw themselves as a simulated oppressed minority were based. As Gamergate supporters flocked to the chans (4chan and 8chan) for more info about the movement, the language of these spaces got sucked into the larger conversation. The in-group of Gamergate were based, the out-group were normies.

Hoff Summers was granted the title Based Mom because she was speaking out on behalf of gamers, and particularly frustrated young white men who felt they were not represented fairly by the media. Women and minorities who supported Gamergate were, like Sommers, based. They weren't the core identity (white men), but they were allies.

Yiannopoulos's first Gamergate story, "Feminist Bullies Tearing the Video Game Industry Apart," was published on September 1, 2014. It was a huge success, celebrated all over the Gamergate gathering places. Yiannopoulos took on Gamergate as a personal project, and claimed, perhaps accurately, that Gamergate wouldn't have become what it was if not for his involvement. The reverse was true: Yiannopoulos would not have become what he was without Gamergate. Those first Gamergate articles propelled him quickly up through the ranks of Breitbart.

Yiannopoulos treated Gamergate like it spoke for all gamers. On one hand, he called it a "consumer movement that rejects sloppy standards in video games, sloppy reporting, journalistic ethics." But in friendly environments, in conversation with others who might have reactionary instincts, he made his true intentions evident: "This is about ritually humiliating people who have ritually humiliated *you*."

Then a smoking gun changed the course of the meme war: the leak of what was called the GamesJournoPros email list. In these leaks, prominent gaming journalists discussed the harassment of Zoe Quinn and strategized on the right way to cover it. It was reminiscent of a similar leak from 2009, of JournoList, a mailing list in which Washington reporters could talk shop off the record. That one, run by star blogger of the left and now *New York Times* columnist Ezra Klein, caused a kerfuffle back then. To the right, both leaks proved that media figures on the left colluded with each other about their agendas, and they served as red pills for those who hadn't previously been against the media.

Yiannopoulos stayed on the beat for a year and was largely welcomed, at first, by the pro-Gamergate community. His attacks on social justice warriors on Twitter, his livestreams, and his guest appearances on gamer channels helped build his image as a man of the (white) people. In a four-hour long interview with the YouTube channel WoodysGamertag, Yiannopoulos claimed that feminism and BLM were chauvinistic, intended to belittle men and bring back segregation. "The current generation of social justice warriors we have," he said, "is just a new generation of authoritarian bullies."

Yiannopoulos hated BLM, despite his many claims that Black Americans were owed a unique social debt for slavery. He also had something of a race fetish, and spared no details in proclaiming his love of being dominated by Black men sexually. These constant reminders of his sexuality, his Britishness, and his racial preferences constantly threw the taboo of race mixing into right-wing conversation. In this way, he was a pioneer in using identity politics to fight against identity politics. In his logic, his status as a gay race mixer made him an impartial observer into the social drama of Gamergate, where he took the position that it was young white men who were truly disadvantaged. He assumed a priori that all "real" gamers were in Gamergate, and that all young white men were on 4chan.

Yiannopoulos paid a lot of attention to /pol/, a beat that had in the past confounded many mainstream journalists, calling the anarchistic anonymous imageboard his "favorite website on the internet." He praised it as being full of people unafraid to speak their mind because no one knew who they were. "Anonymity . . . gives rise to these beautiful valuable fragile subcultures," he said. "4chan is like a really essential pressure valve for a lot of young boys who increasingly don't have anywhere else in life to let off that steam. If they're in the playground and they get a little bit too boisterous, they get whacked on fucking psychotropic drugs? So what do they do, they go to /pol/ and they pretend to be antisemites because it's shocking and it's fun.

"I find it funny. If you don't find it funny don't fucking go there," he went on. "People from /pol/ don't go out into the rest of the world and force havoc unless they have to."

Yiannopoulos's language all came from 4chan, as did a lot of his labor. Allegedly, he also barely wrote his own work. His Gamergate journalism was coauthored or ghostwritten by tech reporter Allum Bokhari or a team of reportedly up to forty-four paid and unpaid interns he called his "truffle pigs," young guys drawn to Yiannopoulos's increasingly high profile and willing to dig up antifeminist narratives from /pol/. "A lot of these guys are young 4chan guys," he told BuzzFeed's Joe Bernstein in 2016. Confronted about the rampant use of the N-word and pro-Hitler language on a Slack group for these interns, he said, "They use it in the sense that message boards use it . . . I know they don't mean it in a racist way."

When asked about Breitbart's shocking antifeminist headlines, Yiannopoulos said, "What we do—something quite rare in journalism these days—we publish satire, we publish provocation, we publish all kinds of journalism that traditionally would have been left wing, this sort of dissident, mischievous, thought-provoking kind of stuff." As his profile rose, he became an in-demand interview subject among conservative YouTubers and right-wing media for the rest of 2015.

His boss, Bannon, himself a skilled provocateur, rewarded Yiannopoulos with his own subdivision, Breitbart Tech, which launched in 2015. Yiannopoulos joked that initially he demanded that it be called "Big Milo," but was rebuffed by Breitbart senior editorial staff and publishers. He stayed on the Gamergate story until the middle of 2015, when Donald Trump announced his candidacy for president. Then he turned his attention—and that of many of his new gaming fans—to Trump.

Social Justice Warrior

When all is said and done, the most enduring meme of Gamergate was the stereotype of the social justice warrior—that is, anyone who held leftist or intersectional feminist political ideas. A riff on the last decade's "keyboard warrior," "social justice warrior" entered internet vernacular in 2011, used largely by Tumblr cringe-watchers calling out particularly outrageous activists. It had been common to question the efficacy of online activism in the real world up to that time, before Occupy and the BLM movement confirmed that posting on social media was a potent way to build camaraderie among activists between real-life events.

Activists would devote Tumblr pages to the matrix of oppression identified by intersectional feminists, and 4chan would mock the most over-the-top of these. It wasn't really about excess, though, so much as identity, and Tumblr's punk feminist aesthetic drew particular ire. As attacks on these posters traveled back and forth between Reddit and Tumblr, social justice warrior was condensed to SJW, three letters that were catchy and unique. SJW made a great keyword for search and hashtags; there was nothing else like it, and liberal activists themselves

didn't use it. Labeling the opposition SJWs allowed their attackers to meme and shape the discourse about feminism and antiracism without engaging much with their opponents' content. Cernovich and other conservative supporters, latching on to SJW's memetic potential, helped take the term mainstream.

In his goodbye to Gamergate on November 29, 2014, Jim claimed that the movement had failed because it didn't focus on SJWs' growing power in politics, business, and academia, and got caught in the more niche ethics-in-gaming-journalism meme favored by other YouTubers like Sargon of Akkad. "It was the opportunity to finally kick the teeth out of social justice warriors and Tumble rats and draw a fucking line in the sand" against "corrupt media and the SJW cultural Marxist bullshit," he lamented. Gamergate was a symptom of the increasing polarization in the West, a dramatic us-against-them distinction, an in-group and out-group that Trump, and others, would later exploit. To Jim's chagrin, though, it didn't destroy the SJWs. Instead, he believed, Gamergate had played itself. "I know what happened to Occupy Wall Street now," he concluded.

Jim had warned Gamergaters not to repeat the mistakes of Occupy, like trying to appeal to moderates, or picking idiots to represent the movement in public. Like many Gamergaters, he'd been inspired by Anonymous and Occupy a few years earlier, and he told Gamergaters that he didn't want their open-source movement to be destroyed by appeasing women and racial minorities. The problem with those movements was the introduction of intersectional feminism and identity politics, in his opinion. But if given the chance and the right fight, the model, he argued, could thrive.

"Look at what you have with the Occupy Wall Street movement," he said. "They were on point from the beginning . . . they got co-opted by people who came in with their own agendas and their own ideas and they poisoned the well. This has happened time and time again." But by November, he had grown disgusted with some of the Gamergate antics. "Gaming is going to die, and these will be the people that cut its throat," he said in a video on November 27, 2014, in which he attacked feminist critics like Anita Sarkeesian, the gaming-journalism establishment, and the "white knights," men who spoke out against the movement and defended the women being brigaded.

What Gamergate certainly succeeded at doing, however, was establishing the media as a battleground and potent wedge issue for meme wars. And it proved that indie online media could outpace mainstream juggernauts like the *New York Times* and influence people directly without the buy-in of traditional gatekeepers.

Gamergate was still active in mid-2015 when Trump's candidacy began, but it was petering out. Trump suffused the movement with energy. The Gamergate meme warriors had honed their tactics, they knew they could get results, and they had some public leaders ready to direct their attention, so they pivoted their efforts toward the 2016 presidential election and set about trying to meme Trump into infamy. No one thought he was going to win anyway, so why not have fun with it?

Chapter 4

Troll in Chief

Trump's Escalator Ride

On June 15, 2015, Donald Trump took the most important escalator ride in American history. Slowly descending into the basement of Trump Tower alongside his wife, Melania, a fully made-up and coiffed Trump waved like a pageant queen to an assemblage of reportedly paid onlookers and rookie journalists.

At the bottom of the golden escalator, Trump joined Ivanka, his daughter from another marriage, at a podium bearing his name. Beaming with pride, he announced that he was entering the race to be the Republican nominee for president. Then he delivered a forty-six-minute speech that set the tone for his candidacy, and his presidency. Shockingly unpolished, it went aggressively against the grain of establishment Republicans. Preaching populism mixed with xenophobia, Trump made specific and memorable allegations: Mexicans were coming across the border to rape American women, for example. He spoke directly to the deepest fears of many white Americans, openly stoking worries about racial replacement that no mainstream politician in decades had dared to allude to. "Sadly," he said with his characteristic smirk, "the American dream is dead. But if I get elected president, I will bring it back, bigger and better and stronger than ever before, and we will make America great again."

For whom would he make America great again? Not the immigrants, that was for sure. He'd make America great again for people who looked like him. He printed the slogan on hats, bumper stickers, T-shirts, posters, flags, cups, and more, making it clear that even if he didn't get the nomination, at least he'd make a killing off the merchandise.

Trump's merch rapidly became a favorite early target of comedians and jokes on Twitter. Screenshots of his "Trump steaks" rollicked through liberal Twitter. Late-night host Jimmy Kimmel described Trump as "a president and an amusement park all rolled into one." Conan O'Brien quipped, "Season 15 of *Celebrity Apprentice* will not air. But not to worry. With Trump running for president, you'll still get to see an irrelevant B-list celebrity not get a job." The metajoke at the heart of everything was that Trump was just trying to get rich however he could.

Trump had to have expected all this. He'd been a target of dismissive humor for years, and in some ways it was this kind of mockery that may have led to his presidential run.

In 2011, the world watched on C-SPAN as President Obama mocked Trump to his face, in front of everyone in D.C., at the White House Correspondents' Dinner. Roger Stone, Trump's longtime friend and political operative, later said, "I think that is the night he resolves to run for president."

The press had a lot to work with in lambasting Trump. And he fit an archetype immediately. Trump was the antithesis of Obama. Where Obama was careful, Trump was loose-lipped. Where Obama was principled, Trump was a flip-flopper, always out for his own gain. While Obama was a mixed-race kid born middle class, Trump had been born rich in New York City, and used his father's money to create a real estate empire known for discriminating against minorities and trying to stop Native Americans from operating casinos. A reality TV star probably best known as that stereotypical rich guy who played himself in cameos of films from the 1980s and '90s, Trump was a playboy and a lout, known for his many divorces, and a regular feature on Page Six. And he palled around with unsavory characters whom most others with political aspirations would assiduously avoid.

Take Roy Cohn, Trump's attorney, for example. Trump met Cohn in 1973, when he needed a tough lawyer to represent him for discriminatory housing complaints from the city of New York. Cohn was known for his ruthlessness. He had personally recommended sending Ethel Rosenberg to the electric chair after she was convicted of espionage. He had enabled the McCarthy trials that sent Red and Lavender scares careening through national politics and media. For many Cohn was a pariah. For Trump, he was a savior. He solved Trump's legal problems, and afterward he and the business tycoon became good friends. According to the notes of Cohn's switchboard operator, Trump was the last person Cohn called before he died in 1986. Among Cohn's other close professional confidants was the dandy Roger Stone, whom he had met during Reagan's presidential campaign in 1979. Stone cut his teeth as an operative for Nixon, and it was Cohn who introduced the tactician to his friend Trump.

He also introduced Trump to Australian media baron Rupert Murdoch. After Cohn's death, Trump, Stone, and Murdoch remained in lockstep, in business and in politics. Murdoch founded Fox News in 1996. By 2011, when the meme war story really starts, Trump had become a frequent guest on the network. After he announced his candidacy, Fox proved to be Trump's greatest ally.

In their own way, both Cohn and Stone lived as reactionary libertines, drumming up right-wing political ops like the Brooks Brothers riot of

2000, where hundreds of people (many of them Republican staffers) stormed the Florida offices where the recount of Bush versus Gore was occurring in order to shut it down. Cohn and Stone were not conservative ideologues but opportunists, and in them Trump had a model for how and why to make deals with anyone helpful to his cause.

And unlike Obama, who had always been a traditional Democrat and whose values seemed pretty much to have tracked in a straight line from his early adulthood up to his presidency, Trump's politics were fluid. No one was quite sure what he believed. He'd been friends with the Clintons. Both Hillary and Bill attended his 2005 wedding to Melania at Mar-a-Lago. He donated over $100,000 to the Clinton Foundation between 2009 and 2010. He switched his party affiliation five times over two decades. He first registered as a Republican in 1987, then switched back and forth between Democrat and Independent, even launching a preliminary campaign as a Reform Party candidate in 1999. For many this would have made him a political nonstarter, but Trump turned it into a strength.

He knew everyone. And everyone knew Trump. He was cozy with politicians on both sides of the aisle, journalists at every publication—especially the tabloids. He knew celebrities, and billionaires who got stuff done behind closed doors.

By the time Trump was descending the golden escalator to change the course of American history, he'd assembled a small but scrappy team of campaign employees, most notable among them Stone and Corey Lewandowski, longtime lobbyist and a director for the Koch-funded Americans for Prosperity advocacy group, which had helped professionalize the Tea Party a few years prior. This inner circle would change and expand over the course of the campaign, with notable departures and fresh blood, but all were drawn from outside the professional class of consultants that catered to Beltway politicians.

Lewandowski had a philosophy he built into the campaign from the start: "Let Trump be Trump." He knew his boss's ego well, and the man's capacity to snag a headline. And when Trump announced his candidacy, he knew he'd get coverage. Trump said in his 1987 best seller *The Art of the Deal*, "One thing I've learned about the press is that they're always hungry for a good story, and the more sensational the better. It's in the nature of the job, and I understand that. The point is that if you are a little different, or a little outrageous, or if you do things that are bold or controversial, the press is going to write about you."

So in June 2015, telling the world that he was running for president to protect America from Mexican rapists surely fit the bill.

The headlines that followed Trump's escalator ride in the daily rags were divergent—and numerous. The *New York Daily News* painted Trump in circus makeup alongside the headline "Clown Runs for Prez," while the *New York Post*—owned by Trump chum Murdoch—applauded, running a cover with Trump's golden logo hanging over the White House. Most papers of record marked the moment with quiet acknowledgment: the *New York Times* ran a small story with the headline "Donald Trump, Pushing Someone Rich, Offers Himself," while *USA Today* had "This Time, Donald Trump Says He's Running." Many had sent their junior reporters to cover the announcement, so sure were they that this was a celebrity publicity stunt and nothing more.

The mainstream media and establishment politicians did not think Donald Trump would be president. They weren't even sure he was serious about running. He'd talked about it for years, and aborted a 2011 preliminary campaign for the Republican party. But in the four years that followed, as meme warriors were honing their skills on social media, so was Trump. He built up a popular presence on Twitter by commenting about everything in the news—sharing his opinions about politics, sports, and entertainment, never shying away from making scathing or outlandish accusations. He shared vaccine misinfo and conspiracy theories, and he congratulated news anchors when they had good performances. He was all over the place. This earned him millions of followers. It also terrified those close to him.

Trump's social media manager from that time, who had previously written tweets on his behalf, recalled the day in 2013 when he realized that Trump had figured out how to log in to Twitter himself: "The moment I found out Trump could tweet himself was comparable to the moment in *Jurassic Park* when Dr. Grant realized that velociraptors could open doors. I was like, 'Oh no.'" By 2015, before announcing his candidacy, Trump was averaging twenty-two tweets a day, with nearly three million followers of supporters and gawkers. No topic was off-limits, and it seemed like Trump had a thought to share about everything. By the time he was running for president, the running joke became that there was a Trump tweet for everything. Every time he was accused of some wrongdoing or dangerous idea, there was a tweet to be found in his archive of him accusing someone else of the exact same thing. These tweets would be presented side by side as evidence of his hypocrisy, though it was never clear if anyone other than liberals cared.

Trump was such a media figure that by 2015, he had become an almost grotesque postmodern simulacrum of himself. Was he a real billionaire, or did he just play one on TV? Did playing one on TV actually make him one? Were his tongue-in-cheek cameos as the "rich guy" funny because he was that rich guy, or was he that rich guy because he played one in the movies? It was impossible to tell, and it didn't matter.

In that way, Trump himself was already a meme. His name, often just the one word—TRUMP—was an aspirational brand, plastered over everything from buildings to ties to boxes of beef. To get back at Trump, celebrities would refer to his original family name, Drumpf, which was changed to Trump before he was born. Referring to him as "the Donald,"

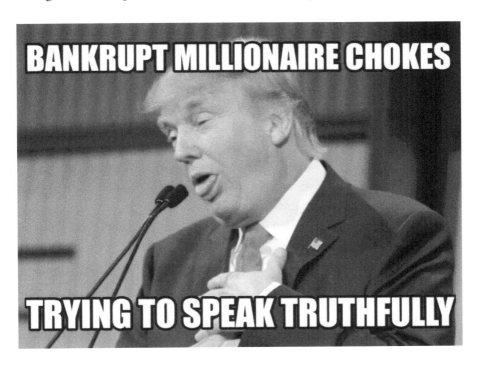

too, was like a remix on the Trump meme. And he seemed to luxuriate in that fact, playing up his love of all things gilded (remember the photos of his mansion apartment in Trump Tower, dripping gold?). All of this made it even harder for the media to take him seriously, so accustomed were they to treating memes as fluff and Trump's bombast merely as the attention-seeking behavior of a celebrity.

But if the media and political establishment had been paying closer attention, they would have realized that Trump had been currying favor with many factions of the extremely online right for years, and had become a sleeper hero in some far-right communities.

Obama had mocked Trump in 2011 because he'd recently launched a full-fledged attack against the then sitting president, amplifying the conspiracy theory favored by the Infowars set that Obama had not been born in America and therefore was an illegitimate president. It was a lie so brazen that only Trump could have sold it. And sell it he did. It dogged Obama throughout his final term in office, eventually forcing him to release his long-form birth certificate after months of press attention to the subject in the lead-up to the 2012 election.

As the "virtual spokesperson for the 'birther' movement," Trump wielded the power to turn nonsense into something real, something that appealed to a swath of right-wing voters, disgruntled in one way or the other with the liberal consensus. This put him in natural alignment with all the people on the far right for whom the Obama years were a nightmare.

Eight long years of Obama's America had existentially threatened these people's values. Gay marriage had been legalized. A Black man with the middle name "Hussein" was president. The only other Hussein known to most Americans was Saddam. Mainstream culture had accepted that diversity was unquestionably "our greatest strength," as the United Nations secretary general Ban Ki-moon and his undersecretary put it. This was a concept that read to some whites as a threat. Jobs were being shipped overseas. Everywhere the far right looked, it saw what Bannon called the "neoliberal globalist agenda" winning—ethnic diversity being celebrated as a virtue while more and more Americans were slipping into poverty.

Speaking to *National Review* on September 11, 2010, at the premiere of his 9/11 documentary *America at Risk*, former House Speaker Newt Gingrich illustrated just how dependent on racial essentialism and conspiracy these fears are. "What if [Obama] is so outside our comprehension, that only if you understand Kenyan, anti-colonial behavior, can you begin to piece together [his actions]?" For Gingrich, Obama was a dangerous "other," whose African blood predisposed him to violent conflict with white people. Even though mainstream white conservatives didn't call this racial essentialism HBD, there were stark parallels to viral racist narratives seeping out of the red-pill right at the time.

In 2015 Trump, Gingrich, and other top birther-theory pushers understood the white backlash brewing in America far better than the Democratic Party appeared to. If the Democrats had sensed how alarmed a large swath of conservative America was after the Obama years, they likely would have picked a different candidate to follow him. Their clear preference for Clinton was seen as aggressive to the right. After six years of slow liberal progress, festering Tea Party resentment, and the successes of Black Lives Matter on top of everything else, the Democrats were nominating a woman for president? A Clinton woman at that? If the establishment's goal was to provoke a strong reaction from the far right, it was succeeding.

So when Trump got to the bottom of the escalator in Trump Tower that day in June 2015, he knew who he was speaking to. Over on Stormfront, the white nationalists worried that he'd blown it immediately by using such outrageous language in public. But to the emergent coalition of his supporters, Trump's forty-six-minute tirade was a call to action. He was speaking their language, and they had nothing to lose by answering the call. An insurgent campaign to help Trump in his quest began to form in the communities that for the last five years had made being a woman or minority on the internet a living hell.

Early Support from 4chan

Anons on 4chan, who always tend to keep up with the news, had been tracking Trump's burgeoning campaign before the announcement, debating his chances and whether he was "hardcore" enough for them—that is, whether he would be willing to take on the Jews, SJWs, and cultural Marxists whom they believed controlled American culture.

Trump's face had been familiar on the chans since at least 2014. They had tons of images to work with. After a life spent in the spotlight, Trump had left a massive media footprint, from press photos to movie clips to decades of television interviews and years of *The Apprentice*, making him the most recognizable candidate of any party by far. Not to mention that he also had an extremely expressive face, verging on cartoonish, which lent itself perfectly to crude caricatures and memes.

There was something fitting about 4chan's interest in Trump. 4chan was a troll empire, and Trump had been influenced for decades by the dirty tricksters of right-wing politics, Stone and Cohn, who were both trolls in their own way, garish and shocking and mean as hell.

Cohn, in particular, lived his life almost like an anon. While Stone would proudly live up to his tabloid-ready playboy lifestyle, Cohn was secretive about his proclivity for young men. According to Alexander von Hoffman in his 1988 biography, *Citizen Cohn*, much of Cohn's life stayed in the dark till after his death from AIDS-related complications in 1986. "His life was spent in a cocoon of filth and disrepair," Hoffman wrote. "The expression used to describe Roy's abodes time and time again was 'shit house.'"

In what would be considered a good example of meme magic by believers in the Cult of Kek, Hoffman also noted that Cohn's bedroom was decorated with frogs: frog drawings, frog paintings, frog decals, frog patterns on sheets, on nightshirts, on wallpaper, froggies everywhere; it was a room "bulging with stuffed animals, in this enormous turn-of-the-century townhouse, the plaster cracking, the paint all but gone from the walls, leaks squirting, and drafts finding their way through the ill-attended cracks."

Cohn's apartment sounded a lot like 4chan. Filth and disarray were signatures of the technologically archaic boards frequented by the nihilistic incels, trading images of racism, misogyny, homophobia, gore, and truly degenerate pornography. A love of toys, cartoons, video games, and other markers of youthful escapism laced the entire site. But for believers in meme magic signs, the frogs are the most significant. Like

Cohn's apartment, 4chan was also littered with frogs—or one frog in particular: Pepe.

Pepe the Frog is such a well-known meme that it almost doesn't need explanation, but you simply can't discuss the Great Meme War of 2016 without acknowledging its mascot. Nowadays classified as a hate symbol by the Anti-Defamation League because of its adoption by online racists, Pepe began as a character in the indie comic series *Boy's Club*, created by the San Francisco artist Matt Furie in 2005.

Furie's style was composed of simple drawings that could be replicated by hand or in basic image software. This allowed memesters to put the goofy characters into any context. In the early 2010s, hundreds of thousands of Pepe remixes were created, clipped, edited, copied, pasted, and redistributed on social media. Anything could be remixed in "Pepe style," from celebrities to fictional characters and even presidents. A market for "rare Pepes" even sprang up, with fans paying thousands of dollars for original copies of these memes for bragging rights.

On 4chan and elsewhere in geek internet culture, Pepe became omnipresent—a flexible reaction JPEG to drop into any conversation, for any circumstance. Pepe became so popular that normal folks on social media liked him too, using the frog for all manner of interactions. Once "normies" had gotten their hands on Pepe, resentful anons made darker, edgier remixes. White supremacists on /pol/ created Pepes in Nazi regalia, engaging in racial violence and other horrific acts. These Pepes quickly became extremely popular with the emergent red-pill right. When Furie saw his frog co-opted by racists, he tried to officially kill Pepe off in an issue of *Boy's Club*, but this backfired. Anons doubled down, making Pepe their official mascot.

These communities of dedicated racists were instrumental in linking Trump with the iconic Pepe meme early in his campaign. There was immediate interest in Trump's announcement on /pol/. Minutes after Trump's escalator ride, the conversation spiked, most notably in a thread titled "Who Else Here / Pumped for Trump/?" Anons are skeptical folk when it comes to real-world politics, and a few vocal anti-Trumpsters spoke out early. Still, there was a lot of excitement about Trump's anti-Mexican comments, and his general chauvinism and anti-immigration stance.

"It's like Lex Luthor is running for president. And I'm OK with it," wrote one anon.

Most anons on /pol/ hated Obama, kind of because he was a Democrat, and primarily because he was Black. The chans and white supremacist forums were filled with racist memes and anger over the fact that it seemed Obama would pass off the presidency to Hillary Clinton, whom they hated as much as him.

A brash white man like Trump was the opposite of the compassionate Obama and "nasty" Hillary, who had tacitly supported left-wing street movements like Occupy and Black Lives Matter after it. They were used to memeing against their enemies, but it had been a long time since they had a politician they could call their own.

The day after Trump's announcement, an anon on /pol/ uploaded a photoshopped meme of Trump's face superimposed on a drawing of the God Emperor of Mankind, a character adapted from *Dune* in the game *Warhammer 40,000*. Set in the grim darkness of humanity's far future, the *Warhammer* mythos depicts mankind as a fascist theocracy, whose sole mission is to systematically purge all alien life from the universe for the glory of their liege, a messianic superhuman imbued with immense psychic powers. Deep cuts like *Warhammer* were popular with /pol/ and most of the red-pilled right, and the God

Emperor meme got a solid first reaction. It's a largely white male fandom, and while it has some social critique of authoritarianism and fanaticism in its text, much of its fiction fetishizes martial power and genocidal religious crusades. While pop culture properties like *Star Wars* and Marvel comics were seemingly lost to the SJWs after Gamergate, *Warhammer* became an important touchstone for /pol/ and online gamer culture in general.

As one anon wrote, "If you sneak across the border and live here without paying taxes and having babies and mooching off the government and justifying it all by saying 'look look I'm a hard worker, I got a job sweeping floors' you are a criminal and a parasite, nothing more; and if Trump wants to fund the construction of real-life Space Marine chapters to hunt your xeno ass down and tear it apart then he has my vote." Trump's extreme statements on immigration would continue to animate the God Emperor meme amongst anons on /pol/ and give body to ultra-nationalist paramilitary fantasies.

It was only after Trump was raised to the level of a god on /pol/ that they blessed him with his own Pepe character. On July 13, a week after the debut of the God-Emperor, an anon posted the first Pepe-style Trump meme. It was the first post in a thread titled "Donald J. Trump: Cure for Neetdom," memetic slang that referred to the scourge of unemployed

and hopeless young white men. The new Pepe had been photoshopped crudely with Trump's signature hairstyle.

The post included a YouTube clip of Trump's job statements from his announcement speech and some German text encouraging the "Amerikanische Volk" (the American people) to help themselves. The poster saw in Trump both the meme power of Pepe and a fascist akin to Hitler. A zeitgeist was approaching. More slowly started trickling in over the course of the month; a notable early Pepe-style meme depicts Trump smirking as a family of Mexican immigrants weeps behind a border fence.

Translating 4Chan

Milo Yiannopoulos, who from the start appeared as excited about Trump as the anons, was clued into these memes bubbling up. His harem of young shitlords, whom he called his "truffle pigs," vociferously watched /pol/ and brought the treats back to him. Yiannopoulos worked to amplify the most promising of the memes on Twitter, in interviews, and in Bannon's Breitbart. "Lovable, mega-rich windbag Donald Trump is trolling the Establishment," he wrote in Breitbart on June 19.

Fresh off his Gamergate victory tour, Yiannopoulos was now singularly devoted to rhapsodic tweets, op-eds, and press hits rallying the internet behind Trump's banner. He painted a picture of Trump as at heart a troll, and therefore the trolls of the nation should get on board with him for the ride of their life. Yiannopoulos built support from the anons by mirroring their own content back at them, and he began dropping "God-Emperor" in interviews and writing. He'd later add his own nicknames for Trump, the signature being "Daddy." Importantly, in the mainstream media, this meant absolutely nothing beyond outlandish and wild statements. They didn't get the subtext or the memes at work.

Yiannopoulos's army of young white boys grew, many of whom were using him as consciously as he was using them. They often kept their identities partially hidden with pseudonyms, the most handsome among them more comfortable with showing their faces in selfies or video clips. Guys with nicknames like Pizza Party Ben, Mike Ma, and Paul Town relentlessly shitposted for Trump on Twitter, creating their own memes and grabbing the best from the chans, and enjoyed the clout that association with Yiannopoulos provided. These guys knew all of 4chan, not just /pol/, and were integral in connecting Trump to the incels of /r9k/ as the year went on. New Pepes, anime, sex appeal, and desperation all fueled this influential recon team that called themselves #Frogtwitter in honor of the ubiquitous Pepe. This energy attracted other factions of the far right that browsed /pol/ and the Daily Stormer for news. The far-right mediasphere egged them on.

Andrew Anglin of the Daily Stormer instructed his readers to "to do whatever they can to make Donald Trump President." TRS was on board as well, seeing in Trump great potential to grow support for white nationalism. It was intoxicating. The feeling on the chans was chaotic and exciting and hysterically funny. It was also nostalgic for any anons who may have been on board for Gamergate.

For Trump's campaign, the excitement on the chans was in stark contrast to the skepticism the campaign faced from the press and the Republican Party. In those early months, according to Matt Brayard, Trump's data lead for much of the campaign, "younger staffers would regularly pass around memes as morale boosters." He told Politico that "a video called 'You can't stump the Trump,' a phrase first popularized on 4chan that mashed up Trump's early primary debate highlights with a narrator from a nature documentary talking about centipedes and other campy effects, [was] a particular favorite of staffers."

As the anons were coalescing around their guy, their guy's staff was taking notes.

The_Donald: Reddit Takes Command

Memeing a president into office was an all-hands-on-deck situation that called for setting aside past grievances, so far-right folks on 4chan and Reddit joined forces.

On June 27, 2015, a new subreddit was created, solely dedicated to Trump's outsider campaign. They called it The_Donald, and it soon drew users who brought the media of their own communities with them— Infowars-tier conspiracy content, chauvinistic Gamergate rage, anti-mainstream-media attitudes, and memes imported fresh from workshop threads on /pol/.

Unlike 4chan's anonymous users, Reddit users need accounts, who accrue "karma," reputation points for high-performing posts. Your commenting history, what subreddits you frequent, all show up in your footprint. Popular subreddits and posts would be boosted by Reddit's main home-page recommendation algorithms, and the more conversation that was generated, the more highly visible the bit of news or photo would get.

Once a free-for-all, Reddit had been adding moderation controls to the site after Gamergate, so to stay online, The_Donald needed to filter out the escalating overt calls to violence and hate speech and bring it up to compliance with Reddit's increasingly restrictive terms of service. The_Donald's moderators made three simple rules: "No trolling, no bigotry, no anti-Trump sentiment."

These guidelines were loosely followed at best. Throughout the rest of 2015, The_Donald slowly gained a following, and within a few months it would grow to dominate Reddit. The subreddit featured "Ask Me Anything" Q&A sessions with Yiannopoulos, Ann Coulter, Tucker Carlson, and even Trump himself. Reportedly, Reddit engineers had to adjust how the entire site handled its recommendation algorithms due in some part to the sheer volume of activity and attention The_Donald was bringing to the site.

Even though Reddit was quick to ban Gamergate organizing in 2014, hundreds of subreddits devoted to anti-SJW content and reactionary politics emerged unscathed. The_Donald flourished in this ecosystem. Its stability and visibility on Reddit helped give the emerging MAGA movement a new vocabulary, taken from years of trolling liberals online in other movements.

If 4chan was the inner bunker where the war plans were drawn up, The_Donald became the frontline for tactical deployment. In this environment, dog whistles and catchy memes with dense meaning could get a lot of white nationalist ideas in front of mainstream audiences without much resistance. They had a term for particularly successful memes, ones that lined up with real-world happenings in the news or politics—*meme magic*.

Meme magic was a joke that wasn't quite a joke. It had been born on 4chan in response to an international breaking news event that bore resemblance to a meme about a character from a Batman film. (The details are wild, but not important—basically there was a plane crash that some anons thought bore resemblance to a Batman movie scene of a plane crash, which itself had already been turned into a popular meme. Combine that with some flight numbers that people thought were clues to a connection with the film, and some anons decided that maybe the memes about the movie had actually crashed the plane. You know, normal shit.) The idea of meme magic became its own meme and precept on /pol/, part of a trend there to embrace the occult. Even as anons mocked SJWs and crystal-toting new age liberals, they embraced their own form of numerology, developing elaborate theories about the number codes generated automatically on 4chan posts. A whole satirical religion was born involving quasi gods such as the froglike Kek, whose name was a transliteration play on the acronym LOL, and who anons said wielded meme magic.

Trump had been such a popular meme on the chans already, and then there he was on June 15, 2015, spouting reactionary ideas in a prime-time announcement of his presidency! That was meme magic in action. Every time Trump, a billionaire political underdog, succeeded where the mainstream said he should have failed, this was taken as more proof that meme magic was real, and perhaps he had a real shot at the White House.

Taking Aim at Cuckservatives

"Donald Trump vs. the Republican Establishment" —CNN

"Republican groups aim to bring down Donald Trump" —*The Boston Globe*

"These Republican Leaders Say Trump Should Not Be President" —NBC News

"Why No One Should Take Donald Trump Seriously, in One Very Simple Chart" —*The Washington Post*

If people were going to understand this new alliance of online racists, sexists, and trolls, they would need first to understand what they weren't. And what they weren't was the GOP. Mainstream headlines from the time made this clear, but the red-pilled right wanted to go further: they wanted to show that eventually the GOP would have to submit to them. A few weeks after Trump announced his candidacy, they found a meme that drew GOP blood: cuckservative. For years, the manosphere and shitlord set had been using *cuck* as slang for men who were weak, subjugated, or useless. Drawn from the egg-replacing sneak attacks of cuckoo birds against unsuspecting nests, *cuck*'s social use conjured images of impotent men whose women were taken by strong alphas, a source of humiliation (and titillation for some). The manosphere's obsession with reproduction strategies had been racialized during the Black Lives Matter era, and now it was about to get politicized.

Cuckservative, a portmanteau of *cuckold* and *conservative*, was floated about a bit before Trump, being applied to any mainstream Republicans deemed insufficiently right wing, soft on immigration and racial issues. From the beginning, the meme was a vehicle for gender and race red pills. While it's not totally clear who created it, Mike Enoch at TRS initially took credit, but attribution popularly goes to the MyPostingCareer forum, a small community for "intellectual" racists and trolls steeped in NRx literature. Like TRS, MyPostingCareer found conservatives and SJWs to be two sides of the same coin, eager to spread racial and gender essentialism into mainstream political discourse.

"The cuckservative is, in habit of mind and sometimes in practice, that pathetic white man with noodle arms and crusted tear tracks sitting hunched on a stool in the corner of his bedroom watching, with willing fervor, his ecstatic white wife get pounded into post-white release by a buck nigra who eats his food and kicks his ass when the fridge needs refilling," was how another NRx blog, the influential *Château Heartiste*, put it.

The meme built strong in- and out-group distinctions between conservatives and the red-pilled right, according to Vox Day, a reactionary blogger. "In some ways, the cuckservative is the counterpart of the SJW (social justice warrior), and they are more alike than dissimilar. You often will hear the cuckservative screaming at an SJW about how 'the Democrats are the real racists.'" All the GOP candidates who weren't Trump were attacked as cuckservatives. The meme surged in use on /pol/ and Reddit, was discussed in great detail on podcasts and blogs, and was weaponized against mainstream conservatives on Twitter.

Conservatives on sites like the Daily Caller and the blog *RedState* noticed, and began hand-wringing; the word was too toxic due to its association with racialized cuckold porn. For a moment, this slowed the meme. So TRS rallied to destroy these sites' comment sections with their counternarrative.

Enoch was on the front lines of these raids. He posted using his known alias so people would know who was attacking them, and convinced conservative readers to get their news from TRS. In the Daily Caller's comments, he made the case for a white voting bloc. "In 8 years it may be demographically impossible for the GOP to win a national election ever again. The cuckservative, blind to race, would continue to fail and lose power. You lost everything, and all because you were afraid a group of communists, atheists and homosexuals would call you racist."

There were thousands of posts like these. The trolling crews exploited the sense of unease and disgust the meme provoked in mainstream anti-Trumpers, and regularly raided the comment sections of publications like *National Review* to discredit their writers and red-pill their readers. As a result, many mainstream conservative sites shut down their comment sections entirely. Analysis of the news shared by Trump supporters shows that these traditional conservative outlets couldn't match the influence of conspiratorial and nationalist alt-news sites like Gateway Pundit and Breitbart that, instead of condemning the energy coming from the red-pill right, celebrated their aggressive memes. This was all part of the wires-to-the-weeds mechanism by which the fringe online influenced the mainstream.

Yiannopoulos, brandishing his bona fides as the "leading conservative authority on interracial intercourse" (because of his claims to have had sex with Black men), took to Breitbart on July 28 to defend the word against the accusation that it was racist. "It's a byword for beta male or coward," he summarized. Whether or not Yiannopoulos was as deeply red-pilled on the race question as his white nationalist counterparts is impossible to know. But he didn't get any love from them in his defanging of *cuckservative*, particularly the downplaying of the racial element at the heart of the meme.

Through the impact of cuckservative, NRx and the manosphere made their early HBD-inflected mark on Trump's grassroots campaign and conservative media: he was an alpha, set against a cast of beta male rivals on the right and a woman on the left. "If the media openly embraces white guilt and feminism, it will be impossible for Hillary to win, even if Trump is third party," wrote one /pol/ anon on September 25. "You'd be looking at a literal society-wide gamergate. I think Trump WANTS the media to attack the regular voter. He wants everyone to abandon the media and most people alive right now would agree with him." As was often the case, anons on /pol/ were seeing a cultural shift that the mainstream press was largely ignoring: the swelling antimedia resentment that had taken hold across the country. A Gallup poll taken in September 2015 found that only four in ten Americans trusted the mass media, tying historical lows set in 2014 and 2012.

TRS, the Daily Stormer, /pol/, The_Donald, and the network of young guys in Yiannopoulos's orbit on #FrogTwitter were learning to goose-step in tandem for Trump while the mainstream media was writing him off. Trump had only been a candidate for two months. One headline read, "Donald Trump Struggles to Turn Political Fling into a Durable Campaign." Then, remarkably, Stone up and quit the campaign in August.

The reason given at the time was that he wanted Trump to focus on policy rather than free-wheeling speeches that got people riled up.

Two fascists in the Right Stuff network soon stepped up to translate the energy from the alt-right into policy talking points—from a white nationalist perspective. They made their own media, as they'd learned, launching a Trump-focused podcast on TRS in August 2015. First called *Cuckservative Insider* and then changed to *Fash the Nation*, it was a weekly deep dive into Trumpworld and political news. The cohosts went by pseudonyms—top dog Jazzhands McFeels and his sidekick and longtime IRL friend Marcus Halberstam, a pseudonym lifted from a character in *American Psycho*. Both hosts claimed they lived in D.C., had worked in "conservative normie politics," and had some insider knowledge.

The name *Fash the Nation* was a parody of long-running political talk show *Face the Nation* and was exactly what the name implied: a show about national politics with a fascist agenda. Unlike *The Daily Shoah*'s shock-jock stylings, meant to be reminiscent of *Opie & Anthony*, *FTN* was pure Rush Limbaugh—a man both hosts worshipped and emulated.

But unlike Limbaugh, *FTN* was more than willing to attack every conservative shibboleth, particularly those Limbaugh tended to avoid, like race science, Israel, or the Jewish question. "Turn off boomer conservative talk radio and tune into *Fash the Nation*," went one of their taglines. Limbaugh, Fox, and all other conservative media that had yet to bend the knee to Trump were holding back the movement, they said, and only *FTN* could be "your guiding light in a sea of *degeneracy*."

Unlike other white nationalist podcasts, *FTN*'s program was buttoned down. They peppered in dog whistles and didn't swear or use foul language. They were wonks, in the weeds, flexing their political knowledge, and even though all their political analysis boiled down to Jewish schemes, the show was designed to appeal to more normie Trump audiences who weren't true anti-Semites. It worked. *FTN* episodes were shared on pro-Trump Twitter and Reddit, so the podcast was a hit. At its peak in the fall of 2016, *Fash the Nation* was SoundCloud's most-listened-to political podcast. High-profile reactionary personalities went on the show, including actress-turned-Hitler-sympathizer Tila Tequila. Some listeners may not have realized that *FTN* was a white nationalist podcast at first—that *fash* was short for *fascism* was hardly mainstream knowledge

at the time—but nevertheless its embrace by the growing pro-Trump movement showed how willing Trump's supporters were to accept whatever hard-right politics supporters brought with them onto the Trump train, so long as those beliefs were delivered with a wink and a nod. Irony was a powerful tactic—it gave cover to those who knew that the humorous statements were not jokes at all and ensnared the unsuspecting, who found themselves drafted into the meme wars by the hilarity of these supposedly ironic memes.

They were all bound together, for the moment, by their support of Trump and his campaign slogan, "Make America Great Again."

It didn't matter that Trump hadn't come up with his quintessential political slogan, though he did trademark it. Five days after he saw Mitt Romney lose to Obama in 2012, he filed the trademark. But it wasn't until a few days after his announcement in June 2015 that the paperwork was finalized, allowing him to deploy the slogan for all manner of campaign uses and merchandise. Variants of the phrase had been used by politicians since the 1940s, passing through the hands of Barry Goldwater, Ronald Reagan, and Bill Clinton before Trump started using it in the 2010s.

The first MAGA hat was white, and it was Trump's. He debuted it during a visit to a border town in Texas on July 23, 2015, when the hats went on sale on his campaign website. The $25 cap immediately sold out. The design was simple, and has been bootlegged countless times ever since. The hat was better than free advertising—it was advertising people were willing to pay for. The *New York Times* style section ran a September puff piece titled "Trump's Campaign Hat Becomes an Ironic Summer Accessory," gathering quotes from Trump fans and apparently some liberals who ironically purchased it because of its catchy slogan. Obnoxiously repetitive, redundant on every platform, it was a very successful meme, eliciting responses and reinforced by the algorithms.

The shortened slogan #MAGA made a great hashtag, as a unique keyword that doesn't have much previous activity in the English language to compete with. After Trump first used the hashtag in March 2016, it took off, unseating #BlackLivesMatter as the leading political hashtag. It still consistently eclipses #BlackLivesMatter on a daily basis. The edgy memes of the trolls and shitposters were all just complementary to the unifying MAGA hashtag, which gave them plenty of opportunities to slip more and more red pills into the thriving networked media ecosystem connecting everyone from Stormfront to 4chan, Reddit, Twitter, Facebook, and YouTube. Because of Trump's status as an outsider to the GOP, MAGA was considered a subversive signal online. Posted as a way to link up with other Trump supporters, put in profiles, and used as a simple response to election-related press, MAGA functioned like a hashtag movement, bringing together different right-wing factions. The movement was helped along on social media by a huge network dubbed the "Trump Train," which used a mix of real and automated accounts to amplify Trump and his allies. Composed of plenty of real Americans as well as international trolls, the Trump Train was proving to be unstoppable online.

Drafting off MAGA's Momentum

Soon opportunists began cashing in on the excitement. YouTube influencers found they could rack up hundreds of thousands of views by producing Trump content. The fascination with Trump's campaign transcended partisanship—people who hated him watched his videos, even if just to repost them in dismay—and the combination of genuine interest and rubbernecking had explosive effects on the YouTube algorithm, which promoted more and more Trump content to everyone. The same thing happened on Facebook, with the help of Trump's savvy social media manager Brad Parscale, who took advantage of Facebook ad targeting tools to get just the right Trump ads in front of those who were likely to see them and share.

All of this interest meant money and clout for folks who could position themselves as important allies to Trump. There were T-shirts and hats to be sold, speaking tours to go on, books to sell, YouTube advertising money to bank. Trump's war with the media became an on-ramp for online influencers, helping them to accrue audiences by offering them an authentic source of information outside of the mainstream bias.

Leading the pack was Breitbart writer Milo Yiannoupolos, who told his audiences that Trump was the final and only solution to the BLM and SJW problems. Like his boss Bannon, Yiannopoulos benefited from the patronage of the wealthy Mercer family, who had been quietly funding Breitbart's operations since 2012. Yiannopoulos soon upgraded his style, appearing with increasingly expensive clothing, bags, jewelry, and various MAGA accoutrements.

Conservative megacelebrity Ann Coulter jumped on the Trump train in mid-August after Trump unveiled his hardcore immigration plans, which included building a wall on the southern border and banning Muslims from the country. Talking Trump up in TV media appearances, Coulter became an extremely influential voice for Trump, especially with GOP women.

Mike Cernovich, who had expanded his audience since Gamergate, saw himself in Trump right away. "I said if a Republican acted like me and ran for office, it'd be a movement. Donald Trump has proven me right. People are tired of pussies," he tweeted the month after Trump announced. He jumped into the cuckservative campaign for the clout. Using his blog, Twitter, and YouTube, Cernovich became ringleader and organizer for many specific hashtag and meme campaigns for Trump over the next year and a half—most notably campaigns attacking Hillary

Clinton. Trump's campaign took him from obscure blogger and lawyer to famous political organizer and pundit. By the end of 2016, having been profiled in the *New Yorker* and interviewed on Fox News, he'd carved out a place for himself in the world of conservative political operatives.

There were all sorts of roles to play in this war. Bill Mitchell, an over-the-top Trump sycophant who gained a huge Twitter following throughout 2015 and 2016 by projecting extreme confidence that Trump would win, carved out a niche for himself as the antipollster. His schtick was to tear down any poll that had Trump behind. Soon he amassed thousands of followers to his @mitchelvii account, earning himself a seat at the pundit table, articles written about him, and a place of importance in the meme war. "They say that opportunity knocks at inopportune times and that's why so many people don't live out their dreams. I won't lie to you, this is fun," he told BuzzFeed in 2016. "I'm on a mission." Liberals and the mainstream press tore him to shreds throughout the campaign, but also elevated him in the process. The fact that he turned out to be *right*—all the traditional polls had underestimated the support for Trump—was an ominous twist.

These pundits and social media influencers were joined by big-league alt-right media powerhouse Alex Jones, who saw Trump as a massive opportunity to align with institutional power. Jones brought with him a massive network of fans willing to mobilize for a cause he believed in. His entire career up to this point had been spent positioning himself as an alternative to the mainstream media, which he called "the lamestream media" or "fake stream media," so he was perfectly set up to draft off the wind of Trump's antimedia campaign.

Jones had become the de facto leader of a large swath of the conspiracist community in America. This community became fluent in Jones's unique terminology and reused it as memes, which often spiked in usage during moments of social terror, like mass shootings. Throughout his rise he criticized the Bushes, Clintons, and Obama, finding reason to attack the establishment no matter which party was in power. Through his involvement with Occupy and the Tea Party, his support for Ron Paul, his fervent pushing of diet supplements and alternative medicine, and his ever-expanding national platform, Jones created an antiestablishment audience primed to support a candidate like Trump for all the reasons people in the mainstream may have dismissed him.

Once Trump announced his candidacy, Jones and his editor at large Paul Joseph Watson gave Trump's speeches plenty of airtime. Watson was plugged into the /pol/ set and brought their ideas to Jones's network. He and Jones kept an eye on 4chan and 8chan happenings, the political energy breaking out in those otherwise obscure imageboards becoming an early warning sign of a happening afoot in the real world.

If Watson spoke millennial, Jones spoke boomer. He was a vital conduit to conspiracy-minded boomers who spent more time watching TV and reading Facebook than going down internet rabbit holes. While anons and their young figureheads were courting young people, someone needed to reach the crucial boomer vote, since the older demographics are the reliable voters in any presidential election. Memes were not the right way to directly target these people, so the memes needed to be translated into sound bites and delivered through familiar channels, such as Infowars, which could then be spread on Facebook for the boomer crowd.

Trump was a good bet for these folks in the right fringes. If he won, he'd mainstream their beliefs and cement their insurgent position in the culture. If he lost, they'd go back to being where they were before, but this time they'd have a much larger network of supporters behind them. And Trump couldn't really lose. If he won the election, he'd be the most powerful man in the world. If he lost, he'd go back to being a celebrity billionaire with an even wider and more fervent fan base.

Trump's more mainstream supporters had a similar mindset. He was a transactional person, and the influencers who rose up to help get him into office were, too. This included people in the entertainment industry, who saw the Trump fever and cashed in. *Saturday Night Live* had him on to host the show in November 2015, and late-night comics like Jimmy Fallon fawned all over him in prime-time interviews. News ratings went up dramatically because of all the interest in Trump and his endless and increasingly hot takes on national issues. Les Moonves, then president of CBS News, famously quipped that Trump might be bad for the country, but he was "damn good for CBS." Trump's anti-media campaign was also one of the most successful and sustained media spectacles of the twenty-first century.

The Establishment Loses Its Grip

By spring of 2016, Trump had courted the conspiracy theorists with his call to Jones, retweeted Pepe to the delight of the chans, and earned the support of anti-immigration hardliners like Coulter. He then secured the vote of white nationalists everywhere when he refused to disavow the KKK's David Duke, claiming he didn't know what the reporter was asking about. In doing so, Trump proved he wouldn't bend to politically correct culture, even about white supremacy. Trump didn't speak much to Black Americans during the campaign. "What do you have to lose?" he infamously quipped when asked what he'd do to earn the Black vote. Trump's racial animus increasingly alarmed the mainstream press and activists on social media, who began engaging in debates about whether to call Trump a racist directly.

This is where the common story told about the 2016 presidential election usually becomes one of international intrigue, focusing on foreign disinformation campaigns and hacks, such as Russia's Internet Research Agency posing as Black people, Muslims, trans people, and others on Twitter, Instagram, and Facebook. And it was true that Russia seeded disinformation into the information ecosystem, and that hacked emails from the DNC released by WikiLeaks beginning in June muddied the waters around Hillary's and the DNC's ongoing email scandals.

But that narrative overplays those contributions and underplays how hard this national, homegrown insurgency had worked to get Trump the nomination, and then the election. Researchers tend to agree that Trump likely would have won without any election interference from Russia or anyone else, so devoted was his US-based troll army to doing whatever it took to bring him into office. This was not meme magic alone. This was the latest version of twenty-first-century political organizing. The Democrats and most of the media, frankly, just didn't see the significance of it all.

Through political trolling they attacked every other candidate in the field, riffing on all Trump's campaign nicknames for his rivals—Lil Marco, Lyin' Ted, and Low-Energy Jeb. Trump's speeches were ready-made memes, where as soon as he said something sticky, meme makers

would rush to be the first to post a reaction. Any remaining Republicans who supported other candidates were constantly swarmed by the pro-Trump online army, silencing any dissent on the road to the Republican National Convention. But the mainstream media was mostly missing this groundswell for Trump. As was most of America. Most Americans were not on the chans, not on Reddit, not tuning in to Infowars, not glued to Twitter, and so the activities of this increasingly amped up meme army went unnoticed for a long time.

By January 2016, Trump had huge leads in the primary polls. Vegas gave him a 32 percent chance of getting the nomination. Those were pretty good odds, but it was far from a sure thing. In the spring of 2016 Roger Stone prepared for Trump's potential loss in the primaries by creating Stop the Steal, an entity that registered a website with the same name on which he seeded the idea that if Trump lost the nomination, it was only because the Republican Party had rigged the race against him.

But then on February 1, Trump had an unexpectedly good showing at the Iowa caucus, the nation's first primary, coming in just behind Cruz. Was it an aberration? No—in the next primary in New Hampshire,

Trump ran away with it. Then again, in South Carolina, he beat Rubio despite Rubio getting the endorsement of the state's governor.

By April the Republican establishment was antsy. Some held their noses and threw their support behind Cruz. Others held out for Rubio. Hastily convened groups with names like Stop Trump tried to slow his momentum in the Midwest. But the Trump Train couldn't be stopped. It barreled forward until May, when Trump had won enough delegates to become the presumptive nominee. Bannon, one of the architects of Trump's massive grassroots support, had predicted the MAGA coalition (here meaning Trump's supporters, not the PAC) back in 2013. "It's going to be an insurgent, center-right populist movement that is virulently anti-establishment, and it's going to continue to hammer this city, both the progressive left and the institutional Republican Party," Bannon said at the time. Despite this appeal to more centrist right-wingers, Bannon's cultivation of the red-pill set helped throw this populist movement much further to the right.

On the other side of the aisle, things were similarly not going to plan. Bernie Sanders was proving to be a real problem for Clinton. Unlike Clinton, who seemed to have moderate support from a wide swath of Dems, Sanders had an energized and devoted base. These supporters put their energy into memes, an online grassroots movement of decentralized campaigning that echoed the best of Ron Paul's 2008 run. Among the online left, Sanders was beloved where Clinton seemed to be barely tolerated. This was absolutely not what the DNC had in mind for this election; Obama was meant to hand the baton to Clinton, and the left was expected to fall in line to support a historic female candidate.

The DNC, it later came out, was working to derail Sanders's campaign, talking directly with the Clinton campaign over email about how to boost her chances while insulting Sanders. In 2017 it was revealed that the DNC had also made controversial agreements with the Clinton campaign, which specified that in exchange for raising money and investing in the DNC, the campaign would "control the party's finances, strategy, and all the money raised."

Clinton's team adopted the pejorative term "Bernie Bros" to criticize the Vermont senator's followers, likening them to Trump's vast MAGA coalition, and played up the idea that the Bros were racist and sexist bullies. It was a sticky meme—rare for the establishment left—and it endured even in the 2020 election, when Bernie ran again. But as the primaries began, Sanders racked up some unexpected wins. He won New Hampshire outright, then proved victorious in other major states, including Colorado, Minnesota, Michigan, Washington, Wisconsin, and Indiana. Sanders ultimately finished with 1,879 delegates, far exceeding initial expectations.

Sanders was hard to get rid of. He stayed in the race long past his welcome with the Democratic establishment, only bowing out after the final primary on June 14 in Washington, D.C. He went on to endorse Clinton soon thereafter, but the Clinton team's misrepresentation of the position of Bernie supporters, together with the Sanders team's unwillingness to play along with the DNC playbook, created a cold relationship between the two politicians and a hot war between their online followers. Postelection interviews suggested that most Sanders supporters did go on to vote Hillary, but few were enthusiastic. Twelve percent of Sanders's fans, by one estimate, voted for Trump.

Clinton supporters kept quiet generally. Her events had smaller audiences than Trump's, and her name trended far less on social media. Research later found that many of her truest supporters didn't feel comfortable openly supporting her due to low enthusiasm for her as a candidate as well as a public lack of trust. They gathered in private Facebook groups to discuss their love for her, which was all well and good, but severely limited their ability to convert others to the Clinton team.

By contrast, Trump's supporters were out there visibly advocating for their guy, loudly haranguing people online and at rallies, and teaching other supporters how to fight the meme war. Channeling the transgression of /pol/, Milo Yiannopoulos went out on the road, holding rallies on his Dangerous F–ggot tour. Yiannopoulos arranged to maximize the media potential at these events, staging press conferences in which he would say controversial things, provoking counterprotesters to show up at his events and try to stop him from speaking. To livestream all this action, Yiannopoulos hired a young former BuzzFeed video producer named Tim Gionet who went by the pseudonym Baked Alaska, in reference to the state where he was born and his proclivity for smoking pot. Gionet had recently quit the liberal-leaning website after becoming red-pilled by what he described as the "wokeness" in the newsroom. Gionet explained that the final straw for him was when a BuzzFeed colleague asked him to stop referring to Justin Bieber as his "spirit animal" because it was an offensive use of a term appropriated from Indigenous people. He got a MAGA tattoo and became the office pariah. Yiannopoulos gave Gionet a place to put his media skills to work for the cause he now believed in. "Who are the underdogs? Who's part of the counterculture? It's the Trump supporters. We're fighting the establishment," he told Breitbart. He was such a MAGA fan that he released a single called "MAGA Anthem," which used Trump's "Build the Wall" slogan as the hook. Despite his best efforts to get it to go viral, it was mostly just passed around the internet as a bad joke. But his videos of near nightly clashes with leftists at Yiannopoulos's tour were a great success. They created high stakes, raw drama that Yiannopoulos and Gionet repackaged to publish on Breitbart and all over social media, amplifying the narrative that conservativism was being silenced on college campuses by overpowering liberals.

The Dangerous F–ggot tour served a critical networking function for members of the red-pilled right who might not have otherwise met in real life. Members of Charlie Kirk's Turning Point USA mingled with others in the campus conservative scene, locally and federally elected Republicans, and Yiannopoulos and Gionet. All of this allowed Gionet to become closer to the Breitbart media entourage. He specifically got to know Pizza Party Ben, one of the many young men in Yiannopoulos's entourage, who would occasionally teach pop-up courses on memeology to conservative students during Yiannopoulos's campus events.

But Gionet quickly started to piss Yiannopoulos off. Embracing his white nationalist views more and more, Gionet kept tweeting flamboyantly antisemitic ideas, which Yiannopoulos considered to be totally unsavvy. Leaked emails from that time show that Yiannopoulos thought Gionet was "becoming a laughing stock." He wrote: "I think we need to replace Tim. . . . [He] has no news judgment or understanding of what's dangerous (thinks tweets about Jews are just fine). . . . He seems more interested in his career as an obscure Twitter personality than my tour manager." It wasn't that Yiannopoulos seemed to disagree with Gionet's views; he just needed a tour manager who wasn't going to get canceled every second. He wrote to another employee, "He needs to understand that 'Baked Alaska' is over."

The Leaky Summer

In July 2016, Trump arrived at the Republican National Convention and proceeded to urge Russia—on primetime TV—to release Clinton's emails. He had secured the nomination two months before, but the GOP had not accepted it yet. Some Never Trumpers, as the press, in a memetic flourish, labeled GOP members who were against Trump, attempted to force a roll call vote at the July 18–21 convention in Cleveland that would have allowed delegates bound to vote for Trump because of the primaries to vote instead for whoever they wanted. All of this procedural fighting came to naught, merely showing Trump and his team who their enemies within the Republican Party were. Back in September 2015, when Trump was just emerging as the front-runner, the GOP had made him sign the RNC loyalty pledge, fearing that his history of vacillating political beliefs as well as his penchant for saying and doing whatever he wanted would be a danger to the platform if he actually won. But Trump and his people proved at the convention that no loyalty pledge would make them hew to GOP norms. They came to Cleveland ready to fight, flaunting their defiance in the face of mainstream Republicans, who seemed apoplectic that the party was suddenly being led by a celebrity they couldn't control.

All the folks who had helped get Trump to the convention showed up. White nationalist Richard Spencer, coiner of the term *alt-right*. Yiannopoulos, of course. Bannon, who declared Breitbart to be the platform of the alt-right. Cernovich. Even notorious pick-up artist Roosh Valizadeh and VDARE founder Peter Brimelow. Laura Ingraham spoke, as did General Michael Flynn. Joe Arpaio, the Arizona sheriff famous for his harsh treatment of immigrants in detention, spoke on the last night. Peter Thiel, rationalist and buddy of Curtis Yarvin, aka Mencius Moldbug, the billionaire representative of the red-pilled right in Silicon Valley, spoke too.

The term *alt-right* was beginning to stick now as a broad descriptor for both white nationalists and this new wave of Trump supporters. Spencer, who'd helped coin the term in a 2008 *Takimag* article, had been trying to popularize it for years, but the various factions of the far right were too splintered for it to catch on. In 2012 Spencer had registered a website called AlternativeRight.com to cater to this larger group of anti-leftists, and now he found a new audience in the Trump coalition. On his site he unpacked popular culture, films, and media that had positive, or negative, examples of white identity and unfettered masculinity. What he wanted, he told the white supremacists at Jared Taylor's American Renaissance Conference in 2013, was a "peaceful ethnic cleansing."

As the media scrambled to understand who Trump's supporters were and what role the internet played for them, they latched on to Spencer's label. The groups that came to be called the alt-right didn't necessarily agree that they were in league together, but during the meme war it was politically convenient to have a common brand identity.

To the establishment GOP, the Cleveland convention with its visible alt-right energy was terrifying. In it they saw the possibility of the RNC's demise and the certainty that Republicans would lose the presidency in the fall. For the alt-right, though, it was a hell of a lot of fun. "It's been one big, bourbon-fueled party all week," Spencer said. "It might be generous to say that the 'alt right' makes up 1 percent of the crowd here. But we've gone from zero to 1. I hope we can go from 1 to 100."

Perhaps no one was having more fun than Yiannopoulos. He and his entourage rolled into the RNC ready to make a splash. Yiannopoulos brought Gionet with him, but he forced him to stay at a hotel far from the rest of the group "to remind him of his place." This wound up being Gionet's final hurrah as an insider with the alt-right's cool kids; Yiannopoulos distanced him from his tight-knit group after that, in a foretaste of the fracturing that would hit the alt-right in the following months. But for now, it was still the best of times.

Yiannopoulos had completely rebranded as an ultraflamboyant gay man, dripping in jewelry, who was willing to challenge the orthodox GOP. And he was becoming the face of the alt-right, too. His image and presence had become a memetic weapon, to be deployed strategically. His entourage made quite a stir as he hosted a Gays for Trump party, among other shenanigans. Now that the Great Meme Warriors had finally met one another, the real networking could begin.

The Democratic National Convention was only a few days later. Clinton needed Sanders to forcefully tell his voters to support her, and the DNC hoped to make a big celebrity splash out of the historical nature of Clinton's nomination. But on July 22, just a few days before the festivities were to begin, Julian Assange's WikiLeaks website published the contents of emails that "Guccifer 2.0" had stolen from the DNC earlier in the spring. The party immediately pointed out the Guccifer persona was likely in fact one or more Russian hackers, suggesting that Russia was actively interfering in the election to help Trump get elected. International intrigue and hacking dominated the news as the Democrats were holding their convention.

But the most problematic aspect of the leaks for the Clinton campaign was what they revealed about the inner workings of the Democratic Party. The emails showed a very anti-Bernie DNC leadership, plotting to keep him from being elected. When he took the stage three days later at the convention, Sanders dutifully told his supporters to vote for Clinton, but the damage had been done.

On July 27, the same night President Obama spoke at the convention heralding Clinton as the future president, Trump held a news conference. The major networks cut away from the DNC to tune in, even running live shots before Trump had actually taken the podium, such was the excitement he generated. When he came on-screen, Trump rambled on about all the reasons Putin wouldn't hurt America, how it would be better for Russian and the United States to get along, and how unlikely it was that Russia had anything to do with the WikiLeaks emails. And then, as an aside, he added, "Russia, if you're listening, I hope you're able to find the 30,000 e-mails that are missing. I think you will probably be rewarded mightily by our press." The press pounced on the call to action, running headlines like "Donald Trump Calls on Russia to Find Hillary Clinton's Missing Emails" (*New York Times*), "Trump Launches Flurry of Attacks, Asks Russia to Hack Clinton's Emails" (*Washington Post*), and "Donald Trump Invites Russia to Find Missing Hillary Clinton Emails" (*Wall Street Journal*). When Clinton took the stage to claim the nomination at the convention the next day, a miasma of controversy trailed her. Things would only get worse.

August was a busy time for Trump's lieutenants. Stone met with Assange for lunch. Then during a conference call on August 4, the *Wall Street Journal* reported, Stone said, "In the background of this entire race going forward is the fact that Julian Assange . . . is going to continue to drop information on the American voters that is going to roil this race."

On August 17, Steve Bannon was appointed CEO of Trump's campaign. This formalized what many already knew: the Trump campaign was a media op, and half the battle was won. Trump's Republican rivals had been defeated, conservative media brought to heel, and under Bannon, Breitbart had been running interference for Trump since Yiannopoulos's early coverage in 2015. It made sense to have a seasoned media guy at the helm to secure the presidency—especially one who hated the opponent and had already turned his Machiavellian attentions to defeating Hillary through his news outlet.

Bannon, like Breitbart before him, skirted the line between media figure and media manipulator. He used the Breitbart platform to push the agenda that Clinton was a lying, sick, old, establishment warmonger, an idea reinforced online through memes showing Hillary looking like she was about to die. Bannon had already been using the site as a mouthpiece for the Trump campaign, publishing stories daily about Hillary's "missing" emails, and he had also been in regular contact with people close to the campaign. This included Stone and the company Cambridge Analytica, which the Trump campaign hired to directly target voters on Facebook using data gathered unethically. In a June 12 email with the subject line "Defeat Crooked Hillary"—unsealed through a Freedom of Information request in the course of the Department of Justice's investigation into Russian meddling in the election—a person from Cambridge Analytica reached out to Bannon and asked to put together a meeting with him and someone else when Bannon traveled to Britain. Parts of the email are redacted, but some speculate that it came from Alexander Nix, Cambridge Analytica's data guy turned whistleblower, and was offering to connect Bannon with WikiLeaks founder Julian Assange, who might be able to get him closer to Clinton's emails.

When Bannon took the helm of Trump's campaign, Clinton took notice. She was very aware of Bannon's power to turn the narrative against her, and she saw in Bannon a chance to make it clear to the left—and particularly to hesitant Sanders supporters—that a vote for Trump was a vote for people like Bannon, in effect a vote for fascism.

On August 25, 2016, six days after Bannon joined the campaign, Clinton attempted to turn the tables on him. At a campaign stop in Reno, Nevada, she deviated from her script to address "something that I've been hearing about all over the country. Everywhere I go," she said, "people tell me how upset they are about the divisive rhetoric coming from my opponent."

Bannon was using Breitbart's audience to turn denizens of the darkest corners of the internet into Trump's biggest boosters, Clinton told her audience. Breitbart, she said, was peddling "race-baiting ideas. Anti-Muslim and anti-immigrant ideas." And then she slowed down and carefully added, "all key tenets making up an emerging racist ideology known as the 'Alt Right.'"

Somewhere in the crowd a man shouted "Pepe!" but Clinton didn't seem to notice. "Alt right is short for alternative right," she continued, as though she were delivering a lecture to a group of poli-sci undergrads. The man who shouted "Pepe!," it turns out, was live-posting the event to /pol/, soliciting feedback from the anons about how best to troll the speech. He posted pics of his place in the crowd to prove he was the real deal, and the board celebrated the moment as their greatest breakthrough to the real world yet. They had someone inside the house. Moreover, Clinton was starting to speak their language.

That "Pepe!" was nothing compared with the cacophony of glee from alt-righters online when they heard their names mentioned. They had been amplified to the highest heights. They'd been recognized by their target, their meme magic the subject of national politics. Their excitement terrified the press: "Hillary Clinton Denounces the 'Alt Right,' and the Alt Right Is Thrilled" was the *New York Times* headline. No amount of shame would stop this mix of hardcore supporters who found communities at Trump's rallies, or the alt-right who found community in the meme wars. According to BuzzFeed reporter Joe Bernstein, who received a trove of Yiannopoulos's emails from this era, Yiannopoulos emailed Bannon, "I've never laughed so hard" following the speech. "Dude: we r inside her fucking head," Bannon shot back.

The fringe had taken control of the system.

But Clinton hadn't learned that the right would outflank her on memes every time. At a fundraiser on September 10, she said that half of Trump supporters would fit into a "basket of deplorables." Within hours the memes started. BuzzFeed's Bernstein revealed Trumpworld's response through an email thread a few days after the speech, started by campaign adviser and YouTuber/podcaster Sebastian Gorka, with the subject line "I presume you Gents approved of this" and the message "As found on Twitter." It included a remix of *The Expendables*' 2010 movie poster, with the actors replaced with Trumpworld all-stars. Recipients were Yiannopoulos, Bannon, and Michael Flynn Jr., the son of Trump's future national security adviser. Flynn Jr. replied within minutes, "THIS IS BRILLIANT. CC'ing LTG Flynn."

Two minutes later, Bannon retorted, "LOL!"

Gorka admitted, "Yes. I'm jealous!!" referring to the fact that he'd been omitted from the meme.

The meme was remixed again as the cast of characters in Trumpworld shifted. On September 11, Roger Stone tweeted it, as did David Duke.

Clinton's social media managers focused on clever comebacks on Twitter, like her reply to Trump over that summer, "Delete your account," which would earn thousands of likes from lefty Twitter folks, seeming to help confirm the false impression that a Clinton victory in November was inevitable.

The Clinton team appeared to think that if they just *explained* that the alt-right existed, and warned the voters of America that a vote for Trump was a vote for *these people*, then she would win. But there were at least two problems with this. One, by naming them, Clinton only gave the alt-right more power. And two, though in fact there were legitimate fascists among the alt-right, actually calling them that was considered incendiary in the mainstream culture, making it easy to assume that Clinton was overstating the problem. She wasn't a widely trusted figure, even among liberals, and so her warning largely fell on deaf ears.

Just as the "Bernie Bros" label had accomplished little else than angering online leftists, calling the Trumpian right a "basket of deplorables"

turned out to be a self-inflicted disaster. The joke, as ever, was on the Clinton campaign.

All-Out Meme Wars

For the next month and a half, the Deplorables gleefully engaged in all-out war. They had more than enough ammunition. News stories about legitimate scandals seemed to break every day, sometimes twice. Trump's online army watched Clinton's every move, looking for weaknesses to exploit. By now they had been working for over a year to make pro-Trump and anti-Clinton memes, and the operation was slick.

In threads on /pol/, anons shared instructions for conducting meme wars. One such instruction manual, from "The Bureau of Memetic Warfare," contained branding and messaging advice to follow when making memes, such as "Find the means of normalizing your message so it can blend in with the normalfags [4chan-speak for normal people]," and advice about how to apply "basic semiotics, assuming people treat the color 'Red' as 'Evil' which can be used to highlight a point you're trying to make." Perhaps unsurprisingly, the example used to demonstrate this best practice for creating memes "painted" the word *JEWS* red.

In mid-September, Clinton appeared to nearly faint while walking to her car after an event. Cernovich and his supporters immediately turned this into a meme that she was very sick, photoshopping images to make her look like she was at death's door, using red letters and other best practices for meme warfare. They spread the memes around with the hashtag #HillarysHealth, playing on rumors seeded by Jones and his Infowars colleague Paul Joseph Watson that she had been hiding some kind of illness. What started as conspiracy theories evolved into memes and then became news in the mainstream press, such as an NBC News piece entitled "Hillary's Clinton's Health Scare: 9 Unanswered Questions."

In particular, anti-Clinton memes focused on making her look as unattractive as possible. Here was a woman trying to become the most powerful person in America, and she wasn't even hot? Photoshopped images making her look sickly and ugly circulated everywhere. Everything she did became meme fodder, and increasingly, every new meme became media fodder.

On October 7, the *Washington Post* published Trump's infamous "grab 'em by the pussy" *Access Hollywood* tape. On the same day, an hour later, WikiLeaks released a cache of John Podesta's private emails with Clinton. MAGA supporters saw the release of the *Access Hollywood* tape (which had been recorded in 2001) as an "October surprise," timed just before the election, as proof that the mainstream media and the DNC were working together against Trump. It was the kind of scandal that could derail a presidential campaign at the last minute, and they professed outrage that the other side would stoop so low. At the same time, Clinton supporters similarly saw the Podesta leak as a brazen attempt by WikiLeaks— possibly in collusion with the Trump campaign—to smother the *Access Hollywood* scandal.

Though Trump would be dogged by the *Access Hollywood* recording for his entire presidency, the right quickly embraced it and turned into a strength. MAGA memelords turned Trump's words into T-shirts and memes that poked fun at Clinton's appearance, alleging that she was too unattractive to be "grabbed by the pussy." To the manosphere crowd and the anons and many factions of the extremely online red-pilled right, Trump's words were not only not offensive but an indication that he was one of them.

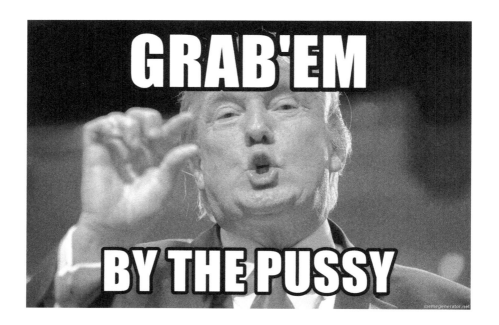

But it wasn't only the denizens of 4chan and The_Donald that embraced Trump's comment. Countless "grab 'em by the pussy" memes hit mainstream social media, especially on the myriad of pro-Trump fan pages and groups on Facebook, populated largely by boomers and Gen Xers. MAGA women began showing up to rallies wearing T-shirts that read "Trump can grab my pussy!" This mystified the left, who couldn't, or didn't want to, recognize how many Americans believed that women should submit to men. What sounded to the left like sexual assault sounded to many in the MAGA faction like a strong man demonstrating his power.

It's hard to know if the *Access Hollywood* tape would have had a larger impact on Trump had the WikiLeaks emails not leaked that same day. They were a distraction from the tape, and because there were so many of them, coverage of them seeped out continuously over the next few weeks. Meme anons got straight to work, looking for anything they could mine for memetic potential. While the Clinton campaign was sighing in relief that there was very little truly damning in then, the Deplorables were finding all sorts of tidbits that they could turn into cannon fodder with a little creativity and innuendo.

Anons claimed to see secret codes in the most mundane messages. Emails about ordering pizza turned into Pizzagate, the proto-QAnon conspiracy theory claiming that a D.C. restaurant that Clinton and many politicians frequented was a haven for pedophiles. Anons on /pol/ found Podesta's password in an email exchange with his assistant, and used it to log into and wipe his other devices. On October 12 his Twitter account was compromised, tweeting "I've switched teams. Vote Trump 2016. Hi pol," an obvious callout to the anons. These hijinks not only spread around the internet but generated considerable news coverage, making the emails into a massive controversy of their own. And embedded in the emails there were some newsworthy items, which the media covered at length.

One such controversy, cited by *USA Today*, involved an email that political commentator Donna Brazile sent to Clinton's team back in March 2016, right before a CNN town hall debate with Bernie Sanders. Brazile told the campaign that she had seen the questions that would be asked in advance, and one of them—about the death penalty—worried her because she felt any answer Clinton gave would make Clinton look bad. Now, in October, this alleged backroom whispering between the media and the campaign became a huge story. People were outraged that CNN would let Brazile see the questions, and that she would share them with a candidate ahead of time. Brazile denied that she had done that. CNN's Jake Tapper, who had hosted the town hall, came out and condemned her. It became a huge thing, and importantly, as an alleged instance of unethical journalistic practices, it tapped into the antimedia sentiment that had been growing exponentially since Gamergate.

But most of the emails had nowhere near that level of newsworthiness. Journalists and trolls alike mined the email dumps, looking for scoops or meme material. *USA Today* ran an article headlined "Four of the Juiciest Leaked Podesta Emails." The emails gave people a look into a normally secret place—the inner workings of political operatives—and so they had the aura of illicit information. People were transfixed.

This created a huge opportunity for meme warriors to satisfy their audiences, delivering scandals, conspiracies, and memes related to the emails. One of the weirdest of these was about, of all things, an avante garde artist.

On November 3, in a long /pol/ thread entitled "Podesta/Pizza PAC Investigation Thread 15," an anon singled out an email from Podesta's brother, inviting him to a dinner party with the artist Marina Abramović, known for her provocative and sometimes disturbing performances. She had written to Podesta's brother, "Dear Tony, I am so looking forward to the Spirit Cooking dinner at my place. Do you think you will be able to let me know if your brother is joining? All my love, Marina." The anon suggested that Spirit Cooking was code for something, and other anons in the thread agreed it was "creepy." "Good find," they told the first anon, and then went about finding Abramović's books and internet ephemera, including recipes that had been part of an art installation, which called for mixing "fresh breastmilk and sperm, serve on earthquake nights."

The next day, former leftist turned MAGA influencer Cassandra Fairbanks published a story about the Spirit Cooking email, embedding a YouTube video of Abramović's performance piece *Spirit Cooking*, in which she wrote in what looked like blood nonsensical instructions, such as "fresh morning urine sprinkle over nightmare dreams." "Hillary Clinton's inner circle keeps getting stranger and stranger, but at this point, we really just want to know what Podesta had for dinner," Fairbanks wrote. Her tone was joking, but vicious—pure /pol/.

WikiLeaks' official Twitter account posted a link to the Fairbanks story hours later. The tweet went viral, and #SpiritCooking trended on Twitter. Spirit Cooking quickly became a meme signifying the cabalistic, sadistic, and corrupt deep state that many on the far right believed was at the heart of Clinton's campaign. Whether Podesta had been there or not, whether it was an art performance or not, didn't matter. It was weird, and it aligned with prior beliefs, so it stuck. Mainstream news articles intended to debunk the story only spread it further. A cycle was born: a meme offense would be born on /pol/ or the like; a member of the right-wing partisan media would write about it; this would get it spread to mainstream social media, where it could go viral, prompting the mainstream media to write about it; which in turn would alert more people to the meme offense even as it also undercut its validity. Often before the mainstream news even hit publish on their articles, the meme warriors were already launching another offense.

The production of pro-Trump memes went into overdrive. There was #DraftOurDaughters, born on The_Donald, which spread fake ads, using Clinton's campaign branding style, suggesting that she was endorsing a new war and planned to reinstate a draft that would include women. There was #DrunkHillary, which, as the *Washington Post* noted, overtook #HillarysHealth in popularity in October. And there were the Benghazi memes, which reminded people of the scandal from the Obama years when the GOP blamed Clinton for an attack on the U.S. embassy in Libya. There were the many, many memes that connected Clinton to dead people—a conspiracy that had a long history dating back to the earliest days of Bill Clinton's term as governor of Arkansas.

Known as Clinton Body Count, the meme functioned as an umbrella term to include many different theories that the Clintons were secretly murderers. The CBC had been memorialized in books and blogs and videos long before 2016, and would later play a large role in the narrative of QAnon. During the 2016 election, this preexisting suggestion that Clinton had covered up heinous crimes turned into the viral memetic slogan "Lock her up," which Trump and his fans chanted at rallies, wrote on signs, tweeted as hashtags, and wore on T-shirts.

The Clinton Body Count meme was born in 1993 in response to the suicide of White House deputy counsel Vincent Foster on July 20. Foster and Bill had been friends since childhood, and right before his death Foster was reportedly overwhelmed by what would be considered a minor scandal by Trump-administration standards—dubbed Travelgate, the controversy had to do with travel expenditures made by federal employees in the Bush administration, who the Clinton administration had fired, a move condemned by the press.

Ten days later an attorney named Linda D. Thompson coined the phrase in a report entitled "The Clinton Body Count: Coincidence or the Kiss of Death?" The report began, "This administration seems to be plagued with an inordinate number of 'suicides,' plane crashes, one-person fatal 'accidents,' and unexplained deaths. The following is a summary of the deaths of people who have died, none of them from natural causes, who are connected to Bill Clinton. The label of 'Insider,' 'NWO,' or 'Bodyguard,' has been applied to the persons below to delineate the manner in which the person could be considered to be connected to Bill Clinton." It then went on to detail twenty-six deaths that Thompson alleged were directly tied to the Clintons.

The Clinton Body Count conspiracy soon included allegations not just of murder but of various other crimes, like fraud, harassment, and blackmail. From then on, when a breaking news event involving the Clintons occurred, conspiracists would bring up the Clinton Body Count. The meme was invoked when the FBI opened an investigation on October 1, 2015, into a computer server Hillary Clinton had at her house. It was a tremendous advantage to Trump that a large proportion of his base (and voters on the left, as well) had already been red-pilled on Clinton by the CBC meme. "It is impossible for the FBI not to recommend criminal charges against Hillary Clinton! What Bill did was stupid!" Trump tweeted on July 2, 2016, as the FBI investigation was wrapping up.

If Trump had been accusing anyone else of crimes, anons wouldn't have been quite so enamored. But because, due to the Clinton Body Count meme, Clinton was already this nearly mythically evil creature, they piled on, mixing allegations of murder with news about the server on social media. The fact that FBI director James Comey recommended no charges against Clinton on July 5 did not quiet the Body Counters down.

On July 10, 2016, under a week later, another person close to Clinton—DNC data director Seth Rich—was murdered while walking home from a bar in D.C. The same day, an anonymous individual on /pol/ who introduced themselves as a "higher-order being" started an "Ask Me Anything" (AMA) thread in which they mentioned an upcoming "mass arrest of the cabal." The next day another anon, identifying themselves, in a foreshadowing of the QAnon phenomenon that would emerge a year later, as a "High Level Insider," started a similar AMA thread on /pol/, saying cryptically: "The lesson you should take from events like Seth Rich is that good intent is worthless without good plans. . . . You need to emerge from your indoctrination into the real world and appreciate principles of reality such as the law of the jungle." The Seth Rich–Clinton connection theories spread to the conspiratorial side of MAGA Twitter, Reddit, and pro-Trump forums. When WikiLeaks released the DNC emails on July 22, people speculated that

Rich had given the emails to WikiLeaks, and this was why he'd been killed.

For Clinton Body Counters, the corpses kept piling up. On August 1, 2016, Victor Thorn, the author of a trilogy of Clinton conspiracy books, was found dead by apparent suicide. His final book, *Hillary (and Bill): The Murder Volume, Part Three*, had not yet published. The Body Counters considered this galling even by Clinton standards, and drummed up outrage about it on the red-pilled right. On August 22, 2016, Trump called for a special prosecutor to "investigate Hillary Clinton Crimes" at a campaign rally in Akron, Ohio.

By the time Comey announced six days later that the FBI was reopening the investigation into Clinton's State Department emails, the internet and the general culture was so awash in anti-Clinton memes, carrying so many different ominous suggestions, it was as if a match had been tossed into a pool of gasoline. Clinton's campaign was toast.

Meme Magic on Election Night

The mainstream media didn't see it that way. The polls said Clinton would win; the experts said so too. Media organizations prewrote articles for either scenario, but they assumed they'd be publishing their stories with the headline "Clinton Elected the First Woman President of the United States of America."

Even Trump was sure he would lose. Yes, there was excitement at his rallies, yes, he was beloved by an eclectic collection of troll youths, militant boomers, white supremacists, and many people in between, but according to his own telling, he didn't think he actually stood a chance.

Neither did Roger Stone. His #StopTheSteal hashtag, coined during the primaries, when it seemed like Trump might not get the nomination, was put back in use to recruit a group of volunteer "poll-watchers" to go to polling places—often in predominantly minority neighborhoods—on Election Day and look for voting irregularities. The Stop the Steal group spent weeks before the election seeding the idea that if Clinton won, it would be because the election had been "rigged," an accusation that Trump amplified in his tweets with regularity.

On the evening of November 8, the online communities who had worked so hard for Trump watched the returns come in live. All week, anons on /pol/ had braced themselves for a loss, even as they clung to hope. They urged each other to not forget to actually vote. They debated the merits of the polls. If it was even close, they said in threads, that would show the power of the MAGA coalition, the power of the internet and memes to make change. And you know what, they argued, just getting to be the nominee at all should be considered a victory!

But then by the evening of election night, it was clear the race was close. Like, really close. It dawned on the anons that Trump might actually, for real, become president. They prayed to Kek. They held their breath. At 1:35 A.M. Eastern Time, as the swing state of Michigan was announced for Trump—a huge surprise to most everybody—they lost it. They praised Kek. "Is this real life?" an anon asked. "It's habbening," said another. "Life can't get much better," answered another, sharing an image of a Clinton supporter on the verge of tears. They cringe-watched liberals freaking out on TV news and Twitter—their tears like manna from heaven for the anons.

At 2:29, the Associated Press called the election for Trump. Though the AP was the epitome of old-guard media who were not to be trusted, Trump's coalition accepted the result and exploded with joy.

"Meme magic is real," supporters declared on The_Donald. "Donald Trump just proved the entire world wrong. Against insurmountable odds, corruption in the media, sabotage from his own party, and the crush of the establishment machine, DONALD J. TRUMP WON. How does it feel, centipedes? The God Emperor said that we would get tired of winning. ARE YOU TIRED OF WINNING YET?"

Breitbart ran the AP's election announcement on its front page, with the headline "Donald Trumps Wins White House in Astonishing Victory." The site had live-blogged the entire election day, taking a journey from hope to glee along with the rest of Trump's supporters.

To Bannon, the bridge between the unbridled energy of the alt-right and the inner Trump crowd, this moment was nothing short of a revolution. "Like [Andrew] Jackson's populism," he told the *Hollywood Reporter*, "we're going to build an entirely new political movement. . . . The conservatives are going to go crazy. I'm the guy pushing a trillion-dollar infrastructure plan. With negative interest rates throughout the world, it's the greatest opportunity to rebuild everything. Shipyards, ironworks, get

them all jacked up. We're just going to throw it up against the wall and see if it sticks. It will be as exciting as the 1930s, greater than the Reagan revolution—conservatives, plus populists, in an economic nationalist movement." The dog whistle about the 1930s was not missed by people on either side of the aisle.

White nationalist David Duke was ecstatic. He credited WikiLeaks' Assange for the victory, tweeting on November 9, "GOD BLESS WIKILEAKS—Julian Assange is a hero -> America owes this man one thing -> FREEDOM!!! Thank you, sir—THANK YOU! #WIKILEAKS."

To the extremely online far right, this was a revolution. Anons on /pol/ stayed up late into the night, trading joyous meme after joyous meme. The alt-right celebrated on every social media platform available to them, rubbing the victory in the faces of anyone who was anxious about this largely unexpected political turn.

For liberals, Trump's election was a tragedy with the magnitude of a coup. It was as if the fabric of reality had been ripped open and the

country had entered an alternate universe. In the coming years, they would recall where they were when they found out Trump won, the way boomers had recalled how they'd found out JFK died. The feeling of shock and horror was summed up perfectly in an image of a woman bawling in agony over the realization that Trump would be president, an image heavily remixed as a meme almost instantly.

Dubbed the "Crying Iowan," the image was taken by a photojournalist working with Reuters news agency in Australia. The *Des Moines Register*, which wrote about its native daughter when the meme went viral, referred to the crying woman as "the international symbol of the inconsolable popular-vote winners of our presidential election." (Online she was zinged as the "poster child for the mentally insane Hillary snowflakes.") In her anguished face, the red-pilled right saw proof of their victory. She was the living embodied of the crying liberal, her tears the lulz-giving rain from Kek.

At Trump's middle-of-the-night victory party on election night, Milo Yiannopoulos responded to the liberal reaction. He told reporters at the scene, "American progressives should be thanking their lucky stars that Donald Trump is the worst thing that happened, because you have been lying to and about people for decades." As Yiannopoulos was celebrating at Trump Tower, his publication was wrapping up its coverage of the night. The final post on Breitbart's live blog was a video from CNN of Trump's face projected onto the Empire State Building as swelling patriotic music played and red, white, and blue lights lit up the darkened sky. The God Emperor had won. America was damn well going to be great again.

Chapter 5

He Will Not Divide Us

The Resistance

On the morning of November 9, 2016, America woke up to the news that Donald Trump had won the election. The thing that couldn't possibly happen—a reality TV star with no political experience was now president-elect of the United States—had happened. If this was possible, what other unthinkable thing could happen next?

The *New Yorker* ran a headline that morning calling the election "An American Tragedy." On the left, bewilderment and mourning turned quickly to rage, and then to a surge of calls to action. People pledged to work hard to stop Trump from hurting America, to make sure he was only a one-term president. On day one, people were already talking about impeachment. Mostly, liberals wanted to do something. The details of what to do were not clear, but the idea was summed up in a word that quickly went viral, becoming a hashtag and a badge of political affiliation: #Resist. Over the next year, #Resistance influencers would rise, some as YouTube and podcast personalities, others as columnists and TV pundits.

In those first few days after Trump won, women on the left in particular were horrified. A man who had bragged that he loved to grab women by the "pussy" was now going to be leading the nation. Quickly the idea for a Women's March fell into place. It began with a Facebook post from Teresa Shook, a lawyer living in Hawaii. The plan came together in a lively pro-Clinton Facebook group called Pantsuit Nation late in the evening on election night, when it had become clear that Trump was the likely victor. Others encouraged Shook to make a new group to organize, and so she did. After a few dozen people had pledged to march, she went to sleep, but by morning more than 10,000 people had signed up to march on D.C. the day after the inauguration. As fall turned to winter, liberal women across the country began knitting "pink pussy hats" to wear during the scheduled mass protest in cities across the country. The hats turned Trump's leaked statement into a kind of reappropriated uniform for the resistance.

Liberals also tried their hand at memeing resistance. This was going to be a bit difficult, considering that one of the most popular memes about liberals was that "the left can't meme." Liberals saw their ideology represented everywhere, in the media, on TV, in movies, and in progressive social policies, and so they had little need for transgressive memes. But now they were the outsiders, and with all the attention on figures in the alt-right, the left seemed to suddenly understand that memes mattered, and they needed to create some of their own. The most successful ones were word-based. The hashtag #NotMyPresident trended, as did #Resistance, #Resist, and various plays on Trump's name—Drumpf (his original name before it was Americanized) and tRump, for example.

Liberals and Never Trump Republicans also got to work trying to figure out who to blame, other than themselves. Sanders supporters blamed Clinton; Clinton supporters blamed Sanders. Many in the liberal press had pointed their fingers at Russia, insisting that Trump could not have won had a foreign dictator not meddled in the process. FBI Director James Comey became a favorite target, criticized for his investigation into the Clinton email hacks, which gave Trump extra legitimacy in the campaign's last stretch.

Obama, as he entered his lame duck period, blamed the Republican Party. "Donald Trump is not an outlier," he told the *New Yorker*. "He is a culmination, a logical conclusion of the rhetoric and tactics of the Republican Party for the past ten, fifteen, twenty years. What surprised me was the degree to which those tactics and rhetoric completely jumped the rails." Clinton herself blamed her defeat on "the epidemic of malicious fake news and false propaganda that flooded social media over the past year," as she put it in December 2016. She went on, "It's now clear that so-called fake news can have real-world consequences." The mainstream media, in its attempt to course correct, dutifully pointed to Clinton's mistakes on the campaign trail and also began to examine in earnest this "fake news" problem.

Trump claimed that he'd coined the phrase "fake news," saying in late 2017 that it was "one of the greatest of all terms I've come up with." In fact, Craig Silverman, a BuzzFeed reporter, coined the term in 2014, using it to refer to web pages that mimicked the stylistic format of a news organization to gain clicks. He described fake news sites as "completely false content, created to deceive, and with an economic motive." Not long after this definition took hold, the "fake news" charge was distorted to include mainstream media outlets. Trump's first clear public use of "fake news" came in a tweet on December 10, 2014: "Reports by @CNN that I will be working on The Apprentice during my Presidency, even part time, are ridiculous & untrue—FAKE NEWS!"

Fake news was a huge meme during the campaign, and sites like Infowars and Breitbart helped turn it into a catch-all insult. During rallies, Trump would point at the press pit and say "CNN, you're fake news!" Calling CNN, the *New York Times*, and the *Washington Post* "fake news" politicized the news itself, and opened space for hyperpartisan media groups and pro-Trump influencers to build trust with audiences. "Fake News" was printed on T-shirts and saturated MAGA communities on Facebook, Twitter, Reddit, and YouTube.

For the mainstream media, Trump's win set off a period of navel-gazing, a so-called reckoning about how they "could have gotten it so wrong." They weren't fake, but many *had* called the election wrong and they wanted to understand why. Eventually they came to the consensus that they had ignored the fringe at their peril. Analysts on the right said that this surprise victory was a product of liberal media bias. They accused the press of carrying water for the Democratic Party, of working intentionally to get "their candidate" Clinton elected. Trump's popularity was hard for the media to take seriously or understand because he threatened so many core liberal principles, and so did his supporters, which challenged the very notion of who and what American mainstream culture was. How could his supporters outnumber the mainstream electorate, if their ideas were such a transgression against America's fundamental beliefs?

Hail Victory

In the weeks after Trump's win, pundits and writers for mainstream outlets vacillated between blaming American racism and Russian interference for Trump's victory, and began to question the team the president-elect was assembling. Steve Bannon, Ivanka Trump and Jared Kushner, and meme-war generals like Mike Cernovich and Richard Spencer were all profiled by newspapers and magazines and interviewed on TV. Regular "Trump voters" were interviewed in small towns across the United States, in an attempt to understand the people who had carried Trump to an electoral college victory. This did not soften the hearts of MAGA toward these outlets Trump and his supporters hadn't really been taken seriously before, and their hatred of the MSM wouldn't subside now they were ascendant. This set the stage for alternative news and influencers to replace mainstream journalists as the news curators of the internet, a phenomenon that increased throughout the Trump era and saw its apex in the QAnon conspiracy movement.

One of the foundational memes of QAnon was born in a speech delivered in the weeks after the 2016 election by General Flynn to a room full of die-hard MAGA supporters, in which he gave a succinct explanation of what exactly the media had done wrong. Now known as the "digital soldiers" speech, it cemented the idea that MAGA had fought a war—and the war was far from over.

"This was an insurgency, folks, this was run like an insurgency. This was irregular warfare at its finest, in politics," he told the room. The territory of that war was the internet, the soldiers were people using media, and their ammo was memes. Flynn and his son had fought alongside these soldiers in the trenches, tweeting memes and conspiracies. "This was not an election, this was a revolution," he said.

Flynn explained that this revolution was necessary because the mainstream media had been entirely against Trump, refusing to give him the time of day. Only on social media, Flynn explained, could people find reports of what was really going on. And who did those reports come from? The audience. "We have an army—OK, as a soldier and as a general, as a retired general—we have an army of *digital soldiers*," he said, coining what would become a resonant meme for the red-pilled right; "what we call citizen journalists, OK, because the journalists that we have in our media did a disservice to themselves actually more than they did to this country. *They did a disservice to themselves because they displayed an arrogance that is unprecedented.* And so the American people decided to *take over the idea of information.* They took over the idea of information and they did it through social media."

He wasn't wrong. For all the media hand-wringing in the fallout of the election, Flynn's description of how the right interpreted the media's so-called arrogance is perhaps the best explanation for why the 2016 election was the nail in the coffin of media trust for millions of Americans. Flynn told the young conservatives on that cold December day that the fight was not over. The mainstream media, the liberal consensus, the establishment—they all would keep coming for Trump, and for them.

Of all these hardworking digital soldiers, the alt-right were perhaps the most dedicated. /Pol/ was awash in victory posts, though critical of Trump's message to supporters to stop harassing minorities after his win. White nationalist podcasters on the TRS network hosted celebratory podcasts, and Andrew Anglin wrote for the Daily Stormer that Trump could now "really make America White Again." White nationalists across the globe were energized, prepared to advance their racist agenda. For those whose stars had risen in this war, the postelection period was their chance to secure leadership positions in the new world.

Richard Spencer in particular wasted no time. On November 19, 2016, he hosted a conference through his National Policy Institute that brought together many of the alt-right players to figure out how to use their new power. It was tricky: the alt-right's most resonant idea was that they were oppressed by the supposedly overarching liberal Marxism of the main-stream culture, but now that their guy was president, the underdog narrative was a little harder to lay claim to. Now they had to convince white Trump supporters to move further right without scaring them off.

In his speech, a suit-and-tie-adorned Spencer suggested how to walk that line. "We willed Trump into office. We made this dream our reality," he said. But the dream was under attack by what he called the "lugen-presse" (German for "lying press"), a slur Nazis shouted at reporters in Hitler's Germany. "The press has clearly decided to double down and wage war against the legitimacy of Trump and the continued existence of white America. But they are really opening up the door for us." By "us," Spencer meant himself. He explained that he would use the media's newfound obsession with the alt-right to red-pill normies by sneaking white nationalist talking points into interviews. Spencer was relatively unknown to the rest of America, and his organization, the National Policy Institute, sounded benign, so he planned to become a Trojan horse for white nationalism.

"No one mourns the great crimes committed against us. For us, it is conquer or die," Spencer said, evoking the ancient Latin battle cry "Aut vincere aut mori." He went on, "To be white is to be a striver, a crusader, an explorer and a conqueror. We build, we produce, we go upward. And we recognize the central lie of American race relations. We don't exploit other groups. We don't gain anything from their presence. They need us and not the other way around." The crowd grew excited and began cheering.

Unbeknownst to the conference attendees, a documentary filmmaker from the *Atlantic* was there that day filming the crowd's reaction. When Spencer shouted "Hail Trump, hail our people, hail victory!" the documentarian captured the Right Stuff's Mike Enoch and others throwing up "Sieg heils," or Nazi salutes, the gesture that Nazis used to pledge allegiance to the party. *Sieg heil* means "Hail victory" in English, so Spencer knew what he was saying when he shouted those words.

The clip went viral and landed Spencer appearances on all the major television, print, and radio shows. This was what he had wanted, though perhaps he had hoped for less of an overt acknowledgment of his Nazi ways. He used these interviews to talk about his support of Trump and the future of white America. He made good on his plan to drop red pills, planting meme after meme in his answers. He would then take those videos and disseminate them himself, pointing out the red pills and celebrating his subversion of the press.

For a mainstream media seeking to understand the mind of the Trump voter they felt they had ignored during the campaign season, Spencer represented an exciting and very serious new storyline: that Trump's victory heralded a vicious new strain of white supremacy returning to America in the guise of professional-looking and -sounding white men like Spencer. Even as the media amplified Spencer, they positioned themselves as opposition, sparking an urge among many in the press to reveal the horrors at the heart of the alt-right. For lefties, the "Sieg heil" video acted as proof that MAGA was swarming with literal Nazis, which justified the outrage pouring from the resistance. In the race to define the opposition, the left had found their lead villain.

The media attention Spencer received didn't please all the factions of the alt-right. More moderate Trump supporters who didn't share Spencer's ethnonationalist ambitions felt he was misrepresenting the movement. Yiannopoulos, influential MAGA media personality Jack Posobiec, and Cernovich split off with other alt-right figures to form a less overtly racist group than the alt-right, calling it the New Right. They were merely the "alt-lite," Spencer shot back, the skim latte to his whole milk. Before Trump had taken office, before the alt-right had even had a chance to fully celebrate their victory, the coalition was already beginning to fray.

Anons on /pol/, increasingly critical of Spencer and his leadership, quickly dubbed the controversy Heilgate. A deep fissure began to grow between the trolls and visible members of the alt-right leadership. For the memelords who had just won the Great Meme War, there was a new battle to be fought: the battle to represent the red-pilled right in the mainstream media. Spencer's position as a media villain solidified after Heilgate, and he had the support of other openly white nationalist factions, like Right Stuff podcast host Mike Enoch. But members of the New Right got busy putting some distance between themselves and their old allies.

Their first move was a celebratory bash they began planning for the night before Trump's inauguration. The Deploraball would be a statement to D.C. that there was a fresh new crew in town. And it would make them money, too. They sold tickets on a sliding scale, $99 for general attendance and up to $2,500 for VIP.

Everybody wanted to go, including Spencer, who reportedly bought a ticket and then was publicly disinvited. The New Right was trying to send a message that they were not part of Spencer's white pride crew. That message failed to reach everyone, including Yiannopoulos's hatchet man Tim Gionet, aka Baked Alaska, hired by Cernovich to help plan the party, though he'd been sidelined by his former boss. But once again, Gionet just wouldn't stop sending blatantly antisemtic tweets. That pissed off Cernovich, who wanted folks with real political power to come to the Deploraball—the kind of folks who wouldn't want to be associated with antisemitic slurs. So he fired Gionet.

"It all boils down to freedom of speech," Gionet explained later in a gossipy interview with Red Ice TV titled "Oy Vey, Banned from Deploraball." "And, you know, these guys are out there saying 'freedom of speech no matter what,' you know, and I started tweeting, as I always do, not anything really out of the ordinary, but I started to get more red-pilled in the last couple months. And there was this weird dynamic where we were talking before the show, where before Trump's election, where we all kind of agreed, you know, don't you know, no infighting, no criticizing each other, no critiquing each other until Trump gets elected, and I think that actually bottled up a lot of emotions, and thoughts and critiques that were actually very healthy that we couldn't talk about." He figured that after Trump won, he could say what he wanted to, which included exploring the "JQ" and the "Jewish influence in media." Gionet claimed that he was being shunned after Heilgate, because telling Nazi jokes was ruining the "brand" of the New Right.

After firing him, Cernovich used Gionet's real name in a blog post that Gionet claimed amounted to a dox, getting him harassed. "I've had people on the right—not on the left!—I've had people on the right tell me I'll never have a job again," he said. "I'm now a neo-Nazi. My whole career is over. No one in media will ever touch me again. And all this stuff. This has made me double down on my beliefs." He began making content using his real name and, like Spencer and the pseudonymous hosts of the Right Stuff, openly embracing his white nationalism.

Anons on 8chan, which had caught a wave of new users during Gamergate and Pizzagate, were not pleased to see folks like Spencer out there carrying the flag for white nationalism. These anons had a far more violent ideology than their peers in the far right, openly celebrating terrorism in their own Politically Incorrect forum. By this time 8chan was becoming known as the worst place on the internet; even 4chan was considered moderate in comparison because its admins were removing Pizzagate content. Now 8chan set their focus on defaming the "respectable" Spencer and the Right Stuff's podcast hosts. Spencer and TRS became targets not just because they were gaining political traction and mainstream visibility; their real offense was "cucking" to the media and profiting. For years across the chans, there had been a fervent adversarial posture toward the press, so the fact that Spencer and Mike Enoch were giving interviews to the *Atlantic* and the *New York Times* enraged the anons, spurring them to a particular style of internet revenge.

On the week of January 16, 8chan anons doxed the Right Stuff hosts, including Mike Enoch, who anons accused of being an illegitimate white nationalist leader because he was married to a Jewish woman. *Salon* reported that this speculation began after Cernovich posted a YouTube video stating that someone in the alt-right "is morbidly obese and is married to a Jewish woman." No detail was so salacious as the fact that Enoch's wife was Jewish. Antifa activists also jumped in, doxing other members of the TRS community and spreading their IDs on social media. Despite the unfolding scandal, Spencer tweeted his support: "I respect, like, and admire Mike Enoch. He will continue to be a force on the Alt Right in the future." However, many in the red-pilled right disagreed with Spencer's generous statement. The popular TRS podcast *Fash the Nation* went dark, removing themselves temporarily from the internet to avoid any further involvement in the controversy. *The Daily Shoah* podcast also went offline for a while as they regrouped, but the public fallout shattered any final semblance of the unity that had been built up during the last days of Trump's campaign. As TRS weighed its options and the alt-right licked its first wounds, the New Right partied.

The Deploraball was held at the National Press Club in D.C. on the eve of the inauguration. Far from the spectacle of Gays for Trump at the RNC, it was a rather staid affair. Yiannopoulos headlined. Micro-influencers and pro-Trump media personalities mingled, drank, and listened to speeches about Trump and the future of western civilization. Trolls rubbed shoulders with journalists sent to cover the event. Outside was a different story: hundreds of left-wing activists showed up to protest. Some of these were self-proclaimed "antifa," eager to fight fascists and racists.

In the United States, antifa—who derived their name from an abbreviated form of Antifaschistische Aktion, the name of an early 1930s forerunner of the wider antifascist movement in Germany—began as a subculture among anti-racist activists in the punk scene of the 1980s. At that time, the hardcore punk and ska music scene was facing a racist skinhead contingent that went to concerts to recruit young people, mostly teen boys. Anti-Racist Action, a loosely aligned political group, found ways to remove or "no-platform" racist skinheads by physically confronting them at shows, or alerting concert promoters to the likelihood of attendance by racist skinheads and urging them to cancel the event.

Now some lefty activists were again embracing the label to express their resistance to the alt-right. A faction of right-wing street brawlers had been watching, and were poised to clash with the antifa. They called themselves the Proud Boys, and their leader was a media-savvy and highly controversial broadcaster named Gavin McInnes, a former punk rocker and media trendsetter who had founded *Vice*. McInnes came out to celebrate at the Deploraball, and brought some of his fighters with him.

The Deploraball was a sort of coming-out party for the Proud Boys. Journalist Andrew Marantz attended the celebration for the *New Yorker* and wrote of the Proud Boys' devotion to McInnes, describing him as both a charismatic leader and front-line general in the scuffles outside the event. As he entered the gala, McInnes took a few swings at the protesters.

McInnes had founded the Proud Boys as a "fraternity," requiring those who joined to take a public pledge: "I am a Western Chauvinist and I Refuse to Apologize for Creating the Modern World. The West Is the Best!" At first the Proud Boys formed as fans of McInnes's podcast and YouTube videos, but quickly morphed into a street-fighting faction of the alt-right.

From the start, the Proud Boys were intended to draw attention. McInnes gave them a uniform to stand out in crowds. He chose a black polo shirt with yellow stripes on the collar and sleeves, made by the designer Fred Perry. These shirts had been popular among nationalist skinheads, back when punk and ska shows became a battleground in the late 1970s and early 1980s. In 1978 the first Rock Against Racism (RAR) show was organized, in response to Eric Clapton's remarks at a 1976 UK concert, when he endorsed the views of then political candidate Enoch Powell, who was running on an anti-Black, anti-immigrant platform. "I think Enoch's right," Clapton had said. "I think we should send them all back. Stop Britain from becoming a black colony. Get the foreigners out, England is for white people, man." (Clapton would later walk this back in interviews.) At that first Rock Against Racism show, the ska revival band the Specials and their fans wore Fred Perry shirts too—but theirs were black and white, reflecting the slogan "Black and white unite . . . and fight!" Rock Against Racism's fusion of punk, ska, and hardcore music would last for decades, but waned in the 2000s, when the political roots of punk became subsumed by pop punk and emo rock.

McInnes was familiar with this musical and political scene. He'd worn many looks in his past that had elements of style from the punk

subculture. McInnes's fashion history shows knowledge of skate, hard-core, crust, and neo-Nazi fashion trends (he famously wore a T-shirt for the hate-rock band Skrewdriver in one photo). His return to skinhead style as the leader of the Proud Boys spoke to those who also grew up with one foot online and the other in the punk scene.

McInnes modeled the logo for the Proud Boys after Fred Perry's, using the same Romanesque garland. Fred Perry as a company had spent decades denouncing association with racist groups, to little effect, and the Proud Boys' adoption of its shirt didn't help. In September 2020 the company officially discontinued the shirt because of its association with the Proud Boys. But counterfeit or copycat items sporting the Proud Boys logo sprang up. From flags to hats, pins, shirts, mugs, bottle openers, and even ammo clips, the Proud Boys made all kinds of merch in the black-and-yellow color scheme of the Gadsden flag and the banner adopted by anarcho-capitalists, a libertarian sect against any and all forms of government.

As McInnes left the gala that night after holding court with his Proud Boys and the other Deplorables, he instructed his crew to "get in forma-tion." When he came into contact with leftist counterprotesters, he joked, "Now I might get loser AIDS." The protesters clashed with police guarding the event and screamed profanities at those entering and exiting the club. Even though he was uninvited, Spencer showed up to catch some attention outside. He stood around smiling and anxiously playing with an unlit cigarette, obviously out of place. Only a few attendees were willing to speak with him.

The whole event revealed new cracks in the MAGA coalition. Reporting on these emergent conflicts, both within the nation and MAGA, the liberal press posed the question: "What now?"

Punch a Nazi

January 20, 2017, the day after the Deploraball, Trump was sworn in as president. He titled his inaugural address "America First," explaining from the lectern that this idea would define his foreign policy.

Pundits and center left and right politicians had speculated since Election Day that Trump might stop acting like Trump once he became president, but the title and tone of his speech proved they had been naive. "America First" had a very long history. First coined by President Wilson as a way to explain American leadership in the world, it was quickly co-opted by isolationists and racists, who argued that the best way to put America first was to care about America only—an argument that people like Nazi-supporting Charles Lindbergh used to argue against involvement in World War II. It was embraced by the Ku Klux Klan over many years in the twentieth century, as expressing the idea that only certain people—white people—could really be Americans, and that it was white people whom the nation must put first. To the embracers of America First, Blacks, Jews, and Catholics were considered not true Americans but rather "hyphenates," whose allegiance to America couldn't be trusted because they were loyal first and foremost to their race or religion. It would be hard to find a political slogan from twentieth-century America more steeped in racist overtones.

Trump had used the phrase on the campaign trail and had denied any intention to evoke these connotations. He liked it, he said, because it sounded strong. In voicing "America First" rhetoric, Trump positioned himself as the strong leader of a nation that wouldn't take anyone's shit. But whether it was an intentional dog whistle or not, the phrase spoke directly to the white male base that had always been its original proprietors. When Trump spoke of "America First," it was their America; he was telling them he would be putting *them* first.

The half of America that opposed Trump was growing increasingly fearful of the potential for real fascist rule under him, and vast coalitions came together to show resistance on Inauguration Day. They asked people to spread the message on Twitter using the tag #DisruptJ20. As one organizer explained, "There has been a lot of talk of peaceful transition of power as being a core element in a democracy and we want to reject that entirely and really undermine the peaceful transition."

Thousands of people protested that day, the majority of them peaceful marchers. But some self-described anti-fascists threw objects, smashed windows, lit garbage cans and cars on fire, and pushed back on police lines at different points throughout the day, earning enough headlines to make their contingent seem much larger than it was. "Make Racists Afraid Again" was their stated mission. More than two hundred arrests were made in D.C. that day for protest-related activities, including arrests of journalists and observers caught up in the melee.

The most well-known face of this new fascism, Richard Spencer, was there in the crowd, though Heilgate had made him a target for both the alt-lite and the emerging anti-Trump popular front. Before entering the National Mall, he went live on Periscope, a streaming service from Twitter, and gave a scene report. Wearing a suit, a red MAGA hat, and a Pepe lapel pin, he talked about what he anticipated for the day's events, saying that he didn't see signs of a massive protest. Comments in the chat about the Pepe pin fluttered across the screen, as did "hail pepe" and "hail victory." He name-dropped his old college friend Stephen Miller, who some speculated may have written Trump's inauguration speech as well as his RNC speech. Spencer went live again right after Trump's speech, now wearing a rain poncho, to say that he thought it was a good speech, describing it as "populist" but not "poetic." Then he walked with the documentary crew that was following him around to a restaurant where, he said, he came face to face with anti-fascist protesters.

In a video he uploaded later that night, titled "The Assault on Me," Spencer told his fans that these protesters had attacked him. The first punch, he said, landed on his cheek and seemed to shock him more than hurt, and the assailant ran away before Spencer could catch him. At this point in the story, the camera crew with him began filming. In that footage, one protester near Spencer holds a sign reading WHITE LIVES MATTER TOO MUCH, and another man behind him holds one reading FIGHT FOR SOCIALISM OVER BARBARISM.

A woman off-camera asked Spencer, "What is your little frog?"

"It's Pepe," Spencer answered, "It's become kind of a symbol—" Before he could finish his sentence, the guy who had punched him minutes before returned and walloped him again on his right ear with a bone-rattling slap.

As Spencer grabbed his face and tried to move away from the crowd, someone spat on him, the saliva mixing with his disheveled hair. Hours later Spencer seemed more regretful than injured, saying, "I'm afraid this is going to become, you know, the meme to end all memes and I'm going to hate watching this."

He was right. The "Punch a Nazi" meme was born, one of the left's most potent contributions to the meme wars. There were thousands of remixes of the punch over the next few days, inspiring a number of media outlets to make "best of" lists. Oddly, the short clip of him getting cold-cocked paired well with music. One video was set to Bruce Springsteen's "Born in the USA," where every time the snap of the snare drum repeated, the strike replayed and whipped Spencer's head back. Sixteen hits in sixteen seconds. Another deftly edited video featured Phil Collins's "In the Air Tonight," a song known for its crescendoing drumming. It was an endless parade of perverse joy, in videos and images encouraging more of this type of direct confrontation.

This meme initiated a media cycle of its own, where it was debated whether it was OK to use violence against Nazis. Twitter pundits and TV personalities swapped opinions on what was an appropriate level of violence to wage against known supporters of fascism. Across anarchist circles, slogans like "Bash the fash" and "Good night alt-right" became protest chants and online sign-offs. The visibility of Spencer getting walloped, coupled with his racist and antisemitic beliefs and his shocking statements to the press, pushed liberal public perception of Trump supporters from Deplorables to actual Nazis. Of course (and we can't believe we have to say this), not many MAGA supporters harbored the same kind of vitriolic positions on ethnonationalism as Spencer, but he

had aimed to become a figurehead for the movement, and now the movement was deeply associated with him.

The more mainstream left developed their own memes in response to the inauguration. "The Resistance" tweeted the hashtag #Resist, along with dire prophecies about the dangers Trump would unleash on America. As the TV cameras showed people gathering before the inauguration speech, Twitter filled with jokes mocking the size of the crowd. High-profile celebrities and pundits compared Trump's sparse crowd to Obama's. As the inauguration was under way, the tenor of the conversation on #Resistance Twitter was effervescent, a palpable mix of gallows humor, incredulity, rage, and puns.

TO BE FAIR...

STARECAT.COM

OBAMA - 2009   **TRUMP - 2017**

The memes trended, and the conversation on TV and the radio as well as online began to focus not on Trump but on the poor showing at his big party. The jokes about Trump's small audience landed even harder the next day, when the Women's March took place in cities around America. Millions of people showed up to demonstrate their disapproval of Trump, in what was estimated to be the largest single-day protest in American history. The crowds were so big that helicopter cameras couldn't capture them in one shot. With the uniform of pink hats in this sea of humanity, the marches were a very powerful visual. The contrast between those swelling crowds and Trump's paltry inauguration audience was stark. Ratings mattered a lot to Trump, ever the showman, and this clearly got under his skin.

In his very first press briefing, the day of the Women's March, press secretary Sean Spicer denied what the photos clearly showed and shot back at the jokes: "Some members of the media were engaged in deliberately false reporting. . . . This was the largest audience to ever witness the inauguration, period, both in person and around the globe." He went on to say, "There's been a lot of talk in the media about the responsibility to hold Donald Trump accountable, and I'm here to tell you that it goes two ways. We're going to hold the press accountable as well. The American people deserve better and as long as he serves as the messenger for this incredible movement, he will take his message directly to the American people where his focus will always be." Spicer resigned six months later, and this press conference would go on to be the laugh track for his return to polite society, where he made light of it at the Emmys and in other public appearances.

The day after Spicer's disastrous presser, Kellyanne Conway, counselor to the president, went on *Meet the Press* and was interviewed by Chuck Todd, who confronted her about Spicer's falsehood. She declared, now famously, "Don't be so overly dramatic about it, Chuck. You're saying it's a falsehood, and they're giving—our press secretary, Sean Spicer, gave *alternative facts* to that."

"Alternative facts" would become another watchword of the Trump presidency—an instant meme, like fake news, that meant different things to different groups. On the right, it came to signify the mainstream press's ignorance; on the left, it represented Trumpworld's obstinacy. Like "Deplorables" before it, "alternative facts" as a meme didn't actually help the left. It became another rallying cry for the right, and as the rest of the year went on, it became increasingly clear that just because the left had lost the election, that didn't mean they would suddenly know how to meme.

Anything Open Will Be Exploited

Many of the loudest voices to come out strong against Trump in the first days of his presidency were from Hollywood, a time-honored institution of the liberal consensus. Anti-Trump social media posts from celebrities were heavily reported on by the press and celebrated by #Resistance liberals on Twitter. Actor Shia LaBeouf, who transitioned from child stardom into leading-man status in blockbuster films like *Transformers*, one-upped his fellow anti-Trump celebrities with a meme that attempted to mix the prestige of fine art with the broadcast power of the internet. The day of the inauguration, LaBeouf launched an interactive digital performance piece entitled *He Will Not Divide Us* along with collaborators from the art world and celebrity friends like Will Smith's son Jaden Smith.

HWNDU, as it came to be called (pronounced win-doo), was a 24/7 livestream video that LaBeouf wanted to last for the entire length of Trump's presidency, an avante garde millennial representation of #Resistance. The idea was that LaBeouf would set up a video camera in various locations that would be streaming all day, every day. When people walked past the camera, they were meant to say into the lens, "He will not divide us," a mantra and promise.

It began with a website, some social media posts, and this call for participation: "Open to all, 24 hours a day, seven days a week, the participatory performance will be live-streamed continuously for four years, or the duration of the presidency. In this way, the mantra 'HE WILL NOT DIVIDE US' acts as a show of resistance or insistence, opposition or optimism, guided by the spirit of each individual participant and the community." LaBeouf mounted the first camera on a wall outside the Museum of the Moving Image in Queens, New York, with the words "He will not divide us" written in black letters above. The frame was a wide-angle static position that overlooked an open sidewalk area. Jaden Smith kicked it off the morning of January 20, chanting "He will not divide us" until a crowd amassed outside the museum. Soon, it turned into a jubilee with Smith and LaBeouf chanting in different tempos and a crowd of looky-loos amassing around them. Spontaneously, the crowd would burst into new rhythms, and a mosh pit would break out.

Very quickly, anons on /pol/ discovered the spectacle and cringed. HWNDU

was an earnest attempt to turn Trump resistance into a meme, to use livestreaming and audience participation to conquer the hate on the internet. The anons wouldn't stand for this audacious display of liberal memeing led by a celebrity. They decided to take it down.

"Lets get a team of /pol/laks [anons] out there, maybe carriing [*sic*] large meme sings or chanting something that will trigger shills," one anon wrote in an early HWNDU thread on 4chan. "Let's finish the meme war with a nuke." By night's end, a young man appeared on the HWNDU stream with a sign that read "#Pepe." As people around him chanted "He will not divide us," this anon abruptly shouted into the camera, "Pizzagate is real," "Obama bombed brown people," "Bill Clinton is a rapist," "Hillary is a warmonger," "Trump won't forget the working class like the Democrats have," and "Shia LeBoeuf is a rich white liberal who doesn't care about the working class." A woman with him giggled as the camera recorded everything.

This was just the beginning. During the night, a masked figure approached the camera with a speaker playing the song "Shadilay," an old Italo disco track that became a MAGA anthem during the Great Meme War. The anon let the song repeat for hours until the batteries ran out. The song was, of course, a meme, written in 1986 by the Italian band P.E.P.E. The cover art for the album featured a frog with a magic wand, which made it a 4chan favorite in September 2016 when it began to circulate in threads about the Cult of Kek meme. Anons remixed it with Trump speeches and turned the song into the ultimate inside joke.

Anyone watching the stream who wasn't a regular on /pol/ would have no idea what the song had to do with, well, anything. When LaBeouf arrived with a cup of coffee in the morning, he removed the speaker. But whether he knew it or not, the war was already on. Hours later someone wearing a Cthulhu mask changed the sign for the Museum of the Moving Image to read "Museum of KEK." /Pol/ was now officially trolling the left IRL.

Over the following weeks, anons and MAGA influencers from many different far-right factions traveled to the sidewalk outside the museum to troll and co-opt the livestream. Though the event garnered little media attention, it had important implications for the meme wars. First, it proved the axiom that anything open could and would be exploited. Second, it became a gathering spot for anons to meet in real life, to emerge from the wires and convene in the weeds now that their guy was in the White House. And finally, it became a fun pastime and a badge of honor. Just as veterans of real wars might compare which battles they had fought, meme soldiers kept track too, and in the battle for HWNDU their participation could be captured for history on the livestream.

LeBeouf lost control by day three. Trolls were dropping red pills and Hitler references on the stream as LaBeouf stood in the frame, growing anxious. "Fourteen eighty-eight!" yelled a guy in military gear, adding, "We must secure the existence of white people . . ." LaBeouf answered by screaming "He will not divide us!" an inch from his face, chest-bumping the troll's shoulder.

"Woooo! Praise KEK!" the anon answered, as LaBeouf ran him off into the back of the crowd. They both came running back about thirty seconds later.

MAGA folks, from Gen Z to biker-gang-style boomers, kept coming, yelling "Lock her up!" and "ShiLeCuck!" Some of these folks used the stream to get popular with the trolls, including Moustache Matt, who appeared that night to say hi to "The_Donald" and to "/pol/" and announce that "Hitler did nothing wrong." After LeBeouf confronted him, he leaned into the camera and said, "I just want to red-pill Shia about the truth about the Holocaust." LeBeouf replied, "Be nice . . . I'm not interested in your truth." Matt went back day and after day, trying to get people to swallow the JQ red pill with constant talk about the Holocaust. He eventually became a main character on /pol/, known as Stachebro. (In a follow-up interview, Matt said he saw HWNDU as an important opportunity to red-pill the masses watching from home through memes. "I think memes are a very important political tool that not a lot of people understand yet. You can create an image, and if you share that image enough, it takes on a life of its own and it shapes the reality that you live in," he said. "There's a saying, 'Make your memes come true.' Well, you know if you repeat a lie enough times it is the truth.)

Well-known internet troll Brittany Venti arrived and started disrupting the recital with a caustic trolling: "He will nut inside us." She'd gotten famous within the extremely online far right by getting banned from Twitch because 4chan raided her stream and posted hate speech in the chat. Venti showed up for several days, taking her cues from /pol/ and a Discord chat room.

On January 28 the undisputed king of trolls, the comedian Sam Hyde, arrived on scene. Hyde was both a man and a meme, his antics the stuff of legends online. His most well-known prank was a meme known as "Sam Hyde Is the Shooter," in which a picture of Hyde would be circulated on social media after every horrifying mass killing, accompanied by "He can't keep getting away with this!" The meme was a way to troll the media, who would sometimes fall for the hoax and report that the image going around was truly of the killer. It was used for the first time in 2015, during the Umpqua Community College shooting, and became a tradition over the next few years. Many journalists know about it, but some still fall for it. It became such a thing that journalists wrote

explanations about the meme that could be shared during breaking news events, in order to warn other journalists not to be misled.

Hyde brought that kind of energy and a new cast of characters from his standup routines all the way to Cartoon Network's experimental *Adult Swim* late-night block in 2016, when he signed a deal to produce a show based on his YouTube sketch comedy called *Million Dollar Extreme Presents: World Peace*. Like his popular subreddit of the same name, *MDE* was riddled with dog whistles and, at times, outright white nationalist references.

The show premiered in August 2016. In one episode, Hyde played a pickup artist who does a makeover on a young man in a wheelchair. After taking the subject shopping, the pickup artist gave the man the nickname Moon Man, followed by a second "secret nickname," David Duke. The skit ended with the pickup artist knowingly smirking into the camera. Racist, homophobic, antisemitic, and misogynist content was common on the show, resulting in an internal battle at Cartoon Network to get it canceled. (By December it was announced that the show wouldn't get renewed.) BuzzFeed's Joe Bernstein reported on Hyde and the controversy surrounding the "alt-right show," and spoke with him in a brief interview to address the allegations.

Hyde recorded the whole conversation and put his combative back-and-forth with Bernstein up on his YouTube channel. This led to a pitched campaign by *MDE* fans and Hyde himself against the BuzzFeed reporter and any Cartoon Network employees who appeared even tangentially involved with the show's cancellation. For MDE fans, Gamergaters, young alt-righters, and assorted internet edgelords, stunts like this, where Hyde seemed to punk the media, made him a legend. His nihilistic, chauvinistic comedy became more politically aggressive after the cancellation of his TV show, and now he turned his energy to owning the libs.

To the folks milling around HWNDU the day he showed up, Hyde was a far bigger star than LeBeouf. Smoking a cigar and sporting a scraggly beard and long hair, he was taller than everyone and easily stood out on the stream.

A few days earlier a group of anons had sung "Happy Birthday" to Hyde over the stream, so the fact that he then showed up in person was meme magic in itself. Hyde's presence seemed to embolden the trolls, who became much more rambunctious. Several were trying to impress him, quoting obscure memes and references from /pol/ to prove how hardcore they were.

Hyde approached the mounted camera and announced, "Heebs will not divide us," an augmentation of the HWNDU meme that replaced "he" with a racist slur against Jews. His acolytes loved it, and their laughter could be heard as he stubbed his cigar out into the camera lens. After that, Hyde got into an altercation with a man holding a #Resist sign who had been at HWNDU for days, whom the anons on /pol/ had dubbed "AIDS Bjorn." They loved that he was now interacting with Hyde—it was like two characters from separate video games meeting in real life for a fight, except all they did was yell "Don't touch me!" and "Don't get close to me!" at each other as the crowd chanted "Build the Wall" and "World peace! World peace!"

Trolls and resisters clashed throughout that day, and that night the cops arrested LeBeouf: he had pulled someone's scarf off, and they had filed a formal complaint. LeBeouf was charged with a misdemeanor and released at 4:00 A.M. The charges were later dropped, and the incident didn't stop LeBeouf, or the trolls, from returning to the HWNDU site.

In the coming days, different key figures on the right showed their faces. Tim "Baked Alaska" Gionet came in a red MAGA hat, camo winter coat, and a mullet. He dropped antisemitic dog whistles, memes, and chants like "Richard Spencer did nothing wrong." Nathan Damigo, head of a white power group called Identity Evropa, showed up on February 4 with Emily Youcis, a woman who was fired from her job after video surfaced of her at Spencer's Heilgate incident. Damigo looked into the camera and with a smile said, "Shia LeBeouf, you will not replace us with your globalism." They started to chant "You will not replace us! You will not replace us! You will not replace us!" as a man played a harmonica loudly off to the side. As more of the Identity Evropa members arrived, Damigo laughed and said, "I feel like I've visited /pol/ in real life."

For the next week, /pol/ made a game out of delivering Hitler jokes while LeBeouf was on stream. A small encampment sprang up on the sidewalk with youths who were either dedicated to defending the stream from literal Nazis, or trolls who did not want to miss an opportunity to shitpost in real life. Trolls had effectively driven out most of the lefty supporters, and the stream had become a place for them to reenact memes and socialize. At this point, they were so far down the rabbit hole that their chants and interactions would have made very little sense to passersby.

Young Identity Evropa members began appearing shirtless on stream, flexing and showing off Nazi tattoos in an attempt to intimidate onlookers and celebrate their particular style of racist bodybuilding masculinity. They also chugged gallons of milk, to the confusion of onlookers, in a holdover meme from the HBD era: racists often cited lactose tolerance in Europeans as proof of their evolutionary superiority over other ethnic groups, a meme on full display at HWNDU that evening.

/Pol/ loved every second of it, and milk emojis and memes were passed around alt-right Twitter and adopted by highly visible figures like Spencer.

While the streams were dominated by the youth wing of the alt-right, some more established older figures showed their faces, like TRS podcast host Mike Enoch. A NYC resident who'd suffered reputational damage in the far right after his recent doxing and the revelation that he was married to a Jewish woman, Enoch took the train up to Queens to plug his network, Spencer's altright.com website, and attack both liberals and his new enemies in the far right. Despite the fallout of his doxing, he wasn't going anywhere.

On February 10, less than a month after it began, the Museum of the Moving Image shut down HWNDU, citing the escalating violence and security concerns that the throng of supporters and agitators was bringing to the area. The trolls celebrated a victory, and LaBeouf promised to restart the installation in another location.

"It's funny that the stream started out as this anti-Trump political rally and you know the whole premise of it was that they believe that Donald Trump is dividing everybody, but in reality it really it brought a lot of people together," said alt-right troll Moustache Matt. LaBeouf and company tried repeatedly to move their installation elsewhere over the next year, but the livestream was met with more pranks, more racism, more sexism, more LGBTQ and religious intolerance. Eventually they placed the camera in an undisclosed location, aimed at a HWNDU flag. Taking this as a challenge, 4chan launched an open-source investigation to find the flag. They'd find it, Lebeouf would move it, they'd find it again. The anons even attempted to light it on fire with a drone at one location.

HWNDU was the red-pilled right's Occupy moment, out of the wires and into the weeds and back again. While they never gained the same numbers of people in the streets as Occupy, it brought together many who would later plan and attend the Unite the Right rally in Charlottesville later that year.

The whole episode was a reminder that memes could not be successful if they were dictated top down and designed by a single author. This was a forced meme: engineered, marketed, and amplified by those who desperately wanted it to go viral. Memes have to be authorless, remixed, crowdsourced, not driven by a volatile celebrity figure like LeBeouf. When Trump amplified memes, he didn't coin them; he sourced them from the oozing sludge of the internet, where the best and most resonant bubbled to the top for people like Bannon and Trump's digital team to find. The HWNDU episode was a reminder to the left that they didn't have the same kind of trolls as the right. Perhaps they never would. Lefty activists were too earnest in their politics, too concerned with actual policy, and lacking the anarchic sense of humor that fueled the far right to be memelords. Nor did the left's most popular online influencers coordinate in the same way as the many factions of the right wing.

Campus Clashes

In the scheme of the resistance, HWNDU was a footnote. While it served as a great distraction and even a community-builder for the trolls, the real resistance battle was being fought in the streets, with protests against the Muslim ban and Trump's anti-science statements, and in the courts with challenges to Trump's executive orders. And it was being fought in California, where Yiannopoulos had decamped to provoke street violence on college campuses.

As with his Dangerous F–ggot tour the year before, Yiannopoulos returned to college campuses in early 2017 to give speeches to conservative groups, knowing that it was on the grounds of academia that the culture wars really played out. His notoriety attracted protests, and his appearances prompted scuffles and shouting matches that he again made sure to catch on camera and use as promotional materials for upcoming engagements. His message was similar to that of General Flynn's in the weeks right after the election: we may have won, but we are still fighting a war. Yiannopoulos framed the war as being about censorship and the oppressiveness of cultural Marxism. The antagonism of the press became a favorite example; the resistance movement on the left, he told audiences, was another clear sign that Trump was still an underdog, and so were his supporters.

On February 1, 2017, Yiannopoulos appeared at the University of California at Berkeley. He often spoke at state schools, because the law did not allow them to discriminate when a student group sponsored a speaker. While over a hundred professors signed a petition asking the administration to cancel the event, it was only when fifteen hundred protesters showed up that the university shut it down. Yiannopoulos's fans and his alt-right supporters violently clashed with anti-fascist protesters outside. This fighting eventually spilled into downtown, leaving massive property destruction in its wake. In response, Trump tweeted that he might withdraw federal funds from UC Berkeley, claiming they were suppressing "free speech" and enabling "violence on innocent people with a different point of view."

On the evening of February 2, Yiannopoulos joined *Tucker Carlson Tonight* to explain this latest dustup to the Fox News host. "Violent riots last night at the University of California at Berkeley, you watched them break out live on this show last evening," Carlson said, referring to previous coverage. "The man who made that campus tremble joins us tonight in the studio for his first interview following the outbreak of violence. . . . Few people are hated more by the left than Milo Yiannopoulos, the gay Jewish immigrant who's become the face of the red-pilled right." Carlson delivered the last line with a slight smirk.

Yiannopoulos seemed pleased to be there and spent a full fifteen minutes in conversation with Carlson. He argued that the fighting outside his speeches was due to Orwellian censorship and the creeping influence of corrupt liberal institutions. "I'm an entertainer. I'm a performer," he told Carlson. "One of the things that authoritarians hate, one thing dictators hate, is the sound of laughter, because they can't control it. They can't control what you find funny."

Playing the dandy and clown prince, Yiannopoulos boasted of having Trump's attention, plugged his upcoming book, and promised to continue to "take the fight to the left," pledging to go past the line where "spineless" conservatives are afraid to cross. "There's a reason there's a sort of parallel conservative media in this country," he concluded. "It is because the establishment, the media, academic and entertainment establishment has made certain sorts of political opinion, respectable, reasonable, mainstream opinion, impossible to express in public."

"The definition of corruption," Carlson agreed. "Unfortunately, we're all going to pay for it."

Chapter 6

Unite the Right

Meme Warriors in the White House

Trump had promised radical things in his bid for the presidency, and the meme warriors who fought so hard for him expected he would follow through. He said he'd bring manufacturing jobs back to the United States from Mexico. He said he'd build a wall to keep the immigrants out. He said he would rid D.C. of the opportunists corrupting the nation. He said a lot. But now that he was the ultimate political insider himself, the man who ate his Big Macs in the Oval Office, those promises were obviously easier said than done.

Early on, Trump's threats to "Drain the Swamp" seemed to have been tempered. He called for unity and for people to put aside "trivial fights" during his first address to joint sessions of Congress in March. When the press noticed the change in tone, Trump fought back against claims that he was going soft. "Someone incorrectly stated that the phrase 'DRAIN THE SWAMP' was no longer being used by me," Trump tweeted after his victory. "Actually, we will always be trying to DTS." Despite his bluster on social media, Trump was struggling to balance his base's expectations with political reality.

Trump's signature slogan Build the Wall faced immediate headwinds. On January 25, Trump issued Executive Order 13767, Border Security and Immigration Enforcement Improvements, tightening immigration restrictions and directing Homeland Security to begin construction on the border wall with Mexico. But who would pay for it? "It's an easy decision for Mexico: make a one-time payment of $5–10 billion to ensure that $24 billion continues to flow into their country year after year," Trump wrote in a 2016 campaign memo. Statements like these, politically unrealistic and rhetorically xenophobic, began to strain US/Mexico relations, and Trump's proclamations drew scorn from Mexican press and politicians.

On the campaign trail, Trump had repeatedly worked these criticisms into his speeches. "They said, 'The president of Mexico said they will not, under any circumstance, pay for the wall, what is your comment?'" Trump proclaimed at a February 2016 rally in Tampa. "I said, 'The wall just got ten feet higher.'" Now Trump had to make good on these threats. His base applauded his early executive order, but there still was no clear path to actually building the wall.

Another executive order issued in January, EO 13769, placed significant travel restrictions on six Muslim-majority countries. For supporters and critics, this "Muslim ban" seemed to be a follow-up on statements Trump made on the campaign trail, particularly a speech in response to the Pulse Nightclub massacre in Orlando, Florida, several months earlier.

Trump had derided Clinton for being unwilling to name the real problem in the attack, which he called "radical Islam." "'Muslims are peaceful and tolerant people and have nothing whatsoever to do with terrorism.' That is Hillary Clinton," he said, incredulously. "With 50 people dead and perhaps more ultimately and dozens more wounded, we cannot afford to talk around issues anymore. We have to address these issues head-on. I called for a ban after San Bernardino and was met with great scorn and anger but now . . . many are saying that I was right to do so." Here Trump employed one of his most notable rhetorical flourishes, "A lot of people are saying," a vague generalization of the will of the American people that he, unlike his political rivals, was listening to.

Trump's base showered him with praise when he actually did restrict the ability of some Muslims to enter the United States. It wasn't an easy win, though. Trump faced resistance even from his own team, and fired his acting attorney general, Sally Yates, for refusing to enforce the ban. She became the one of the first of many political casualties of his presidency. By the end of his presidency, there would be a 92 percent turnover of senior executive staff members, many of whom Trump forced out in messy public spectacles.

After serving as national security advisor to Trump during the campaign, General Michael Flynn was sworn into the same position as part of the cabinet. This tenure was short-lived. Soon an FBI investigation into Flynn's activities advising foreign entities unearthed inappropriate lobbying work for the Turkish government and an uncomfortably close relationship with Russian intelligence agencies. Trump and his proxies supported Flynn's position in the cabinet until it was revealed that he had apparently lied to Vice President Pence about his history with Russian ambassador Sergey Kislyak. Flynn was forced to resign on February 13. But even afterward, Trump blamed Flynn's predicament on liberal collusion and coordinated lies from the left; "Mike Flynn should ask for immunity in that this is a witch hunt (excuse for big election loss), by media & Dems, of historic proportion," he tweeted on March 31.

Trump continued using Twitter to both circumvent and shape media narratives in his first months in office. Even throwaway posts would result in press, all of which was "good." He also tweeted to spread accusations. "Terrible! Just found out Obama had my 'wires tapped' in Trump Tower just before the victory," he tweeted. "Nothing found. This is McCarthyism!"

A new president is expected to make the global rounds, meet with world leaders, and discuss how their tenure will extend, or improve upon, the policies of their predecessors. Trump's first months in office did not ingratiate him to many of Obama's strongest allies, foreign or domestic. In his first year on office, Trump's unfiltered tweets sparked diplomatic tensions with several countries, angering Swedes, Australians, and beginning a long war of words with North Korean dictator Kim Jong-un. On June 1, 2017, Trump announced withdrawal from the Paris Agreement on climate change, upsetting European allies and domestic environmentalists but delighting those in his base who believed neither that climate change was real nor that any global body should influence American energy policy.

As President Trump attempted to assert dominance over Republican critics like Ted Cruz and John McCain, and tried to wash away remnants of the Obama administration like the Affordable Care Act, he gave his people a new enemy to keep them mobilized. That enemy could no longer be the government, because he was the government. So he gave them the resistance, and lumped the media in too, for good measure.

There were many groups of people calling themselves part of the resistance, from activists to Democratic lawmakers to the viewers of CNN and MSNBC. MSNBC's Rachel Maddow was drawing huge audiences by hitting Trump hard nightly on her show. She reported about the child separation crisis and the Muslim ban, and never stopped beating the drum for the Russian collusion story from the election. Maddow dissected every little lead in the case, every rumor and accusation. In this way she got viewers frothed up, thinking there was a chance that Trump might soon be going to prison. Liberal boomers tuned in religiously to discuss the latest updates on the case and then share their thoughts on Facebook pages or in their family's group chat. MSNBC's viewership went through the roof, hitting record highs in mid-2017.

The resistance caused many headaches for Trump, from the initiation of his first impeachment proceedings to constant bad press, but it also gave him a gift: a way to claim he was still the underdog, despite being president. He drummed up support from the antiestablishmentarians of America by invoking the many ways he, like them, was victimized by the left. Together they'd fight the liberal powers that be.

The MAGA coalition continued their online crusade against liberals, but the grassroots power of their movement was diminishing as the alt-right committed serious tactical errors. Spencer had already fallen from mainstream grace, having been labeled a neo-Nazi in the press after Heilgate, and Milo Yiannopoulos was soon to follow. In late February 2017, the Reagan Battalion, a conservative outlet critical of Trump and the growing antisemitism the alt-right was bringing into mainstream politics, surfaced statements Yiannopoulos had made years earlier on the podcast *Drunken Peasants*, in which he condoned sexual relations between older men and underage boys.

In the fateful interview, Yiannopoulos claimed that these illegal liaisons were "hugely positive experiences" for the young boys impacted, himself included. "I'm grateful for Father Michael. I wouldn't give nearly such good head if it wasn't for him," he said of the priest who allegedly molested him as a teenager.

This was the kind of thing not even champions of free speech were willing to support. Despite—or maybe because of—Trump and Bannon's close relationship with Yiannopoulos, the scandal cost him his job at Breitbart. He also lost his book deal with Simon & Schuster and a prime speaking gig at CPAC and became, for a time, a pariah. While he'd worn his Twitter ban for instigating a racist hate mob against actress Leslie Jones in 2016 as a badge of honor, there was no way to spin his defense of pederasty to his advantage, and he had few allies left to come to his aide. His former tour manager Gionet was first out the gate to criticize him, again trying to ride the attention of the falling star and pick up new fans along the way.

Yiannopoulos's cancellation, though, was less about Yiannopoulos and more about conservatives landing a blow against the emergent alt-right and Trumpism. The battle for the soul of the Republican party was at stake. While liberals took heat in the press for backing away from Yiannopoulos, the real story was the wedge in the party that had learned to wield cancellation as a cudgel. His fan base had eroded as he was banned from mainstream platforms. For 4chan anons and the folks who'd been at HWNDU, Yiannopoulos was now seen as a grifter and a degenerate whose flamboyant homosexuality didn't need to be tolerated anymore. He may have helped popularize the term that Richard Spencer coined, but the alt-right didn't belong to either of them anymore. Meme wars like the great #CNNBlackmail would prove that these factions worked better together when they were simply slinging memes.

#CNNBlackmail

CNN bashing was a favorite pastime of Trump's. He was at his best when he was in opposition to someone or something else with power, and CNN was a very useful enemy. Throughout his career and into his presidency, Trump regularly engaged in confrontations with critical reporters and negative press, and focused a lot of his negative attention on CNN. Anti-CNN memes had become popular in the MAGA coalition, with

early meme war threads on /pol/ targeting the network. On July 2, 2017, Trump posted one of those memes to Twitter and kicked off a war.

A short GIF file, the meme remixed a famous video of Trump staging a comical fight with his longtime friend WWE CEO Vince McMahon at Wrestlemania 23 on April 1, 2007. In an event billed as the "Battle of the Billionaires," McMahon and Trump bet on rival wrestlers in a title match. The loser would be forced to have his head shaved. Trump and McMahon, both famous for their signature coifs, gave the bit their all. Trump's wrestler won, and during the match the future president tackled McMahon to the ground before restraining him in the ring and shaving his head on live television. Moments like these, where he asserted dominance over even friendly rivals, made Trump a media legend long before his 2015 campaign.

The fateful meme Trump uploaded remixed the fight and superimposed the CNN logo over the WWE CEO's face, to symbolize Trump beating CNN into submission. This relatively simple meme delighted his fans and supporters and quickly went viral in the MAGAsphere.

The meme drew immediate condemnation from liberal twitter pundits and mainstream press, most notably CNN's Brian Stelter, who reacted by asking his followers to identify the creator, sharing the Reddit username of the meme's creator—HanAssholeSolo, a regular of /pol/ and The_Donald, who had previously shared antisemitic memes about Jews' control of media.

Trump's top Twitter trolls delighted at the chaos ensuing from one of "their guys'" memes. "What a time to be alive with President @real DonaldTrump, God Emperor of the meme-lords," Ricky Vaughn tweeted. Trump's top general, his son Don Jr., fanned the flames by claiming that conservatives faced a doubled standard in regards to free speech: "CNN & dems calling Trump assassination play 'artistic expression' but WWF [sic] joke meme is 'a call for violence'? Hilarious reinforcement of FNN [Fake News Network]."

HanAssholeSolo was initially delighted with the attention from the president. "Wow!! I never expected my meme to be retweeted by the God Emporer [sic] himself!!!" he posted on Reddit. That excitement would soon sour. On July 4, after being contacted by CNN's Andrew Kaczynski, HanAssholeSolo posted a lengthy apology for the meme. Kaczynski claims that CNN "discovered HanAssholeSolo's identity through bits of biographical data left on his Reddit," and related how the meme creator reportedly called CNN to alert them of his apology, hoping to preserve his pseudonymity. "Trolling is nothing more than bullying a wide audience," he said. "Don't feed your own self-worth based upon inflicting suffering upon others online just because you are behind a keyboard. We as redditors and as Americans are better than this. So to the members of this community, the site, the media (especially CNN), and anyone offended by the posts, again I apologize." HanAssholeSolo then deleted himself from the internet, in what seemed to many like an attempt to avoid being doxed by CNN.

While liberals on Twitter celebrated the defanging of yet another of Trump's troll army, the red-pilled right perceived the incident as nothing short of blackmail, and HanAssholeSolo as a victim of the mainstream media's coercion. WikiLeaks condemned the media spectacle, tweeting "CNN extorts amateur satirist who made video tweeted by Trump: if you make fun of us again we will harm you." "How brave of CNN, a multibillion dollar corporation, to go after a private citizen," tweeted Mike Cernovich. Jack Posobiec jumped into the gathering storm: "The geniuses at CNN thought it would be a good idea to pick a fight with the American people on the 4th of July #CNNBlackmail." Gamergate legend Jim saw this as more proof anonymity on the internet was under attack. "If you try to mock the mainstream media," he said in a YouTube video, "CNN is going to come after you and your fucking family. And there isn't a god damn thing you can do about it because they're the truth tellers." All the attention from top right-wing influencers helped get the hashtag trending number one in the United States, with a huge volume of tweets driven by MAGA and trolls.

The anons on /pol/ were watching the developments closely. "Did CNN declare war on us?" wrote one anon in response to the negative attention the MAGA memesphere was receiving from CNN reporters. "Let's go full gamergate on their advertisers," wrote another anon, calling back to the 2014 antimedia campaign. Some launched meme contests to solicit more anti-CNN images to share on social media, while others on 4chan, 8chan, and other anonymous imageboards had a more sinister plan: dox any and all CNN reporters they could. Anons began passing

WHO WOULD WIN?

#FakeNews	*A Nation of Meme Farmers*

around what they believed to be home address of reporter Andrew Kaczynski, and of any other notable CNN personalities they could find. In their harassment of the CNN journalists they joined the MAGA coalition on Twitter, fueled by a cocktail of antisemitism and antimedia fury. "WE'RE GOING TO WAR /POL/, OPERATION ASSHOLE COUNTER OFFENSIVE," wrote one anon. A rumor spread on the chans that HanAssholeSolo was a teenager (according to his Reddit history, this is certifiably untrue), a claim that may have originated with Jack Posobiec and was spread by Donald Trump Jr.

Writing for the Daily Stormer, the notorious neo-Nazi hacker weev had far more radical intentions than those of the comparably mainstream MAGA coalition. In an article laced with explicit antisemitism and murderous intent against journalists, he wrote:

> Any CNN employee that does not want to be tracked down along-side their families will have one additional week to quit CNN and denounce their act of blackmail against a private citizen. After that, it is game on.
>
> Do you understand what is coming? This is going to be ironic punishment. You are going to have the exact thing done to you that you've been doing to us for ages. You have an easy chance to

stop this, so don't say that we don't play fair, and don't pretend you didn't have it coming.

We didn't make these rules—you did—and now we're going to force you to play by them. Hope you enjoy what is coming, you filthy rat k–ke bastards.

Kill yourselves, k–ke news fakers. You deserve every single bit of what you are about to get.

Unite the Right

The left had painted the MAGA coalition as a bunch of racists, and for the white nationalists in the group, this posed a question: Should they embrace this designation, or deny it? How open should they be with their red-pilled beliefs? Stephen Miller, an anti-immigration radical who Richard Spencer claimed as a friend and mentee while both were students at Duke, was writing presidential proclamations, for goodness' sake. While Miller disputed this relationship with Spencer, many of the white nationalists on the Trump train figured that close associations like these meant their chance to wield real power was soon to come.

In anticipation of this new political influence, Richard Spencer moved to Washington, D.C., and set up shop. As his relationship with the MAGA coalition began to fray after Heilgate, he found himself allied out of necessity with more traditional white supremacist street gangs and neo-Nazis, not the Beltway power brokers he'd hoped for. His relevance in mainstream politics rapidly waning, Spencer helped organize a rally in Charlottesville, Virginia, on August 12, 2017, that would go down in history: Unite the Right (UTR).

The alt-right had set their sights on Charlottesville because it was in the midst of a public debate about the removal of Confederate monuments. Spencer had attended the University of Virginia, so he knew the city's pain points all too well. Plus, it was close to D.C.

Unite the Right came at a time when lines were drawn between the coasts, but also between local groups, as the alt-right splintered and individuals fought with one another for dominance. The West Coast factions Proud Boys and Patriot Front were primarily known as roving street gangs, decked out in weapons and battle armor, while Spencer and his East Coast ilk fought with words, honing their brand as "dapper" intellectuals (courtesy of *Mother Jones*), more interested in political power than their more violent white nationalist peers.

Strong divisions between the alt-right and alt-lite were being drawn in right-wing media, as the ethnonationalists' blatant racism and antisemitism risked damaging the reputation of the more moderate alt-lite. This tension was made clear on June 25, when the formerly allied factions held dueling rallies in D.C.

Spencer, along with a bunch of other alt-right personalities who embraced public displays of racism, had helped to plan the Rally for Free Speech. But given his increasingly high-profile association with Nazism, some members of the alt-right refused to appear onstage with him. Mike Cernovich and Jack Posobiec, who along with Yiannopoulos had been calling themselves the New Right to gain distance from Spencer, decided to hold instead what they called the Rally Against Political Violence, with Roger Stone to headline.

Before the rallies, Spencer sneered to the *Washington Post* that a better name for the New Right was "alt-lite," a name that would stick for many people. "If these were really top-notch thinkers, scholars, human beings," he told the *Post*, "I might try to reach out to them. Being that they're not, I think it's good to just cut off the fat. . . . They are going to look like losers."

The "top-notch thinkers" who stayed loyal to Spencer and spoke at his rally included reliable gadfly Tim Gionet, aka Baked Alaska, who took the stage dressed in the Proud Boys' signature black-and-yellow Fred Perry shirt, more as a sign of respect than of true allegiance. Gionet spent most of the time making jokes and referencing memes. He joked about how people were so afraid of getting called racist and antisemitic, proudly telling the crowd—in a brag reminiscent of Yiannopoulos's boast about losing his Twitter account at the Gays For Trump event—that Twitter had suspended him for a "gas chamber meme." "I thought it was funny personally," he said. The crowd roared.

America, Gionet said, had lost its way if it couldn't handle jokes about people's ideologies and religions without being labeled as racist. "I've got pride in who I am, in my identity, as a white person," he said to more cheers. He closed by saying he was excited for the future of "Generation Zyklon," referring to the name of the poison gas used during the

Holocaust—a shout out to the Gen Z far right, who made up the mass of his audience.

The other speakers were not so subtle. Daily Caller contributor Jason Kessler invoked the trope that Jewish people held undue influence over the media. TRS's Mike Enoch went on an antisemitic, anti-Black tirade about diversity being antiwhite. Chris Cantwell, a former libertarian broadcaster who had been flash-radicalized just a year earlier by exposure to HBD, told the crowd that if they didn't change their tactics, they would lose to the more organized left. "We lack the networking and camaraderie of our leftist counterparts," he said. "They are building teams, figuring out who the leaders are, sizing up strengths and weaknesses, acquiring resources, and honing their propaganda to become efficient mechanisms of radicalization. To put it simply, they are preparing for open warfare while we prepare for structured competition like debates and marksmanship. Either that changes or not only will we lose, but we will be scrubbed from the historical record. Inside of a generation, it'll be as though we never existed. Other than some false historical narrative, like Hitler's Germany."

Spencer was the closer. After again jeering at the "alt-lite," who were too cowardly to stand by their beliefs, he proclaimed that the most radical thing a person could say these days was "I am white, my life has meaning, my life has dignity, I am part of a family, I will fight for my children's future!" It was a clear dog whistle to white nationalist David Lane's Fourteen Words, and a public attempt to define white identity politics under the Trump administration.

Over at the other rally, where antisemitism and explicit white identity politics weren't welcome, Cernovich and Posobiec were joined by numerous right-wing attendees like Gateway Pundit's Cassandra Fairbanks and Lucian Wintrich and conservative operative Ali Alexander (who would later go on to spearhead #StopTheSteal in 2020). Roger Stone never showed up, organizers blaming his absence on "security concerns." In an interview with the *Daily Beast*, Spencer suggested Stone bailed because the more moderate gathering was "pathetic," afraid to touch the third rail of white identity. The New Right disavowed the racism of the alt-right, making it clear they would no longer run cover for them.

After that, the factions of the fringe right became more defined than ever. Those who would attended Unite the Right the next month were not coming from the alt-lite. No, they were all those who most committed to fascism and neo-Nazism, explicitly antisemitic, white nationalist, and for now, still pro-Trump. Gavin McInnes, who alongside his Proud Boys fraternity was scheduled to be at the event, pulled out as it became more obvious this was not just a right-wing but an explicitly white nationalist event. Even as these groups took shots at one another online and off, an effervescent collective spirit took over on the right as the date for UTR approached and more groups began to climb on board, including militia groups, memelords, libertarians, and unabashedly proud Nazis.

Join or Die

The call to "unite the right" came after a small demonstration by Spencer and others in Charlottesville's Emancipation Park (formerly Lee Park) in May 2017. The Robert E. Lee statue that towered over the park served as a monument to the Klan's brutality in Charlottesville and shaped how many residents viewed the park as a "whites only" space. Locals had petitioned the city government to remove the statue and were awaiting the results of a lawsuit when the alt-right seized on the park as a place for their public demonstrations.

The online hype for the UTR rally was unprecedented in the history of digital white supremacy, with Facebook organizing, crowdsourced flyers, factions preparing their own memetic propaganda, and the exploitation of gamer tech like chat app Discord to coordinate communication. The overt organizing for this event troubled those tracking the far right but was largely ignored by law enforcement. Drunk on clout and lusting for blood, the alt-right followed notorious trolls and podcasters into a two-day event that would forever change the trajectory of their own movement and right-wing politics under Trump.

Spencer did not need the press to cover the fiery event; he could use social media to generate his own news cycle. As the tweets and images spread, mainstream coverage soon followed. Using social media as an access point for journalists ensured that even if a rally did not conjure press in person, it could captivate online audiences. Not long after, the plans for UTR began to circulate on message boards, social media, and chat apps. Even those who thought it was dumb helped spread the memes.

The online promotion of the event included a series of posters that remixed propaganda, memes, and other historically significant cultural symbols. A simple blue-tinged poster included only an image of the Lee statue, the heading "Unite the Right," a list of speakers, and the date, time, and place, providing no links to other information, and concluded sharply "We Will Not Be Replaced." Another was rife with imagery from /pol/, including an army of Pepes and Wojaks holding Confederate flags, while famous Civil War statues formed a background silhouette. Above them were flying Nazi eagles and the names of the speakers. Another in the 1980s retro "fashwave" style, in shades of neon pink, blue, and purple, featured headshots of the speakers taken from the June free speech rally, with the #UniteTheRight hashtag at the bottom. Another featured a man and woman drawn in an iconic 1950s varsity sports poster style, spelling out the rally's intention more clearly as "a pivotal moment for the pro-white movement in America." Lastly, the Daily Stormer made its own flyer, which invoked the strongman imagery popular in Soviet propaganda of the interwar period. Instead of a sickle and hammer to connote the working class, a man aimed a sledgehammer

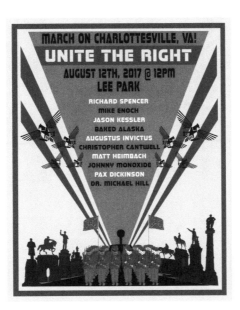

at a Star of David, above the line "Join Azzmador and The Daily Stormer to End Jewish Influence in America." (Azzmador was the pseudonym of a well-known Daily Stormer.)

The most important rallying call for the Unite the Right rally was a remix of Benjamin Franklin's original "Join, or Die" woodblock cartoon of a rattlesnake cut into pieces, the precursor to the Gadsden flag. Whereas that first snake had been divided into eight segments, standing for the regions of the thirteen colonies, this one was cut up into different factions of the red-pilled right, and along with the call to join or die was a location and date: Charlottesville, August 12, Lee Park.

The first version of this remixed meme was posted to Discord on June 28, 2017, and included a typo. The digital flyer was fixed and reposted by "Commander Davis (TWP)," a screen name believed to belong to a known white nationalist and supporter of the Traditionalist Worker Party, Derrick Davis. From left to right the snake segments were labeled

"K" (for Kekistan), "A.C." (Anti-Communist), "L" (Libertarian), "N" (Nationalist), "I" (Identitarian or Identity Evropa), "S.N." (Southern Nationalist), "N.S." (National Socialist), and, as the head of the snake, "A.R." (Alt-Right). Each snake section was patterned with the flag of these different factions. Rhetoric online about UTR eschewed adopting different ideologies and emphasized putting divisions aside in favor of building momentum for the movement as a whole.

However abhorrent, many of the groups on the flag had become familiar and legible political positions in U.S. politics. The inclusion of Kekistan, however, was particularly telling as a nod to internet culture's influence on the rally. Invented by shitposters on 4chan's /pol/ and later popularized in a stunt mocking the census by UK right-wing YouTuber Sargon of Akkad, Kekistan was a parody of U.S. identity politics: a country that didn't exist, with a vocal exiled population cast off to the internet, represented by a banner that mimics a Nazi war flag. It was a troll born of reactionary meme culture. Its inclusion in the "Join, or Die" meme served as a catchall callout to online communities, if only for the lulz. Ironically, the original Kekistan flag was designed as a way to recognize one another in the throngs of Trump's inauguration crowd.

On August 9, two days before the torch march, Andrew Anglin of the Daily Stormer published a lengthy blog post outlining the reason for the rally and his expectation of attendees. He viewed the rally as a way to market the ideas of the alt-right, he wrote: "The core of marketing is aesthetic. We need to look appealing. . . . We have to be hip and we have to be sexy. This means we have to look good, we have to look dangerous, we have to have humor, we have to look powerful and we have to look like we are in control." Bottom line, he said, "People who see us have to want to be us. That means you have to go to the gym."

Anglin spent much of the article discouraging behavior that would make the marchers look bad to mass audiences. "We have worked out a very good aesthetic for the internet. However, that isn't going to translate directly to real life. That means that Pepe banners are a non-starter. This is cringe. We do not want that." Despite his extensive list of "don'ts," Anglin did encourage his followers to enjoy themselves and "have fun." "We are fighting a war," he wrote. "But what is the point of fighting it, if we can't enjoy it?"

Friday

While UTR was certainly not the first white nationalist gathering in the United States' history, it was the largest in the twenty-first century. As hype grew among the alt-right and alarms were raised by anti-fascist activists, national media and local government took notice. Concerns over potential violence were raised, and extra resources devoted to keeping the peace on the day of the rally.

When the city of Charlottesville sought to move the UTR permit to a larger park farther from downtown for safety, the ACLU deployed resources to defend the UTR rally's location and won. The rally would be moved back to Emancipation Park, formerly known as Lee Park, where the statue of General Robert E. Lee still remained in place pending a court decision. Using a combination of gamer chat apps and message boards, the UTR organizers gamed out a contingency they called "Plan Red." In the event that the police would not let them into the park, they would take it by force.

The weekend began with a surprise torchlight march on the evening of August 11, when a procession of young white men clad in a uniform of white polo shirts and khakis marched through UVA's campus. This mass was designed to be terrifying to casual onlookers, and exciting to those who had been waiting for such a media moment. There was no need to alert the media, as the participants, and their hastily rallied opponents, livestreamed the ominous march and the chants for white supremacy on YouTube, Facebook Live, and Periscope.

From the outset the alt-right put a lot of planning into Friday night's torchlit march, led by Jason Kessler. Spencer's faction, headed up by a man going by the pseudonym Eli Mosley (also a member of Identity Evropa), used a Discord chat to explain details and convene organizers; Mosley also offered instructions for the rally. On the Charlottesville 2.0 Discord server, organizers were asked to buy torches on their way to the rally, but to avoid speaking about the torchlight vigil publicly. In the instructions, Mosley asked that the marchers learn the song "Dixie" and be prepared to perform it. It seemed as if Mosley believed that, like the smaller demonstration in May, the event would go off without a hitch. Someone also posted this set of instructions from the alt-right Discord chat to /pol/ as a way to recruit more people.

What happened was very different. Kessler kicked off the march with a speech about white genocide, telling Ford Fisher of News2Share in an interview before the torch march that "our people are being torn down and replaced through immigration policies." Torches lit up the night sky. The serpentine march through campus was caught from multiple angles and livestreamed. Fisher caught the very beginning, when people chanted, "Out of our sight, antiwhite," "One people. One nation. End immigration," and "Fuck off commies! This is our town now!" This eventually gave way to the familiar protest chant, "Whose streets? Our streets!"

The livestream of Tim Gionet, aka Baked Alaska, was prominently featured online as he marched alongside rallygoers, chanting and giving commentary. Chants of "You will not replace us" shifted into mechanical laughter as intermittently some substituted "Jews will not replace us," which had become an Identity Evropa slogan after Nathan Damigo first said it into the camera at HWNDU.

Wearing a blue jacket and a hat emblazoned with the Gadsden snake and the slogan DON'T TREAD ON ME, Gionet exclaimed into the camera,

"You will not replace us! You and your cultural marxist f–ggot bullshit will not replace us," just as the march turned a corner and spilled out into the campus quad. A stunning visual of orderly flaming torches dotted the screen as the march moved toward the Thomas Jefferson statue and split into two lines. Gionet, flanked by his bodyguard, exclaimed "Beautiful!" as another person shouted "Heil victory!" at the camera. "Guess what?" Gionet said ominously. "We're standing up for our rights! We're proud to be white." At that moment, more people reached out to shake his hand and give thumbs-ups to the camera.

About five minutes into the march, a small group came onto Gionet's screen holding a sign that read "VA Students Against White Supremacy." They huddled around the statue of Jefferson, chanting, "No Nazis. No KKK. No Fascist USA." Hundreds of alt-righters surrounded them, their torches enclosing them in flame.

"This is antifa!" Gionet yelled.

"White lives matter!" the crowd chanted in a roar.

And then the altercations began. Someone shoved Emily Gorzenski, a local protester, yelling "Move, bitch!" Punches and kicks were thrown in the melee, much of which Gionet captured on his stream. "Holy shit! Holy shit!" he screamed. "Pray for us! They're attacking us! The Communists are out!" He panned the camera away from the clash and then back to the statue. At its base stood several men, sieg heiling. Chants of "White lives matter" and "Antiwhite" swelled as the crowd broke apart after some chemical dispersant filled the air.

Moustache Matt, part of Gionet's entourage, quipped, "Isn't it ironic that we got gassed?"—an obvious dog whistle about the murder of Jews in concentration camps.

Gionet responded with dramatic effect, as though he was delivering the voice-over for a movie trailer: "This shit is absolutely bonkers. . . . We are going big tomorrow. . . . This is just the beginning!"

By the next day over thirty-five thousand people had viewed Gionet's thirty-eight-minute stream, and clips from it were bouncing across every platform. Millions more watched the story via mainstream news. Though universally critical, the coverage was still a boon to the alt-right, who came off as dangerous, powerful, and full of conviction. Online, the alt-right cheered the tiki torch assembly, mocked anti-fascist activists' calls for backup, and valorized the marchers in memes. Both sides braced for what was to come in the morning.

Saturday

It was a sunny day as rallygoers marched through the city center, dressed in paramilitary gear and helmets and brandishing homemade shields and batons. The crowd of white nationalists had begun gathering at 8:30 A.M. to make their way to Emancipation Park. After the highly publicized tiki torch march of the night before, so did anti-racist counterprotesters, chanting "Kill all Nazis" and "Follow your leader, kill yourself" as the far right amassed a large and unwieldy presence. Roving groups assaulted locals as police stood back, awaiting instructions from commanding officers.

As Gionet had promised, the events of Saturday made the Friday night torch march look tame in contrast. But it was over in a matter of hours. Whereas the Unite the Right marchers on Friday had a cohesive look and demeanor, Saturday was a free-for-all. The atmosphere was tense and chaotic.

Vice profiled Chris Cantwell as he arrived, wearing a shirt with the name of his podcast *Radical Agenda* emblazoned on the front and a silhouetted body falling out of a helicopter on the back, a familiar alt-right meme that was a nod to a gruesome method used to execute Communist opponents by Chilean dictator Augusto Pinochet. As more people began to show up, Cantwell's free-helicopter-ride dog whistle was overshadowed by Nazi flags and burly men with white supremacist tattoos and patches. The National Socialists, League of the South, and hardcore militants had arrived, together representing a diverse group of white nationalist factions. The small clique of online trolls circled around Gionet, many of whom had attended HWNDU antics a few months earlier. They wandered the crowd, seemingly out of place amongst older extremists and militia folk.

Among the throngs of attendees and counterprotesters shouting at one another, chants of "Blood and soil" and "Whose streets? Our streets!" gave way to screaming matches, and clouds of mace and tear gas filled the air. By 10:30 violence had begun to break out. An hour later police declared an unlawful assembly in Emancipation Park, followed by the declaration of a state of emergency by Virginia governor Terry McAuliffe.

Some of the marchers began to disperse quickly, while others stayed around to brawl. Spencer and other organizers, furious at this outcome, reluctantly left what was meant to be the greatest day for the alt-right. Cantwell ran too. People yelled "Heil Cantwell" at him as he jumped in a van, flanked by a writer for the Daily Stormer.

David Duke, a KKK member and former politician, also gave numerous interviews to eager journalists and other videographers from the march. "We're going to fulfill the promises of Donald Trump" to "take our country back," Duke told the *New York Times*. *Vice* kept rolling as Cantwell's entourage hopped in a van headed to McIntire Park, where the city was going to allow them to congregate. Matt Heimbach, leader of the white nationalist Traditionalist Worker Party, explained to *Vice* that they had organized the largest nationalist rally in twenty years.

As the day devolved into street brawls, reporters were punched, and people got pepper sprayed, beaten, and bloodied, the nation watched on TV and social media. Trump's opponents blamed the disaster on the president's enabling of white nationalists, and he was forced to address the situation. At 1:19 P.M. Trump tweeted vaguely, "We ALL must be united & condemn all that hate stands for. There is no place for this kind of violence in America. Lets come together as one." Twenty minutes later James Fields, a young man who had traveled from Ohio to be at the rally, according to the *New York Times*, slammed his Dodge Challenger into the largest part of the remaining crowd at high speed before fleeing the scene. The attack killed a white leftist protester named Heather Heyer and injured several others.

The hit-and-run was captured from several angles by journalists on the ground, and online sleuths from the right and the left raced to ascertain the subject's identity. Fields's arrest wouldn't be announced by Virginia police until later that evening. Before the suspect was confirmed, /pol/ anons spread false info on social media about the attacker's identity. Most were gloating over the death of a leftist woman and the other counterprotesters' injuries. Within a few minutes, they'd turn Fields's attack into a gruesome series of memes. Despite UTR organizers' insistence that this would be a peaceful gathering of well-intentioned white men trying to preserve their cultural heritage, their gathering had become a crime scene.

"Very Fine People on Both Sides"

Responses from politicians began to roll in, kicked off by a rare statement from First Lady Melania Trump. As he was signing a bill from his golf resort in Bedminster, New Jersey, Trump made this statement to the press: "We're closely following the terrible events unfolding in Charlottesville, Va. We condemn in the strongest possible terms this egregious display of hatred, bigotry and violence on many sides, on many sides." Trump later tweeted another quote from the press conference, recalling his inauguration speech in January: "We must remember this truth: No matter our color, creed, religion or political party, we are ALL AMERICANS FIRST."

Several critics pointed out that "America First" was also a well-known slogan of the KKK. Trump was getting the full-court press from reporters anxious to hear him disavow the white supremacists, but he remained coy on the issue, reportedly meeting with Bannon and Stephen Miller privately.

All of the more mainstream conservative figures denounced the rally, and on August 13, 2017, even The_Donald backtracked on support for Unite the Right. But when Trump addressed the fallout of UTR in a twenty-minute press conference on August 15, 2017, he lambasted the press for ignoring the violence of the "alt-left." He then uttered the line that became a meme that would define his presidency: that there were "very fine people on both sides" of the deadly gathering. Anons on /pol/ took this as support, as did many in the alt-right that day. "HAIL TRUMP," some anons wrote. "The future is looking brighter by the day lads."

Many liberals would agree that Trump clearly sided with those who wanted the Confederate statues preserved, and was at least sympathetic to the alt-right. As the press kept up questioning, he began to push back, asking the press to define the alt-right and asking them to admit that the "alt-left" were also perpetrating violence. But "Very fine people on both sides" would go on to dog his presidency. Joe Biden reported that Trump's response to Charlottesville was what inspired him to run.

The death of Heather Heyer, the terrifying images of fascists with torches marching in America, and Trump's response excited his critics. Here was irrefutable proof that the president's supporters in the alt-right were no different from the KKK members and neo-Nazis who marched alongside them in the streets of Charlottesville. Alt-right figurehead Richard Spencer had built a career off attaching his name to Trump's, and now his association with Unite the Right would be difficult to shake. Only a few days after Unite the Right, on August 18, 2017, after months of private and public disagreement, Bannon left his position at the White House and returned to Breitbart.

Though by 2016 Bannon had spent years cultivating right-wing internet movements like Gamergate and alt-right support for Trump, he had no control over the movement after, earlier that year, Yiannopolis was displaced when his pro-pederasty comments resurfaced. Anons on /pol/ debated whether Bannon's sudden departure was bad news for their movement. Many blamed the influence of Fox News baron Rupert Murdoch; others blamed Jared Kushner and Ivanka, describing their influence as distinctly "Jewish." "Once bannon leaves is there really a point?" one anon wrote. "He in [*sic*] unironically /ourguy/ in the WH. Now this stupid rally is being attached to him somehow to make him a fall guy. Maybe Trump is just using him to make it seem like he is getting fired for leaking and not his connections, but still, he will be gone."

The day he left the White House, Bannon told the *Weekly Standard*, a conservative magazine, "The Trump presidency that we fought for, and won, is over." He went on to say, "We still have a huge movement, and we will make something of this Trump presidency. But that presidency is over. It'll be something else. And there'll be all kinds of fights, and there'll be good days and bad days, but *that* presidency is over."

Anons on /pol/ didn't take kindly to Bannon's comments, nor his dismissal of Trump. Despite their initial support for his departure, it seemed that now he wanted nothing to do with the assortment of white nationalists who'd marched in Virginia a few days earlier. While in 2016 he'd given them their most significant platform, Bannon now was forced to disavow the white nationalists in the alt-right, severing any lingering ties with a movement that had already served his purposes.

Deplatforming

Unite the Right was a disaster for all who planned it. The most bloodthirsty of the digital army celebrated the death of Heather Heyer in memes, but mainstream conservatives and the reluctant New Right, who viewed the descent to street actions with explicit racism as detrimental to Trump's political power, universally condemned it. Jason Kessler, the local organizer who pulled the permits for UTR, was admonished by Gavin McInnes and the New Right publicly on McInnes's YouTube show. The lawyer Roberta Kaplan took up the charge and put together a number of civil cases against the organizers of the UTR rally. Luckily for Kaplan, a group of anti-fascist citizen journalists called Unicorn Riot had been monitoring the chat rooms where the alt-right organized the rally, and were able to give Kaplan the evidence she needed to ask for other forms of discovery, including the seizure of laptops and phones.

The most telling pieces of evidence in Kaplan's arsenal were the memes, as she told a reporter: "A lot of the pre-Aug. 11 communication these guys had was about driving vehicles into protesters." Evan McLaren, executive director of Richard Spencer's white supremacist National Policy Institute, told ProPublica that references to car attacks were "irreverent banter" and "not relevant to what happened." But regardless of Fields's intention, he'd lived the meme. And the online far right had reacted to the killing with collective exuberance and the exchanging of vile car-as-weapon memes.

When a social media company suspends or deletes someone's account, it is called deplatforming. In the week leading up to UTR, Facebook deleted the event page, while Airbnb canceled reservations for many rally attendees, including Richard Spencer. After the event, corporations such as Google (including YouTube), Twitter, Facebook, Cloudflare, Go Daddy, Airbnb, Uber, PayPal, Discord, Patreon, and others removed the accounts of UTR organizers and groups. This left the communication infrastructure of the movement largely in disarray, and foiled attempts to control media narratives from the alt-right.

Unite the Right splintered the alt-right irrevocably. Some saw it coming—like Gavin McInnes, who backed away from the alt-right before Charlottesville. While many of the organizers of Charlottesville faced charges, Gionet did not. Jason Kessler and Christopher Cantwell (who, as the "Crying Nazi," became his own meme) took much of the blame both legally and online. Not long after, Gionet, Jared Taylor, and many other alt-right figures lost their Twitter accounts in November 2017, though Kessler and Spencer somehow retained their accounts.

UTR proved to be the line in the sand between the edgy conservatives of the New Right, led by Yiannopoulos, Posobiec, and Cernovich, and the committed ethnonationalists of the alt-right, led by Spencer. The violence destroyed old allegiances as those more deeply entrenched in mainstream conservative circles condemned the violence of Kessler and Spencer's street Nazis and KKK members. The online left responded with the viral meme "It's ok to punch a Nazi."

Between Bannon's departure and the waves of deplatforming and infighting that followed Unite the Right, the old MAGA coalition had been shattered. White nationalists, including Spencer, began to sour on Trump, disappointed by his mixed response to the rally and claims that "bad people" were among his ranks. Many other stalwarts in the movement, such as *Fash the Nation* and TRS, followed suit. Trump had already disappointed them when he bombed Syria in April, and despite the occasional retweet of an alt-right meme, he hadn't meaningfully addressed white people in a way that satisfied them. Perhaps Trump was a bad bet, just another neocon interventionist acting on behest of Israel, and the lack of progress on the border wall or a meaningful halt to immigration over the first several months of his presidency was also the result of Jewish meddling. Rallying in public was a bad idea; the popular front of liberals and leftists were becoming increasingly organized and effective at pushing back against white nationalist Trump supporters. As summer turned to fall, the alt-right leaders lost much of their influence, and the anons grew restless.

Now Spencer was too toxic to have much clout. On October 19, 2017, when Spencer, Mosley, and Enoch held an event at the University of Florida, the governor preemptively declared a state of emergency. After the event, two Nazi-saluting supporters of Spencer were convicted of firing shots at counterprotesters, terrible optics for a movement attempting to redefine itself after UTR. The alt-right leaders were left looking both foolish and dangerous, and so they retreated back from IRL into the wires. Many more were driven from the movement.

Infighting and Retreat

Milo Yiannopoulos, who hadn't been at UTR because of his earlier exile from the coalition, capitalized on the deplatforming of Spencer and his many other rivals in a planned four-day event at the University of California–Berkeley in September, a reprisal of the battles that had brought him so much attention in the spring. He booked Bannon, his old boss, to headline, and he named the whole thing Free Speech Week. The intent was to force what the right believed was the hypocrisy of liberals out into the open. Who among them would be able to argue against Yiannopoulos delivering the Mario Savio Award for Free Speech on the same hallowed grounds where the free speech movement began?

But in the aftermath of UTR, the backlash against Free Speech Week from liberals, leftists, and even some conservatives was so strong that the event never happened. Most of the guests never confirmed, space on campus was not secured, and the threat of a riot was too imminent. What was planned as a four-day event ended up as a single speech given by Yiannopoulos to a small crowd. He'd lost access now to two of his most important platforms—Twitter and college campuses—and the fight to stay relevant would prove to be an uphill battle for the British provocateur.

In early November, Yiannopoulos started hawking T-shirts with the slogan "It's Okay to Be White," a post-UTR /pol/ meme campaign. After the debacle of organizing and marching in real life, Yiannopoulos retreated back to memes. The IOTBW campaign began October 24, 2017, after someone on /pol/ suggested printing it on flyers and placing them on high school and college campuses. Their hope was to generate debate on social media and instigate mainstream press coverage. An anonymous poster wrote, "Based on past media response to similar messaging, we expect the anti-white media to produce a shit-storm about these racist, hateful, bigoted fliers . . . with a completely innocuous message."

Some anons made comparisons between the IOTBW and HWNDU campaigns, and how anonymity and trolling served them best. As the campaign picked up attention in the alt-right, it was endorsed by several of the higher-profile leaders. This wasn't a welcome development to the anons. "Mike Enoch and Richard Spencer show up again to ruin

everything, trying to turn IOTBW into another Charlottesville," wrote one. They held special vitriol for Yiannopoulos's attempt to cash in on the meme. His co-option clearly violated the rules around anonymity, and by connecting it to himself, he connected it to racists and the alt-right by extension. The irony was not lost on Spencer and others, who responded by denouncing the T-shirt sale with antisemitic dog whistles by tagging their tweets with #MerchantRight. #MerchantRight suggested that Yiannopoulos, of partial Jewish ancestry, was exploiting the movement, and the shitlords of 4chan, for profit.

Be it the alt-right, New Right, alt-lite, or any other group, the mainstream media lumped together all Trump supporters; to them, these factions' names were distinctions without a difference. The term *alt-right* was now rightly paired with white supremacy in articles about the movement, and Spencer was unable to conjure mainstream media attention as he had in the past. While Spencer, Enoch, Gionet, and others retreated to the safety of their online social worlds, companies were now feeling public pressure to prevent the far right from using their platforms to coordinate and plan violent events. But it was already too little, too late; these groups had finally met each other in person and were bonded by their shared experiences and by public condemnation. The leaders of the movement were no longer considered edgy and provocative. Now they seemed defeated, seeking donations to support their court cases. But in this power vacuum, a small-time influencer with an ardent interest in right-wing populism and white identity was gearing up for a takeover.

Chapter 7

Joker Politics

Eighteen-year-old Nicholas Fuentes flew into Charlottesville, Virginia, with a friend around 11:00 A.M. on August 12, 2017, and immediately started streaming to his small but interested fan base.

"It's a beautiful day in the South," he reported, except for the fact that "some dumb woman" had mass-reported all his misogynistic tweets and gotten him locked out of his account. "I can't wait to see my people. It's gonna be a real powder keg."

Fuentes and his friend got into an Uber outside the airport. Fuentes told the stream the driver had "some exotic name." He joked that he hoped he didn't identify as a white nationalist on the way to the rally. "There was some trendy liberal reporter on the plane next to us," he said with a coy smile. "I wanted to get all up in his face and be like 'Hey buster, we're gonna consolidate the white race today and we're gonna win bigly.'" He hadn't.

The day before, from his freshman dorm room at Boston University, Fuentes had expressed doubts about his trip. He told the audience of his show, *America First*, which he'd been airing on the pro-Trump Right Side Broadcasting Network (RSBN) for the past few months, that he was going to attend Unite the Right, but he was "a little bit worried."

"I'm excited to go," he said on the stream. "I'm excited to meet everyone that's coming out there. I saw Sam Hyde is gonna be there. I love Sam Hyde! I met him at He Will Not Divide Us in New York City, but I am a little bit worried as much as I am excited to go and meet people of like-mind, people that know what's going on, people that are not dumb, and are in the matrix, and on the blue pill. People that we can talk about how we're gonna fix the country, fix the demographics. As excited as I am for all of that, I'm nervous." He said he worried the whole thing could be a trap to gather "the top guys, the top brass, all the tin-pot soldiers" in one place and take them down.

Now, as he and his friend approached Emancipation Park, he told his followers, "In choosing to go here we basically decided that if push comes to shove we may have to die for our beliefs."

"I didn't decide that. I don't wanna die," the friend chimed in. He had been quiet this whole time.

"I decided that," Fuentes told him. "I'm ready to lay it down on the line for my people, my heritage, the blood and the soil."

His friend didn't answer.

The Uber dropped Fuentes and his friend off at Emancipation Park, and they quickly found his online friends, like Tim "Baked Alaska" Gionet. Sam Hyde wasn't anywhere to be seen, to Fuentes's disappointment. The small crew stopped to greet the few fans that recognized them, live-streaming the whole time on Periscope. At one point, they came across an Infowars reporter with a camera and proceeded to drop red pills on stream about Jews and demographics. And that was about as exciting as it got for Fuentes at Unite the Right. He stayed on the edges of the rally and cleared out early. He wasn't anywhere near the violence. He didn't carry anything that identified him with other white nationalist groups. And he wasn't able to tweet from the protest, because his account was locked. But he did post on his personal Facebook.

"Wow—what an incredible rally here in Charlottesville," he wrote. "A tidal wave of white identity is coming." He ended his note with a quote ("The fire rises!") from a Batman film that was a popular 4chan meme. Like his heroes, Fuentes used memes as a lingua franca to reach people with similar ideas.

His presence at the rally would cost him, after a former friend leaked a screenshot of his Facebook post. The uproar at his college, and from the CEO of the network where his show was broadcast, was intense. When he returned to campus, he received "death threats," he told the AP in a video interview, and so he retreated to his parents' home in suburban Chicago. "The fix is in, it was a setup," Fuentes fumed on a livestream after the event. He blamed everyone from George Soros to federal narcs, but mostly he blamed mainstream conservatives. UTR cost him his show, and lost him more moderate conservative friends. Fuentes believed the subsequent violence gave conservative pundits an excuse to condemn the entire alt-right movement as antisemites and Nazis once and for all.

Too green to be a ringleader, and not as extreme as some of the white nationalist militias that drew national attention, Fuentes continued broadcasting, tweeting, and writing after UTR. He was ready to play the heel, and thrived equally on positive and negative attention. Back in 2016, Fuentes introduced himself to the world in an essay titled "The Villain America Needs." The title was a reference to Batman, but instead of a hero like the titular caped crusader, Fuentes was writing himself as a bad guy.

"I was born 3 years before the World Trade Center fell," he wrote. "5 years before Saddam Hussein fell; 10 years before the election of a fifth columnist to the Presidency; and 18 years before the stakes of a Presidential election were raised to the fate of a civilization." He traced his lineage as a pundit to Trump, Yiannopoulos, and Pat Buchanan, and described himself as "a devilishly handsome 17 year old mischief maker with grit, a full head of hair, and some balls."

Born August 18, 1998, to an Italian mother and a father of mixed Mexican descent, Fuentes had been brought up Catholic and conservative in the Chicago suburbs. He was vice president of the student council at his school and in Model UN. On November 5, 2015, he started the first show to bear his name: *The Nicholas J. Fuentes Show* on his school's TV station. He honed a careful, deliberate delivery, aided by his naturally baritone voice.

Throughout high school, Fuentes won speech tournaments and devoured classic libertarian and conservative texts, drawn to the paleoconservatism of Pat Buchanan. He enrolled as a freshman at Boston University in the fall of 2016 and quickly became red-pilled. After being exposed to revisionist World War II documentaries and befriended by some other hard-right BU students, Fuentes said he started to "notice things" that made him conclude that "ethnic conflict is real, that we can't all live together in the same country."

On his personal political blog, Fuentes began writing his way through these new ideas. On September 12, 2016, he published "The Ascendancy of the Madman," in which he wrote, "Donald Trump is the George Washington of this century, a war-time president who we entrust with our lives and the lives of our families to lead this people once again to that shining city on a hill, to wage a guerilla campaign, with only God on our side, to defeat the forces of tyranny which have infected our republic." Heady words for a college freshman.

"For years the Alex Joneses of the world were called madmen," he went on, signaling the impact Jones had in the MAGA community Fuentes was growing up in. "Hillary Clinton and her globalist sponsors snicker at the deplorable hordes of alt-right psychopaths rejecting the great globalist lies erected over the past 25 years. The ascendancy of the madman heralds the end of the old regime, and they know it."

Fuentes's rhetoric grew more revolutionary as the election grew closer. On October 30, 2016, in a piece titled "America Needs Trump More Than Democracy," he wrote, "To hell with the democratic process if we continue down the rabbit hole of corporatist, globalist tyranny." The next day he was featured in a BU student roundup where he stumped for Trump and revealed his newfound obsession with demography. Decked out in a red MAGA hat, with the practiced delivery provided by years of broadcasting experience, Fuentes used this platform to praise Trump's anti-immigration attitudes, but took it one step further: "The multi-cultural movement in America is subverting any efforts that a conservative could ever make to change the country."

The video made Nick infamous—and despised—on campus. The BU student body president challenged him to a debate, in which he accused Fuentes of being a "crypto Nazi" and a "digital brownshirt" on Twitter. Fuentes's high school years had prepared him well for this style of debate, and he mercilessly mocked his opponent, to the delight of campus conservatives.

On the evening of November 8, 2016, he livestreamed his reactions to Trump's victory, excitedly asking his audience, "Are we living through the rapture, because it certainly feels like it." Elated, Fuentes and a friend (an Iraqi student who also supported Trump) went around campus to a bunch of liberal student viewing parties and rubbed Clinton's loss in their faces.

His notoriety attracted the attention of some campus conservative leaders in Massachusetts, particularly Mount Holyoke student Kassy Dillon, who helped him get a show on RSBN. At that time, according to former friend Will Nardi, she called Fuentes "the next rising star in the Republican party." Fuentes's show, *America First*, was a hit with edgy right-wing Gen Z kids. Fuentes prioritized engagement with his audience, replying to questions in his livestream chat at the end of every show, sometimes for upward of an hour. These questions ranged from national politics to thinly veiled racial dog whistles. And Fuentes relished engaging with it all, not shying away from reactionary comments around race and gender. He gave his audience the feeling that he wasn't just talking at them but enjoyed their company and valued their anonymity, solidifying the bonds within his growing online community. Fuentes's increasingly radical rhetoric and caustic style led many of his more establishment conservative friends to distance themselves, particularly Dillon, who denounced him and leaked his celebratory Facebook posts after the Unite the Right rally.

When asked by a viewer who would be his dream debate, Nick replied without hesitation: "Ben Shapiro." "He's sort of a character foil for me," he said. "We fought a bit on Twitter before, I fought a lot of his followers, minions and friends." The media darling Shapiro, he said, was basically a liberal, along with the rest of what Fuentes called "Conservative Inc." With a massive audience on YouTube and hundreds of thousands in book sales, Shapiro had a significant reach and a devoted following, and was something of a meme himself. Shapiro was also Jewish and, despite his right-wing leanings, was openly critical of the alt-right and their overt antisemitism. While Shapiro may have begun as an inspiration for Fuentes, now he was a target.

Halfway through his second semester, Fuentes grew even more red-pilled. "Who runs the media? Globalists. Time to kill the globalists," he said in an April 24, 2017, broadcast on RSBN. "I want people that run CNN to be arrested and deported or hanged." The clip came to the attention of watchdog Media Matters, and RSBN was forced to apologize. Fuentes didn't lose his show, but he did learn a lesson about explicit calls to violence; he'd be careful about crossing that line in the future. Even though he was barely able to contain himself, he was one of many young men red-pilled during this period. What made him different was his willingness to put his real name on his hard-right shitposting, and to follow the memes into the real world in Charlottesville.

Fuentes faced personal repercussions from the fallout of UTR and felt the weight of disappointment and disillusionment. The alt-right leaders who organized UTR and urged people like Fuentes to show up had seemed to know what they were doing. Fuentes and everyone else had trusted them. Now it turned out they were losers, too.

The world was a clown show.

Fuentes Embraces His Power Level

Unlike many others who organized and attended UTR, Fuentes hadn't lost his Twitter or YouTube accounts, and he was able to reach a growing audience via his nightly broadcasts. He also became a frequent guest on the anti-social-justice-warrior YouTube punditry circuit that had grown out of Gamergate. In the aftermath of UTR, when the alt-right was no longer welcome in more mainstream spaces, this community still offered the red-pilled fringe a place to gather, and an increasingly lucrative way to make money.

On November 6, 2017, Fuentes proved himself a ruthless debater during a YouTube stream that brought together various alt-right, alt-lite, and leftist influencers—the kind of people Fuentes was dead set on bringing down. These sorts of large debate streams were pulling in serious viewership, sometimes more than 500,000. Fuentes argued traditionalism and racial realism, attacking trans YouTuber ContraPoints (Natalie Wynn). This was the first time Fuentes appeared on a stream with Gamergate legend Jim, who was still the preeminent tastemaker in the red-pilled right. Fuentes's viciousness was praised by fans. From there, he quickly became a star in the debate space, embraced by Jim as a rugged individual with no equal or mentor.

But if Fuentes was going to use this new underground fame—as well as his moderate fame in the mainstream—to dethrone the elders of the conservative and alt-right movements, he'd need an army.

He found one in a new trolling faction that had been growing on /pol/ for a few months. The group took on the name of Groypers, a neologism first used by a beloved troll on 4chan's /r9k/ board in 2015. As the year was coming to a close, the Groypers were popping out of their holes and emerging on Twitter just as the Pepe posters of the 2016 meme war had littered the site with their cartoons. Groyper became a character, a mascot, and a meme. Just like Pepe, Groyper was a green frog (some would argue, a toad), smug and calm with folded hands. Groyper was described by *Slate* as a "Fatter, More Racist Pepe the Frog."

"Groypers like to relax and drink tea. Groypers are all WWII revisionists in the sheets, but proper and almost non offensive in the streets. They show a bit more class," a Groyper fan told reporter Will Sommer. Groypers stayed home, cozy, behind their screens. Fuentes gravitated to this new pseudonymous community, increasingly disconnected from the alt-right that was left in disarray after UTR.

There was a decidedly misogynistic streak to this new subcommunity. The sexism of the Groypers appealed to Fuentes, and when they tuned in to his stream, he celebrated them. This turned him into the highest-profile Groyper, and therefore their de facto leader. Like them, Fuentes hated women and prided himself on his hypertraditional sexual values, his virginity, and his essentialist views on gender. This differentiated him from the mainstream views of the anons on /pol/ or even 8chan, who

were antifeminist but low-key still wanted to have sex with women. On the message board Kiwi Farms, one poster wrote of Fuentes, "This dude and his legion of incel followers are just stealing /pol/ memes and bringing them outside of the internet."

By December 2017, with a growing fan base of young right-wing men, Fuentes's popularity scored him invites to livestreamed debates about race realism, gender essentialism, and the Jewish question, which he dominated. These debates were so based and depraved that the troll Jim named them "Internet Bloodsports—the Jerry Springer of YouTube content," and devoted himself to covering their drama. Nothing was off the table. People pushed the idea that the white race was experiencing a genocide caused by immigration, and they embraced the meme "White Sharia," the idea, rooted in dark irony and Islamophobia, that white men should invoke laws to control white women—a concept first promoted by neo-Nazi hacker weev. Fuentes used these debates to further a "thot war" against women of the alt-lite and alt-right, which he and the Groypers waged by attacking female and trans content creators. Thot was an acronym for "that ho over there," popular rap slag referring to a woman with many partners. To the Groypers, all women were thots, and thots had no place in politics at all.

As he got more and more attention, however, the doubts about whether Fuentes was white enough to be a white nationalist also got louder. After all, his last name was Spanish, and he had admitted to some Mexican ancestry. The established white nationalists in the far right demanded that he take a DNA test.

Fuentes was skeptical of DNA tests, and 23andMe in particular, believing that Jews could be messing with the test results to "deracinate" the white population. But he agreed to take a test, and he liked the results he got: primarily European, with a small percentage of Sub-Saharan African. To his relief and pride, his results showed no Jewish ancestry, so he shared them on stream in December. The white nationalists were happy with that. Fuentes was white enough, despite the marginal African traces. This became a running joke for Fuentes, who would refer to himself as "Afro-Latino" in ironic attempts to escape accusations of white supremacy.

Fuentes just got stronger. He launched *America First* as a donation-based show on YouTube that he could control entirely on his own, and began taking direct shots at the millennial alt-right leadership, like Spencer, whom he called a "pedophile CIA LARPer" based on passing comments Spencer made about the merits of using child pornography to reduce sex offenses. This was the same basic allegation that had gotten Yiannopoulos canceled, and it irked Spencer enough that he reportedly called Fuentes and angrily called him a "spic."

The fact that Fuentes, who just six months before had almost no real connection to the alt-right leadership, could make Spencer that mad showed how much power he had been accruing as the old guard was in tatters.

Optics Debate

Perhaps the biggest lesson from UTR was the necessity of controlling public perception of contemporary American white nationalism, and the importance of good optics for recruiting. Apparently, just because Trump was in the White House, that didn't mean people could wear their racism on their sleeve—the mainstream culture could still destroy you when overt racism, antisemitism, and misogyny went from the privacy of the wires to the scrutiny of the weeds. And so throughout the months that the Internet Bloodsports were taking place and Fuentes was becoming the leader of the Groyper army, all across the extremely online far right— from /pol/ to Reddit to 8chan—people debated what constituted good optics. What was the best way to red-pill normies and exist in the world? Should they hide their beliefs, and not say explicitly racist things, or should they put it all out there?

Journalist Luke O'Brien described this divide between "the real-world extremists who want to continue holding rallies and mixing it up in the streets, and the 'optics cucks' who think the best approach to the mainstream is to keep pushing alt-right ideas through better propaganda." Optics cuck or not, here Fuentes was generally more cautious with his words and appearance than someone who would describe themselves as a conventional neo-Nazi. He advised his followers to be smart, not explicitly using antisemitic or anti-Black slurs on Twitter, for example.

At the start of the year, the alt-right leadership and Fuentes endorsed one of these followers—a self-described "America First" candidate for Congress named Paul Nehlen, who had swallowed the JQ red pill and run a failed but admired campaign in 2016 that had drawn approval from Bannon and Trump. But as 2018 wore on, Nehlen got on the wrong side of the optics debate. He would not stop making openly racist comments on Twitter, so the site banned him.

Spencer condemned Nehlen, saying that he "clearly couldn't keep a lid on it." "Paul Nehlen is out of the movement, he's gone!" Fuentes declared on his show in early April. Wrapping himself in a Trump flag, Fuentes held a knife to a Nehlen campaign sign and said, "Knife nation, raise your knives. We are declaring War. The America First coalition is here, we're smart, we're vindicated, we're not going anywhere." His menacing theatrics soon earned him the nickname Nick the Knife.

The movement infighting and optics debate came to a head in August 2018, when disgraced Proud Boy Jason Kessler attempted to hold another Unite the Right Rally on the event's one-year anniversary. Every major figure of the alt-right urged their followers not to attend, from Fuentes to Spencer. Andrew Anglin warned readers in the Daily Stormer to "lay low," and that attending UTR 2 could ruin their life. Anons on /pol/ also believed it to be a trap. One wrote, "Seriously, don't go to the UTR. it's a false flag. Just like the last one, it's infiltrated with AntiFa types and only 1 or 2 boomers who actually want to unite the white." "Even CIASpencer is telling people not go to UTR 2.0," wrote another. Kessler and about thirty supporters showed up for a short march, washed out by rain and vastly outnumbered by thousands of counterprotesters. The showing was pathetic.

By this point, most of /pol/'s faith in the last generation of leadership had been permanently shaken. Within the greater movement, condemnation of street Nazis like Matthew Heimbach of the Traditionalist Worker Party intensified, their bumbling antics being blamed for setting back the greater good. /Pol/ and the zoomers under Fuentes began referring to these aggressively misguided and often uneducated white nationalists as "wigger nationalists," or wignats—low-class neo-Nazis with no subtlety or sophistication. Just as Gen Z referred to everyone older as "boomer," for Fuentes and the Groyper army, everyone they didn't like was a wignat.

Later that year, on October 27, 2018, a man named Robert Bowers, who had been flash-radicalized on the far-right internet by memes about white genocide, carried out a lone-wolf attack that would further shake the remains of the alt-right. In his last post to the alt-tech platform Gab, Bowers wrote, "Screw your optics, I'm going in." He then proceeded to attack the Tree of Life Synagogue in Pittsburgh, Pennsylvania, killing eleven Jewish worshipers. The event was widely covered by the press and condemned by public figures.

/Pol/ reacted with the expected celebration of violence and vicious antisemitism, though many visible far-right leaders distanced themselves from the killings, or found ways to avoid talking about it as either a positive or a negative event. They did, however, universally bemoan how Bowers's reckless action was about to make their lives on the internet a whole lot harder. Gab temporarily went offline, after being dropped by its service providers. Big Tech, the government, law enforcement, and media were paying closer attention to the scattered remains of the alt-right than ever before.

The Great Replacement

Brenton Tarrant was twenty-eight years old on March 15, 2019, when he strapped a GoPro camera to his head and broadcast live on Facebook as he murdered fifty-one Muslims in a mosque in Christchurch, New Zealand. Right before he began shooting, he said, "Remember lads, subscribe to PewDiePie."

This was a reference to a massively popular meme about Swedish YouTuber PewDiePie, who was defending his crown as most popular YouTuber of all time and had recently gained massive support from the far-right and more mainstream conservatives for his edgy humor and

right-wing dog whistles. His fans launched a meme war to keep him on top, spreading the slogan "Subscribe to PewDiePie" on social media, billboards, and even through hacking escapades. The most notorious of these stunts came when someone hacked into fifty thousand home printers and got them to print out the phrase. After being named by Tarrant, PewDiePie issued a public disavowal, calling an end to the great subscriber war.

Tarrant had orchestrated the heinous crime to be a social media spectacle, posting the above message on 8chan and Twitter, along with a link to view his massacre live and an eighty-seven-page PDF titled "The Great Replacement." He tweeted the manifesto, as well. It opened with a thrice-repeated phrase: "It's the birthrates," detailing his obsession with Europeans being outbred by immigrants. He followed up with links to Wikipedia pages, detailing how fast demographics were changing in different countries. For Tarrant, the only way to reverse course was to commit violence so that "terror" could make political change possible, urging (white) readers to "do your part by spreading my message, making memes and shitposting as you usually do." He focused on immigrants as "invaders" and saw New Zealand as an extension of Europe.

Tarrant's manifesto quickly turned into a self-interview, in which he posed questions and then answered them. He self-consciously laced the answers with memes and ironic misdirections, for instance jokingly blaming Candace Owens, a Black conservative pundit, for his radicalization. He also made several calls to action throughout the manifesto. "Inspirational terrorism" is the name for acts like this, where the attacker explicitly encourages more violence and copycat murders. Definitely a product of the internet age, he also wanted to bring about a culture war by inspiring more memes:

> Humans are emotional, they are driven by emotions, guided by emotions and seek emotion expressions and experiences. Monotonous repetition of immigration facts and statistics will simply bore the masses, and drive the people away from the stale and uninspired speakers that propagate them. Be creative, be expressive, be emotional and above all be passionate. These are the things that speak to people, connect people, drive people. Paint, write, sing, dance, recite poetry. Hell, even meme. Create memes, post memes, and spread memes. Memes have done more for the ethno-nationalist movement than any manifesto. Above all, just don't be stale, placid and boring. No one is inspired by Jeb Bush.

After his arrest, Tarrant was not done memeing. On March 16, 2019, he flashed an OK hand sign, a reference to a 4chan meme, while shackled and facing the judge, signaling back to those watching online that he was most definitely "their guy." For many, the hand gesture still simply meant "OK," but for white supremacists it had become an in-joke, and for some MAGA folks it was a way to mimic Trump's hand gestures. Tarrant signed the OK hand gesture as one of his last messages to his online community.

While Tarrant titled his manifesto "The Great Replacement," it wasn't a theory of his own design, and the replacement anxiety that fueled his hateful rampage was not unique. The theory that demographic change was orchestrated and that white Europeans were being replaced in their own countries by design had been around for over a century as an anti-semitic trope. It was updated by French author Renaud Camus in his 2011 book of the same name to suggest that African and Muslim immigration was to blame for the decline of Europe. When Tarrant said, "It's the birthrates," he meant that demographic change would lead to cultural shift, just as American fascists had chanted "Jews will not replace us" at UTR back in 2017. This style of white nationalism was a global phenomenon. Before his rampage, Tarrant had donated $1,700 to Martin Sellner, the founder of Generation Identity, a European counterpart to the United States' alt-right.

Racist, antisemitic, and—particularly in Tarrant's case—anti-Muslim narratives were traded back and forth between international white nationalist groups during the 2010s. In *The Islamophobia Industry*, writer and religious scholar Nathan Lean details how right-wing news, blogs, and talk radio cultivated decades of anti-Muslim sentiment during the so-called War on Terror following the 9/11 attacks, and how these sentiments were deployed by reactionary broadcasters and politicians during the European migrant crises of the early 2000s. What began as an existential threat to Western civilization in the form of terrorism morphed into replacement anxiety, a "demographic jihad" to replace native European populations with Muslims migrants and refugees. Tarrant's 2019 Christchurch attack was celebrated by the most bloodthirsty anonymous communities in the far right, like 8chan, as a brave attempt to stop the Islamic replacement of white people in nations that were supposedly theirs by birthright.

Support for a mass shooting was a third rail that even Fuentes wasn't brave enough to touch. That kind of bad optics could get you kicked off social media. Still, Tarrant and Fuentes's ideology wasn't that different— they both ascribed to some version of the Great Replacement theory, believed in racial essentialism, and felt they were doing their part to defend Western civilization from decline and degeneracy.

Clown World

While the Great Replacement was brewing in the far right, and celebrations of violence were reaching obscene levels, the more moderate side of the red-pilled right was also pushing back against multiculturalism, albeit with less bite. "Diversity is our greatest strength" had become a mantra repeated by liberal politicians and celebrities, meant to be a uniting phrase, connecting citizens across divides of race, religion, gender, and sexual orientation. On a September 2018 episode of his nightly program, Tucker Carlson addressed the slogan directly, challenging its assumptions and questioning the legitimacy of its claims. "How precisely is diversity our strength? Since you've made this our new national motto," Carlson said, "please be specific as you explain it. Can you think, for example, of other institutions such as, I don't know, marriage or military units in which the less people have in common, the more cohesive they are? Do you get along better [with] your neighbors or your coworkers if you can't understand each other or share no common values?"

Many on the right were focused on this mantra, and it became a parody in alt-right memes, portrayed as a spoon-fed narrative that brain-dead white liberals were accepting with no challenge. Diversity, the alt-right argued, was a circus, and those who accepted it blindly were clowns. A new Pepe variant that got popular a few months before Chirstchurch, Honkler, encapsulated this attack on cultural diversity. A frog wearing a rainbow wig, red nose, and polka-dot bow tie, Honkler was deployed as a mockery of diversity narratives, yet another culture hack the anons on /pol/ could sneak into mainstream conservative publications. Some suggested that Honkler, and the "Honk, honk" used to critique liberal diversity, could be "the next OK sign," a way to take back rainbows from the LGBT community.

In an investigation for Right Wing Watch, journalist Jared Holt traced how Honkler evolved into "clown world," a more resonant and widely used meme. The viral phrase "We're living in clown world," meaning that liberal democracy and diversity are responsible for social decline, became a popular refrain in reactionary circles throughout 2019. Sometimes the meme was expressed with the Pepe clown variant, sometimes with the Clown and Globe emojis. It was used as a critique of liberal orthodoxy around things like trans rights and immigration, reframing social progress as cultural and demographic suicide of the West. Using the guise of a seemingly innocent clown, right-wingers of all variants used Honkler and Clown World to memetically express a range of grievances.

Much like the NPC Wojak variant meme a year earlier, Clown World was a new way to mock normies. The NPC (non-player character) was a normie, a mindless drone spoon-fed SJW propaganda and a proud inhabitant of Clown World. Cultural degeneracy, compliance with liberal

institutional language, and the Great Replacement were just as much a threat to the red-pilled right. Despite their God Emperor being in power, things weren't getting better. Trump, perhaps, was either set up to fail or in on the game from the start.

Many alt-righters, oddly enough, threw in support for Andrew Yang in March 2019. The Chinese American entrepreneur emerged as a wild-card outsider who gained a diverse online following when he entered the Democratic presidential primaries. /Pol/, TRS, and even Fuentes, sincerely or ironically, briefly joined the "Yang Gang," excited by his willingness to address working-class white people and the economic hardships they faced. Trump, despite his racial dog whistles and travel bans, didn't speak directly enough to white people for red-pillers, rarely using the word *white* at all. But when Yang was forced to thoroughly denounce the insurgent white nationalist support for his campaign, the ironic support from the far right ended. Trumpism still seemed their best and only option for electoral power. Accelerationist violence, like the Christchurch massacre, wouldn't get them there, but trolling and memes still held magical potential.

The Groyper Wars

As all of this was happening—an upcoming election, the haze of memes steeped in clowns and white genocide, rapid realignments, and accelerationist violence—Fuentes was commenting on it nightly on his show, guiding the Groypers through the disintegration of the alt-right, commenting on pop culture, and orchestrating ops. That fall, Fuentes and the Groyper army distilled their approach to meme wars in a reaction to Joaquin Phoenix's film version of the DC Comics character Joker. The character was an important meme to Fuentes already, embodying a lot of his own nihilistic approach to life, and so Fuentes and the Groypers had a heyday trolling liberals who were outraged about the film.

There was a lot of hype and controversy about *Joker*, which featured a nihilistic Joker who goes on a killing rampage because he feels society has betrayed him. Some worried about a copycat-style killing during the film's release, suggesting that the franchise was toxic. Others dreaded a film focused solely on the Joker, believing it would lead to other kinds of violence. For decades, parents had blamed music, movies, and video games for teenage angst, and this movie in particular was hyped to be the devil's work.

The Joker character from DC Comics' Batman series had supplied fodder for memes since the mid 2000s, after the success of *Batman Begins* (2005) and *The Dark Knight* (2008), the latter with Heath Ledger playing a maniacal Joker who had been pushed over the edge by the absurdity and unfairness of the world. After Ledger died tragically in 2008, his version of the Joker became a sort of hero to the online set—a tragically disturbed white guy willing to destroy the world to make a point. The character's recognizability became a way to make a statement about people—photoshop Joker makeup on someone, and you indicate that they are at heart a trickster, a nihilist, and a villain.

Obama first got this treatment, becoming "jokerfied" on November 2, 2008, at Florida State University, where "Why So Socialist" signs were hung outside a Joe Biden appearance two days before the election. But it was on January 18, 2009, that the meme took a form that would stick when college student Firas Alkhateeb made a mockup of Joker Obama from a *Time* cover. That April, the image was plastered around downtown L.A., with the word "socialism" added underneath. *Guardian* film blogger Ben Walters referred to Joker Obama as "the American right's first successful use of street art," one of the first of their memes that would stick. The mainstream press critique of the meme made it even more popular among conservatives.

socialism

On August 30, 2009, Alex Jones painted his face in Joker makeup and announced an Obama Joker contest, offering cash prizes for those willing to stand up to "censorship."

Throughout the Great Meme War of 2016, Trump got the Joker treatment, as did Hillary and many other candidates. But in the case of Trump, it was done with ironic admiration. He was their joker, and he broke tradition in obscene and comic ways. This was when the Joker meme took on its most powerful form: the Ironic Joker, the Joker Fuentes would begin to embody.

"The biggest reason [behind my activism] is that it's hilarious to me," he told a Lyons Township student newspaper in 2017. "I'm not going to pretend that I put on my 'Make America Great Again' hat and get the Trump flag out because of some political crusade. It's just fun for me to go and engage with people." Like the Joker, Fuentes's amusement, and politics, came at the expense of others.

Ironic Joker memes are supposed to be both dark and pathetic, the text seething with rage and the threat of violence, executed with purposeful misspellings and poor grammar. The Joker was becoming synonymous with gamers, mocking them, mocking oneself. His awkwardness, strange sense of humor, and forced isolation made him into the antihero gamers saw in themselves. The Joker was flawed, depraved, and indifferent, poisoned by society's shit.

After the failure of UTR, the Joker meme evolved into a new form: Gamers Rise Up, a parody of older memes from the HBD and Gamergate eras that still held the potential for chaotic play. Gamers Rise Up wasn't just a right-wing meme—its origins lay in mocking entitled, toxic Gamergaters, incels, and internet racists. Still, young far-right guys, many of whom grew up spewing racial slurs in the chatrooms of online games, took the meme into their lexicon. In the subreddits where these memes flourished, alt-righters would drop in memes that blurred the line between irony and sincerity, often passing off racial statements or nods to alt-right influences under the guise of parody.

One of these memes, a chaotic YouTube video entitled "Gang Weeders Rise Up" from July 2018, showed how the memes connected to politics. "Gang Weed" was a Facebook page dedicated to gamer memes, and the Joker specifically, and was sometimes used as internet slang for gamers who smoked pot to suppress feelings of rage against society.

Anyhow, the video begins with Trump in Joker makeup saying, "The world is a mess. The world is as angry as it gets." It then jumps to Alex

Jones, talking about the "incel rebellion" and deriding the government in full Joker face paint, and footage of Sam Hyde's alt-right standup comedy routines. Elliot Rodger then appears, to explain that he's the ultimate gentleman, "But you girls will never give me a chance." The final scene of the video is a Joker meme, proclaiming "Gang Weeders Rise Up." It was all jokes, but for Gen Z reactionaries like Fuentes, Gamers Rise Up and its variants became a coded way to talk about suppression of white grievance.

Gamers, trolls, incels, and zoomers took the fearmongering around the new movie as an opportunity to meme, even creating a petition to make Joaquin Phoenix say "We live in a society," a line from *Seinfeld* that had somehow become a meme for zoomers. To them, the line ironically mocked growing up in a world full of contradiction and disappointment, and became synonymous with the Joker in meme culture, so much so that they campaigned to have it included in the upcoming film.

On October 4, 2019, *Joker* was finally released to rave reviews, though it didn't include the "society" meme the fans were clamoring for. While many questioned the film's politics, there were no mass acts of violence at any screenings around the nation. The Joker's trick, it seemed, had

worked. In *Joker*, the chans and zoomers saw an earnest representation of the nihilistic fury that fueled their social detachment. The film both critiqued and glamorized an anomic violence that echoed the chaos of the online culture war they'd grown up in. The film would go on to gross a little over a billion in the worldwide box office, landing multiple Academy Award nominations, including a Best Actor win for Phoenix's Joker. His titular portrayal resonated with far more people than just reactionary kids on the internet, and the film itself became a global phenomenon, full of memeworthy moments that could be adapted to many cultural contexts outside the United States.

The culture wars leading up to the film's release, and the concerns about its potential to inspire violence, subsided after its success. This was not the first, nor would it be the last, portrayal of Joker, but it was the one adopted by the young red-pilled right. In the next few months Fuentes would go on to embody the Joker politics of this era as the general in a meme war of his own: the Groyper wars to take down Conservative Inc. and the remaining alt-right leaders, who he felt had betrayed them all in some way.

With allies like former Tea Party star Michelle Malkin, too edgy for conservatives but too pragmatic and polished for wignat street fighting, Fuentes set out to build a new right-wing coalition heading into the election year of 2020. But this was not going to be a big tent; who was excluded was just as important as who was included. The first target of what would become the Groyper wars was Charlie Kirk, as the most visible and therefore most reachable face of the young conservative movement.

Kirk was about to embark on a national campus tour titled "Culture Wars," where he was supposed to build a broad student coalition in support of Trump. A veteran of the college circuit, Kirk was poised to lead the young Republican wing of the party. He and his TPUSA had taken heat for their proximity to the alt-right at political and campus events in 2017 and 2018, and Kirk publicly denounced white supremacy after Unite the Right.

For Fuentes, Kirk and TPUSA embodied everything that was wrong with conservatives who upheld the liberal consensus by promoting Israel, gay rights, and softer immigration policies. Kirk had been in Fuentes's sights over the years as he soured on campus conservatives. Getting to the top tier of Trumpworld was nearly impossible for someone as marginal as Fuentes, but opportunity struck in October 2019, when Kirk took TPUSA's "Culture War" college tour on the road. Kirk brought Trumpworld to campuses across the nation with special guests like Senator Rand Paul, Donald Trump Jr., Kimberly Guilfoyle, Lara Trump, and congressman Dan Crenshaw. Like when Richard Spencer, Shapiro, or Yiannopoulos would book campus tours, Kirk's events too often attracted protest from left-wing student groups. But this time, the attacks would come from their right.

Beginning on October 7 at the University of Nevada, Kirk set a tone where debate was encouraged, even allowing those who disagreed with him to move to the front of the line during Q&A. Ever since Charlottesville, Kirk had been particularly careful to avoid association with the alt-right, and went so far as to fire any TPUSA representatives who were in close proximity to confirmed Groypers, especially Fuentes. Kirk started his speech in Reno with a countersignal to the alt-right, proclaiming, "The evil, wicked ideology of white supremacy has no place in our organization." He continued, "We repudiate it, we reject it, whole-heartedly and completely as should any decent American."

Over the next few weeks, Groypers swarmed TPUSA events, waiting for the opportunity to ask Fuentes and his guests questions and

grandstand for the livestream. Even though TPUSA was aware of the Groypers' plan, they didn't have a strategy for defending against them. The popular "debate me" style of conservatives online made any effort to shut down Q&A seem anti-free-speech. Kirk was caught in a trap of his own design, and the Groypers knew it.

It all began on October 21, 2019, when Donald Trump Jr., Kimberly Guilfoyle, and Kirk were taking questions, and a young man dressed in a suit approached the mic. He said he was asking his question from "an America First perspective," and he wanted to know why the United States provided so much aid to Israel even after the attack on the USS *Liberty*. Kirk shot back, "Do not peddle conspiracy theories at our event," hoping to shut him down. He then went on to answer that Israel is the only place in the Middle East where people of "all three monotheistic religions" are in the government and where gay people are not thrown off the top of buildings if found out, and that it's the only partner in the fight against radical Islamic terrorists. The crowd clapped, and Kirk seemed to have "won" the debate.

Then, on October 22, Fuentes sent this message to subscribers on his channel on Telegram, a chat app where many white nationalists moved following the wave of deplatforming after UTR:

> Go to TPUSA events. Pack the line. Ask intelligent, well-rehearsed questions. Ensure the audience begins questioning TPUSA's milquetoast conservatism. It's clear that a growing body of young people want something more authentic than what Charlie Kirk has to offer.
>
> Suitable question topics:
> - Charlie Kirk's support for mass immigration
> - TPUSA's promotion of identity politics for every group but white people
> - TPUSA's focus on economics above all else
> - Demographics and voting patterns
> - White people becoming a minority in a few decades

Just as his *America First* podcast was gaining name recognition, Fuentes partnered with Patrick Casey, who had founded the American Identity

Movement (AIM), a rebrand of Identity Evropa. Casey, a longtime member of Identity Evropa, had changed the name after their chat logs and real identities were leaked at an anti-fascist website, and to distance themselves from the UTR disaster. He called upon AIM to join the Groypers to confront Kirk at Politicon, a bipartisan conference dedicated to debate across the aisle, set for October 26–27, 2019. Kirk was set to make an appearance, and Fuentes planned to attend and ask a question. After several hours inside, suddenly Fuentes was physically stopped and asked to leave the conference. The Q&A portion of the Kirk event was canceled too.

The Groyper wars reached a fever pitch on October 29, 2019, at Ohio State, when Kirk and Rob Smith, a Black gay conservative, were confronted by a long line of Groypers, including Casey. "How does homosexual sex help us win the culture war?" asked one, while another asked, "Can you prove that our white European ideals will be maintained if the country is no longer made up of white European descendants?" On it went for eleven of fourteen questions that evening, one of them even encouraging the audience to look up "dancing Israelis," a reference to a meme claiming that Israel had orchestrated 9/11, by couching it in a question about "awesome fun dancing parties" in Jerusalem.

On a Halloween podcast, Spencer criticized the Groypers for not having learned from the alt-right's inability to institutionalize, and then insinuated that Fuentes was quintessentially alt-right. This made Fuentes furious, as he did not want to be considered a revolutionary, or changing the culture. More than prepared for this critique, he lashed out at any of Spencer's followers willing to debate: "I'm not a left-wing person. I'm Catholic, I'm reactionary, I'm hard right." Insulting their brand of identity-forward politics, he said, "The alt-right is basically a collection of racist liberals—left wing people who don't care for racial minorities." Finally, he summed up his views on Spencer with this retort: "I can't think of a single person whose life has gotten better after coming into contact with Richard Spencer."

Fuentes continued, despite Spencer's antagonisms, and on November 5 at UT Austin, Groypers confronted Dan Crenshaw. Initially, they tried to limit Q&A to students with a campus ID, but that quickly devolved into shouting as the Groypers pushed Crenshaw on his support of Israel.

Crenshaw decided to address the crowd: "What you're seeing here is a fringe on the right that we do not associate ourselves with."

Someone in the audience yelled, "Here comes that N-word that you pointed out in the introductory video!" Crenshaw had played a video where a woman called him a "Nazi."

"What was the N-word?" Crenshaw replied. "Nick Fuentes? Your little leader? Nick Fuentes? Is that the N-word? That's their leader. That's these guys' leader. Nick Fuentes is a Holocaust denier. That is not something we associate with in the conservative movement." One man stood up and shouted, "I'll be on my way out, but in your introductory video you mentioned calling people Nazis as a way to silence them!" The crowd erupted in applause.

Groypers went after Crenshaw again at another event at Arizona State University, and again it turned into a shouting match. By now all of Conservative Inc. knew about Fuentes's Groyper army and were preparing to counter as best they could. It was nearly impossible to avoid the Groypers, though, since a big part of their shtick was to call out leftist students who dared to confront them at live events. What were they going to do about those punching right?

On November 8 Ben Shapiro gave a long speech at Stanford blasting Fuentes, though not by name, and the alt-right for the Groyper wars. Fuentes reacted on his YouTube livestream, exuberant that Shapiro had read, word for word, an antisemitic meme about the Cookie Monster and the Holocaust that Fuentes had read on stream. Fuentes then attacked one of Shapiro's writers, Matt Walsh, calling him a "shabbos goy race traitor" due to his condemnation of the El Paso shooter earlier that summer. It was evident that Fuentes was now living rent-free inside their heads, and the major event was yet to come.

Donald Trump Jr. was set to give a book talk on November 10, organized by Kirk and TPUSA, at UCLA. It was a Sunday. The Groypers came with a game plan, laid out by Fuentes in his Telegram chat. "COOL IT WITH ISRAEL," he demanded. "The Optimal Strategy is to ask Kirk questions that expose his 'never Trump' past," thus exposing him in front of Don Jr. as a "fraud." Fuentes even recommended that attendees wear MAGA hats and not be too disruptive, save for booing Kirk.

The set for the event that day was simple: some TPUSA branding in the background and three stools. Kirk sat between Trump Jr., who was in a dark suit and white shirt, with no tie, and Guilfoyle, in a black leather dress. About twenty minutes into the talk, some in the audience broke out into a garbled chant of "USA" mixed with "Q and A." It was confusing. As Guilfoyle spoke about record low unemployment for people of color and human trafficking, the crowd chanted, "Build the wall."

Then Trump Jr. announced that there would be no Q&A, enraging the 450-person crowd. "It's because people hijack it with nonsense looking to go for some sort of sound bite," he said. "You have people spreading nonsense, spreading hate, trying to take over the room." While Don Jr. was trying to win back the crowd, Guilfoyle stood up and antagonized them further. "No, it's because you're not making your parents proud by being rude and disruptive and discourteous. We are happy to answer a question. Respect the people around you so that they can hear." Then she called them incels in her own special way: "Let me tell you something, I bet you engage and go on online dating because you're impressing no one here to get a date in person. How many people have you catfished?" Trump Jr. tried to hand the mic off to Kirk, who shook his head and said "No" as the crowd cheered and wailed.

Meanwhile, over on Fuentes's stream, he was rocking back and forth, arms snapping to an unheard song, dancing like the Joker and savoring every second of trolling Conservative Inc. He had finally arrived.

Trump Jr. only found out later that the jeers were from the Groypers.

Some on the online right responded to the Groyper wars with admiration. Fuentes managed to control optics without it careening into physical violence. The ultimate sign of respect came from Jim, who watched closely, tweeting support for Fuentes. He made a video detailing Fuentes's exploits and pointed out how flawed Conservative Inc.'s response to the Groyper insurgency was. Yiannopoulos took notice too, and interviewed Fuentes about the Groyper wars. Fuentes now had the approval of both Jim and Yiannopoulos, two of Gamergate's most high-profile generals and consistent critics of mainstream conservatism.

For Fuentes, 2019 was ultimately a clumsy experiment, with a few high-profile moments of sending his followers into the weeds while he coordinated like a supervillain from his command center. A persona non grata within conservative politics himself, he showed up to large events just to IRL meme on his enemies. He crashed the annual TPUSA conference and happened to run into his dream nemesis Ben Shapiro crossing the street in Miami. Fuentes and his entourage followed Shapiro for two blocks, but the optics were bad: Shapiro wasn't alone, but pushing a stroller and walking with his children and wife. The conservative establishment condemned Fuentes yet again, resurfacing jokes he'd made about physically assaulting Shapiro in the past.

The Groyper wars only lasted a few months, and many would suggest that they were just the antics of a dumb radical fringe. But they mattered, not least because they cemented Fuentes's position in the red-pilled right. On his stream, as Fuentes delighted in taking down Don Jr., he blasted music from the film *Joker*, swaying to it as the character had, in an impersonation of a madman. It was clear that a new leader had been crowned king. In an interview with the *Hill* during the Groyper wars, Fuentes took a victory lap. "We have figured out the game. The algorithm," he said of the attention he'd generated with the Q&A stunt. "We've hacked the conversation where if you say sensational things like we do, you get attention. I don't want it to be like that. I wish I could ascend with ideas."

Fuentes may have hated the conservative establishment, but he still needed their attention. Just like his alt-right forebears, like Spencer, his only strategy was antagonizing conservatives until they acknowledged the Groypers and America First. The nihilism of Fuentes and Joker politics would go on to fuel right-wing Gen Z in the coming year on their mission to "Destroy the GOP." Trump, and Trump alone, was all that was to be salvaged from the disappointing mess of the Republican Party.

Chapter 8

These People Are Sick

The Calm Before the Storm

On October 5, 2017, President Trump and First Lady Melania stood for a photo op with Trump's military leaders, who had come to the White House to discuss growing tensions with Iran. Trump had repeatedly threatened to back the United States out of its nuclear treaty with Iran, and the suspicion at the time was that he was about to do it. (Spoiler: He did.)

"You guys know what this represents?" Trump asked the press, going off script, as he often did.

"Tell us, sir," a reporter replied.

"I don't know. Maybe it's the calm before the storm."

"What's the storm?" the reporter asked.

"I don't know, maybe it's the calm before the storm," Trump riffed.

"What's storm, Mr. President?" another reporter asked.

"You'll find out," he shot back.

This cryptic exchange made headlines instantly, nationally and globally. The mainstream news scrambled to make sense of the remarks, but largely chalked it up as another weird thing Trump said that made no sense. The vagueness was catnip for Trump supporters, conspiracists, and anons alike. It was a mystery that needed to be solved.

MAGA believers on reddit and anons on /pol/ dissected Trump's riff with enthusiasm. That evening, in a thread titled "REAL ACTUAL HAPPENING," one anon solicited speculation on what world event Trump was referencing. This particular anon was serious, writing in all caps, pulling out an old 2012 Ron Paul happening meme for emphasis.

"NORTH KOREA??? HILLARY GETTING LOCKED UP??????????? WHATS GONNA HAPPEN POL!?!??"

A lot happened. It was that same day, October 5, that the *New York Times* broke allegations of rape and sexual assault against Hollywood mogul Harvey Weinstein. An A-list producer, who palled around with the Clintons, was an evil sex fiend? For anons watching media trends and measuring them against Trump's agenda, this revelation was too good to be true. When a few days later, on October 10, 2017, the *New Yorker* published Ronan Farrow's detailed exposé on further sexual assault accusations against Weinstein, it looked like the storm was hitting Hollywood.

For the folks who were skeptical of the mainstream narrative and who craved explanations, these two nearly simultaneous events—Weinstein's depravity and Trump's bewitching promise—were critical to the development of what would soon be known as the QAnon movement. For pro-Trump online communities, already steeped in Pizzagate, Weinstein's real, material connections to Clinton and other Democratic elites was one of the abuse scandals that helped make the QAnon movement the political force it became.

Twenty-three days after Trump said some kind of storm was coming, the conspiracy movement known as QAnon formally came into existence. It arrived in the form of a cryptic post by an anon on 4chan's /pol/ on October 28, 2017. This anon, who later self-identified as a "Q Clearance Patriot," announced, "HRC extradition already in motion effective yesterday with several countries in case of cross border run. Passport approved to be flagged effective 10/30 @ 12:01am. Expect massive riots organized in defiance and others fleeing the US to occur. US M's will conduct the operation while NG activated. Proof check: Locate a NG member and ask if activated for duty 10/30 across most major cities."

This self-consciously cryptic post was published exactly one year after the FBI reopened its case into Clinton's emails at the end of the election. The comment was in response to an anon who claimed "Hillary Clinton will be arrested between 7:45 AM—8:30 AM EST on Monday—the morning on Oct 30, 2017."

From the first post, Q had two main characters in mind: Trump, the hero and defender of all things good; and Clinton, the villain and representation of evil on earth. This first message was largely ignored by most of the anons. But that "drop," as Q posts came to be called, was the first of many, which grew increasingly detailed and militaristic and tantalizing as they went and accumulated more and more followers. Breaking news became something Q would anticipate and try to predict, but the number of failed prophecies would later come to dog QAnon followers as they continually were led to believe the storm was on its way.

This anon, known in the community as Q, posted 4,953 times (give or take about a dozen "lost drops" discovered by researchers at the Q Origins Project) from October 2017 through December 2020 across three websites: first 4chan (until the local anons turned against Q), then 8chan (until the site was taken down following the Christchurch massacre), and then 8kun (where 8chan was resurrected). From the earliest days, Q's storyline was clear: the world was being run by a cabal of evil, secretive, baby-eating, sex-obsessed pedophilic monsters, and Donald Trump was on a mission to root them out and save the world. How did we know all this? An operative inside the deep state, who went by the name Q, was leaking the secrets.

Here's what we don't know: who Q is, whether it's one person or many, what their motivations were, and why they stopped posting immediately after Trump lost the 2020 election. These are details that many, many people are obsessed with finding out, but for the purposes of this book, they are not that relevant, and it's nearly certain Q was not some Beltway insider like they insinuated. Who Q is does not change the impact of the posts on Q's believers and the subsequent impact those believers had on history.

So here's what we do know. We know Q's posts undermined trust in government among their followers, some of whom participated in the insurrection on January 6. We know Q supporters rallied and campaigned for Trump's reelection. We know that professional conspiracy theorist and 8kun site owner Jim Watkins and his son Ron have back-end access to Q's credentials. And we know that none of what Q said would happen actually came to pass.

Materially, QAnon is an aggregation of older conspiracies, a bucket into which centuries-old anxieties and myths could be dropped, chewed up, and spit out in a new form. QAnon flourished due to a number of factors, some social, others technical. The salacious intrigue of Hollywood perversion that was brought to light by the Weinstein and Epstein scandals reinforced that some elites were criminals hiding behind their wealth and fame. The QAnon movement was able to grow its influence because of the MeToo years, which pedophile-obsessed Pizzagate followers interpreted as proof of their conspiracies about the depravity in Hollywood. Each new MeToo revelation fed the media cycles in QAnon online communities. Q supporters would go in search of further proof, looking at the social media of celebrities, specifically for unusual dress or hand gestures that could be perceived as occultist or Satanic.

All of these particular events of October 2017, along with the tumultuous first months of the Trump presidency, set the stage for dedicated operators to connect hundreds of years of American conspiracy theory to breaking news events. Creating unwavering support for President Trump, they built a powerful conspiratorial faction of believers across the nation. This community, connected by memes and outrage, became an echo chamber of disappointment and paranoid hate.

Indeed, with the alt-right splintered and holed up in the wires, the president needed a foe and a foil to cast him as a hero battling the evils of the land, and the Q conspiracy supplied a doozy. Over the course of three years, QAnon adherents developed a robust toolkit to explain what Trump was up against and to reinterpret and excuse his many failures, in the form of their own media system. And they spread their message far and fast and effectively, inspiring people to commit violent acts, abandon their lives, and get lost so far down the rabbit hole that their family members had to form support groups to try and pull them out.

None of it would have been possible without the internet's disinformation economy and the resonance of the two historical political memes QAnon built its foundation upon: the New World Order and the "deep state."

New World Order

The New World Order as an idea was born not as a conspiracy theory but as a practical way to describe a global governance body designed to prevent war. Variations of the phrase were used first during the presidency of Woodrow Wilson in the aftermath of World War I to discuss Wilson's insistence on creating a League of Nations that would keep the world in a state of peace and order. The New World Order, the idea that powerful nations should and must collaborate to avoid such costly conflict in the future, was long a political project before it became a slogan of conspiracists. In 1932, in response to the unstable geopolitical landscape after World War I, British writer Aldous Huxley published *Brave New World*, which painted a dystopian picture of what a unified global government could be. While some, like Huxley and hardline nationalists, responded negatively to the world governing body, others embraced the idea with technocratic optimism. Renowned science fiction author and political commentator H. G. Wells published his own treatise on the subject of global governance, *The New World Order*, in 1940, in the early months of World War II.

In *The New World Order*, Wells argued for a humanistic technocratic alternative to the "terrors of modern warfare" plaguing Europe, one with greater force of will and power than the outcome of the Treaty of Versailles that ended World War I. In it, Wells foreshadowed the theories at the heart of many ideas about technology in Silicon Valley today: the idea that technology must be included in the solution to global disorder, and that technology itself influences social relations and organization. "That is where the League of Nations broke down completely," Wells wrote. "It was legal; it was political. It was devised by an ex-professor of the old-fashioned history assisted by a few politicians. It ignored the vast disorganisation of human life by technical revolutions, big business and modern finance that was going on, of which the Great War itself was scarcely more than a byproduct."

These early formulations of NWO were decidedly liberal and optimistic in their politics, based on the belief that global governance was possible and could be democratic at its heart. Adolf Hitler built off these theories, but put a fascistic bent on them. A global world order was possible, he decided, but not the liberal formulation. He laid out his fascist version of a new global governance, *Neuordnung* (New Order), a promise to unify a fracturing Europe under eugenic fascism.

After the Allied nations defeated Hitler and his Axis allies, conflict between Western liberalism and Eastern communism would fuel a new cold war. Soviet president Mikhail Gorbachev popularized NWO in a post–Cold War context in a historic speech to the UN on December 7, 1988. The influx of neoliberal economics into the Eastern Bloc following the collapse of the USSR brought about the need for a reassessment of the NWO, as America assumed a position of hegemonic global power.

NWO was put into service to justify and describe America's long "war on terror" in the destabilized Middle East, invoked multiple times by then president George H. W. Bush. In his 1991 State of the Union address, Bush laid out "a new world order, where diverse nations are drawn together in common cause to achieve the universal aspirations of mankind—peace and security, freedom, and the rule of law." Instead, America got decades of endless wars and a surge in retaliatory Islamist terrorism for the destruction wrought in the Middle East, culminating in the World Trade Center attack on 9/11. The failure of these wars, and a growing distrust of the government officials who championed them, led to a rise of conspiracism in the United States throughout the late twentieth and early twenty-first centuries, sped along by the emergence of the internet, the possibilities of independent broadcasting, and the general and growing disenchantment with modernity.

NWO paranoia flourished during the 1990s, though it's still a byword in American conspiracy subculture today. It's used as shorthand by a variety of "truther" movements to describe whatever they don't like about modern society, but it's been used by all manner of public figures, from academic Noam Chomsky, billionaire philanthropist George Soros, and televangelist Pat Robertson to institutions like the United Nations, which is the closest governing body to the League of Nations, which inspired the idea in the first place.

For those in the greater QAnon movement, the existence of a *malicious* New World Order is a given, and there were decades of conspiratorial literature extrapolating and manipulating real world events to draw from. Q directly mentioned the New World Order in the first few months of the conspiracy's life cycle, on November 11, 2017.

The QAnon community's understanding of the New World Order comes, whether they know it or not, from A. Ralph Epperson, a seminal figure in the revisionist history community who wrote a book in 1990 on the topic. Epperson represented a grand unifying theory of conspiracy, beginning in the 1800s and ending in the late 1980s. In classic "do your own research" tradition, he proved his point through analysis of the Great Seal of the United States. The front displays the well-known eagle, America's national bird, while the back has a pyramid topped with an all-seeing eye accompanied by two Latin phrases that can be translated as "He [God] has favored our undertakings" ("Annuit cœptis") and "A new succession of ages" ("Novus ordo seclorum"). Epperson viewed the seal and every detail on it as the key to understanding a "secret destiny" playing out in American history, orchestrated by a cabal who had for hundreds of years planned global conflict and manipulated world leaders to bring everyone under one satanic government.

Epperson, like many in the so-called Silent Generation, was deeply affected by the great world wars and the rapid shifts in global power that followed. While the New World Order narrative is used to describe the evils, or virtues, of global governance, a separate term is used to describe the secret cabals within one's own government. The deep state meme sums up the worldview that there is a unelected, undemocratic administrative state that truly governs the United States, deciding who is president

and when to go to war. It's easy to see how this belief fits with the idea of a new world order—for people who believe both theories, it's the deep state who is executing the vision of the New World Order. This is the aspect of the deep state that proved to be so helpful for Trump, who, once he was president, found himself in the uncomfortable position of trying to be antiestablishment even as the embodiment of the establishment. By positioning himself as against the deep state, which was trying to illegally and secretly enact a neoliberal New World Order, Trump could be the most powerful man in the government without taking singular responsibility for the government's actions.

As an idea, the deep state is old, but it did not go by that name in the United States until 2013, and even then it was not common. Before that it was referred to as a "state within a state." In 1903, this state within a state was identified as the corporate interests of the railroad industry, which, like tech companies today, had wealth rivaling that of the entire nation. "An Empire has been slowly rising within the Empire of the United States, and today the new and privately owned Empire, virtually overshadows the Nation, and holds it by the throat," socialist newspaper editor Daniel De Leon wrote of the railroad at that time. This fear of a privatized and militarized state rising within the legitimate U.S. republic was raised to the level of national concern on January 17, 1961, when President Dwight Eisenhower conjured the threat of state subjugation to the military-industrial complex during his farewell address, warning that "potential for the disastrous rise of misplaced power exists, and will persist."

In the American context, this state within a state wasn't abbreviated into "the deep state" until 2007, when a UC Berkeley English professor named Peter Dale Scott used the term in a book entitled *The Road to 9/11* to describe "deeper forces" that threatened civil society, particularly intelligence interests and military spending. Alex Jones latched onto Scott's definition—naturally, as 9/11 conspiracies were the golden goose for Jones at that time—and interviewed Scott about the deep state on his show repeatedly in the spring of 2008. This led to the phrase's usage among Jones's audience, but it was hardly mainstream. It was the acclaimed spy mystery novelist John le Carré (David John Moore Cornwell) who popularized the phrase in *A Delicate Truth*, his 2013 bestseller set against the corruption and collusion of the Bush-Blair era of international insecurity.

In 2014 retired GOP congressman Mike Lofgren wrote a piece called "The Anatomy of the Deep State" for *PBS NewsHour* and—having read the le Carré book from the year before—borrowed the phrase to describe the animating idea of his piece: that "there is another government concealed behind the one that is visible at either end of Pennsylvania Avenue, a hybrid entity of public and private institutions ruling the country."

In early 2017, the combination of a mass of defections from the government in protest of Trump and a mass of leaks from within the government, trying to shed light on Trump's dangerous policies, convinced the right that a liberal deep state was working against Trump inside the government. Trump tweeted the phrase for the first time, according to an archive of his tweets, on November 18, 2017, and he would go on to use it throughout his presidency.

It wasn't until after Trump tweeted the words "deep state" that Q used the meme in one of their drops. It came on May 10, 2018, as allegations of the Trump campaign colluding with Russia in the 2016 election were mounting. Q conflated the swamp—Trump's preferred term for any establishment government official and politician in D.C.—with the deep state, suggesting that perhaps the entire government outside of Trump and his appointees were part of the cabal. The *New Yorker* ran an article headlined "Trump vs. the 'Deep State,'" which would have read to liberals like a manufactured conspiracy theory and to Q supporters and other red-pilled right-wingers as proof that Trump was focused on the right thing.

On May 23, 2018, Democratic congressman Ted Lieu felt it necessary to get Secretary of State Mike Pompeo on the record saying the deep state didn't exist. "I don't believe there's a 'deep state' at the State Department," Pompeo insisted in a public hearing. Which, of course, is exactly what a member of the deep state would say.

Trump, with the help of the red-pilled right, had fully co-opted a term that started out as a critique of American military spending, and turned the deep state into a certified right-wing conspiracy theory he could use to his advantage.

Digital Soldiers

Members of the QAnon movement saw themselves as soldiers in an information war. Q called them patriots, but soon they began calling themselves digital soldiers, a term they took from retired general Mike Flynn's rousing speech the week after Trump won the presidency in 2016: "We have an army of digital soldiers, what we are now, what we call, what I call them, 'cause this was an insurgency, folks, this was run like an insurgency. This was irregular warfare at its finest, in politics."

The digital soldiers researching Q's provocative questions saw other hints in Flynn's speech about what to care about and how to fight this insurgent war. He told them that the United States had "two huge problems: one is Hollywood, and one is right down the street here, okay?" By this Flynn meant Washington, D.C.—the swamp, the deep state.

Less than a month after Trump was inaugurated, Flynn resigned on February 13, 2017, amid allegations that he had misled Vice President Mike Pence and other White House officials about conversations with the Russian ambassador. New allegations followed and Trump was taking considerable heat. The FBI had questioned Flynn the month before.

Two months later, in April 2017, Flynn reportedly asked the FBI for immunity in the Russia investigation in exchange for his testimony.

"WE HAVE AN ARMY OF DIGITAL SOLDIERS."
GEN. MICHAEL FLYNN

He was denied. That same month, he capitalized on his growing support from the insurgent right and registered a "Digital Soldiers" website. He would go on to use it and similar sites to raise money for his mounting legal bills. He later filed to trademark the name, and went on in the summer of 2019 to form a media company with a high-profile QAnon influencer called Digital Soldier Media LLC, according to public records.

Some anons, MAGA diehards, and the diffuse members of the former alt-right and alt-lite coalitions loved Flynn (and his son Flynn Jr.), his culture warrior rhetoric, and his use of social media. On October 31, 2017, three days after Q's first post on /pol/, Q dropped the first message about Flynn. A few days later, on November 2, Q instructed followers to "focus on Flynn." This led to speculation that Q *was* Flynn, and cemented Flynn's position as one of the good ones fighting on the right side of justice with Q. When Flynn pleaded guilty on December 1 to charges that he had lied to the FBI, he officially became a hero to Q: he had proved he would rather take the fall than turn on Trump. Trump praised Flynn the next day, even while announcing his firing: "It is a shame because his [Flynn's] actions during the transition were lawful," he tweeted. "There was nothing to hide!"

Q took to /pol/ on December 5 to assure followers that all was well. "Who knows where the bodies are buried? Flynn is safe. We protect our Patriots," Q posted. All people needed to do was "trust the plan." To a QAnon believer, the future was predetermined: Trump had won, and would continue to win. But to truly understand Q, and decipher the many codes in the posts, you had to put in work yourself. You had to do the research, which included learning the importance and history of the deep state, the New World Order, and more esoteric threats like the Illuminati. As part of "The Greatest Intelligence Drop in History," QAnon adherents were active in disseminating the secrets hidden in plain sight that would bring about the Great Awakening, the downfall of the cabal. Each anon had a crucial role in spreading the forbidden knowledge that Q was so desperately trying to reveal to the world. Like other networked social movements that rallied around a hashtag—Anonymous, Occupy, Black Lives Matter, MeToo—QAnon was participatory across all platforms, memetic, and self-defining. Most importantly, participants made their own content, not just for infotainment but to mobilize.

The interactive feedback loop of this anon style of research was not only emotionally rewarding but reinforced ideas and created a quick cycle of acceptance and rejection. Nothing was off-limits, but if Q or other anons rejected the premise or found it wanting, it could be discarded, no big deal. Anons, in what was rapidly becoming a movement, would move on. They were fighting a war, a war to end evil, and there was no time to pause to fight about specific details. This pattern of "proofing" specific claims was all-consuming for those with an internet connection and time. Q was encouraging participation, hedging bets against failed predictions with the early caveat "Disinfo is necessary."

Open-source intelligence (OSINT) dates back to governments monitoring the media of other nations. It's a style of research that relies on piecing together information available in the public domain, hence "open source." With expanding access to the internet, OSINT techniques developed in hacker circles, where digital traces often held clues as to the who, what, when, where, and why of financial transactions, communication trails, and networked coordination. OSINT research exploded with the advent of social media, as everyone from private detectives to celebrity gossip columnists, law enforcement, and the public searched for clues to who was behind certain scandalous events and crimes. Anonymous had popularized a version of this participatory open-source research during its heyday, allowing anyone to join investigations and join the cause, ferreting out facts and clues to push their agenda. QAnon's digital soldiers built off that style of communal hacktivism as they dug into their "intelligence drops," some of whom saw themselves as extensions of Anonymous's tradition of digital organizing.

With the QAnon community, however, there was no hacking going on, just a lot of posting and memeing and searching in vain. This kind of collective digital sleuthing has become a widespread pastime online. With the help of the internet and social media, the same information available to police can be available to everyone else. The power of the crowd isn't in surfacing evidence, but in its chorus of support for whatever explanation seems to stick.

The other power—and weakness—of anon-style research is that it removes the middleman. If someone asks a question and invites you to seek out the answer, whatever you find feels like your own discovery. This is very different from the process of learning that happens when, say, you watch the news or listen to a friend tell you what they believe. With information from journalism or other Cathedral institutions, an expert is telling you what is true. This, for insurgents, is highly suspicious. But if someone, like Flynn or Q, just asks a question and tells you to figure out the answer for yourself, it is empowering. Whatever you find has the aura of personal discovery, which engenders a feeling of ownership and pride. If you are looking for a like-minded community set against the corrupt, dystopian world of the liberal consensus, this participatory, do-your-own-research—and share it—aspect of the Q conspiracy was emotional gold.

As interest in Q grew with every post, anons began organizing dedicated Q threads to keep everything in one place. They labeled these threads "The Calm Before the Storm," and they would go on to become the backbone of the QAnon community on /pol/. The organizers of these threads would do their best to filter out dissenting opinions, of which there were many. Many seasoned anons accused Q of being a fraud, a hoax, and a distraction, but all dissent was stripped out of the videos increasingly appearing on YouTube, which translated the prophesies of Q to more people. This manufactured consent as to Q's legitimacy was reinforced by an emerging meme aesthetic, separate from the alt-right miasma that had dominated /pol/ for so long.

Broadcasting the Conspiracy

For anons on /pol/, the Calm Before the Storm threads made it easy to keep track of Q's drops and contribute to the growing crowdsourced investigation. But anons knew that most MAGA supporters were not on the chans. Q's message—that Trump was in danger of being taken down by the deep state unless more people helped uncover its crimes—needed to be translated to a wider audience.

Dozens of bloggers and YouTubers were already covering what happened in the intersection of conspiracy and politics, and they were poised to take on the duty of amplifying Q to normies. Three days after

Q's first post, one such journalist, a woman named Tracy Diaz, stepped into the role.

It was 8:42 A.M. on November 3, 2017, and Diaz was whispering into her microphone. The mother and host of a moderately popular YouTube channel devoted to explaining things like Pizzagate and WikiLeaks, Diaz, who went by Tracy Beanz on her social media, was making another video. But this one, she cooed, was different.

"As many of you know, I do not typically do videos like this," she announced in a perfect ASMR hush, aspirating her *s*'s and allowing her breath to audibly hit her mic. "However, due to the very specific and kind of eerie nature of what's been going on over on /pol/, I've decided that it's important for me to cover this, just in case this stuff turns out to be legit, because honestly it kind of seems legit, to be honest."

She was talking about QAnon, and specifically the first Q drops. For the next thirty-five minutes, Diaz introduced her YouTube audience to "someone who says they have Q clearance," and then monologued a carefully curated list of Q posts and predictions in full, interrupting herself now and then to point out that some of these prophecies had already come true (such as a few politicians announcing they wouldn't seek reelection).

It was almost exactly a year since Donald Trump had been elected president, and less than a week since Q first posted, and it was this YouTuber, recording at home on a quiet, chilly fall day, that helped turn a bunch of anonymous posts from a message board most people ignored into the full-on Trump-revering QAnon movement that in part led to Stop the Steal and the storm of the Capitol. It was Diaz, quiet, earnest, curious, who made QAnon accessible, and it was that accessibility that let it spread so far, and so wide, and so dangerously. That, and the apparent appetite among a surprisingly large segment of the population for big answers to their experience of persistent malaise and the reasons behind it, no matter how out there.

"If nothing happens, then this is the hugest, most detailed, amazing LARP ever," she ended the video saying. "Or Q really has a Q clearance. Make up your own minds. Buckle up, I guess."

Watching the video from the future, after the siege on the Capitol and the second impeachment of President Trump, is eerie indeed, to use Diaz's language. Though Q's grand predictions did not come true—Hillary

Clinton was never arrested, for instance—watching this seminal video about them reveals that actually, a lot of what Q said would happen did take place. Just not the way Q said it would.

"We will change the GOP fundamentally," she read, and asked questions that sound prescient now, such as, "Was the election meant to be rigged, and did good people stop the rigging?" She recounted how the military would take over D.C. to restore the nation from chaos—another prediction that came true after the siege.

People with Q-level clearance, Diaz told her audience, have "the potential to cause exceptionally grave or inestimable damage to the national security of the United States," which also proved to be true. Whether Q was a real person with top-secret security clearance or not, the movement Q inspired played a major part in the nation's second insurrection and the deaths of at least five people, as well as the total reorienting of the Republican Party, just as promised.

Years before Diaz brought Q from 4chan to the open web, she was in Zuccotti Park representing the Tea Party wing of the Occupy Wall Street movement. "We got some folks to open up their eyes," she has said of her time in Occupy. "But back then talking about anything that was outside of the mainstream in terms of the government, how it worked, if there was a deep state—those words have become very popular, we were looked at as crazy. People thought we were absolutely nuts."

That taught Diaz to become her own source of news. She identifies as a journalist, and even in her first Q video, she described herself "reporting" on this crazy thing happening on /pol/. Like Alex Jones and many others in conspiracy media and the alt-right, she had been watching 4chan ever more closely since /pol/'s creation in 2012 for potential leaks and fresh rumors. For Diaz, Q was a cut above the other insider anons who used /pol/ as a dumping ground for all manner of hoaxes. She, like any others willing to do their own research, could become part of the story.

"It is our hope that this message reaches enough people to make a meaningful impact. We cannot yet telegraph this message through normal methods, for reasons I am sure everyone here can understand," Diaz said. The audience listening understood that to mean that it was their job to spread the message. And from that point forward, they came to her YouTube channel for the latest information on the Q movement. More professional conspiracy theorists and YouTube truthers would begin to cover Q drops as news, translating the work of QAnon researchers for a growing audience.

The next day, November 5, Q used a phrase that brought the QAnon movement into the spiritual realm: "The Great Awakening." This phrase had a historical association with Protestant religious movements in the United States, emphasizing that the individual could have a relationship with God outside the structure of church doctrine, but it's unclear if Q meant to evoke those ideas. It came to mean something akin to a rapture, an event of enlightenment that would take place en masse once enough people had been red-pilled to the truth of QAnon.

In response to Diaz and other supporters' popular videos on YouTube, normies were entering the QAnon rabbit hole and making their way to /pol/, where they were shocked at what they found. Their outrage and confusion started harshing the vibe. Anons on /pol/ who weren't into the Q stuff—those who just didn't care and the many who saw the whole thing as a delusional live action role-play (LARP) excursion or a hoax—had already been growing annoyed at how much oxygen Q was getting on the board. This sent some over the edge. On November 12, 2017, an anon posted, "We've become a whore house, pimping out slut Q anon vids all over boomer youtube. I hope you're all real proud of yourselves."

/Pol/ was the beast in whose belly QAnon was born, but less than a month into the phenomenon, it had become an inhospitable host. Conflicts between boomer QAnon followers new to 4chan and the hostile reactionaries native to /pol/ threatened to expose Q as a hoax. On November 25, 2017, Q began to migrate the movement to 8chan, a less restrictive imageboard founded by software engineer Frederick Brennan and sold to Jim Watkins, both men having made it clear that Q was more than welcome on their site. (Brennan later vigorously disavowed Watkins, and 8chan, and devoted much time to debunking the QAnon movement.)

Q, or whoever had control of the Q handle at that point, first tested the waters on 8chan's /pol/ board, but the extremists who occupied that niche community were overwhelmingly hostile to Q's message and followers. Too cringeworthy for the hardened neo-Nazi anons of both the 4chan and 8chan /pol/ boards, the QAnon movement needed a stable new home where they could set the house rules.

During the messy transition from 4chan to 8chan, Trump retweeted the first of many QAnon Twitter accounts that he would go on to amplify in the following years. To the digital soldiers, this was reason to keep the faith. Crumbs of proof that digital soldiers were on the inside with Trump kept coming. Hardcore QAnon followers built subreddits and Facebook groups, expanding the movement's net across the web, all the better to ensnare folks.

In March 2018, one of Q's high-profile early adopters, America's ultimate boomer, Roseanne Barr, tweeted "Who is Q?" and "Tell Qanon to DM me in the nexxt [*sic*] 24 hrs." This sort of boomer attention, and cringeworthy earnestness, was not welcome in the vicious world of 4chan. This was normie behavior. By January 2018 the boomers who'd heard about Q had found their way over to 8chan. The 8chan official account tweeted, "We joked about it for years, but #QAnon is making it a reality: Boomers! On your imageboard."

As the movement was moving to more and more platforms, increasingly decentralized Q posted a new slogan: "Where we go one, we go all." This came at a time when many anons were confused about who to trust after the move from 4chan, but needed to stay together.

Q was warning followers not to trust impostors. The weirdly ungrammatical phrase "Where we go one, we go all" was a reference to the 1996 Ridley Scott movie *White Squall*, about a group of kids trying to survive a massive and unexpected storm. Its usage implied a coming storm, or a storm that had already arrived—itself another important Q meme, and a reference to Trump's comment from the weeks before Q first posted. "Where we go one, we go all" would go on to become a hashtag, a T-shirt, a rallying cry, spoken at the Capitol on January 6, 2021, as well as at the ballot recounts of the 2020 elections. Q eventually abbreviated it as WWG1WGA, creating a coded message digital soldiers could share as a hashtag, print on stickers and on signs to hold at rallies, and wear on shirts. In this way, WWG1WGA was a mechanism for moving the wires to the weeds: when people saw it on clothing and protest signs during news coverage, they could google it and find their way down the Q rabbit hole.

Q Versus Infowars

At this point QAnon was rapidly turning into an alt-media network, a unifying theory of reality, and a profitable open-source brand for entrepreneurial conspiracists to merchandise. This meant that it was on the radar of OG conspiracists like Alex Jones. Some elements of the movement—the NWO and deep state parts, and the adoration of Trump, whom he had supported in the election—spoke to Jones and were inspired by his years of broadcasting. Throughout the early part of 2018, Jones gave the movement airtime on Infowars, but by May 2018 he had written it off.

Here's how that went down.

On January 9, 2018, truther and Infowars Washington bureau chief Jerome Corsi—author of such books as *Killing the Deep State* and *Where's the Birth Certificate?*—went on Jones's show and excitedly told the audience about Q. "The Storm is upon us," Corsi said. "2018 will be the year of the counterattack that Donald Trump is going to wage against the deep state. This is going to be a battle of enormous proportions which will determine whether or not the American republic as a constitutional republic sustains or does not. Depending upon Donald Trump's success or failure, we will have a coup d'etat which will replace the Constitution with a globalist, socialist state."

On January 11, 2018, Corsi went on Tracy Diaz's show and told her audience that he had uncovered "irrefutable proof" that Q was real. The evidence was a photo of a pen that Q had posted, with the words: "Look familiar? Note the desk." "That's the Laurel desk," Corsi told Diaz's audience, describing the generic woodgrain surface visible in the photo. "It's the one that Obama used and apparently Trump is also using at Camp David. That's the desktop at Camp David."

This early endorsement from an influential 9/11 truther and birther provided an on-ramp for other truthers to join the movement. The influx of folks from Infowars audiences onto Q threads was disrupting alt-right conversations. Q was no longer welcome on 4chan's /pol/ board because anons despised how their militant white identity politics had been subverted by the QAnon community, who cared far less about racial politics than about countering normie mainstream attacks on Trump. Redditors didn't like them either, especially because they didn't stay in their own board and spammed Q explainers everywhere they went. The_Donald members began pushing back on the conspiratorial influx in any conversation around breaking news, which had a different tenor than that of the MAGA loyalists who still frequented The_Donald and the remaining alt-right subreddits. On March 15 Reddit banned Tracy Diaz's Q subreddit.

After too many failed predictions, Corsi too turned on Q in May 2018, publicly disavowing the movement on Twitter and his YouTube channel. Q shot back with his own response, accusing Corsi of being a grifter. "Some are building a big following off this movement only then to retreat and go mainstream," Q wrote, "The only profit we should all be striving for is TRUE FREEDOM."

Corsi, Jones, and other professionalized conspiracy theorists read this as a subtle jab from Q. Rather than say the whole thing had been a lie from the start, they announced that QAnon had been "completely compromised," and withdrew their support. But it didn't matter. The Q loyalists turned on Infowars. Jones, who had enjoyed a stranglehold on online conspiracy movements for years, now faced a conspiracy movement that he couldn't control.

Jones's position as the king of conspiracy was further threatened a few months later, when after years of pressure from activists, journalists, and lawmakers, the big tech companies finally booted Infowars off their platform. In quick succession in August 2018, Jones's shows were banned from Facebook, Twitter, Spotify, Apple Podcasts, and YouTube. While QAnon followers were running free on social media, Jones and his Infowars empire were now massively kneecapped. The veteran broadcaster became the most censored man in America, and he was pissed. Not just at the deplatforming, which he saw as political retribution, but also because QAnon, which was shaping up to be a fearsome rival for the crown of conspiracy king, was being allowed to run amok unmitigated.

Trump Needs Q

By now, Q was well known enough to be the butt of jokes on TV, as well as to receive coverage throughout mainstream journalism. On June 28, 2018, *Time* named Q one of the most influential people on the internet, alongside online celebrities and culture makers like Matt Drudge and Kylie Jenner, as well as Trump himself. That influence was increasingly being felt offline as well, and just a few weeks later QAnon adherents showed up at Trump's Tampa rally bearing Q signs and wearing Q shirts. If QAnon's digital soldiers could draw blood from the liberal establishment through Twitter campaigns, could they be mobilized politically as well? Whoever was posting as Q certainly thought so, and from August to September of 2018 Q worked hard to get out the vote for the midterm elections, with frequent posts supporting pro-Trump America First candidates.

The QAnon supporters' attention to real politics and visibility at Trump events was growing impossible to ignore. On August 2, 2018, Sarah Huckabee Sanders was questioned about QAnon at a press briefing. The heat from the press was starting to draw attention to the more noxious elements of the movement, and Q sites got their first taste of deplatforming. On August 10, 2018, The_Donald banned QAnon discussion. The biggest QAnon subreddit, r/GreatAwakening, had grown to seventy thousand-plus members when Reddit banned it in early September, marking the official end of QAnon's time on the platform. No matter. Sure, that made it harder for some to find Q, but where they went one, they went all. Tracy Diaz and other Q YouTubers were still there, Twitter was an open battleground for red-pilling campaigns, 8chan still harbored the most hardcore digital soldiers, there were backup communities on all manner of alternative tech platforms, and by this point there were all sorts of repositories keeping track of everything Q had ever said. Being taken off one platform did not slow the movement's growth.

On March 22, 2019, Department of Justice special counsel Robert Mueller concluded his investigation into Trump's possible collusion with the Russian government during the 2016 election. This investigation had been a source of growing agita not just for QAnon followers but for Trump himself, whose tweets and statements about Mueller had grown increasingly myopic. Amateur politicos of all political stripes, as well as Congress, were extremely eager to read the lengthy tome that had taken more than two years to compile. And yet it was redacted, so at first the press, the public, and many in Congress—except those on certain committees—were unable to read Mueller's findings for themselves. All they had to go on was then attorney general William Barr's summary, which gave the impression that Mueller had cleared Trump of wrong-doing. This was great news for Trump, whose reelection campaign was about to begin. On May 1, Mueller himself stated that Barr's summary was misleading, and Barr refused to testify to Congress about it. That day Trump retweeted messages of support from several QAnon accounts. Q, and the movement, had his attention, and he'd go on to retweet them more and more into election season. By this point he had already retweeted Q-related accounts roughly 315 times, a privilege previously granted only to a handful of alt-right memelords during the 2016 campaign. No matter what the negative news story about Trump might be on any given day, he could count on QAnon Twitter accounts to provide praise for the God Emperor. QAnon adherents adopted and discarded beliefs as needed, but they were always loyal to Trump.

Alt-right leaders, who had long since given up on MAGA and were still licking wounds from UTR, were skeptical of Trump and particularly of Q. "My #QAnon conspiracy conspiracy—," Richard Spencer speculated on Twitter, "which I present as speculation—is that the author actually is a high-level person in the Trump admin or similar org, and he's engaging, quite successfully, in masterful propaganda. (Or I might be wrong and it's all done for the lulz by some troll.)"

"Trump was elected on the basis of deep White anxiety," Spencer continued, noting that the insurgent energy of 2015 would be difficult to recapture. "It's doubtful that mainstream, FOX-level 'conservatives' will embrace Q. But they won't denounce him either. The phenomenon serves their purposes, and they will put forth a slightly less wacky version of the Q narrative." As usual, Spencer proved an observant commentator on the motivations of the various factions of the right. Without the alt-right to meme him into office for his second term, Trump's next best option for an online army was the digital soldiers of QAnon, who proved adept at repackaging the same anxiety in more elaborate, if more wacky, and less overtly offensive ways.

With no support from the leaders of the alt-right, QAnon was unencumbered by associations with white nationalists, despite the common ground they shared online and in their language, memes, and belief systems. While QAnon gatekeepers and influencers worked hard to maintain good optics, moderating out most overt racism and antisemitism, these attitudes lurked below the surface. "We are saving Israel for last. Very specific reason not mentioned a single time," Q wrote in March 2018, early in the movement's development. It's unclear what Q meant exactly, but that ambiguity allowed for both pro- and antisemitic interpretations by their followers. The deeper into the anonymous QAnon community on 8chan, the more explicit the antisemitic language became, though not the deliberate, political sort employed by white nationalists like Spencer.

Despite the friction between the alt-right and QAnon, they were bound by their belief that the troubles of the world could be blamed on an "other"—in the alt-right's case, a different race, and in QAnon's, a cabal of elites, who might or might not also be Jewish. Either way, this other had their tendrils in our institutions, our government, and our entertainment.

Pedowood and the Power of Pop Culture Red Pills

Despite Trump's well-known associations with and cameos in the entertainment industry in the twentieth century, by the twenty-first, he had become nearly universally reviled by Hollywood's liberal intelligentsia. As the arbiter of American pop culture, Hollywood had always been seen as suspect by the far right. With their disdain for the president, anti-Trump celebrities became the frequent targets of MAGA social media mobs.

When in October 2017 powerful Hollywood producer and Democratic donor Harvey Weinstein was accused of rape and years of abuse, few in the liberal mainstream publicly defended him, and those who did, like Woody Allen, Donna Karan, and Oliver Stone, were met with waves of criticism. Few conservatives dared defend Weinstein after Matt Drudge made a particularly tone-deaf tweet about a "magical evening" spent with Weinstein, "talking about movie music," which drew a lot of criticism from the right and showed that Drudge might be losing touch with the pulse of the online insurgent right. While liberal and leftist activists took the cause of sexual assault mainstream, the remainders of the alt-right and MAGA coalition sought ways to spin the situation to their particular advantage. Weinstein was Jewish, after all, a confirmed Democrat, and a friend to the Clintons and other powerful elites.

Though the QAnon movement at this time was rarely directly acknowledged by mainstream MAGA outside of occasional curiosity, they were happy to join in with MAGA influencers like Mike Cernovich, Pizzagate pusher and architect of the alt-right purge during the Deploraball, on anti-Hollywood campaigns. In revenge for the industry's refusal to support Trump, Cernovich painted Hollywood as a den of pedophilia and immorality. When on July 20, 2018, Disney fired director James Gunn over tweets he'd sent years earlier that seemed to condone pedophilia, it was in response to an anti-Hollywood (and anti-pedophile) crusade led by Cernovich. "The Harvey Weinstein case showed us that Hollywood is rotten to the core," Cernovich said. "We are continuing our investigation into the conduct and behavior of members of the Hollywood elite."

The Gunn firing proved to the digital soldiers that they could get results by collaborating with the alt-lite and Conservative Inc. when their goals aligned. They went on to target many more celebrities, such as Chrissy Teigen, pulling up their old social media posts and scouring them for potentially controversial statements. People within Hollywood began to notice the ferocity and impact of these campaigns, including those of a D-list actor named Isaac Kappy. Kappy had held small roles in the movie *Thor* and the TV show *Breaking Bad* and was currently under investigation by law enforcement for choking a woman at a party. In Hollywood he was basically a nobody, but he soon became a hero to the QAnon community.

In July 2018 Kappy began amplifying Q's claims about pedophiles in the entertainment industry. Speaking as an insider, he told anons that he could verify allegations that Hollywood elites were pedophiles, murderers, and baby eaters. On Periscope on July 28, Kappy said he'd been on the Q train since the beginning. He baselessly alleged that Steven Spielberg and Tom Hanks were pedophiles, and part of a larger cabal. "I want to talk about how this is all connected," he said, and then told everyone to look into the Rothschilds and cannibalism at the root of "Pedowood."

"They want you in the dark, they are losing their control, but at this point they cannot do anything, it's over. The only thing that needs to happen is the people need to see what is going on, the people need to wake up," Kappy said. "You need to wake up, you need to do the research. You need to get out of the mindstate that the mainstream media is the arbiter of truth, because they are not. The *New York Times* lied, and lied, and lied and got us into the Iraq War."

The QAnon community ate it up. This was as close to proving Q's prophecies as they had ever seen—an actual actor in Hollywood saying Tom Hanks ate babies! On August 2, 2018, a few days before Alex Jones was deplatformed, one of his final Infowars shows to air across the major platforms featured Kappy making these claims. As Will Sommer put it in the *Daily Beast* a few weeks later, Kappy was "QAnon's Newest Hero." Though Kappy had never attained real fame as an actor—his name was not known widely, nor was he a topic of gossip in the rag mags—now, with QAnon, he was a star.

He didn't enjoy this stardom for long. The broadcasts that brought him infamy revealed that he was a deeply troubled man. Kappy jumped from a bridge to his death on May 13, 2019. In his final post on Instagram, he apologized to Q for abandoning the movement. Yet even with this suicide note, QAnon followers were not convinced that he had killed himself, particularly as he'd previously claimed to not be suicidal. Nothing, Q had taught them, was ever as it seemed. In death Kappy was canonized, becoming part of a group of several high-profile Hollywood suicides that they came to believe were actually murders. These men, they believed, were assassinated because they were attempting to blow the whistle on Hollywood's sex trafficking.

Back in December, Q had drawn attention to the deaths by suicide of friends Chester Bennington, a musician and actor, and musician Chris Cornell, both sexual abuse victims. "Everything has meaning," Q said, which followers took as an indication that Bennington and Cornell's deaths were tied to the evils of the cabal, aka Hollywood. The same conclusions would be drawn about Swedish superstar DJ Avicii, who'd made a music video about sex trafficking, and who killed himself in April 2018, and about beloved chef and writer Anthony Bourdain, who killed himself in June of that year. As the world mourned Bourdain—why would this successful, brilliant man take his life?—the QAnon community claimed it was all part of the same sickness. Bourdain had been a loud critic of Weinstein. Either Bourdain was saddened by the gross injustice of the pedophiliac world he inhabited as a TV star, or, like Avicii, he'd been murdered because he knew too much. Kappy's death almost a year later made him a meme and a martyr. His wild accusations while he was alive carried more weight for conspiracy theorists in his death, who remixed and shared quotes from the hours of livestream video he left behind.

During the summer of 2019, QAnon adherents were turning up at Trump rallies looking mainly like regular white folks, like the family whose baby, wearing a onesie emblazoned with "Trump" on the front and "Q" on the back, the president pointed out at an event in North Carolina. "Wow, what a baby. What a baby! That is a beautiful baby! That's like from an advertisement, perfect! Look how happy that baby is! So beautiful, thank you, darling. That's really nice." In an interview with *Rolling*

Stone, the parents of the "Q Baby" praised the movement as "empowering because it's a lot of patriots that are following Trump when a lot of media is bashing our president, and it's exciting to know there's someone out there fighting for us and trying to bring the darkness to light." Predictably, the QAnon community saw this a wire-to-the-weeds moment, which was shared widely in the community, as a sign that Trump was looking out for the children preyed upon by the unseen cabal.

The cabal would strike back, however. QAnon took a major infrastructural hit on August 4, 2019, when Cloudflare terminated service for 8chan in the wake of the outcry following the Christchurch terrorist attack. The site was now synonymous with terrorist manifestos in the international press. In a rare public statement, CEO Matthew Prince compared Cloudflare's decision to removing the Daily Stormer from their services: "While removing 8chan from our network takes heat off of us, it does nothing to address why hateful sites fester online," he wrote. "It does nothing to address why mass shootings occur. It does nothing to address why portions of the population feel so disenchanted they turn to hate. In taking this action we've solved our own problem, but we haven't solved the Internet's."

Prince was correct. For 8chan site owner Jim and his son and technical admin Ron, this meant finding a new host and a rebrand of the imageboard now associated not only with neo-Nazis, child-sex-abuse material, and conspiracy theories but now also with terrorist manifestos. While this wasn't a direct attack on Q, it did impact the community, whose leader temporarily had nowhere to post. No 8chan meant no Q drops, and before 8chan was relaunched as 8kun, several months went by with no updates. Influencers filled the gaps with daily news analysis. Q's old posts had been saved and reaggregated on numerous websites, where followers counted the days since the last drop. Q had gone silent before, and would again, without destroying the movement. There was still plenty to talk about.

On August 10, 2019, accused sex trafficker and billionaire Jeffrey Epstein died in his prison cell less than a month after he had been arrested. His death was officially ruled a suicide. For the QAnon community, this was far from surprising. They saw it as fitting into the same old pattern: a person who knew too much died, and the death was made to look like a suicide. When Epstein was arrested in July 2019, the jokes about his impending death at the hands of the Clintons had begun immediately. Interest in him was not confined to QAnon; mainstream pop culture followers as well as conspiracists of all ilks were interested in Epstein's story, so when anons got interested too, it provided yet another entry point for outsiders to fall into the rabbit hole. They may have come for the Epstein theories, but they would stay for Q.

Rumors about Epstein online ranged from the banal to the insane. His death was either the result of a guilty man knowing his fate, or an incredibly suspicious cover-up arranged by Clinton herself. He was a rich pervert with a close circle of powerful friends, or perhaps an intelligence asset running a global honeypot operation with his partner in crime Ghislaine Maxwell, daughter of a world-renowned spy.

With such a high-profile list of friends, from Hollywood royalty to tech giants to Trump himself, Epstein *had* to have been murdered. Never mind the rumors about famous musicians and the small tragedy of Isaac Kappy; this was a real hit by the cabal. Indeed, it became a joke, a big one. MAGA folks were invested, as was pretty much anyone who wasn't buying the mainstream narratives. The mainstream narratives at the time were mainly focused on a much bigger story, and one with more real-world import for Trump: the impeachment, on charges that he had pressured the Ukrainian government to investigate his political rival, Joe Biden, in exchange for aid money, that was about to get under way. #EpsteinDidn'tKillHimself, whether ironic or serious, was a powerful memetic distraction from Trump's impeachment.

While the meme circulated far and wide across all platforms and in all mediums, from 4chan to Facebook to Fox News, Trump supporter Paul Gosar, the U.S. representative from Arizona, took it to the limit by creating a twenty-three-tweet-long-thread with a secret acrostic hidden in the first capitalized letter of each tweet, spelling out "E-P-S-T-E-I-N D-I-D-N-T K-I-L-L H-I-M-S-E-L-F." Gosar, or a member of his communications team, posted the thread during Trump's impeachment hearings. If the internet was fixated on Epstein while the government tried a complicated impeachment case, the two universes of "facts" would compete for attention, and memes had a chance of outweighing matters of utmost national importance.

Q started posting again during the hearings, on November 11, a few days after 8kun launched. There was a lot of breaking news to catch up on, particularly the death of Epstein and Trump's crusade against the cabal. During Trump's impeachment, Q posted to assure followers that all this was merely part of the plan, and that despite the political turmoil it created, "Attempts to slow/block the inevitable [Justice] will fail." Nothing in Q world was a coincidence, and nothing was as it appeared. "These people are sick," Q concluded. "We, the People, are the cure."

And the people were also getting rich.

By the end of 2019, QAnon had metastasized into something that couldn't be killed by pulling the plug on a single server, as the Cloudflare deplatforming proved. And it had also become a lucrative merchandise racket for anyone who wanted to use it to become an internet influencer. Books, hats, T-shirts, private spiritual counseling—all this and more was available with Q branding. No one held a trademark. It was perhaps this fact that most irked Jones, who was at heart a supplement salesman, after all. Infowars conspiracy theories were merely content in which to wrap ads for supplements that could cure any ailment, and QAnon influencers making bank off unfulfilled Q prophecies were a threat to his bottom line.

"I watched this Q phenomenon start a few years ago," Jones said in an episode of his daily broadcast devoted entirely to Q in the summer of 2019. He equated his distrust of the Q movement to his reservations about Anonymous from years back. In his own logic, Jones was different because his name was attached to all his brands. He wasn't some shadowy anon! He was also more legitimate because he talked to the president "many times on the phone," and because Trump tweeted out Infowars content "all the time."

Jones, who had claimed and would claim again in the future to know Q's real identity, got angrier as he began addressing Q believers directly. "I don't just talk to the president. My listeners got him elected. We're the dog, Trump's the tail. The American people are bigger than Trump, you stupid ass Q cult members." And they were also, apparently, more desperate and gullible than possibly even Jones could imagine.

Chapter 9

Fuck Around and Find Out

Pandemonium

Long before the COVID-19 pandemic hit the United States in January 2020, many in the red-pilled right were already tuned in to faint reporting coming out of China that a deadly disease was spreading in the Wuhan region. 4chan anons always kept up with the news, particularly stories that could involve a lot of dead people. The first post about Wuhan on /pol/ came on January 1, 2020, linking to an article in the *Independent* about a possible "mystery" SARS outbreak in Wuhan.

Anons on /pol/ talk about China frequently for all sorts of reasons: Some praise what they see as a successful authoritarian state, others share the more conservative attitude that China is a threat to U.S. global hegemony, and many bring it up simply to be racist. In the emerging disaster of COVID, they made a new meme for the virus ravaging Asia: Corona-Chan.

There had long existed a popular meme format in anime fan communities that used mascots of cheerful girls to represent anything—from countries to operating systems to planets. Anons on /pol/ adopted this meme format to create friendly female avatars meant to represent calamitous events, most famously pandemics. In 2014 the anons popularized Ebola-Chan, a smiling female nurse holding a bloody skull, meant to represent the thousands who had died of the viral fever. Mixing anime girls and dark humor about global tragedies had fueled many 4chan meme wars of the past, and their early interest in COVID-19 gave them a head start on setting the stage for the far right's attitudes to the pandemic.

An anon posted the first anime-style Corona-Chan mascot to /pol/ on January 21, 2020. Other anons immediately began iterating on the sketch, improving the coloration, adding details like bottles of Corona beer and, after new rumors suggested the virus originated in local bat populations, bat wings. Anons began jokingly referring to Corona-Chan as a beloved fictional character, just as anime or *My Little Pony* fans would pine after cartoon girls, human or not. "Corona-Chan spreads love to all peoples of a nation. God speed, Corona-chan," one anon said of their ironic mascot for the deadly new disease.

Other anons were immediately skeptical that *any of it was actually happening.* "Coronavirus and the quarantining of Wuhan IS NOT REAL!! It is all an elaborate hoax by a group of students from Yale University. The goal is to measure how information spreads across the internet if it originates on 4chan. It's fake," read a post on /pol/ on January 22, 2020. This was accompanied by an image of Pepe the Frog wearing a Communist soldier's helmet. Many news-obsessed anons on /pol/ were quite alarmed, but China's drastic government actions to

You have been visited by *the Ebola-Chan of Pestilence & Death*

Excruciating pain and death will come to you unless you post an

"I LOVE YOU EBOLA-CHAN!"

in this thread

curb the spread inspired an immediate counternarrative: that COVID was a government psychological operation, an idea shared by some in the QAnon community on 8kun, Twitter, and YouTube.

Q addressed the coronavirus news with vague generalizations and unprovable claims, spreading and amplifying preexisting disinformation rather than generating any particularly fresh theories. Independent conspiracy influencers and content creators did the job of connecting the dots, incorporating Q posts and proofs from the past into memes and infographics that described the pandemic as part of the same global system of control behind every other ill in the world.

Some of the most circulated of these memes came from graphic designer Dylan Louis Monroe and his Deep State Mapping Project. Monroe created a series of high-resolution maps, each reiterating tenets of revisionist history and conspiracy moments of yesteryear, to explain the COVID moment. From the Illuminati to the Bilderberg Group to JFK, these images named anything that could be connected to the cabal. For many newcomers to QAnon, these COVID memes became essential guides to their journey of research and red pills.

Veteran right-wing tastemakers like Jim took note of the brewing conversations about COVID on the chans and across the Q internet. On January 23, three days after the first COVID case was confirmed in America, he made COVID the focus of his livestream. "Lemme get comfy in my recliner, have a cup of cocoa, and watch the world go to shit," he said in the first of a dozen livestreams about what he called the "Wu Flu." These YouTube videos outpaced mainstream news coverage, which was not yet treating COVID like a front-page news story. Jim claimed to be suffering with serious health issues and was by no means a COVID denier. He took particular issue with Western news outlets' initial downplaying of COVID's transmissibility and severity, and the U.S. media's refusal to place the blame for the outbreak on China.

But the mainstream, liberals and conservatives alike, were focused on other things, like Trump's impeachment trial that kicked off January 16.

For his supporters, the impeachment was seen as yet another coordinated attack from the left, just like the Russian collusion investigation, and when he was acquitted on all charges on February 5, they celebrated.

Now Trump could focus on gearing up for a second term. His campaign adopted "Keep America Great" as its new slogan.

COVID soon interrupted the campaign's plans. America, like the world, was heading quickly not toward greatness but a public health calamity. Trump began his pre-campaign rallies in February, right as public health officials like chief medical adviser Anthony Fauci warned that the lethal virus would not be eliminated by the spring. Trump issued a travel restriction to parts of China, which some on the left decried as racist. Before February was out, it was clear the pandemic threatened to upstage his campaign. At a February 28 rally after securing the South Carolina primary, he accused the Democrats of "politicizing the coronavirus." "This is their new hoax," he claimed.

This became the theme of 2020: the politicization of "facts." Trump declared a national emergency on March 13, but this did not bring about consensus. Something as simple as a face mask, and whether it was helpful against a virus or damaging, became the object of intense disagreement. Dual realities emerged down partisan lines in the United States. Each camp believed the science was on their side, that the beliefs they held were factual, and that the others' beliefs were idiotic. The president fed this division by consistently downplaying the threat.

Whether Trump's insinuations and outright false statements about the virus were meant to win him reelection or just calm the nation, they were immune to the fact-checking complex that had grown up during his presidency to correct his many misstatements. No debunk could cause him to course-correct on COVID, nor could it change his followers' minds. No Politifact article shared on Twitter could fight the disinformation engine that the internet had become by 2020. All the incentives of the internet had conspired to make it an ideal host for a thriving disinformation ecosystem. And a news industry that had grown increasingly bifurcated during Trump's presidency didn't help— while channels like Newsmax and Fox News painted the picture of a president handling a global crisis with acumen, the mainstream and liberal media filled with alarming stories of government dysfunction.

Political and social truths became so subjective that it was difficult to build consensus, and where people stood on these empirical wedges was very much tied to issues of identity. Online pro-Trump factions like QAnon made sharing disinformation a form of community building, expanding their ranks to include anti-vaxxers and otherwise apolitical conspiracy theorists who were already comfortable with alternative facts. But the hotbeds of the red-pilled right, like 4chan, weren't as universally pro-Trump as they once had been. Their denizens bemoaned the fact that boomers and normies were moving into a new disinfo ecosystem, outside the influence of anonymous trolling operations. Trump fanned the flames of this epistemological polarization, actively dealing in lies to fire up his base, but in doing so set the stage for a year of unprecedented political chaos that ultimately cost him the election.

Polarizing a Public Health Panic

In an appearance on *Fox & Friends* in late February, the president's son Don Jr. went so far as to claim Democrats were maneuvering the virus for political gain. "For them to try to take a pandemic and seemingly hope that it comes here, and kills millions of people so that they could end Donald Trump's streak of winning, is a new level of sickness," he said. "You know, I don't know if this is coronavirus or Trump derangement syndrome, but these people are infected badly."

Early on, Jared Kushner reportedly axed a coordinated national COVID response, which led state governments to adopt radically different approaches to the pandemic. Democratic-run states initiated public health orders to combat the virus, while many Republican-led states did not. For swing states like many in the Midwest, where a large population was conservative but the leadership was Democratic, this created internal tensions. Some school districts closed, others did not. The disparity led not only to a dangerous public health environment where the virus was able to spread freely in some places but not others, but also increased the sense that the red and blue Americas were two totally different places. In one, school was out, everyone who could was working from home, and people were afraid for their lives. In the other, people were eating in restaurants, going to concerts, and wondering what the hell was wrong with the uptight liberals in their neighboring states.

These feelings were summed up in a series of memes comparing cases and death rates in Democrat- versus Republican-controlled states that

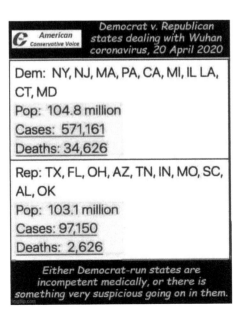

circulated in the spring, appearing to show blue states were being hit harder. Trump supporters shared these explainer memes as "proof" that the Democrats had the wrong strategy, or perhaps that the virus was targeting their populations more specifically. This contrasted with the burgeoning theory on the left that the Trump administration's response was designed to harm Democratic electoral prospects, a notion *Vanity Fair* published in an article citing unnamed sources. This idea that the response to COVID was driven by election math outraged liberals, who spread it across social media as proof that Trump was not just incompetent but also cruel.

In tweets and press conferences Trump began referring to the pandemic as the "Chinese Virus" and the pithier "China Virus." His embrace of the #ChinaVirus hashtag made it clear who Trump blamed for the pandemic, but this wasn't a Trump-coined phrase. An anon on /pol/ had first posted it back in January 2020, when the virus was still only reported in China. The term spread from the far right to the MAGA internet, assisted by the common speculation that the Chinese practice of selling wild animals as meat in "wet markets" could have sparked the pandemic. During that time, both conservative and liberal politicians attacked Chinese wet markets and the consumption of animals not familiar to Western palates, and Western meme makers made them out to be sites of viral outbreaks. One meme in particular, a viral "bat soup" video, was one of many bits of misinfo and decontextualized media that drove up anti-Asian sentiment domestically and internationally.

The first high-profile use of the #ChinaVirus meme came from Turning Point USA's Charlie Kirk, who tweeted on March 9, 2020, "Why is no one talking about punishing the Chinese governemnt [*sic*] for the ChinaVirus? They are destablizing [*sic*] the world economy because of their lies, deceit, and unsanitary conditions. They need to pay a very steep price for what they are doing to our country Make China pay!" The next day he tweeted, "Now, more than ever, we need the wall / With China Virus spreading across the globe, the US stands a chance if we can [*sic*] control of our borders / President Trump is making it happen / I explain why this matters & SO MUCH MORE!," followed by a link to subscribe to his podcast. Trump retweeted that tweet, which amplified the phrase to the whole world. After that, Trump began using the slogan, as did much of the right-wing media sphere.

#ChinaVirus and all that it implied was pushed by influencers and politicians all over the right, including sitting politicians like Senator Tom Cotton and House minority leader Kevin McCarthy. But in particular, it was Trump's long-lost ex-campaign CEO Steve Bannon who did the heavy lifting in not only building the case against China as the site of COVID's initial outbreak but also suggesting that COVID might be part of a large-scale attack on America.

Bannon had been busy since leaving Trump's staff after the Unite the Right rally in 2017. He spent most of his time trying to build a global populist movement and raising alarm bells about the "threat" of China. For him and fellow China hawks on the right, COVID presented a great opportunity. Alex Jones and Rush Limbaugh joined Bannon's quest to single out China as enemy number one. But by far his most significant ally was a wealthy fugitive from China named Guo Wengui, aka Miles Guo. Guo was a self-described billionaire who had once worked with businesspeople and the government of China but left the country in 2014 after being charged with fraud. In 2017 he officially applied for asylum in the United States, and it was that year that Bannon linked up with him, according to a profile of the two's partnership in the *Washington Post*. They bonded over their shared enemy, the Communist government in China. "While my pairing with Mr. Bannon may seem a bit odd, an enemy of my enemy is my friend," Guo told the *Post*.

Guo was on a mission to paint himself as an anti-Communist whistleblower and build up a movement that he would lead for Chinese dissidents, using media as his tool. On his YouTube channels, he made daily videos for his supporters and showed off a flashy, rich lifestyle, peddling conspiracy theories and singing the praises of capitalism.

In 2018 Bannon signed a $1 million deal to be an official consultant for Guo Media, a social media company Guo ran that was headquartered in New York, according to the news site Axios. Guo Media would become a vehicle for Bannon to enact his operational philosophy of political change via disinfo. That year, 2018, he laid this strategy out for journalist Michael Lewis in an interview: "We got elected on Drain the Swamp,

Lock Her Up, Build a Wall. This was pure anger. Anger and fear is what gets people to the polls. . . . The Democrats don't matter. The real opposition is the media. And the way to deal with them is to 'flood the zone with shit.'" It was a strategy that came fully into its own in 2020, one that exploited the emotional and economic turmoil of the pandemic and built a new outsider identity for MAGA 2020: a movement of political dissidents and whistleblowers fighting back against communism, the deep state, and the New World Order.

Bannon had an office in Guo Media's headquarters and flew around on Guo's jet, even appearing in it in a scene from a documentary about him that came out in 2019. That year, Bannon launched a YouTube show and podcast called *War Room*, on which he had Guo as a frequent guest. The theme song for the show was "Let's Take Down the CCP."

In 2020 Guo and Bannon took their partnership much further. In the spring, Guo launched GMedia and appointed Bannon as chairman. GMedia consisted of the website GNews.org, which pushed anti-CCP stories and worked as a clearinghouse for Guo's allegations of corruption against President Xi, and GTV.org, which published video content in the same style. Guo also commanded the "Himalaya movement," a vast network of digital soldiers that promoted the content from GNews, GTV, and related anti-CCP rhetoric on social media. Throughout the spring and early summer of 2020, this network spread the #ChinaVirus hashtag and tons of coronavirus-related disinformation about China.

This complex of people, accounts, and websites worked as an enormous disinformation engine throughout 2020, spreading medical misinformation about COVID-19 across the world and turning a health emergency into a mass political polarization red pill. As early as January 2020 the Himalaya and GMedia networks and YouTube influencers pushed the idea that COVID was a bioweapon created by the CCP to destroy America using #ChinaVirus and #CCPvirus. "[Guo's media] is spreading misinformation. I think it's trying to interrupt the United State elections," John Pan, a former member of Guo's media empire, told an Australian news outlet in the run-up to the election. Pan reported being involved in meetings about how to push anti-CCP misinformation, and even spoke with Bannon a few times.

This disinformation team was just one of many groups coordinating to support Trump in the 2020 election, through political hijinks, memes, misinformation, and old-fashioned rallies. Trump was an incumbent this time, but because he had been recently impeached, he came into the election season before COVID with the same underdog status he'd held in 2016. He and his supporters blamed the impeachment, and his many broken campaign promises, on a deep-state witch hunt, attempts to discredit Trump's accomplishments by hostile intelligence services.

Despite or perhaps because of his hyperpolarizing effect in media and polling, Trump still had a tight control over the right-wing base, and had continued to hold rallies around the country during his presidency. After three years in office, Trump was as popular as ever with his base, with his approval ratings among Republicans staying at a consistent 87 percent, while holding a 6 percent approval with Democrats in August 2020. Over the last four years, loving and hating Trump had become an identity. MAGA labeled liberals as sick with "Trump derangement syndrome," and liberals labeled pro-Trump conservatives as cultists and fascists.

But Trump's reelection campaign was dogged from the beginning by the high turnover of his inner circle, damaging leaks, and his continued public spats on Twitter. In preparation for the 2020 campaign, Trump's team courted influencers and corny, professionalized meme makers, the top tier of whom were even invited to the White House for an official social media summit in July 2019. Power dynamics in right-wing media were also changing. Fox News had competition from the right for the MAGA audience from growing pro-Trump networks OANN and Newsmax. Both these smaller networks branded themselves as even more loyal to the president than Fox, and more likely to repeat blatant disinformation on air than the conservative news giant.

But there was no alt-right meme engine overwhelming social media this go-round. Support from more libertarian-minded pundits was weaker than in 2016, and the QAnon network introduced an open-source means of spreading disinfo that was proving impossible for traditional right-wing gatekeepers to control. While Nick Fuentes and the Groyper army were out there, they were doing as much harm as good, far more optical than the older fascists they replaced, but just as committed to biting the ankle of the conservative establishment in hopes of recognition and amplification. Plus, this time social media platforms were quicker to ban fake news clickbait, abuse of advertisements, automated activity, and overt bigotry than they had been in 2016. Many of the best trolls and meme warriors from the past campaign had received permanent suspensions for violating updated terms of service. Further, they took unprecedented steps to curb COVID misinformation, actions that became as politically polarizing as the virus itself. As COVID began dominating the news cycle, a litany of conspiracy theories and disinformation campaigns began taking hold, but the most prolific at that time was the idea that the death toll was being exaggerated. None of this was helped by contradictory statements by public health officials, changing mandates around public distancing and masking, and the media's struggle to keep up with both the CDC's and Trump's increasingly conflicting positions on how to stop the spread.

As COVID disrupted the world and drove up global internet use, social media moved faster than any institution could respond, fostering doubt, skepticism, and vitriol. The Trump administration's response to COVID further polarized Americans and brought into question the very mechanism by which Americans would vote in November—would it be safe to vote at voting booths, or would Americans need to use mail-in ballots? As early as May 2020, Trump was fighting hard against the use of mail-in ballots, even threatening social media companies for allowing information about mail-in voting to proliferate across their sites.

Trumpworld found new villains in Democratic governors like Gretchen Whitmer of Michigan and Andrew Cuomo of New York, and most importantly Anthony Fauci, the country's top infectious disease expert.

On March 11 Trump began giving long-ranging press conferences on COVID, eventually inviting a cast of national health experts, including Fauci, to give daily updates. Fauci proved to be popular with many Americans. "He's become a major television star for all the right reasons," Trump said of the chief medical advisor. But the goodwill lasted only so long as Fauci agreed with the president.

Some high-profile businessmen and Trump supporters had been sharing the claim that a drug called hydroxychloroquine, used to treat malaria and some autoimmune diseases, could treat or prevent COVID. On March 19, Trump suggested that it was a promising potential treatment that the FDA and drug companies were looking into. The next day, reporters asked Fauci about this idea. His reply insinuated that Trump's optimism about the drug was unfounded, noting that there had been no clinical trials. Trump rebutted Fauci's downplaying of hydroxychloroquine's effectiveness based on "a feeling." "I'm a smart guy," he told the press. "I feel good about it."

So did many of his followers, who declared hydroxychloroquine some kind of miracle drug. The headlines that ran after this exchange declared Trump and Fauci at odds. Liberals turned Fauci into the anti-Trump realist, lauding him as "Saint Fauci" in memes. The rift between him and Trump grew, and so did the calls from supporters to #FireFauci. His arrest, and even assassination, became the subject of increasingly dark images shared in conservative boomer and red-pilled communities.

Liberate Michigan

As COVID denialism and misinformation around magical cures circulated online, Trump's briefings became even more unmoored from the science. He famously joked that maybe people could inject bleach to kill the virus during one such conference, which led to people actually trying that at home.

And Trump began to align himself with the emergent anti-lockdown communities, who were becoming increasingly vocal. As states went on lockdown throughout the spring, militia types and libertarians took to state houses to protest. Trump made it clear that even though he was the president, he could not control state governors, and refused to condemn any of these anti-government actions. This was a way of not only harnessing the growing insurgency of COVID downplayers and deniers but also showing favor to state governors who supported his administration.

"Liberate Michigan!" he tweeted on April 17. Then, "Liberate Illinois!" "Liberate Wisconsin!" These tweets, as with all his tweets during his presidency, carried the weight of the president behind them, and his followers took them as a sign that he was paying attention. After the tweets, the protests multiplied in cities across the United States, as did the idea that COVID restrictions were an overreaction, yet another federal overreach into personal liberties.

For militia types in particular, the lockdowns and closures to curb the coronavirus felt like one of their longest-held fears coming true: an excuse to trample the Constitution and shut down their way of life. Groups like the Proud Boys, the Three Percenters, and the Oath Keepers began protesting and speaking out against the lockdowns online. They were joined by newer pop-up militias that formed in response to COVID, such as the group in Michigan called the Wolverine Watchmen, who hatched an unsuccessful plot to overthrow the sitting governor of Michigan, Gretchen Whitmer.

One of the members of that group was a man named Adam Fox, who was outraged that Governor Whitmer had closed down inessential businesses in the state. He and several acquaintances from Facebook, some of whom were later revealed to be FBI informants, put together a group chat called "Fuck Around Find Out." A popular meme at the time, FAFO is a memetic way to say, "Try me, I dare you," implying that if someone pushes you the wrong way, you will retaliate.

In 2020 the FAFO meme went viral as both the left and the right took to the streets for increasingly violent protests. Proud Boys picked up the

FUCK AROUND AND FIND OUT

phrase as a motto, wearing it on T-shirts and patches. Some leftists embraced it too, a warning to both the far right and centrist libs who they believed were actively sabotaging Bernie Sanders's 2020 chances in favor of more moderate candidates. In June 2020 FAFO adorned an unofficial antifa flag, a play on the Gadsden flag with an alligator in the place of the snake and "Fuck Around and Find Out" where "Don't Tread on Me" would normally be.

The Wolverine Watchmen weren't part of the established Michigan militias, of which there were many. They did, however, align with the loosely affiliated Boogaloo movement—a younger brother to the more established Patriot movement that grew up in the 1980s and was filled with boomers and Gen X anti-government, pro-gun militia folks. Boogaloos share those beliefs; they are not classically white supremacists, though some are.

On April 30, the Michigan State Senate met to decide whether to continue the coronavirus lockdowns. The Wolverine Watchmen draped their rifles across their military vests and went to the state capitol in Lansing. There they joined the American Patriot rally organized by Meshawn Maddock, a pro-Trump lawmaker. (Maddock later arranged for nineteen busloads of people to go to the January 6 siege in Washington, D.C.) It was rainy that day in April, but "well over a thousand" people showed up to the steps of the state capitol, according to witness reports, waving signs and Gadsden flags. Two young girls did a dance wearing sequined American flag leotards and face masks—one a minstrel-style blackface Obama mask, the other a Trump mask. Turning Point USA's Benny Johnson livestreamed the event, taking time to tweet updates and pose for photos with members of the Boogaloo movement, easily recognizable by their Hawaiian shirts. "My private security," he joked. The Boogaloo on the left of Johnson wore a patch on his vest that read "Meme War Veteran."

After hours out in the rain, hundreds of protesters, many armed, moved into the building. Despite the FBI's informant telling his handlers that the militia guys he was with were trying to get into the capitol, the doors of the capitol building had been left unlocked. Security guards made people leave their flags and signs at the door and submit to a temperature check, but the protesters were allowed to bring in their weapons.

Some members of the alleged plot to kidnap Whitmer went upstairs and entered the Senate gallery, where they "loomed," according to Michigan state senator Sylvia Santana, as the lawmakers passed resolutions about COVID. The hundreds crowded inside the lobby faced the main Senate doors and chanted "Let us in" and, more ominously, "Lock her up!" As if they were at a Baptist revival, the protesters sang American hymns and then switched to chants, surging forward ever so slightly as they spoke. If past is prologue, the video from the lobby is eerily reminiscent of the January 6 insurrection that would follow almost a year later. As with January 6, thousands watched the events unfolding in real time on Twitter.

Liberals responded with the hashtag #covidiots, which trended throughout the day. This only charged up the anti-lockdown protesters in Michigan. While the center and left mainstream media embraced Governor Whitmer's courage in bucking Trump, she had been transformed into Hitler in popular right-wing memes.

This was just one of many anti-lockdown protests that sprang up all over the country around this time, largely in red counties in blue states, such as those in western Oregon, or in swing states under Democratic control like Wisconsin, Minnesota, Virginia, and Michigan. The feeling in the country was one of fear, frustration, and confusion. Areas that would vote for Trump in the 2020 election proved to have much lower vaccination rates than in states that voted Biden. As a result of the year of disinfo and disarray, many of his most devoted followers refused the vaccine that Trump himself had proudly claimed as one of his greatest accomplishments.

Pastel QAnon and the Red-Pilling of Millennial Moms

On May 17, tech billionaire Elon Musk tweeted his followers, "Take the red pill." Musk, a fifty-year-old white man born in South Africa who regularly communicated with his massive following using the language of memes, had defied COVID lockdowns, refusing to stop manufacturing his Tesla electric cars despite California mandates. This defiance was praised, privately and publicly, by Trump, and for a time Musk became a celebrated figure of resistance within the MAGA world.

The timing of Musk's tweet made many think he was flirting with the hordes of alt-righters, QAnon digital soldiers, and Trumpsters. Then Ivanka Trump retweeted him, proudly proclaiming "taken." A slew of liberal press published yet another wave of explanations about the origins of the term.

Lilly Wachowski, who with her sister wrote and directed *The Matrix*, took offense to the co-option of the term. "Fuck both of you," she replied on Twitter, having watched closely over the last decade as her metaphor for enlightenment was hijacked by neo-Nazis and pickup artists. This exchange—a filmmaker condemning the use of a meme hijacked by a powerful CEO and the daughter of a sitting president—in a different year would have been a very significant meme moment. In 2020 it was but a footnote in a chaotic timeline no one could have predicted, where obscure references and otherwise fringe ideas became front-page headlines.

Of all the memes and movements that coalesced in 2020, none captured the chaos of the moment better than the surging popularity of QAnon, which managed to act as a news curator for conspiracy-minded people trying to figure out what the hell was really going on.

The Q community took Trump's vague assertions and accusations against political opponents and helped get them trending on social media while seeding their own disinfo. Beliefs popular in the Q community, old ideas about the New World Order and cabalistic blood sacrifice, were adopted more widely, giving birth to the so-called Pastel QAnon movement of new age influencers, hippies, and paranoid moms.

The COVID summer was boom times for the do-your-own-research crowd; there was so much to look into, so many competing stories and events to try to understand. QAnon influencers made it simple. They told people what to care about and what to ignore. In this way, QAnon was like a sneak attack on the populace. If BLM and COVID protests were the battles happening out in the open, QAnon was the stealth mission, working in the shadows, in the comments, to build an army of unsuspecting normies who would become digital soldiers and spread the message far and wide. For many who didn't know its murky origins, Q became a marker of antiestablishment political identity both online and off. The open-source Q branding on products ranging from books to shirts to disinfo memes proved to be effective advertisements, an easy way of branding decontextualized truths and outright fabrications. Anyone could hijack the hashtags to make whatever cryptic claims they wanted. From the deep boards of 8kun to Fox News, any information, true or false, that ultimately supported Trump was celebrated. While Trump and his team were responsible for many falsehoods, the disinformation spread by the QAnon community helped lead many angry and uncertain Americans down the rabbit hole in communities previously untouched by MAGA.

This was increasingly visible on Instagram in particular. Instagram became the sea in which to fish for new QAnon believers, especially in the wellness and anti-vax communities, which were amped up and gaining followers due to coronavirus. QAnon hashtags began to be dropped in the comment sections of these accounts. QAnon memes went viral over and over again on the app, and people posted them without realizing what they were perpetuating. To target the wellness community, which was predominantly made up of millennials, QAnon influencers began making memes that matched the preferred aesthetic of white Instagram momflu-encers, with pastel pinks and lots of plants and white space.

QAnon became a red pill for a much wider audience than ever before, starting in July 2020. This was when the movement successfully snatched the #SaveTheChildren hashtag from under the nose of the social media companies and turned it into QAnon hashtags that led to adrenochrome theories. Celebrities were posting selfies with no makeup because they were stuck at home, and some QAnon believers interpreted that to mean that their supply of adrenochrome—which they believed was harvested from the blood of tortured children—had been disrupted by global supply chain issues, and that they therefore couldn't keep themselves looking young and beautiful.

This trap snared unsuspecting parents of young kids, who came upon memes about missing or murdered children and had no idea they had anything to do with QAnon. The adrenochrome conspiracy was a modern take on an ancient antisemitic myth, the blood libel, which dated back to the Middle Ages and was created to tap into the deepest fears of humanity. As Jews were moving into Europe, some non-Jewish Europeans spread rumors that Jews ate children. The purpose of this was to justify shunning and excluding the Jewish people from society. In QAnon, it functioned the same way: to prove that "elites" (often but not exclusively Jewish) were demons out to destroy the world.

People who may not have been open to such wild conjecture were more so during the pandemic, when the whole world really did feel upside down. As anxiety was high everywhere, posts on TikTok and Instagram about the horrors of missing children slid right into the panic of the moment.

It makes sense. The year of coronavirus lockdown, the entrenched disinformation networks of the QAnon community, and the amped-up political rhetoric of the 2020 campaign season created the conditions for an explosion of conspiratorial belief. This perfect storm was destabilizing emotionally, economically, and intellectually. One response to the disaster was to desperately seek an answer for why all of this was happening. And so much was happening.

If people thought coronavirus was bad, wait until they found out about something even worse, something so evil and horrible people could only whisper about it, or make ten-part documentaries on YouTube. This evil thing was that a global cabal of elites, and mostly Hollywood elites, but also political elites like the Clintons and the British royal family, were eating babies. Sucking their blood. Crunching their bones. They were sometimes having sex with them, and other times they were ingesting the babies whole. They were stealing them from their parents and shoving them in furniture that they would mail to pedophiles and baby eaters through the internet.

Again, this was an old idea. It had been part of Pizzagate before QAnon; it had been an idea spread around /pol/ long before that; and before that it had lurked on websites and pamphlets and myths told as urban legends passed down by word of mouth. COVID gave it new life.

In March 2020, Dutch UFO truther Janet Ossebaard released a ten-part documentary on YouTube entitled *Fall of the Cabal*. These twenty-minute videos worked as a gateway to the QAnon movement for thousands of people who were stuck at home watching social media more and more because of the pandemic. The video series stepped in to answer the unanswerable: Why is this happening? Why? Because of this plot to eat our babies. It was all part of the cabal's plan to do terrible things to regular people and keep the world from being truly free—unless people like Ossebaard and her viewers could stop them.

"We are about to witness one of the greatest events in human history," Ossebaard announced in the introduction to the first episode. "The world as we know it is crumbling before our very eyes and the majority of the world population is not aware of it. Power structures that have been in place for thousands of years are taken down as we speak. Soon we will be shown evidence of an elite plan so evil, so all-encompassing, that people will be shocked to the core. This documentary was made to help you deal with what's coming. Are you ready? Join me on a journey down the rabbit hole."

The videos employed extremely persuasive rhetoric. Ossebaard narrates, and her voice is comforting, familiar, and authoritative. Before she started pushing Q conspiracies, she was an alien crop circle truther—more proof that there were many on-ramps to QAnon, from political extremism to generic antiestablishmentarianism to all forms of trutherisms.

It is hard to watch Ossebaard's films. They are extremely upsetting. She shows footage of children in pain—most of which is staged or taken from entertainment sources—as well as horrifying footage of real refugees in crisis whom she accuses of being paid actors, using every smile or clean cheek of a baby to prove that the migrants are liars. The videos cunningly suck you in—they begin with Ossebaard explaining that she was skeptical of all of this, and she was a liberal who worried about migrants and believed the news—just like you. She presents herself as a reasonable regular person who, like the viewer, is just seeking answers. "Why is sex with children so important?" she asks in episode 5. "What is going on here?! Let's follow a lead." She then introduces the audience to Pizzagate: "The more I studied Pizzagate the more I realized this was quite likely conspiracy fact, not theory."

By July 2020, these people were mobilizing in the streets at rallies to save children from human trafficking, using much of the language of Ossebaard's films. A number started circulating: 800,000. This was how many children were supposedly missing or trafficked every year, according to comments and videos put out by Q influencers. These posts were accompanied by Q hashtags like #WWG1WGA, once obscure phrases from 8chan now used as symbols in a protest movement. Child trafficking conspiracy theories like WayfairGate—the false viral claim that kids were being sold on the furniture retail site Wayfair—helped propel Q beliefs further into the mainstream.

"Has anyone else noticed what's going on with your normies friends on Facebook Etc? People who have no idea who or what Q is are sharing #SaveTheChildren memes and dark to light related info. We are watching the #GreatAwakening in real time," tweeted a QAnon on July 31, 2020. July 31 was the UN's annual World Day Against Human Trafficking, and #SaveTheChildren QAnon campaigners made the most of it, throwing a "Child Lives Matter" protest in Hollywood complete with #adrenochrome and #WWG1WGA signs, and protesting at CNN's offices.

Throughout the summer of 2020, the meme war hit the streets again. In battle after battle, from Washington, D.C., to Portland to Texas, the arguments of the internet spilled out everywhere. And it didn't let up for the rest of the year. The movement was good for Trump, who retweeted Q accounts repeatedly throughout the election and never disavowed the movement.

When asked by NBC's Savannah Guthrie about the QAnon movement in the final weeks of the campaign, Trump was initially evasive. "I know very little," he said. "You told me, but what you tell me, doesn't necessarily make it fact." Trump dismissed Guthrie's description of QAnon as the "theory that Democrats are a satanic pedophile ring and that you are the savior," but he seemed proud of the ridiculous attention from the movement and willing to give them some praise, despite minutes earlier having denounced white supremacists and antifa. The alt-right was now a burned asset for Trump, but if he was going to win the election and the meme war, he needed QAnon despite their bad optics. "I do know they are very much against pedophilia," Trump said of the movement. "They fight it very hard."

Whose Streets?

At the beginning of the summer, the death of yet another Black man at the hands of the police exploded like a bomb in a country that already seemed to be tearing itself apart along partisan lines. In normal times the leader of the country might offer words of healing and solace at such an obvious tragedy, but such was not to be.

When George Floyd was murdered by a police officer in Minneapolis, Minnesota, a young girl at the scene recorded a video of his painful and excruciatingly long execution. It quickly went viral around the world. A nation already deeply on edge exploded with anger over the horrifying video of Floyd's obviously wrongful death. Liberals and BLM supporters left their homes in droves and showed up in the streets for the first time since the national pandemic had been declared in March, and many corporations adopted the BLM meme to signal political correctness in social media posts and PR statements. Protests were staged in the streets, the word spreading on Instagram stories, the For You page of TikTok influencers, Facebook groups, and the nightly news.

Floyd's name wasn't the only name chanted by the resurgent BLM protests across the world—from Trayvon Martin to Breonna Taylor and Ahmaud Arbery, other Black victims of police or wrongful killing were represented too. Riots accompanied some of the protests, as did looting and arson, particularly in communities most directly impacted by police violence, though the vast majority of protesters weren't involved in any form of criminal activity. In fact, the majority of BLM protests were entirely peaceful.

In the Northwest, this new street movement sparked a near-permanent occupation by anarchists and anti-fascists of a part of Seattle eventually dubbed the Capitol Hill Autonomous Zone, or CHAZ. The Seattle Police Department reportedly spread false rumors that armed Proud Boys were planning an incursion into CHAZ, and days later members of the Proud Boys, along with other groups, did visit the zone's border and violently clash with leftists. Other right-wing militias, like the Oath Keepers, issued calls to dismantle the area, calling it an "international terrorism and insurrection campaign." Participants livestreamed clashes between left- and right-wing street protesters, as did well-known streamers who showed up to broadcast this "riot porn" on their own social media or on partisan websites, where they wrote scathing articles about how Black people and antifa were burning America to the ground. The spectacle reached fever pitch when in Washington, D.C., BLM protesters were tear-gassed to clear the way for President Trump to walk through the crowd like Moses parting the Red Sea, so he could hold a Bible up for a photo op outside a church.

This energy from the left was matched by armed outrage on the part of the right, who showed up to counterprotest, condemning the BLM protesters as tools of Marxists and the Democrats. The right felt that allowing the BLM marches and publicly commending them despite lockdown orders was a glaring contradiction. Once again the reactionary meme #BlueLivesMatter was seen online and on protest signs and T-shirts. It fought for recognition on social media, and protesters clashed with police and counterprotesters in cities across the United States. As the violence and outrage grew, Trump and the red-pilled right circulated propaganda implying that the unrest was the work of "antifa" extremists, who they claimed were being bussed into cities across the United States to foment chaos and throw cans of soup. In late June Trump threatened to designate antifa a terrorist organization, furthering the narrative that the left was to blame for the unrest, though in fact it was largely being perpetuated by fake Twitter accounts, convenient straw men used to stoke conservative panic.

The red-pilled right media and influencers took the protests seriously, sending reporters and streamers to cover marches and counterprotests all over the country. The explosive footage of arson and late-night clashes with police captured by these on-the-ground reporters set the tone in national media. Mainstream outlets relied on it to report on what was going on, thereby painting a broad picture of violence and chaos. The left had innovated streaming journalism to help validate their social movements earlier in the decade, but now their tools had been completely co-opted by the right.

On May 29 Trump tweeted "When the looting starts, the shooting starts," referring to the "thugs" protesting George Floyd's murder. In response to this call for violence, Twitter added its first ever public warning to one of the president's tweets, a measure it would resort to increasingly through the rest of the election and postelection period.

For the last generation of alt-right leaders, most of whom had long since lost their social media platforms and mainstream recognition from the MAGA movement, history seemed to be repeating itself. Many called the protests following the killing of Trayvon Martin in Florida and Michael Brown in Ferguson, Missouri, their awakening, the red-pill moment that led them to white nationalism. The *Daily Shoah* and *Fash the Nation* podcasts blamed the usual cast of characters for the chaos— Jews instigating Blacks, enabled by white liberals. But this time around, they put equal responsibility on Trump, for both his chaotic handling of COVID and his duplicity in dealing with the protesters. A true strongman, in their estimation, would have crushed the national protests with the National Guard.

/Pol/ was experiencing deja vu as well. But they knew what to do. The familiar game plan called for them to follow the breaking news, look for clues and new information, dig into the past of any individual involved, and encourage others in mocking Floyd's death. They collected as many videos and photos of Floyd as they could and, in an echo of 2012's Trayvoning meme, engaged in "George Floyd challenges," in which people posed to re-create the infamous image of Derek Chauvin crushing Floyd's neck with his knee.

As the BLM protests spread around the United States, reactionaries claimed an unlikely set of heroes: the McCloskeys and Kyle Rittenhouse. One a middle-aged married couple and the other a Gen Z teen, they became highly polarized symbols of white resentment and reactions to racial justice movements in mass media, politics, and memes.

On June 28, 2020, Patricia and Mark McCloskey became the face of fed-up white boomers when they were photographed and videotaped brandishing weapons at a group of BLM supporters marching past their house in Saint Louis, Missouri, to protest outside the mayor's private residence a few blocks away. The images were extremely memorable— Patricia was barefoot, and Mark looked like he'd just stopped grilling long enough to pick up his gun. They drew polarized reactions: mocking and condemnation from the left, joking approval from the right, expressed in memes, videos, tweets, and think pieces. After the social media outburst following the incident, Mark McCloskey appeared on Fox News's *Tucker Carlson Tonight* and CNN's *Cuomo Prime Time*, describing the moment as "the storming of the Bastille." He rationalized his behavior by saying he believed that he would be murdered, his house burned down, and his pets killed. The McCloskeys pleaded guilty to misdemeanor charges and had their weapons confiscated following the incident, but they had become anti-BLM cult heroes among the Republican base, and in 2021 Missouri governor Mike Parson pardoned them.

Both the left and right framed the McCloskeys as comic vigilantes in memes. This tendency to treat vigilantism as something to mock or celebrate took a dark turn when on the evening of August 25, at a BLM protest in Kenosha, Wisconsin, a boy named Kyle Rittenhouse killed two people and maimed another. After his arrest, online investigators of all political affiliations pored over every available minute and angle of footage of his actions that night, including two of the shootings. Anons on /pol/ followed the events in real time, tracking his arrest and the response to it by the press and libs. In one of those first threads on /pol/ on August 26, an anon urged everyone to work together to set the record straight that Rittenhouse did nothing wrong and get the hashtag #FreeKyle going. It worked. The hashtag trended and became the name of a movement to support Rittenhouse and crowdsource his $2 million bail.

Though Rittenhouse didn't appear to be one of theirs—from what they could find on his public social media, he didn't use white supremacist lingo, or even express anti-Black or anti-Jewish racism—the anons saw that he had potential for massive meme magic. They claimed him as a saint, albeit a goofier one than the cold, calculating, and unrepentant mass murderers Elliot Rodger and Brenton Tarrant. They also dug up the criminal charges of the men Rittenhouse had shot. Memes depicting Kyle as an innocent young saint were cranked out for propaganda purposes, now paired with claims that those he'd shot were not racial justice protesters but violent abusers and pedophiles. A popular running linguistic meme in the far right, asking "Have you Seen Kyle" (Sieg Heil), attempted to reframe the boy as some kind of Nazi youth.

Rittenhouse was obsessed with law enforcement, though he was not formally associated with any white nationalists or militias, and in statements given in 2021, he even claimed to support the BLM movement. These details didn't really matter: to the left he was a white supremacist terrorist; to the right, a white hero. Slowly conservatives who had initially condemned the street violence fell silent, and by August 28, Republican establishment and right-wing media were openly endorsing #FreeKyle. Unlike the mass shooters of the red-pilled right, Kyle had a plausible claim to self-defense and no white supremacist footprint online. Trump himself suggested that Rittenhouse had acted in self-defense, and reportedly called to congratulate him when he was acquitted on all charges in November 2021.

In the support for and antagonism to BLM, we can see how resonant it was as a meme—and how powerful a cultural dividing line it proved

to be. As a force that brought so many out into the streets during a global pandemic, BLM was an incredibly powerful motivator to move people from the wires to the weeds, from sharing hashtags to marching through towns across the world. In terms of online buzz and real-world mobilization, Black Lives Matter could be considered the meme of the decade, the single most popular slogan of the early 2000s. Yet very few, if any, policy changes were implemented as a result. And BLM's mobilization into the streets in the summer of 2020 was used by some on the right— many of whom counter-organized under the banner of Blue Lives Matter—to argue that it was not policing but racial justice activism that was destabilizing America. According to polling from Pew Research, support for BLM actually declined after the George Floyd protests, from 67 percent of the U.S. population in June to 55 percent in September 2020. It then remained steady at that level over the next year, yet another indication of the hyperpartisan divide around transformative racial justice in America.

When Memes Are Just Not Enough

In June 2020, Biden clinched the Democratic nomination and named Kamala Harris as his VP. Since Harris was of mixed race, that move looked politically savvy in light of the country's racial justice momentum. Trump tried to meme Biden as "Sleepy Joe," using the moniker repeatedly, but it wasn't very catchy, and didn't electrify people like "Crooked Hillary" had. Biden was just too boring and familiar to make a very convincing fuss about. Unlike Hillary Clinton and her campaign advisers, Biden declined to comment on most of the provocative things Trump said about him, insisting repeatedly that he wanted to stick to what mattered to the American people: fighting coronavirus and getting the economy back on track. Biden's refusal to take the bait as Clinton had in 2016 made it hard for Trump to fight a meme war against him.

By now the election was rapidly approaching, and things were not going according to plan for the meme warriors. But it was also growing increasingly difficult for the Republicans to even run a normal campaign. Trump began signaling that if he lost the election, it would be because it was rigged in some way. He harped on the risk of mail-in ballots, which conservative pundits surmised would favor Democrats. As Biden's double-digit lead in the polls endured, Trump seemed to be growing desperate. In late July he said that the election should be delayed due to COVID, which many saw as an undemocratic power grab.

After having paused his rallies in the spring, Trump insisted on holding one in Tulsa, Oklahoma. For the date he chose June 19—also known as Juneteenth, a federal holiday celebrating the date when, in 1865, two years after the Emancipation Proclamation was signed, slaves in Texas were finally freed. Trump's campaign staff sent out a barrage of text messages asking supporters to be there, and tickets sold quickly, leading Trump and his campaign to believe it would be a packed house. It wasn't. Anti-Trump teens on TikTok claimed they had reserved tickets for the event with no intention of showing up, making it seem as if it had sold out. Though it was sparsely attended in comparison to previous Trump events, the rally still proved lethal for Herman Cain, who contracted COVID and died six weeks later. "Trump Staffers Blame Themselves for Herman Cain's COVID Death," read one headline, though in their official statements Trump and the White House denied that Cain had contracted the virus in Tulsa.

Trump continued to hold rallies until Election Day, though they were not as big as he might have liked. In the absence of the large Trump rallies that they craved, his supporters improvised and organized their own rallies, such as the Trump Trains, caravans of supporters driving down U.S. highways with MAGA gear draped over their cars and trucks, and the infamous Trump Boat Parade in Florida, which ended in disaster when five of the flag-bedecked boats took on too much water and sank.

Throughout late summer and fall, things kept going wrong in Trumpworld. Trump himself contracted COVID and had to be flown by helicopter to the Walter Reed Medical Center, which was a difficult media spectacle to square, in the final weeks before Election Day, with his campaign's insistence that COVID was under control. Digital guru Brad Parscale was detained (but not charged) for a domestic dispute, and the video went viral. Federal agents boarded Guo's yacht and arrested Bannon, charging him with fraud for his role in the Build the Wall campaign. While Bannon and his business partners raised $25 million using crowdfunding, Bannon allegedly misused nearly $1 million on personal expenses. When asked about Bannon's arrest in late August, Trump was dismissive. "I feel very badly," he told reporters, "I haven't been dealing with him for a very long period of time." After pleading not guilty, Bannon was released on a $5 million bail bond.

With Trump facing so many headwinds—the terrible optics of the COVID response, Biden's surging poll numbers, and a lack of energy and cohesion in the meme wars—his generals got to work trying to turn things around. Bannon, Giuliani, and other Trump operatives made multiple efforts to destroy Biden's campaign. They'd been seeding the meme "Biden Crime Family" for months as a catchall, like Clinton Body Count, that would evoke wrongdoing without being specific. But it didn't seem to be cutting through the noise, and the social media platforms began banning it as a hashtag. Senate Republicans launched an official investigation into Biden's Ukraine dealings, which they hoped would be a problem, cast aspersions on the conduct of Biden's son Hunter, who had worked in Ukraine during the Obama years. But with the country distracted by COVID and nationwide protests, this didn't become the scandal Trump needed. Trumpworld was going to need a smoking gun, a specific artifact or statement about Ukraine and Hunter and Biden, something like the WikiLeaks drops and Podesta's emails in the 2016 election that had made Hillary Clinton look like a criminal. In September, they seemed to have found it.

On September 28, Bannon brought Dutch journalists onto his now very popular *War Room* show and boasted, "We have the hard drive. I have the hard drive of Hunter Biden."

"Oh really, what's on it?" the Dutch journalist asked.

"You'll see, stand by."

"Releasing it before the debate?" The debate was the next night.

"Stand by," Bannon said.

The laptop contents did not get mentioned in the debate the next day, but the words that Bannon had used—"stand by"—did, and they would reverberate around the far right. Fox News host Chris Wallace asked Trump, "Are you willing, tonight, to condemn white supremacists and militia groups and to say that they need to stand down and not add to the violence in a number of these cities as we saw in Kenosha and as we've seen in Portland?"

"Proud Boys," Trump said directly into the camera, "stand back and stand by. But I'll tell you what. I'll tell you what. Somebody has got to do something about antifa and the left because this is not a right-wing problem, this is a left wing. This is a left-wing problem." The attention from the president delighted the Proud Boys, who celebrated Trump's seemingly affirmative statement and turned it into memes, patches, and T-shirts. "Standing by, sir," Proud Boys national chairman Enrique Tarrio wrote on Parler that night.

It wasn't until early October that Trump operatives gave Hunter Biden's laptop to the *Wall Street Journal* as an exclusive story, but when it looked like the *Journal* might not publish anything scandalous enough to hurt Biden, Giuliani gave it to Trump's hometown broadside, the *New York Post*, as well. The *Post* published a story with the headline "Smoking-Gun Email Reveals How Hunter Biden Introduced Ukrainian Businessman to VP Dad," but it was not corroborated by any other news outlets at the time, and social media companies promptly took unprecedented action to censor the link, muting its impact. The *Journal* eventually published a short article concluding that the laptop didn't prove Biden had done anything wrong, as the final debate was unfolding live. The contents of the laptop were relegated out of mainstream news and to the likes of Guo and Bannon's GMedia empire. The last few days of October, GNews was practically nothing but pictures of Hunter Biden's nudes and sex videos reportedly taken from the hard drive. Its video sister site, GTV, published videos of the naked images, stitched together with anti-CCP rhetoric and text that alleged the Chinese Communist Party had used the images as blackmail against candidate Biden in order to control his agenda. It was the same allegation Never Trumpers and resistance fighters had lobbed against Trump in regard to his alleged "pee tape" and Putin's supposed use of it to blackmail him. A YouTuber named Lude, reported by former Guo associate John Pan to be the "number one propagandist for Guo Wengui," pushed the Hunter laptop pictures hard.

The notoriously uncensored 4chan became a dumping ground for Hunter's nudes, which were completely banned on mainstream social media, and the chaos-loving anons on /pol/ spent hours and hours looking at Hunter Biden's penis, hoping to find some evidence of a crime. Other anons who weren't on the Trump Train mocked them mercilessly. As

GNews's daily video updates focused on the laptop, claiming more evidence was about to drop, anons kept up hope there would be something damning, outside of photographs and videos of Hunter's sexual escapades and drug use. Some tried to make the case, unsuccessfully, that he'd been cavorting with underage women.

Soon the anons worried that they might be getting played, that they were being tasked by Bannon and Guo's team to make up for the media silence. "There has been zero mention of the hard drives on any of the MSM sites beyond some boilerplate bs," an anon said on October 26. "Nobody knows anything other than a vague 'hunter Biden has porn on his laptop'. No mention of GNews, of the photos/videos, of Bannon and Guo, etc. Total media blackout, so most normies here are in the dark as a result. That goes for MSNBC, CNN, and Fox. It's painfully obvious WHY they're being silent. Fucking grifters on all sides."

By October 27, anons were growing weary of looking at Hunter's genitals and turned on Guo and Lude's attempt to court their digital warrior energies. That day one admonished /pol/: "/pol/ sure loves to click, save and then post a whole lot of dick pics while hinting about corruption they don't post about," adding, "Ya want a different narrative, start with less

TO HONOR ALL
WHO SERVED

2019 - 2020
DICK PIC WAR

cock." "Less Hunter Biden dick pics. More Hitler," one anon begged on November 5, two days after Election Day, when MAGA was still holding out hope despite most votes having been counted and Biden showing an unbeatable lead.

It's clear from the conversation on /pol/ that a lot of the reason why Hunter's nudes didn't have anywhere near the stamina (pun intended, sorry) of the Pizzagate allegations against Clinton was that (a) Hunter was a man and so harder for /pol/ to hate, and (b) he appeared to be a virile man who slept with hot women, the kind of alpha male who anons aspired to be.

Despite Trump operatives trying to "pizzagate" the Hunter Biden laptop, with some assistance by Alex Jones and the QAnon community, they couldn't make it stick. After being banned from so many online services for his role in spreading Sandy Hook conspiracy theories, Jones didn't have the access to social media that he did in 2016, and QAnon was dealt a major blow when the social media companies began deplatforming their accounts en masse in October.

Trump wasn't deterred. He continued to push the idea that Biden was a criminal, his family was sketchy, and he was in cahoots with China. He called Biden a globalist, a liar, a bought-and-paid for establishment shill who was going to outlaw the auto industry and big oil and ship more jobs overseas. On November 2, the eve of Election Day, he tweeted dozens of times, including meme-war-style gems like this thread:

> Every corrupt force in American life that betrayed you and hurt your [sic] are supporting Joe Biden: The failed establishment that started the disastrous foreign wars; The career politicians that offshored your industries & decimated your factories; The open borders lobbyists . . .
>
> . . . that killed our fellow citizens with illegal drugs, gangs & crime; The far-left Democrats that ruined our public schools, depleted our inner cities, defunded our police, & demeaned your sacred faith & values; The Anti-American radicals defaming . . .
>
> . . . our noble history, heritage & heroes; and ANTIFA, the rioters, looters, Marxists, & left-wing extremists. THEY ALL SUPPORT JOE BIDEN!

But tweetstorms and memes weren't going to be enough this time. On November 3, as initial exit polling showed a reasonable Trump lead in eastern states, MAGA prepared to celebrate a second term and victory over the libs. Champagne waited on ice to be popped at Trump HQ. However, election experts had been warning for months that the early returns would create a "red mirage," showing a temporary Trump lead that would vanish as the full counts came in. The right discounted this warning, believing it would either not pan out or, worse, was part of a plot to steal the election from Trump.

Late at night after all the polls were closed, Fox News became the first media outlet to confirm that Trump had lost the election, by calling Arizona for Biden. Trump fumed and refused to concede—a final act of transgression that showed once again why he had been such a hero to the red-pilled right. MAGA turned on Fox, lashing out at the network that had, largely uncritically, supported the president for so many years. Trump fumed on Twitter: "Last night I was leading, often solidly, in many key States, in almost all instances Democrat run & controlled. Then, one by one, they started to magically disappear as surprise ballot dumps were counted. VERY STRANGE, and the 'pollsters' got it completely

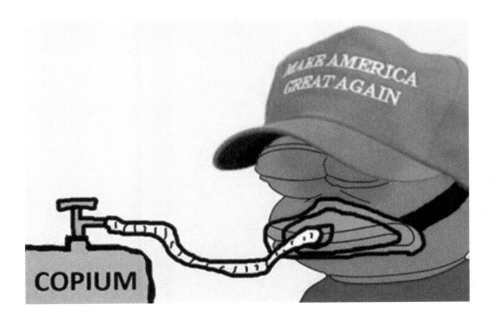

& historically wrong!" He and his team ramped up their sloganeering: "Stop the Count," "Stop the Fraud," and other such incantations.

As the weeks went on, and the numbers were clearly in Biden's favor, MAGA began publicly dealing with the reality that Trump might not get a second term. This "coping," denialism, and wishful thinking was widely mocked by Trump detractors on the left and right, eager to see his failed presidency taken off life support.

If Americans were hoping that Election Day would bring closure to a chaotic year, they were in for an unfortunate surprise. What happened next, in the postelection period, became the final absurd happening of the Trump era. Soon, the red-pilled right's insurgent mindset would turn into a literal insurrection.

Chapter 10

Stop the Steal

How Did We Get Here?

"If you don't fight like hell, you're not going to have a country anymore," President Trump told thousands gathered near the White House the morning of January 6, 2021. "So we're going to walk down Pennsylvania Avenue—I love Pennsylvania Avenue—and we're going to the Capitol, and we're going to try and give our Republicans—the weak ones, because the strong ones don't need any of our help—we're going to try and give them the kind of pride and boldness that they need to take back our country."

Tim "Baked Alaska" Gionet, former alt-right hanger-on and full-time MAGA troll, was livestreaming Trump's speech from the crowd, exclaiming, "Exactly! Exactly. They want us to back the blue, they got to back us!" He was one of thousands who took Trump's words literally, breaching the U.S. Capitol while Congress was in session to certify Biden's win. A veteran of the 2016 meme wars and one of only a few insurrectionists to have attended Unite the Right back in 2017, Gionet was an avatar for the red-pillers watching his livestream of the insurrection. His viewers told him where to go inside the building—"The boomers are storming the building! You're missing it!"—controlling him almost as if he was a live-action gaming character. They goaded him in the chat with shitposts, memes, and calls for violence: "America First!" "I just want violence," and "WHEN ARE PEOPLE GOING TO DIE BORING."

People were dying already, though the chat didn't know it yet. A woman was trampled on the steps as people broke past the police barrier and rushed toward the building. And in a few short moments, a Capitol police officer would shoot and kill a protester named Ashli Babbitt as she attempted to break into the House Chamber. Others would die in the aftermath. Four rioters lost their life on January 6. On January 7 Officer Brian D. Sicknick of the Capitol Police, who had been pepper-sprayed by rioters, died of a stroke in hospital. And four more police officers took their own lives in the following months.

Gionet missed the violence outside, but he captured the joyous chaos inside the building, the feeling that patriots were throwing an enormous party, that this was their moment. At one point he entered an office in the building and picked up the phone, entertaining the other protesters and his audience with a fake call to Trump. "America first is inevitable? Let's go! Fuck globalists!" he yelled into the phone. A young man near him laughed hysterically.

The events of that day were captured from hundreds of angles. Tens of thousands of video clips and photos from inside the insurrection were posted across the internet and uploaded to TV news. It may very well have been the most well-documented crime in human history. A steady diet of repetition on social media and memetic warfare had united a tacit coalition of white nationalists, conspiracists, religious zealots, zoomers, and boomers, alongside 147 representatives of the Republican party who had descended on the Capitol that day, to contest the 2020 presidential election results and place Donald Trump, illegally and unconstitutionally, in a second term.

It took all of the events of this book—all of the meme wars—to turn the brewing insurgency in America into an actual insurrection. The meme wars of the decade leading up to 2021 created movements, burnished the bona fides of movement leaders, entrenched ideologies, drafted new believers, and changed the landscape of the media ecosystem. If not for Occupy and BLM's innovative wires-to-the-weeds organizing tactics, assembling massive protests via online coordination would not have been possible. Without Gamergate, Milo Yiannopoulos and Mike Cernovich, for example, would not have been in the position to funnel young reactionaries to MAGA. Without the human biodiversity meme wars, white nationalists wouldn't have had enough troops to rally to Unite the Right. Steve Bannon and Michael Flynn might not have been able to build armies of digital soldiers

without Alex Jones's decades of NWO conspiracism. Without Anonymous-style hacktivism, you would not have gotten WikiLeaks. Without Pizzagate, QAnon could never have grown into a global conspiracy movement. And none of the above would have happened without the evolution of social media and the intensification of community building that took place online over this period and factored into it all.

Perhaps a January 6–like event would have taken place without Trump, and without any of these meme wars. We will never know. That a significant swath of the American public is profoundly unhappy with the way things are is now more of a given than ever. But it is undeniable that Trump harnessed and encouraged the antiestablishment energy found online, and that his status as president helped this energy move from the wires to the weeds. Stop the Steal, Trump's last gamble, showed him ready to exploit the very people who had voted for him and who he surely knew were susceptible to his lies.

The thing about meme wars is that winning them doesn't necessarily work out well for the fighters, nor does a win necessarily result in meaningful policy change. Stop the Steal failed to get Trump into the White House. Hundreds of people caught on camera that day were later arrested, Gionet included. In terms of resonance, the meme war definitely got ratings. It brought people from the wires to the weeds; it threatened the stability of an entire nation, became a household phrase, changed lives, changed the course of history. But to what end? If this book has demonstrated one thing, it's that memes can be popular and powerful and persistent while hurting the very people who spread them, and even the causes they represent. Still, if the intent was to disrupt the system, to spread the distrust that memes signified in their images and phrases, to flood the space with shit, as Bannon said, the meme war succeeded. The fallout lingers. Memes, like Melania Trump's famous jacket, really don't care. They have a life of their own.

The 2020 Stop the Steal meme war had its first big outing back in August 2020, when Trump announced at a rally, "The only way we're going to lose this election is if the election is rigged; remember that." It was an idea he would go on to repeat—in tweets about mail-in voter fraud, RNC speeches, and answers to press questions—throughout the election period. In September, as his poll numbers dwindled and mainstream media and the Cathedral classes publicly fretted about what he would do if he lost—a question they had been posing as a thought experiment since the earliest days of his presidency—Trump was asked point-blank at a White House press conference whether he would commit to a peaceful transfer of power. He demurred: "We're going to have to see what happens."

This comment belied the many different efforts that would soon be under way—from blocking recounts to filing lawsuits to contemplating the use of executive orders to stop the certification of the vote—to keep Trump in power. They all came under the heading of "Stop the Steal," a memetic phrase that actually dated back to Trump's first campaign. Roger Stone had come up with the meme in 2016, registering a website by that name when Trump had not yet been named the Republican nominee. Stone had done it because he anticipated that Trump wouldn't get the nomination at the Republican National Convention that year, and he planned to use the website to claim that the nomination had been stolen. Alex Jones picked up the meme back then, using it to organize a motley crew of bikers, white nationalists, and activists to force the RNC to nominate Trump. The plan was—in a foreshadowing of the events of 2020—to protest outside the convention center, and disrupt the proceedings if things did not go Trump's way. But in 2016 the RNC did nominate Trump, so the meme was put on ice.

When it was redeployed in 2020, the Stop the Steal meme had grown much bigger. And it represented Trump's last chance at remaining in the White House. As street fights, shootings, and stabbings involving militia groups and the Proud Boys ramped up, Trump's campaign sent out donation requests, asking people to join the "Army for Trump." Trump's old hatchet man, Bannon, devoted his morning and evening broadcasts to pushing rumors of ballot tampering and fraud. The Hunter Biden laptop fumble meant he had something to prove, and his *War Room* podcast would be devoted to Stop the Steal henceforth.

The MAGA coalition understood the gravity of a Trump loss. It was willing to risk everything to prevent it, even uniting uncomfortable bedfellows like Kirk's Turning Point USA with Infowarriors and Fuentes's Groypers to reach a common goal. Right-wing activist Ali Alexander

worked with Roger Stone to rally under a sprawling big tent using the hashtag #StopTheSteal, which morphed from a set of Facebook events into a traveling sideshow jumping from election-counting sites to state capitols in an effort to stop vote certification. On November 19, 2020, for instance, Alex Jones and Nick Fuentes shared a megaphone at a rally in front of the Georgia governor's mansion. Throughout November and December, some of these rallies were well attended and made for popular content on social media. Bannon promoted #StopTheSteal from the beginning, which led Facebook to terminate several of his pages, with a combined over 2.45 million followers.

Trumpworld repeated the same claims multiple times a day, redundantly across internet, cable, radio, and print, reinforcing the meme in search and recommendation algorithms. Finally center and left media had to respond, if only to acknowledge its totally ludicrous claims.

QAnon adherents universally supported Stop the Steal, and though Q seemingly tapped out on December 9, their final post being a video edit of "We're Not Gonna Take It," the movement continued in deeply entrenched alt-tech communities they'd been building out since getting kicked off the major platforms in October. The QAnon army would be mobilized by their community influencers in the coming weeks.

The online-distributed campaign strategy of Stop the Steal, combined with local actions in key states where counts were contested, created a potent mix of action in both wires and weeds. With all this excitement and buy-in for the meme on the right, #StopTheSteal quickly took on the feeling of a movement—a movement filled with frenzy.

Giuliani, who had urged Trump to declare he was the winner on election night, took the lead in setting an absurdist tone for the postelection period. As Trump's personal lawyer, he was on a crusade. On November 7, 2020, as ballots in Philadelphia were still being counted and Biden had yet to be officially named the president-elect, Giuliani called a press conference in the area. "Lawyers Press Conference at Four Seasons, Philadelphia. 11:00 A.M.," Trump tweeted. While reporters were preparing to make their way to the conference, Trump followed up and corrected himself. It wasn't at the Four Seasons Hotel, he said—but at Four Seasons Total Landscaping! The . . . what? The jokes wrote themselves. CNN reporter Jim Acosta tweeted, "Trump advisor tells me the campaign has 'nothing concrete' in terms of voter fraud," to which Hollywood producer Andy Lassner replied, "Yeah well I bet they got concrete at Four Seasons Total Landscaping."

The event became a meme in its own right within communities on both sides of the ideological divide. It was just too crazy to be true, and yet . . . it was happening. Worse still for Giuliani, once he assembled the press and began to make an announcement about . . . something, the phones of every reporter in the crowd started pinging like mad with breaking news alerts that it was all over: Biden had been declared the official president-elect. Many reporters ditched the Giuliani conference as he was still talking. The die-hard Trump supporters still hung on every word, however, and distributed the news of every court case and state senate hearing. They took every loss as a sign that the deep state was working against Trump, and time was running out. So they turned to the courts to try to get the election results overturned.

D.C. outsiders Lin Wood and Sidney Powell became the Trump campaign's legal team. They pushed the specific claim that certain voting systems made by a company called Dominion had been rigged in some way. Powell immediately made herself memorable by invoking a meme that dated back to 2010 to explain her legal strategy. She would, she said on Lou Dobbs's Fox News show on November 13, "release the Kraken"—a reference dating back to the 1981 film *Clash of the Titans* that was also a popular battle cry in meme culture.

"It's gonna be biblical," Powell said on Newsmax on November 21, 2020.

With financial and motivational support from Mike Lindell, the CEO and founder of the direct-to-consumer pillow company MyPillow, as well as reportedly from Patrick Byrne, the former CEO of Overstock.com, Wood and Powell filed more than sixty lawsuits trying to overturn the election outcome. Every case was thrown out, except for one, which wasn't about fraud and according to fact checkers had no bearing on any election results. The cases were "fantastical," as one judge put it. None had their intended result, but the flurry of legal filings gave the red-pilled right something official to point to, and kept hopes alive that one of these might result in a change to the election count. Even months into Biden's first term, STS supporters like Lindell continued to fan the flames of election fraud to increasingly smaller, and angrier, audiences.

As a meme, Stop the Steal functioned like a throwback to the technopolitics of the 2011 Occupy Wall Street campaign. It mobilized all the red-pilled right that was still on board with Trump, from the Groypers to QAnon to the Proud Boys. They began staging rallies and protests across the country—the most notable of which was perhaps a protest in D.C. on December 12, which resulted in multiple stabbings and the Proud Boys burning BLM banners. While Stop the Steal shared some of the open-source participation and distributed protest tactics of Occupy, it was born of elites who were reaping massive benefits from being close to Trump. Like the Tea Party, moneyed interests helped organize working-class white Americans' grievances for their own gain, leaving patriots to foot the bill and serve the time. The red-pilled right were merely the foot soldiers, cannon fodder that would go on to bear the heaviest costs for their participation.

On December 19, 2020, Trump accelerated, tweeting that his followers should plan to show up for a "wild" protest on January 6. If any other person had called for a wild protest, there would not be so much debate about Stop the Steal. But Trump was the sitting president of the United

States, and in that role was the commander-in-chief over the U.S. military. He had refused to concede the election, calling into question America's entire electoral process. On January 2 he called Georgia's election "illegal and invalid," right before an important Senate runoff that ended up going to the Democrats. Now he was calling on his supporters to show up in person at the nation's seat of government and be "wild."

The Gathering Storm

People heeded Trump's call. Their president had told them to be in D.C., and so thousands of people came. Trump's trusted operatives and supporters planned a rally for January 6 in the President's Park, south of the White House in an area known as the Ellipse, put on by Women for America First. They secured permits and lined up an explosive list of speakers, including Eric Trump and Representative Paul Gosar. Trump would be the closer.

The protesters and people drafted into the meme war had their own plans for the wild protest, too. Partaking in the January 6 Stop the Steal protest was not as simple as sharing an image on Facebook; they had to buy plane tickets and bus tickets, figure out hotel rooms, and learn whether they could carry their gun on their flight into D.C. They organized caravans and even booked private jets, and many, like the militia groups scattered among the crowd, came prepared to detain, or harm, government officials. Some protesters even brought lumber and schematics for erecting a gallows on the Capitol steps.

Anyone watching Trump-dedicated Twitter or forums on sites like Reddit replacement TheDonald.win in the days before and the morning of the insurrection would have seen conversations between insurgents trying to decide whether a gallows or a guillotine would be more effective, or figuring out the best places to park for the riot, or wondering whether a garage's three-hour limit would allow enough time for the insurrection.

Livestreamers promoted the event on their channels. Flights into D.C., which had still been relatively underbooked due to the ongoing COVID pandemic, filled with Stop the Steal protesters. They came from every state in the union to do what their president told them to do: protest an undemocratic subversion of freedom. Attendees bought new clothes and flags and hats and camera equipment. They made signs that read "Stop the Steal," "Jesus Is King," "1776," "Don't Tread on Me," 'MAGA," "Q," and "WWG1WGA." Someone even made a green flag for /pol/'s imaginary kingdom Kekistan. Militia groups trained in the woods. Hotels filled up. As thousands descended on the nation's capital, their plans and actions were out there for anyone paying attention to see.

Though Facebook had officially banned the phrase Stop the Steal and groups going by that name, Bannon and others easily got around the ban by changing the names of their groups. On January 5, 2021, Bannon posted to a Stop the Steal Facebook page that he ran, "TAKE ACTION. THEY ARE TRYING TO STEAL THE ELECTION." On his *War Room* podcast that day, he announced, "All hell is going to break loose tomorrow."

Many were already in D.C., getting ready for the next day's happening. At the eight-hour Save America rally put on by Ali Alexander at Freedom Plaza, crowds and audiences online heard from people like Flynn, Stone, Wood, Jones, and a litany of elected officials from all across the United States, as well as religious leaders and minor social media stars. All manner of red-pilled-right beliefs were on display—from QAnon talking points to evangelical pro-life positions to libertarian idealism to fascistic idolizing of strongman leaders. "Lock her up" chants broke out when Nancy Pelosi's name was mentioned. On the stage were Gadsden and MAGA and Trump flags billowing along with the Stars and Stripes. Behind the stage a huge sign read "Jesus Is King."

"I'll tell you who I am excited here to see," Jones screamed to the assembled crowd that night. "It's you, the American people, a unified resistance to the new world order!" He was joined by members of a wide assortment of hardcore MAGA factions, from QAnon adherents to militia groups.

"Tomorrow is a great day. We don't quietly take the election fraud," Jones said. "This will be their Waterloo; this will be their destruction. Whatever happens to President Trump in fifteen days, he is still the elected president of this Republic and we do not recognize the Communist Chinese agent Joe Biden or his controllers!" In his classic screaming style, he declared: "We commit to war against the globalists and we commit to truth and we will NEVER SURRENDER!" The red-pilled right was readying for war.

The next day was gray in D.C., though the rain had let up. The Women for America First rally officially started at 9:00 A.M., but people began milling around early. News crews were on scene to cover the event live, some of whom witnessed people telling other protesters to forcibly enter the Capitol after President Trump's speech. The word of this plan spread through the growing crowd.

While the speeches were still going on at 11:35 A.M., video shows Proud Boys members already near the Capitol, yelling, "Let's take the fucking Capitol!" Tarrio had told them this was their D-day, and they were early, and ready. Reporters wrote that they saw different groups of men in tactical gear preparing for the assault in different places around the Capitol.

At 11:57, Trump took the stage. He spoke for an hour and fourteen minutes. In that time, members of the Proud Boys had led other insurgents through the first row of flimsy barricades set up outside the west side of the capitol, and the Senate and House had convened in the Capitol Building to certify the vote. The rest of the crowd at Trump's speech made their way to the Capitol, too. By 1:52 P.M., Alex Jones was screaming into his bullhorn, telling insurgents to turn around. It was far too late. They were climbing the scaffolding set up for Biden's inaguration stage, attacking police with bear spray and their own shields, using their flagpoles to push in doors and windows. Jones said he had expected the president to walk with everyone, to walk with him. They expected Stone to walk with them, too. But that didn't happen. In fact, though high-profile red-pilled-right influencers like Jones and Fuentes did walk to the Capitol, they did not enter the building.

When people began clashing with police and defacing the Capitol, Jones screamed into his megaphone for them to stop: "We are not antifa! We are not BLM! You're amazing. I love ya, but let's march around to the other side and let's not fight the police and give the system what they want! We are peaceful. We won this election. As much as I love seeing the Trump flags flying over this, we need to not have the confrontation with the police. They're going to make that the story."

The MAGA crowds did not listen. Over the din of the insurrection, most couldn't even hear him.

The War for the Story

The optics of the insurrection were, to put it bluntly, insane from the start. The foot soldiers of Stop the Steal recorded themselves breaking windows, ransacking offices, and screaming meme slogans in the hallways of the Capitol. Members of the Oath Keepers, Proud Boys, and other militia groups, who were major instigators of the day's violence, stood out clearly in their uniforms and tactical gear on video, appearing extremely well prepared for what they would later claim was spontaneous violence. All of this was watched live by their fans and their families, as well as by law enforcement, the media, and a stunned nation and world. The "story" of what was happening before the world's eyes was pretty clear on its face: Americans were attacking their own government, and seemed to be having a lot of fun doing it.

The massive online footprint the insurrectionists left was picked through as it was happening by civilian researchers and law enforcement—an open-source investigation following an open-source insurrection. Streamers like Gionet left crucial trails of evidence behind, capturing characters in their feeds later identified by their loved ones, online sleuths, or police. Many boasted on social media of their presence, with little concern for the ramifications of that, or awareness of the laws they were breaking. Some stole mementos like podiums or computers or documents and posted photos of those too. Others smashed windows and smeared feces on the floor, documenting their antics in selfies and videos. One sheriff's lieutenant who had traveled from Texas to the Capitol that day posted on Facebook, "Not gonna lie. . . . .aside from my kids, this was, indeed, the best day of my life." She was later fired for her participation.

The reaction from the establishment, including the right-wing establishment, was initially one of shock and horror as they watched it all live. For the right, the politically savvy thing to do seemed to be to distance themselves from this mayhem. Even Fox News hosts Sean Hannity, Laura Ingraham, and *Fox & Friends* host Brian Kilmeade were horrified, frantically texting Trump's chief of staff, Mark Meadows, that Trump needed to come out and condemn the violence. "Please, get him on TV. Destroying everything you have accomplished," Kilmeade texted Meadows, imploring the president to urge his supporters to leave the Capitol.

Instead, as Trump's supporters attacked police and roved the halls of the Capitol looking for Vice President Pence, he tweeted, "These are the things and events that happen when a sacred landslide election victory is so unceremoniously & viciously stripped away from great patriots who have been badly & unfairly treated for so long. Go home with love & in peace. Remember this day forever!"

On TV, these same hosts were downplaying what was happening or blaming it on leftists. The initial narrative of what exactly was happening was chaotic, and mainstream media struggled to tell the story of what memesters have come to call "J6." The rundown of the day quickly became a cacophony of partisan positions fighting for prominence, while journalists and law enforcement ran down footage and compared the thousands of hours of streams forensically. The insurrectionists were allowed to board their buses and their private jets and go home. Congresspeople returned that night to certify the election, and Biden was named the president-elect. For a brief minute, time seemed suspended. It appeared like most insurrectionists were going to walk away from the breach of the U.S. Capitol without so much as a slap on the wrist. Only a few people were arrested that day, but law enforcement used all the evidence that the insurrectionists had left online, as well as tips from family, friends, and the public, to arrest more than six hundred people who broke into the Capitol that day over the course of the next year.

Though these arrests took time, the tech companies deplatformed insurrectionists en masse much faster. On January 7 Facebook banned Trump from the platform for two years. Twitter kicked him off permanently the next day. Stop the Steal content was banned across both platforms. Twitter deleted more than seventy thousand QAnon-related accounts. Nick Fuentes was finally banned from Twitter. YouTube promised to suspend any videos with false claims about election fraud. Ali Alexander was kicked off every social media platform, as well as PayPal and Venmo. Mike Lindell, Lin Wood, Sidney Powell, 8kun administrator Ron Watkins, Roger Stone, and Steve Bannon were all kicked off Twitter. Many of the Himalaya movement Twitter accounts Bannon and Guo had used through 2020 to push disinformation campaigns were also removed. Within days, corporate America, realizing that there was no way to deny the role their platforms had played in enabling the insurrection that the entire world had watched unfold on their sites, removed tons of seditious content and many accounts that they had previously allowed.

The immediate bipartisan consensus from elected officials was that an assault on the Republic had taken place. Many clearly placed the blame on Trump. "It breaks my heart that my friend, a president of consequence, would allow yesterday to happen," Republican senator Lindsey Graham said the next day. "And it will be a major part of his presidency. When it comes to accountability, the president needs to understand that his actions were the problem, not the solution." Similarly, Kevin McCarthy, who had been a strong Trump supporter throughout his presidency, said, "The President bears responsibility for Wednesday's attack on Congress by mob rioters. He should have immediately denounced the mob when he saw what was unfolding."

But soon this consensus would unravel. As the danger of that day receded, and the evidence was deleted from social media, the battle for how the event would be remembered and who would be blamed for it began. Democrats demanded that Trump be brought up on impeachment charges again and charged with sedition. Taking cues from right-wing media, many Republicans downplayed what had happened, just as they had entertained dead-end investigations into the election results and machines. Most importantly, they didn't want to give any credence to the idea that Trump should be impeached for a second time for his actions leading up to and during the insurrection. "We must come together and put this anger and division behind us," Ted Cruz said two days after the insurrection. The mainstream GOP didn't want to take any responsibility; they were clearly invested in putting this matter aside as quickly as possible.

With the facts and optics of the day not in their favor, conservative pundits and far-right influencers got to work spinning conspiracy theories and alternate interpretations of the insurrection. Laura Ingraham suggested that antifa could have been among the rioters. Sean Hannity made similar claims, as did Rush Limbaugh and elected representatives Matt Gaetz, Mo Brooks, and Paul Gosar.

On January 13, President Trump was brought up for a second time on articles of impeachment, this time for his role in inciting the insurrection. A month later, on February 13, a Republican-led Senate acquitted him. The line the Republican Party repeated was that it would be best for the country to just move on. The day after the impeachment trial ended, Senator Graham changed his tune: "The speech on Jan. 6 was not an incitement to violence. Every politician has used the word 'fight,' 'fight hard,' so I don't think that he caused the riot." McCarthy too walked back his condemnation of Trump, after it was clear that, even without a Twitter account or a presidential seal, he would maintain his stronghold on the party and its now red-pilled base.

By April, half of Republicans polled said the insurrection was either a peaceful protest or staged by antifa. The pro-Trump meme wars presented Americans with a binary choice: Were you for him or against him? Despite what they had seen with their own eyes, for the GOP to condemn the people who had stormed the Capitol on January 6 as insurrectionists would be to condemn Trump, and the identity of their own base. They couldn't risk distancing themselves from the red-pilled right, which had been schooled to line up behind Trump. Right-wing influencers and pundits had their work cut out for them in shaping a counternarrative, not only about the direction of the GOP but about objective political truth as well. Tucker Carlson rose to the challenge at the year anniversary mark with a three-part documentary series arguing that the insurrection had been a deep state trap to persecute conservatives. "The U.S. government has in fact launched a new war on terror," he said. "But it's not against Al Qaeda, it's against American citizens."

Following the insurrection, and the subsequent arrests of many attendees, MAGA began turning on cops, just as they had turned on the security state. Pro-police memes like Blue Lives Matter and Thin Blue Line were called into question for the first time, as the people fighting the police on J6 were previously those who loudly supported militarized law enforcement. As Officer Daniel Hodges was fighting off the insurrectionists, he saw one of them carrying a Thin Blue Line flag. One video even showed an insurrectionist using the pole of a Thin Blue Line flag to pummel a Capitol Police officer—an irony that liberals were quick to point out.

Liberals mocked the conspiracy theories and frantic coping strategies employed by MAGA to justify January 6. And for many in the Cathedral— especially historians of autocracy as well as "thought leader" resistance fighters—the main reaction was "We told you so." When Trump first became president, prognosticators in academia and on the left and some on the right had warned that he could destroy America, destroy democracy. People who had lived under dictatorships and fascist regimes published articles in major U.S. newspapers and magazines warning Americans that the United States could be next. At the time, many if not most of these warnings were considered by the mainstream to be hysterical; America, after all, had enough checks and balances in place to ensure that its democracy would survive an unpredictable president. American democracy, scholars and journalists wrote, was far bigger than one man, or even one political party. It could not so easily be threatened. But on January 6, it became clear that those assumptions were naive.

The idea that American democracy was special, better than the fragile democracies elsewhere in the world, has been a key factor in the concept of American exceptionalism held across both right and left. American democracy was supposedly inviolate. But then a mob managed to break into its house and stop the certification of the election of a president. How were checks and balances supposed to deal with an insurgency that came from the Oval Office itself, and that was backed by thousands of citizens who believed not only that they were acting as patriots but that the only way to save America was by subverting its democratic processes?

America Made Meme

At the first hearing of the Select Committee to Investigate the January 6th Attack on the United States Capitol, which finally convened on July 27, 2021, Capitol Police officer Harry Dunn testified that after fending off insurrectionists that day, he found himself overcome with emotion. On a bench outside the Capitol afterward, he sat comparing notes with another Black officer. "I began yelling, how the *blank* could something like this happen? *Is this America?* I began sobbing. Officers came over to console me."

Moments before, Dunn had described trying to keep insurrectionists out of the building, fighting them off, hearing them plot to steal his gun, administering aid to fellow officers, and realizing in horror that law enforcement had been completely overrun. As the crowd first surged toward him, Dunn said he asked a group of people to please leave the Capitol grounds. They refused, telling him they had been invited by the president. They insisted the election had been stolen because no one had actually voted for Joe Biden, Dunn recalled.

> I'm a law enforcement officer and I do my best to keep politics out of my job, but in this circumstance, I responded, "Well, I voted for Joe Biden. Does my vote not count? Am I nobody?" That prompted a torrent of racial epithets. One woman in a pink MAGA shirt yelled, "You hear that, guys? This n–gger voted for Joe Biden." Then the crowd—perhaps around 20 people—joined in, screaming, "Boo, fucking n–gger." No one had ever, ever called me a n–gger while wearing the uniform of a Capitol Police officer. In the days following the attempted insurrection, other Black officers shared with me their own stories of racial abuse on January 6. One officer told me he had never in his entire 40 years of life been called a n–gger to his face

and that streak ended on January 6. Yet another Black officer later told me that he had been confronted by insurrectionists in the Capitol who told him, "Put your gun down or we'll show you what kind of n–gger you really are."

After Dunn spoke, Representative Adam Schiff, Democrat from California, returned to the question the officer had posed that day: "Is this America?" It was the same question that had haunted him since January 6, Schiff said. "I'm very interested to know your thoughts on the answer to that question. Is this America, what you saw?"

"To answer your question, frankly, I guess it is America," Dunn answered. "It shouldn't be. But I guess that's the way that things are. I don't condone it. I don't like it. But if you look at our history, American history, our country existed because they won a war, our colonies and state lines and boundaries exist because of violence and wars, so, it sounds silly, but I guess it is America. We represent the good side of America, the people that actually believe in decency, human decency, and we appeal to the good in people."

The exchange was powerful. News organizations covered it live and referred back to it often. Schiff choked back tears as he thanked Dunn and his fellow officers for protecting elected officials that day. "I believe in America," Schiff said, "because of people like you." The America that Schiff and Dunn described was the one that had been assaulted, the multiracial democratic republic that they both served, the America of the American dream, of Martin Luther King Jr's dream, a place that despite its mistakes was always trying to be better, more fair, more equitable, more just.

But the insurrectionists were fighting for a different America. On January 6, parties on both sides of the barricades around the Capitol Building were representing America, fighting for America, believing that they were doing their duty for their America. But their ideas of America couldn't have been more different. The left and the mainstream saw America as a multiracial democracy whose arc of history bent toward justice. The red-pilled right saw America as a once-great nation that was increasingly slipping away from them. The multiracial part of America's democracy, to them, was a bastardization of American democracy. In fact, it was a betrayal of the pure America they believed in.

Competing interpretations of what America is and who it serves are older than the nation itself. As the historian Colin Woodard put it in his book *American Nations,*

> Americans have been deeply divided since the days of Jamestown and Plymouth. The original North American colonies were settled by people from distinct regions of the British Islands, and from France, the Netherlands, and Spain, each with their own religious, political, and ethnographic characteristics. Throughout the colonial period, they regarded one another as competitors—for land, settlers, and capital—and occasionally as enemies. . . . Only when London began treating its colonies as a single unit—and enacted policies threatening nearly all—did some of these distinct societies briefly come together to win a revolution and create a joint government. Nearly all of them would seriously consider leaving the Union in the eighty-year period after Yorktown; several went to war to do so in the 1860s. . . . There isn't and never has been one America.

As Woodard notes, white men who did not want to pay taxes to the crown managed to come together to create America in 1776, and less than a century later it would be race that drove them to go to war with each other. These white colonists of means were unwilling to legally recognize the Indigenous inhabitants already on the land or extend citizenship to people of other races.

This was the contradiction at the heart of the American project. The settlement of the land now known as America was the result of genocide, and the economic engine that turned the new society into a global powerhouse was built on the brutal labor of enslaved Africans—and yet America was also a place of asylum for white colonists fleeing the English monarchy. America was from the start both a place of oppression and a bastion of freedom. America's very name encapsulates these contradictions: the nation was named after Amerigo Vespucci, who first argued that the lands Columbus conquered were not the West Indies but a whole new continent. Amerigo is an Italian version of the German name Emmerich, which can mean "ruler of the universe," "ruler of labor," or "ruler of the home." America would give its colonists the freedom to rule the world through the oppression of those deemed unworthy of being American themselves.

Birthright citizenship was not codified until 1868, three years after the Civil War, when America began searching in earnest for its identity as a nation. Even then, it did not grant Indigenous people, Black Americans, or women the same rights as property-owning white men. America itself was a meme, one whose identity has shifted across institutions and time, especially across politics and the media, where race is the penultimate wedge issue.

What Does It Mean to Be American Today?

It is the laws and the constitution that make a nation, where in exchange for consent to be governed, citizens enjoy rights, freedoms, and security. French historian Alexis de Tocqueville came to revere American democracy as something unique, but also dangerous due to the tendency of Americans toward individualism. In *Democracy in America*, he warned that such individualism could cause Americans "to draw apart with his family and his friends; so that, after he has thus formed a little circle of his own, he willingly leaves society at large to itself."

The best way to guard against too much individualism gumming up the works of democracy would be to maintain a strong free press, Tocqueville argued, educate the public, and uphold that "the gradual progress of equality is something fated." Thomas Jefferson agreed. In a letter dated January 6, 1816, Jefferson wrote of the importance of education and a free press in maintaining America's tenuous democracy. "If a nation expects to be ignorant and free, in a state of civilization, it expects what never was and never will be," he wrote, suggesting a "literary fund" devoted to educating American youth as a means of ensuring that the new nation remained engaged in the business of governance, and protected from "toryism, fanaticism and indifference." Yet Jefferson, remembered as the author of the Declaration of Independence and an exemplary president, was himself a slaveholder, who sired children, through sexual coercion, with Sally Hemings, a woman at the time considered to be his property.

Over time, to be "an American" meant to be a full citizen of the United States, a status reserved for free white men. After the Civil War, the U.S. government created hundreds of treaties with Native Americans, only to break those treaties and exact extraordinary violence against the country's original inhabitants while driving them westward. At the beginning of the twentieth century, when Woodrow Wilson popularized the slogan "America First" as an argument against fighting in World War II, the question quickly became "Who exactly are we putting first, if we put America first?" The belief that "real Americans" were Protestant white people of Anglo descent was pervasive enough during the "America First" debate in the following years that whoever did not conform to that designation was considered a "hyphenate American," defined by their African, Italian, or Catholic heritage.

In the early 2000s, as DNA ancestry tests became more popular, there was an effort to redefine the meaning of Native American by locating that trait in blood. The attempt to classify Native Americans by paternity testing and DNA ancestry was a return to the same white logic of citizenship offered throughout American history. Equality under the law is not fated; it's fought for, like the fight against slave ownership that motivated the Civil War and the long battle for civil rights for Black people that followed emancipation.

But in the decades after the Civil War, as the definition of who counted as American shifted, there emerged a new need to define national identity. Theodore Roosevelt responded with a call for a "new nationalism," one that exemplified a "melting pot" of nationalities, even as he privately believed—as historian Jill Lepore points out in her book *This America: The Case for the Nation*—the metaphor was only applicable to Europeans. Not long after Roosevelt lost the election to Wilson in 1912, there was a global rise of white nationalism as the Klan began to reassert itself in the south and Hitler came to power in Germany. The 1964 Immigration Act opened the doors to an unprecedented wave of immigration to America, setting a course of demographic change and newfound cultural diversity that likely would have troubled the (white) Founding Fathers.

So what does it mean to be an American today? The answer depends on which group you are in and which group perceives you as their enemy; it depends on whether you view America as a land mass or an idea, as a nation of immigrants or a nation of conquerors.

Is America just a meme—an authorless idea that's been remixed and reinvented countless times since its first use to describe the "new world"? It's a legally defined entity with material borders, certainly, but also an abstract idea that resonates across history, creed, class, and nationality. Memes pass through generations and cultures and mean different things to different people. One of the most enduring and oldest meme wars ever fought on U.S. soil is who gets to be considered an American and who gets to define what America really is. And it's a war that the red-pilled right is still fighting today, in meme-driven online culture wars and in very real battles against voting rights and racial justice in school curriculums.

America Online

In the months after the insurrection, the question of how such a thing could have happened to America was continuously debated. We hope this book has provided some answers and made it clear that one enormous factor boils down to this: the internet moves faster than society's institutions.

The architecture of the internet, and social media in particular, creates the perfect conditions for community in-groups to form and bond over shared interests, even though, in most instances, their members don't know each other in real life or form the solid friendships they might develop through membership in, say, a bowling league or some other offline group. The algorithmic reinforcement of social media platforms and search engines leads, through repeated and constant exposure to similar ideas, to the intensification of belief systems, and creates community around shared grievances. The incentives baked into the design of social media—from the clout gained by likes and retweets to the power bestowed by virality—influence how people behave online. These incentives lead people and media organizations to post more exciting, inflammatory, or polarizing information so as to reach the most people, since tech companies have trained their algorithms to boost that kind of content.

Internet memes take advantage of all of these conditions. Like a bacterial infection that grows in a compromised immune system, political internet memes evolved to dominate the networked internet age. They are tiny packets of emotion-laden information that in a few words or images can convey worldviews. They can become red pills and lead people down rabbit holes. Over the course of the last decade such memes spread from their origins as reactions in Reddit threads and 4chan boards to everywhere—Instagram comments and TikTok videos and hashtags. They not only spread from obscure corners of the internet to larger platforms but also jumped out of the online world into the weeds, showing up on billboards, T-shirts, and flags, coming out of the mouths of presidents and elected officials and celebrities.

The internet accelerated the culture wars, allowing a piece of misinformation or a slogan to travel the world in seconds. When the president of a nation has the speed and scale of social media at his fingertips, a tweet can instantly become a matter of national concern. This speed also completely changed the role that the old gatekeepers played in the culture wars. The media and pundits of former eras had time to think through arguments about a given social debate and present them in the pages of the newspaper or on a TV screen. As communications scholar Manuel Castells explains in his 2009 book *Communication Power*, social media has ushered in an era of mass self-communication. "The message is self-generated, the definition of the potential receiver(s) is self-directed, [and] the retrieval of specific messages (or content) is self-selected." More than simply delivering content, social media provides emergent groups an opportunity to find one another, coordinate, and create social change without channeling their momentum through the mainstream media.

In the era of Walter Cronkite, the press had a monopoly on the presentation of ideas, picking which writers to feature in the pages of magazines and who to invite on TV. In this way, the press also maintained control of its own image and its purpose in a democracy. Now opinion is formed in hordes of online accounts, consensus shaped by the people with the loudest voices and biggest followings, and often by whoever is willing to eschew ambivalence and nuance in favor of certitude. And the media landscape itself is fragmented in countless ways—small websites and big ones, platforms and paywalls, partisan positions and business models.

After the success of Fox News in the 1990s, the rise of the internet inspired the creation of partisan media ecosystems and echo chambers. All of this has changed who wields influence in the culture, and contributed directly to a massive loss of trust in the people presenting facts, and even in the facts themselves. On the internet, separating truth from lies is extremely difficult, a fact that meme warriors and propagandists can capitalize on to deny reality or present an alternative world.

And internet memes made the culture wars funny and easy to engage in, in contrast to the dour Christian conservatism of the twentieth century, enlisting millions of digital foot soldiers who didn't need to take religion or politics seriously to partake. Memes function as the social glue for communities, binding them together in a common language, with shared in-jokes and sworn enemies. And in this way, they also help different subcultures online form alliances for specific reasons, as we've seen so many times in the past decade—from He Will Not Divide Us to "Subscribe to PewDiePie."

And memes are badges of identity. The hashtag #Resist in a Twitter bio conveys membership in a political group and a certain approach to politics. Ditto "America First." For young people who are forging their identities in the crucible of the internet, memes are a way to practice politics. Instead of having to join a bunch of different college clubs or political organizations, young adults can try on being a fascist or Communist behind the veil of pseudonymity.

The most powerful memes trigger an emotional response, be it laughter or rage. They are powerful shortcuts to provoking reactions. And participating in meme wars is fun, and rewarding: it taps the dopamine button in our brain that craves feedback and acceptance. Memes reinforce an individual's worldview and help define their enemies. The emotion involved in meme wars is a huge part of what makes them intoxicating, what drafts people into them in the first place and keeps them burning. When someone gets red-pilled, a reasonable emotional response is anger: they've been lied to. And that anger leads to the natural question: What else have I been lied to about? The further they go down the red-pilled rabbit hole, the more angry they likely become. You would be pissed, too, if you sincerely thought the story you'd been told about the world was a lie. This anger is a driving force behind any meme war.

During the course of the events in this book, Trump became the most important political avatar of meme culture, and as we have said, this had a lot to do with his charisma, his transgressiveness, his desire to be in the spotlight. But his success as a meme warrior also came from his ability to tap into the emotions motivating people, their grievances and their desires. Like the best memes, Trump resonated with his audience. He reflected their anger back to them; he became the symbol they wanted him to be—both a strong patriarch and a political outsider.

By explicit or tacit approval, Trump legitimized the extreme world-views of reactionary online communities, inviting them from the wires into the weeds of the government. His political playbook has been to tap into and amplify people's fears—fears of economic insecurity, of others surpassing them in the class hierarchy, of falling behind. To the white men who felt that the twenty-first century was moving away from them, prioritizing the rights and needs of everyone but them and at their expense, Trump said: I am one of you. But it's important to realize that Trump didn't create these grievances, and they did not end when he left the White House. He capitalized on them.

Trump's prolific use of social media to shape political reality in real time, coupled with a reactionary online army, accelerated the meme wars and brought them into the streets. He acted as a mechanism to move memetic ideas from 4chan to Reddit to Twitter to the pages of executive orders. Moving fringe ideas from the wires into the weeds was his super-power, and one of the ways he kept the red-pilled right in thrall.

So what was the result of all these meme wars? Not many material policy changes. Occupy didn't lead to policies that lessened the economic divide in this nation. Gamergate didn't kick women out of gaming—in fact, gaming companies responded by doubling down on their desire to diversify their audiences. Games are filled with more nonwhite male characters now than ever before, and the industry that makes them is shoveling in money. It is true that racial red pills sown during this decade to justify white supremacy have led not only to historic rises in neofas-cist street organizing but to the idea that somehow white people are under attack from our nation's legal and educational institutions. Ideas like the deep state and the New World Order, once the language of the fringe, are common terms in political debate. This is a legacy we will be wading through for years.

But these meme wars were not a win for the Republican Party or the Democrats. They were not a win for the people who fought them, many of whose lives they ruined. Rather, they caused pain and grief and death and harassment and distraction and an insurrection. And fleeting laughs, perhaps—but the message of the past decade of meme wars is still that the only way to win is to not play.

There's no single magic technocratic solution. Meme wars are a tactical adaptation of culture wars, and in the networked age, they are here to stay. Platforms like Facebook (now Meta) often argue that they are not responsible for the content on their websites because they are merely displaying what users post, but that argument is false. Platforms directly shape the world by sorting, ranking, filing, and broadcasting information in different proportions to different groups based upon platform companies' algorithms.

But meme wars and the impacts they have on lives and culture are not something we can fix with a single tweak to an algorithm or a new free speech law. No social media company employs a single algorithm, but rather they are composed of hundreds if not thousands of inter-locking instructions that can be tweaked to increase or decrease the proportion of different kinds of content. These algorithms can also be manipulated directly by hackers who can take over accounts or overrun servers, influencers who ask their followers to take a specific action, and networked factions who come together spontaneously to meet the moment. Politics plays an immensely important role in how communi-cation infrastructure is designed, distributed, maintained, and trans-formed locally, nationally, and globally. The wedge issues of the United States are not the same as those in Myanmar, Brazil, or Russia, but networked propaganda has come to play a significant role in most coun-tries where there is robust access to the internet.

While Andrew Breitbart used to say "Politics is downstream from culture," our research into a decade of meme wars demonstrates that culture is downstream from infrastructure. From Occupy to the January 6 insurrection, the communication infrastructure adopted by insurgents, coupled with favorable social conditions maintained by political, news, and economic elites, has shaped how they reach new audiences and proliferate. Perhaps ironically, a fringe group's ability to sway main-stream media and political agendas depends upon their ability to be noticed and amplified by the same institutions they revile. As Whitney Phillips and Ryan Milner note in *You Are Here: A Field Guide for Navigating Polarized Speech, Conspiracy Theories, and Our Polluted Media Landscape*, journalists get caught in the crosshairs of meme wars more and more frequently as they traverse and attempt to decipher online communities, where extremist groups see them as a political opportu-nity to spread red pills to the public. Rarely do internet users depend on only one platform for communication, and the more contentious their activities, the more specific these groups will be about adopting infra-structure that openly commits to anti-surveillance and free speech prin-ciples. For global tech companies, this creates a conundrum, where they must meet opposing demands from consumers, especially governments and advertisers.

Safiya Noble and Sara Roberts, information studies professors at UCLA, argue that tech companies have a moral and ethical responsibility to ensure that their systems are delivering high-quality information, a role librarians have played in the past. Global tech companies must build products that conform to the standards and regulations of many nations, and if they cannot meet those standards, they must either choose not to do business in that country or to build a product that can. However, in the United States especially, tech companies have consistently lobbied to keep their products free from government oversight, often claiming—like the red-pilled right—to embody the ethos of the U.S. Constitution in their strong commitment to free speech, particularly for U.S. citizens. Politicians employ soft power to influence the design decisions of platform companies both overtly, by calling them out publicly in the news and holding congressional hearings about the safety of their products, and covertly, by holding close relationships among these powerful elites. As a result, politicians willing to employ dirty tricks like disinformation, brigading, and botnets tend to benefit from the hands-off approach that Facebook and Google adopted in the 2020 election. Twitter has taken a different line, employing much more strict terms of service. Advertisers, supported by campaigns designed by advocacy coalitions like Change the Terms and Stop Hate for Profit, exercise soft power to challenge tech companies to implement their own policies on users.

You might have seen memes going around about that. You might have shared them. You might have laughed. Like all memes, some were quite funny. And like all memes, they carried with them a history, an agenda, and the power to get you to spread them, whether you wanted to or not.

We urge voters and lawmakers of both parties to disengage from the meme wars, to resist the easy reactions that inflammatory content can generate. While memes may be effective at drumming up engagement and getting folks incensed, they do not communicate the necessarily complicated and nuanced reality of public policy and legislation. Knowing what you now do about how meme warriors use the internet to advance their fringe beliefs in the real world, you will think twice before sharing a political meme you might not fully understand the provenance of. As we hope this book has taught you, the meme wars are a no-win game for democracy.

And yet individual knowledge is not enough to create social change. Knowledge can help us thwart our own descent into the meme wars. But this individual approach is not a solution to the wider systemic problems that underlie meme wars. Meme wars are a continuation of culture wars by digital means, and it's perhaps no longer fitting to imagine a difference between what happens online and off. Nor is the fact that a troll-in-chief is no longer president of the United States any kind of guarantee that meme wars will have less direct impact on U.S. politics. No one person should hold so much command over a political party, a country, or the globe. Trump's power was certainly derived from the legitimacy of the office of president, but it was intensified by the mainstream media's obsession with his every provocative word and gesture.

Social media is no longer an emerging technology imbued with the possibility of fostering social change by giving voice to small groups; it has instead become a tool of the powerful, used to dominate, harass, and coerce vulnerable groups. It has taken a decade for social media to be co-opted by political operatives after social movement activists proved its usefulness and seeded it with purpose. If we do not acknowledge this shift, the freest speech will benefit only those who are already powerful. It should go without saying that there is an unfathomable amount of money and power at stake, and it's the rich and powerful who now see how much they have to lose. Tech CEOs have been called in front of governments who levied fines on their companies, but they continue to remain at the helm of platforms spiraling out of their control. While it took decades to regulate print, radio, telephone, and television, it will take the will of the people pushing their governments to introduce protocols for a public-interest internet—an internet designed not to divide but to bring together, a pro-social internet. It's easy for us to forget that underneath the hood of social media and the internet are a bunch of tubes and wires connecting the wires to the weeds physically.

Trump's promises to build the wall, drain the swamp, and lock her up didn't pan out. Instead, they were replaced with new memes like Release the Kraken and Stop the Steal, which in part mobilized thousands to storm the Capitol on J6. And all of these meme wars succeeded in distracting from the real policy needs of the nation—from holding tech companies accountable for the reactionary rhetoric and violence they enable to recognizing the shifting demographics and economic needs of a nation racked by growing inequality and replacement anxiety.

Stop the Steal, and the subsequent insurrection on January 6, changed the internet forever. It kicked off the largest and most sweeping dragnet to find and remove accounts and content complicit in the coordination of that event. That effort didn't target only individuals like the president himself; entire online communities were knocked out. But the digital insurgency will continue, drafting soldiers to fight another meme war, exploiting grievances to distract from the real work of governance. To help people, to truly address the common material instabilities and inequities in our nation and in the world, we have to move away from using memes for political communication, and be more critical of those who rely on them to campaign and govern.

January 6 was the rattle of the snake's tail: a warning of how fragile a multiracial democracy in America truly is. What happens now is not exactly clear, but as the next era of meme wars begins, at least now you understand the playbook.

EPILOGUE

In coining the word *meme*, Richard Dawkins chose the word for its similarity to *gene*, viewing memes as genes' cultural equivalents in the way that they replicated ideas. Another way to think of memes is linguistic: as units of culture that, like words or phrases in a language, can be used to transmit ideas through and across generations. The researcher Susan Blackmore in her book *The Meme Machine* takes the gene comparison a step further, arguing that memes, like genes, are selfish objects. Like genes or viruses, Blackmore posits, memes are out for themselves; their goal is to replicate, whether that destroys the vessel or person doing the replicating or not. Many of the memes in this book have grown in power even as they upended the lives of the people who spread them. The biological comparison between memes and genes has its limitations, however. Blackmore, like Richard Dawkins before her, has struggled to prove that memes behave exactly like genes, or can be used to explain away the entirety of human culture. She does argue that memes may be bad for people, and based on the decade of meme wars we've outlined in this book, we tend to agree.

For many of the people drafted into it, the Stop the Steal meme war that ended in insurrection was personally devastating. More than seven hundred people were arrested. People lost their jobs and their friends, and were turned in to law enforcement by their own children. Even those red-pilled right-wingers in this book who had very little to do with the insurrection were impacted by the day's fallout. Power dynamics within the red-pilled right shifted. People lost and found platforms and allies. Just as UTR had reorganized the landscape of the fringe right, so too did the Capitol siege—a reorganization that continues even now, more than a year later.

Members of both the Oath Keepers and the Proud Boys appear to have been major instigators of the violence at the Capitol that day. After January 6, sixteen members of the Oath Keepers would be charged with conspiracy. Oath Keepers founder Stewart Rhodes, though he had stayed outside the Capitol, was eventually charged himself. Alex Jones was not arrested that day, but his status as a leader had been irretrievably damaged by video that captured the mob ignoring his attempts to rein them in as it went wild, just as Trump had tweeted weeks before. Many others were charged with crimes. Beyond legal repercussions, the red-pilled right as a whole experienced a massive deplatforming in the days after January 6, losing access to the social media sites on which they had spread their rhetoric as well as the commerce sites that had allowed them to sell merchandise to subsidize their movements.

QAnon, in particular, was deeply destabilized by the outcome of the 2020 election and the failure of the January 6 insurrection to make Q's promise of the Great Awakening come true. Q never again posted after December 8, 2020, and nothing that he had predicted ever came true. After the world watched people in Q T-shirts and waving Q flags attack the Capitol, QAnon accounts were massively deplatformed across the internet, and many lost their friends and families too. Others left the movement completely after that day, beginning a painful and arduous journey out of the rabbit hole. The remaining QAnon community, now relegated to dysfunctional alt-tech platforms, are led by a rotating cast of influencers vying to make money off their lingering belief system. Q boosters like Tracy Diaz and Michael Flynn moved on to other ventures, while some increasingly radicalized QAnon factions spun out into cults.

Groyper general Nick Fuentes was finally kicked off Twitter in the aftermath of January 6. A year later, he was subpoenaed to testify before the Select Committee to Investigate the January 6 Attack for "promoting unsupported claims about the election, including at the November 14th, 2020 Million MAGA March in Washington, D.C. and the December 12th, 2020 Stop the Steal rallies." In its summons the committee called out the

Groypers by name, stating that Fuentes and former friend Patrick Casey were the leaders of the "'America First' or 'Groyper' movement."

Fuentes's rival Richard Spencer largely withdrew from right-wing organizing after the fall of the alt-right following Charlottesville. In 2020 he voted for Biden. And in 2021 he and other Unite the Right organizers, among them neo-Nazi Jason Kessler and white supremacist Chris Cantwell, were ordered to pay $25 million in damages in a civil lawsuit brought against them by nine plaintiffs from Charlottesville.

Milo Yiannopoulos had fallen from his pedestal as a hero of the alt-right before Trump even took office, but in 2021 he made a strange return: he disavowed his former proudly gay lifestyle and claimed to have found a cure for homosexuality. In the months after January 6, Yiannopoulos produced a series of interviews with several of the insurgents, giving his former friends or enemies a platform on which to describe their side of events, defend their actions, or audition narratives of remorse.

Tim Gionet, aka Baked Alaska, was arrested on January 15, 2021, and charged with violent and disorderly conduct on Capitol grounds and knowingly entering a restricted building without permission. He faced up to a decade in prison, and spent a week in solitary confinement before he could make bail. In July, after being released from federal prison, he went on Yiannopoulos's show to discuss his predicament and speculate on the state of MAGA after Trump.

"Tim, we've known each other a long time," Yiannopoulos said at the beginning of the interview. "Did you think we'd meme him into office?"

"I always thought we probably would," Gionet replied. But the rest of the interview was far more somber.

"You found yourself, thanks to an invitation from the president of the United States, attending a rally on January 6," Yiannopoulos said. "You could be going away for a decade."

"Oh this would ruin my life, like, absolutely." Gionet said, adding, "I've had the fed come to my door trying to put me in jail for tweeting out a meme."

Toward the end of the interview, Yiannopoulos questioned if J6 had shaken Gionet's allegiance to Trump. "If Donald Trump won't say your name, and won't say Ashli Babbitt's name, why on earth are you still supporting him?"

"Well, I'm still going to be supportive to the man who I put into office," Gionet said. "I am disappointed that he didn't stand up for me. I think we should have all gotten pardons . . . but at the same time, I'm not going to turn on Trump just for one thing that he does. I just would love Trump to acknowledge us."

In January 2022, Trump did indeed acknowledge the rioters. "We will treat them fairly," Trump told a crowd at a rally in Conroe, Texas, while teasing a 2024 presidential run, "And if it requires pardons we will give them pardons. Because they are being treated so unfairly."

ACKNOWLEDGMENTS

Special thanks to the Shorenstein Center and its directors, Nancy Gibbs and Laura Manley; Technology and Social Change team members Rob Faris, Jenn Nilsen, Marya Mtshali, Dwight Knell, and Kaylee Fagan for research and support; Catesby Holmes, Chris Gilliard, Jazilah Salam, Jennifer Preston, and Jenna Ruddock for close reads; and project manager Megan O'Neil for keeping everyone safe and stable.

This book couldn't have happened without the tremendous editorial support of Anton Mueller, Morgan Jones, and all the Bloomsbury team. We also are deeply indebted to Michael Signorelli and Aevitas Creative Management.

Special thanks to domain experts Erin Gallagher, Matt Goerzen, Ben Lorber, Martin Rooke, Nathan Schneider, and the Q Origins Project for their critical reads and insights during the writing process.

Thanks to formative conversations with Daryle Lamont Jenkins, Brandi Collins-Dexter, Becca Lewis, and Daniel Harper as we prepared for the challenges of transcribing this history.

Thanks to the many journalists whose work informes our own, specifically Brandy Zadrozny, Ben Collins, Julia Carrie Wong, Jared Holt, Luke O'Brien, Michael Hayden, Andrew Marantz, Jane Lytvynenko, Craig Silverman, and Abby Ohlheiser.

We recognize the invaluable tools that help make any of the historical research possible, specifically the Internet Archive, Know Your Meme, RationalWiki, 4plebs, and the InVID Project.

Love and thanks from Joan to mentors and colleagues across academia and beyond. Inspiration from Martha Lampland, Chris Kelty, Aaron

Panofsky, Ruha Benjamin, Alondra Nelson, Safiya Noble, Sarah Roberts, Whitney Phillips, Alice Marwick, Danah Boyd, Jessie Daniels, Brooklyne Gipson, Biella Coleman, Mary Gray, Catherine Gutherie, Kim Fortun and the Fortun family, Tom Boellstorff, Dean Bill Maurer, Kevin Driscoll, Lana Swartz, Latanya Sweeney, Kelly Nielsen, David Pinzur, Will, PQ, Tram, and my mum.

Thanks from Emily especially to Seth Shipman, Mariana Ayala (for providing essential childcare during the writing process), friends in the group chat who didn't kill me when I wouldn't shut up about red pills for eight months, Jeramie Dreyfuss and Jen McCann for their lifelong support, Huxley and Asa Shipman for celebrating with me along the way and never making me feel like a bad mom for working so hard on this, and my neighbor Tom, who talked to me about politics and memes over the fence.

Special respect and recognition from Brian to Matt, Xu, Yulan, Dhana, Micah, Marco, Leon, Sasha, Linda, and Robert for tolerating and moderating me during my red-pill overdoses.

NOTES

INTRODUCTION

3   they held up green Kekistan flags: Don and YF, "Kekistan," Know Your Meme, December 12, 2021, https://knowyourmeme.com/memes/kekistan.

14   "cancer" called feminism: Sravya Jaladanki, "One Feminist's Thoughts on Milo Yiannopoulos and 'Feminism Is Cancer,'" *Daily Bruin*, May 26, 2016, https://dailybruin.com/2016/05/26/one-feminists-thoughts-on-milo-yiannopoulos-and-feminism-is-cancer.

16   ubiquitous computing environment: Paul Dourish and Genevieve Bell, *Divining a Digital Future: Mess and Mythology in Ubiquitous Computing* (Cambridge, MA: MIT Press, 2011), https://mitpress.mit.edu/books/divining-digital-future.

17   "surveillance capitalism": Shoshana Zuboff, *The Age of Surveillance Capitalism* (New York: Public Affairs, 2017), https://www.publicaffairsbooks.com/titles/shoshana-zuboff/the-age-of-surveillance-capitalism/9781610395694/.

19   "connective action": W. Lance Bennett and Alexandra Segerberg, "The Logic of Connective Action," *Information, Communication & Society* 15, no. 5 (June 1, 2012): 739–68, https://doi.org/10.1080/1369118X.2012.670661.

20   "something about a given image": Whitney Phillips, "In Defense of Memes," Spreadable Media, accessed February 4, 2022, https://spreadablemedia.org/essays/phillips/index.html.

21   Governments use cyber troops: Samantha Bradshaw, Hannah Bailey, and Philip Howard, "Press Release: Social Media Manipulation by Political Actors Now an Industrial Scale Problem Prevalent in over 80 Countries—Annual Oxford Report," Oxford Internet Institute, January 13, 2021, https://www.oii.ox.ac.uk/news-events/news/social-media-manipulation-by-political-actors-now-an-industrial-scale-problem-prevalent-in-over-80-countries-annual-oxford-report.

CHAPTER 1: WE ARE THE 99 PERCENT

24 temporary deportation reprieve: Julia Preston, "U.S. Issues New Deportation Policy's First Reprieves," *New York Times*, August 22, 2011, https://www.nytimes.com/2011/08/23/us/23immig.html.

26 for the fourth year in a row, to $50,054: Rakesh Kochhar, *A Recovery No Better than the Recession*, Pew Research Center, September 12, 2021, https://www.pewsocialtrends.org/wp-content/uploads/sites/3/2012/09/median-household-incomes-2007-2011.pdf.

26 "I tell you what, I have an idea": Heritage Foundation, "CNBC's Rick Santelli's Chicago Tea Party," YouTube video, 4:36, February 19, 2009, https://www.youtube.com/watch?v=zp-Jw-5Kx8k.

26 got on the phone: Kate Zernike, "Unlikely Activist Who Got to the Tea Party Early," *New York Times*, February 27, 2010, http://www.nytimes.com/2010/02/28/us/politics/28keli.html.

27 "After a while the people paying for it": "Rush Limbaugh Remarks to Conservatives," *C-SPAN*, 1:32:57, February 28, 2009, https://www.c-span.org/video/?284357-3/rush-limbaugh-1951-2021.

27 leaving negative reviews: Taki Oldham, director, *The Billionaires' Tea Party*, Larrikin Films, 2011.

27 shareable and shocking images: Ashley Fantz, "Obama as Witch Doctor: Racist or Satirical?," *CNN*, September 17, 2009, https://www.cnn.com/2009/POLITICS/09/17/obama.witchdoctor.teaparty/.

28 first *Time* cover of 2011: "The Vault: Cover—Jan. 17, 2011, Vol. 177, No. 2," *Time*, January 17, 2011, https://time.com/vault/issue/2011-01-17/page/1/.

28 *Time* cover for June: "The Vault: Cover—June 20, 2011, Vol. 177, No. 25," *Time*, June 20, 2011, http://time.com/vault/issue/2011-06-20/page/1/.

28 8.9 percent: *News Release: Regional and State Unemployment—2011 Annual Averages*, Bureau of Labor Statistics, February 29, 2012, https://www.bls.gov/news.release/archives/srgune_02292012.pdf.

28 long decline in the wealth of American families: Rakesh Kochhar and Anthony Cilluffo, "How Wealth Inequality Has Changed in the U.S. since the Great Recession, by Race, Ethnicity and Income," Pew Research Center, November 1, 2017, https://www.pewresearch.org/fact-tank/2017/11/01/how-wealth-inequality-has-changed-in-the-u-s-since-the-great-recession-by-race-ethnicity-and-income/.

29 Amped Status: David DeGraw, "Full Report: The Economic Elite vs. The People of the United States of America," AmpedStatus, March 9, 2010,

https://web.archive.org/web/20111001165905/http://ampedstatus.org/full
-report-the-economic-elite-vs-the-people-of-the-united-states-of
-america/.

29   A99 platform: "Original A99 Platform," AmpedStatus, November 10, 2011,
https://web.archive.org/web/20111110123908/http:/ampedstatus.org
/network/original-99platform.

31   memetic infrastructure of #OccupyWallStreet: Nathan Schneider, *Thank
You, Anarchy: Notes from the Occupy Apocalypse* (Berkeley: University of
California Press, 2013).

32   In June, the magazine had tweeted: Oleg Komlik, "The Original Email
That Started Occupy Wall Street," Economic Sociology & Political
Economy, December 27, 2014. https://economicsociology.org/2014/12/27
/the-original-email-that-started-occupy-wall-street/.

32   The hashtag was also a way: Joan Donovan, "Keyword," Society for
Cultural Anthropology, March 29, 2018, https://culanth.org/fieldsights
/keyword.

32   the *Guardian* coined the term: Eric Augenbraun, "Occupy Wall Street and
the Limits of Spontaneous Street Protest," *Guardian*, September 29, 2011,
https://www.theguardian.com/commentisfree/cifamerica/2011/sep/29
/occupy-wall-street-protest.

33   "They just confirmed it": Malcolm Harris, "I'm the Jerk Who Pranked
Occupy Wall Street," *Gawker*, December 14, 2011, https://www.gawker
.com/5868073/im-the-jerk-who-pranked-occupy-wall-street.

34   the NYPD arrested seven hundred people: Natasha Lennard, "Five Years
After the Brooklyn Bridge Arrests, the Occupy Wall Street Worth
Remembering," *The Intercept*, October 1, 2016, https://theintercept.com
/2016/10/01/occupy-wall-street-brooklyn-bridge-five-years/.

34   display of state violence: Christopher Robbins, "Video: NYPD Uses Pepper
Spray, Force On Wall Street Occupiers," *Gothamist*, September 25, 2011,
https://gothamist.com/news/video-nypd-uses-pepper-spray-force-on
-wall-street-occupiers.

34   witnesses captured footage: "Hacker Group Anonymous Targets UC-Davis
Pepper-Spray Cop," *Yahoo!*, November 23, 2011, https://news.yahoo.com
/blogs/cutline/anonymous-hackers-target-uc-davis-pepper-spray-cop-1817
22285.html.

35   "Can you still move up in America?": "Time Magazine Cover: Can You
Still Move Up in America?," *Time*, November 14, 2011, http://content.time
.com/time/covers/0,16641,20111114,00.html.

35 Later a disclaimer was placed on the post: Lloyd Hart, "Forum Post: Proposed List of Demands for Occupy Wall St Movement!," Occupy Wall Street, September 25, 2011, http://occupywallst.org/forum/proposed-list-of -demands-for-occupy-wall-st-moveme/.

36 "fatal weakness": Slavoj Žižek, "Occupy Wall Street: What Is to Be Done Next?," *Guardian*, April 24, 2012, sec. US news, https://www.theguardian .com/commentisfree/cifamerica/2012/apr/24/occupy-wall-street-what-is -to-be-done-next.

36 coordinated a massive crackdown: Joe Weisenthal and Robert Johnson, "Here's How Occupy Wall Street Came To A Sudden, Unexpected End Today," *Business Insider*, November 15, 2011, https://www.businessinsider .com/how-police-cleared-occupy-wall-street-2011-11; Ian Lovett, "Occupy Los Angeles to Be Evicted From City Hall Park," *New York Times*, November 25, 2011, https://www.nytimes.com/2011/11/26/us/occupy-los -angeles-to-be-evicted-from-city-hall-park.html.

38 "very healthy movement": Michael Tracey, "Ron Paul Reaches Out to the Youth of Occupy Wall Street," *Reason*, January 4, 2012, https://reason.com /2012/01/04/ron-paul-and-occupy-wall-street/.

38 "The internet will provide": Charlie Spiering, "Transcript: Ron Paul's Farewell Address to Congress," *Washington Examiner*, November 15, 2012, https://www.washingtonexaminer.com/transcript-ron-pauls-farewell -address-to-congress#.UKaJyvOe9yd.

38 "The online enthusiasm for Paul": David Weigel, "The Paul Paradox," *Reason*, May 25, 2007, https://reason.com/2007/05/25/the-paul-paradox/.

38 like Aaron Russo's 2006 *America: Freedom to Fascism*: Revolutionize Your Mind, "America: Freedom to Fascism—Full," YouTube video, 1:47:45, May 11, 2011, https://www.youtube.com/watch?v=uNNeVu8wUak.

41 "the bottom of the internet": "Another Online Community Joins Our Grassroots," Ron Paul Forums: Liberty Forest, November 6, 2007, http://www.ronpaulforums.com/showthread.php?32574-Another-online -community-joins-our-grassroots&highlight=4chan.

41 sloganeering threads: "Sloganeering," Ron Paul Forums: Liberty Forest, September 2, 2007, http://www.ronpaulforums.com/showthread.php?15269 -Sloganeering&highlight=Meme.

41 "Angry White Man": James Kirchick, "Angry White Man," *New Republic*, January 8, 2008, https://newrepublic.com/article/61771/angry -white-man.

42 "It's kind of like the rabbit hole": Reid Cherlin, "The Matrix Revolutions, Starring Ron Paul as Morpheus," *GQ*, February 8, 2012, https://www.gq.com/story/ron-paul-supporters-and-the-matrix.

44 "I learned that there was an agenda": Nate Blakeslee, "Alex Jones Is About to Explode," *Texas Monthly*, March 2010, https://www.texasmonthly.com/news-politics/alex-jones-is-about-to-explode/.

44 having "predicted": Al Jazeera English, "Alex Jones Predicts 9/11," Dailymotion video, 2:17, September 24, 2007, https://www.dailymotion.com/video/x31xfd.

45 Occupy San Antonio: JMacQ77, "Alex Jones Speaking at the Occupy The Fed San Antonio Rally," YouTube video, 10:24, October 9, 2011, https://www.youtube.com/watch?v=PBqITiT_Tl4.

45 Occupy Bilderberg: "'Occupy Bilderberg'—Alex Jones Calls for Thousands to Protest Upcoming Meeting of Global Elite," *RT International*, May 1, 2012, https://www.rt.com/usa/bilderberg-jones-elite-years-331/.

45 seeing Occupy: Sage Antone, "Andrew Breitbart—War," YouTube video, 0:24, September 29, 2018, https://www.youtube.com/watch?v=FhSy-6VqIww.

45 "committed to the destruction": Frank Ross, "Andrew Breitbart: Enemy of the Left with a Laptop," *Breitbart*, August 3, 2010, https://www.breitbart.com/the-media/2010/08/03/andrew-breitbart-enemy-of-the-left-with-a-laptop/.

46 "My goal is to take down": Lisa DePaulo, "Please Let Andrew Breitbart Finish," *GQ*, March 18, 2011, https://www.gq.com/story/andrew-breitbart-lisa-depaulo.

CHAPTER 2: A SAFE SPACE FOR HATE

50 These "hate facts": George Leef, "'Hate Facts'—When the Truth Is Intolerable," National Association of Scholars, July 8, 2013, https://www.nas.org/blogs/article/hate_facts_when_the_truth_is_intolerable.

51 Under the name LilAryan: "Restricted Material: GOVERNMENT Exhibit 505," October 28, 2015, https://www.uscourts.gov/courts/scd/cases/2-15-472/exhibits/GX505.pdf.

51 "Let's face it!": Joseph Bernstein, "The Surprisingly Mainstream History of the Internet's Favorite Anti-Semitic Image," *BuzzFeed News*, February 5, 2015, https://www.buzzfeednews.com/article/josephbernstein/the-surprisingly-mainstream-history-of-the-internets-favorit.

53 "Where they preach materialism": Andre (Andrew Anglin), "Hail Victory: Brutal Extremism Is the Way Forward," Total Fascism, January 2, 2013, http://archive.is/epKKA.

54 Anglin created the Daily Stormer to establish a bridge: Keegan Hankes, "Eye of the Stormer," Southern Poverty Law Center, February 9, 2017, https://www.splcenter.org/fighting-hate/intelligence-report/2017/eye -stormer.

54 "If you read this site with any regularity": Andrew Anglin, "Internet Activism vs Street Activism," Daily Stormer, March 30, 2015, https://web .archive.org/web/20201116203602/https://dailystormer.su/internet-activism -vs-street-activism/.

55 "I had always been into 4chan, as I am at heart a troll": Brett Barrouquere, "Family Ties: How Andrew Anglin's dad helped his neo-Nazi son with the Daily Stormer," Southern Poverty Law Center, December 20, 2018. https://www.splcenter.org/hatewatch/2018/12/20/family-ties-how-andrew -anglins-dad-helped-his-neo-nazi-son-daily-stormer.

55 Leaders like David Duke: David Duke, "Ferguson and the Jew Media Plot," Daily Stormer, November 28, 2014, https://web.archive.org/web/202010 05072335/https://dailystormer.su/ferguson-and-the-jew-media-plot/.

56 Roof was on the Daily Stormer forums: "Dylann Roof Appears to Have Regularly Commented on a Neo-Nazi Website," *BuzzFeed News*, June 22, 2015, https://www.buzzfeednews.com/article/ellievhall/dylann-roof-appears -to-have-regularly-commented-on-a-neo-naz; Keegan Hankes, "Dylann Roof May Have Been A Regular Commenter at Neo-Nazi Website The Daily Stormer," Southern Poverty Law Center, June 22, 2015, https://www .splcenter.org/hatewatch/2015/06/21/dylann-roof-may-have-been-regular -commenter-neo-nazi-website-daily-stormer.

56 Roof's Facebook profile: Frances Robles, Jason Horowitz, and Shaila Dewan, "Dylann Roof, Suspect in Charleston Shooting, Flew the Flags of White Power," *New York Times*, June 18, 2015, https://www.nytimes.com /2015/06/19/us/on-facebook-dylann-roof-charleston-suspect-wears-symbols -of-white-supremacy.html.

56 eighty-eight "friends": Rachel Kaadzi Ghansah, "A Most American Terrorist: The Making of Dylann Roof," *GQ*, August 21, 2017, https://www .gq.com/story/dylann-roof-making-of-an-american-terrorist.

56 Rhodesia: John Ismay, "Rhodesia's Dead—but White Supremacists Have Given It New Life Online," *New York Times*, April 10, 2018, https://www

.nytimes.com/2018/04/10/magazine/rhodesia-zimbabwe-white-supre macists.html.

58   "Justice for Dylann Roof": Jacob Geers, "'Justice For Dylann Roof' Is A Real Facebook Page," *Thought Catalog*, June 18, 2015, https://thoughtcatalog .com/jacob-geers/2015/06/justice-for-dylann-roof-is-a-real-facebook -page/.

60   "terrible student": Beth Fouhy, "Trump: Obama a 'Terrible Student' Not Good Enough for Harvard," *NBC New York*, April 26, 2011, https://www .nbcnewyork.com/news/local/trump-obama-wasnt-good-enough-to-get -into-ivy-schools/1924291/.

60   Obama presented a complication for race relations: John McWhorter, "Racism in America Is Over," *Forbes*, December 30, 2008, https://www.forbes .com/2008/12/30/end-of-racism-oped-cx_jm_1230mcwhorter.html.

60   questioned if he was truly Black: Chris Cillizza, "Is Barack Obama 'Black'? A Majority of Americans Say No," *Washington Post*, April 14, 2014, https://www.washingtonpost.com/news/the-fix/wp/2014/04/14/is-barack -obama-black/.

60   "Beer Summit": "The White House 'Beer Summit,'" Boston.com, July 30, 2009, http://archive.boston.com/news/politics/gallery/073009_beer_summit _obama/.

60   "worsened under Obama": Jennifer Agiesta, "Most Say Race Relations Worsened under Obama, Poll Finds," *CNN*, October 5, 2016, https://www .cnn.com/2016/10/05/politics/obama-race-relations-poll/index.html.

61   "capable of creating, shaping, and remixing popular culture": Jason Parham, "A People's History of Black Twitter, Part I," *Wired*, July 15, 2021, https://www.wired.com/story/black-twitter-oral-history-part-i-coming -together/.

61   Quick-witted Black reaction memes: Andre Brock, "From the Blackhand Side: Twitter as a Cultural Conversation," *Journal of Broadcasting & Electronic Media* 56, no. 4 (December 12, 2012): 529–49, https://doi.org/10.1080/08 838151.2012.732147.

61   #ByeFelicia: Jenna Graham, "16 Memes That Prove You Need Black Twitter In Your Life," *Elite Daily*, February 6, 2017, https://www.elitedaily .com/social-news/black-twitter-breaks-the-internet/1779294.

62   wore hoodies and posted selfies: M.E., "Celebrities, Athletes and Thousands More Wear Hoodies in Support of Trayvon Martin," Dre Black So Fresh, March 25, 2012, https://dreblacksofresh.com/2012/03/25

/celebrities-athletes-and-thousands-more-wear-hoodies-in-support-of
-trayvon-martin/.

62   "the hoodie is as much responsible": "ColorOfChange.Org Responds to
      Geraldo Rivera's Characterization of Trayvon Martin," Color Of Change,
      May 22, 2012, https://colorofchange.org/press_release/colorofchangeorg
      -responds-geraldo-rivera/.

63   internet hate machine: andcallmeshirley, "Internet Hate Machine," Know
      Your Meme, October 10, 2020, https://knowyourmeme.com/memes
      /internet-hate-machine.

63   "Trayvoning": Ryan Broderick, "'Trayvoning' Is a New Horrible Trend
      Where Teenagers Reenact Trayvon Martin's Death Photo," *BuzzFeed News*,
      July 16, 2013, https://buzzfeednews.com/article/ryanhatesthis/trayvoning
      -is-a-new-horrible-trend-where-teenagers-reenact-t.

63   Black journalists like Brande Victorian: Brande Victorian, "Trayvoning:
      This Trend Has to Stop," *Clutch Magazine*, May 17, 2012, https://web
      .archive.org/web/20120519014403/http:/www.clutchmagonline.com/2012
      /05/trayvoning-this-trend-has-to-stop/.

64   "more and more oppressed": Kyle Munzenrieder, "Trayvoning Meme
      Emerges on Facebook," *Miami New Times*, May 25, 2012, https://www
      .miaminewtimes.com/news/trayvoning-meme-emerges-on-facebook
      -6546233.

64   Skype-bomb his testimony: tsg600, "Zimmerman Trial Skype Bombing,"
      YouTube video, 3:47, July 3, 2013, https://www.youtube.com/watch?v=VfJ1
      tTGjySo.

64   meme-ification of Black death: Jalen Banks, "Black Death as Spectacle: An
      American Tradition," *Berkeley Political Review*, November 23, 2019,
      https://bpr.berkeley.edu/2019/11/23/black-death-as-spectacle-an-american
      -tradition/.

65   first Breitbart article about Trayvon: William Bigelow, "Media Labels
      Hispanic Man White in Shooting of Black Teen," *Breitbart*, March 19, 2012,
      https://www.breitbart.com/the-media/2012/03/19/sharpton-martin-media/.

65   "white hispanic": Ben Shapiro, "Obama Continues Racial Zimmerman
      Narrative While Hispanics Targeted," *Breitbart*, July 20, 2013, https://www
      .breitbart.com/politics/2013/07/20/obama-profile-zimmerman-trayvon/.

66   published all of Martin's tweets: David Martosko, "The Daily Caller
      Obtains Trayvon Martin's Tweets," Daily Caller, March 26, 2012, https://
      dailycaller.com/2012/03/26/the-daily-caller-obtains-trayvon-martins
      -tweets/.

66   *Business Insider* found an image: Ryan Chittum, "Sourcing Trayvon Martin 'Photos' From Stormfront," *Columbia Journalism Review*, March 26, 2012, https://www.cjr.org/the_audit/sourcing_trayvon_martin_photos .php.

66   *Good Morning America* then used the same image: Ryan Chittum, "Audit Notes: Chart of the Day, Trayvon Martin Sourcing, Updates," *Columbia Journalism Review*, March 28, 2012, https://www.cjr.org/the_audit/audit _notes_chart_of_the_day_t.php.

66   Adrian Chen reported at Gawker: Adrian Chen, "White Supremacist Hacks Trayvon Martin's Email Account, Leaks Messages Online," *Gawker*, March 29, 2012, https://www.gawker.com/5897485/white-supremacist -hacks-trayvon-martins-email-account-leaks-messages-online.

66   outlets like the *Daily Mail*: "Trayvon Martin Was Angry about Losing a Fight in the Hours Before He Was Shot Dead by George Zimmerman, Claim Defence Attorneys," *Daily Mail*, May 25, 2013, https://www.daily mail.co.uk/news/article-2331100/No-angel-George-Zimmermans-attor neys-want-villainize-Trayvon-Martin-photos-smoking-pot-texts-fighting .html.

66   far-right and conservative backlash: Max Read, "Your Guide to the Idiotic Racist Backlash Against Trayvon Martin," *Gawker*, March 27, 2012, https://www.gawker.com/5896490/your-guide-to-the-idiotic-racist -backlash-against-trayvon-martin.

66   "2013 /pol/ was fuckin amazing": Anonymous, "/Pol/—Politically Incorrect » Thread #310341696," 4chan, March 2, 2021, http://archive .4plebs.org/pol/thread/310341696/#310347668.

68   guinea pigs for medical research: Harriet Washington, "Medical Apartheid," Penguin Random House, January 8, 2008, https://www .penguinrandomhouse.com/books/185986/medical-apartheid-by-harriet -a-washington/.

68   "Bad Scientific Arguments Used by White Nationalists": "RE: Bad Scientific Arguments Used By White Nationalists," Stormfront, March 14, 2004, https://www.stormfront.org/forum/t120656-4/.

69   began pushing race science: Angela Saini, "Why Race Science Is on the Rise Again," *Guardian*, May 18, 2019, https://www.theguardian.com/books /2019/may/18/race-science-on-the-rise-angela-saini.

69   This new racial "inquiry": James Wilson, "Human BioDiversity Reading List," Human Biological Diversity, accessed February 7, 2022, http:// humanbiologicaldiversity.com/.

69 "It is rare for a professor to birth a meme": George Leef, "'Hate Facts'— When the Truth Is Intolerable," National Association of Scholars, July 8, 2013, https://www.nas.org/blogs/article/hate_facts_when_the_truth_is _intolerable.

72 the Chimpire: Jewish_NeoCon2, "CoonTown: Home of the Chimpouts," Reddit, April 28, 2015, http://archive.is/SK9sJ.

73 r/CoonTown: "CoonTown: Home of the Chimpouts," Reddit, April 28, 2015, http://archive.is/SK9sJ.

73 finally banned it in August 2015: Annalee Newitz, "Reddit Bans /r/ Coontown For All the Wrong Reasons," *Gizmodo*, August 5, 2015, https:// gizmodo.com/reddit-bans-r-coontown-for-all-the-wrong-reasons-172235 6507.

75 the Synagogue: "The TRS Lexicon," The Right Stuff, April 30, 2017, http://archive.is/uZWK4.

75 Culture of Critique series: Southern Poverty Law Center staff, "Kevin MacDonald," Southern Poverty Law Center, accessed February 10, 2022, https://www.splcenter.org/fighting-hate/extremist-files/individual/kevin -macdonald.

75 Spectre: "Week 28: Spectre," *Fash the Nation*, podcast, 2015, https://archive .org/details/ShitlordNews/Week+32_+Spectre.mp3.

76 "I find myself constantly engaging": Ragnar Talks, "Memetic Monday: Operation Redpill," Daily Stormer, August 1, 2016, https://web.archive.org /web/20201117050720/https://dailystormer.su/memetic-monday-operation -redpill/.

CHAPTER 3: GAMERS RISE UP

79 "My Twisted World": Elliot Rodger, *My Twisted World: The Story of Elliot Rodger*, Document Cloud, accessed February 7, 2022, http://s3.document cloud.org/documents/1173619/rodger-manifesto.pdf.

79 Supreme Gentleman meme: Rose Rose, "Involuntary Celibacy / Incel," Know Your Meme, May 30, 2019, https://knowyourmeme.com/photos /1497760-involuntary-celibacy-incel.

80 He began by making a video: "Elliot Rodger—Why Do Girls Hate Me so Much (Retribution)," Dailymotion video, 6:22, June 11, 2015, https://www .dailymotion.com/video/x2tlfww.

80 posted on a bodybuilding forum: Eyder Peralta, "Alleged Shooter in California Left Vast Digital Trail," NPR, May 24, 2014, https://www.npr

.org/sections/thetwo-way/2014/05/24/315624700/alleged-shooter-in
-california-left-vast-digital-trail.

81 tracked developments of his rampage in real time: Anonymous, "/R9k/—
ROBOT9001 » Searching for Posts That Contain 'Elliot Rodger' and in
Ascending Order," Desuarchive, May 24, 2014, https://desuarchive.org/r9k
/search/text/%22Elliot%20Rodger%22/order/asc/.

81 aka Wojak: YF, "Wojak," Know Your Meme, February 7, 2022, https://
knowyourmeme.com/memes/wojak.

82 "So ignore the shoddy, opportunistic posturing": Milo [Yiannopoulos],
"Killer Virgin Was a Madman, Not a Misogynist," *Breitbart*, May 27, 2014,
https://www.breitbart.com/europe/2014/05/27/virgin-killer-was-not-a
-misogynist-but-a-madman/.

82 "shit-talking insurgent": Sargon of Akkad, "A Conversation with Milo
Yiannopoulos about #GamerGate," YouTube video, 2:26:35, April 18, 2015,
https://www.youtube.com/watch?v=DzK7VqGfGSs.

82 "virtuous troll": ABC News, "Milo Yiannopoulos Interview: No Regrets
on Leslie Jones Attack: Part 1," YouTube video, 5:58, September 2, 2016,
https://www.youtube.com/watch?v=jkrY6Ny7pMg.

83 "I get paid to be me": WoodysGamertag, "PKA 264 w/ Milo
Yiannopoulos—Milo Loves Kyle, Relationship Advice, Politics," YouTube
video, 4:20:08, January 9, 2016, https://www.youtube.com/watch?v=R7
Fka3EbtYc.

84 "He was really cool": Milo Yiannopoulos, "Milo on the Gavin McInnes
Show Talking SJWs, #Gamergate, and Free Speech," YouTube video,
November 2, 2015, https://web.archive.org/web/20151103060601/https://
www.youtube.com/watch?v=7sQ5OWIgFUE.

84 particularly Stephen Fry: Milo Yiannopoulos, "My 'Twitter Row' with
Stephen Fry," *Telegraph*, November 16, 2010, https://www.telegraph.co.uk
/comment/personal-view/8137164/My-Twitter-row-with-Stephen-Fry
.html.

84 early profile in the *Guardian*: Ben Dowell, "Milo Yiannopoulos—Meet
the 'Pit Bull' of Tech Media," *Guardian*, July 7, 2012, https://www.the
guardian.com/media/2012/jul/08/milo-yiannopoulos-kernel-technology
-interview.

84 hadn't paid any of his contributors: Charles Arthur, "The Kernel to
Close as Debts Stay Unpaid," *Guardian*, March 5, 2013, https://www
.theguardian.com/media/2013/mar/05/kernel-close-debts-unpaid-sentinel
-media.

84 *The Sociopaths of Silicon Valley*: "Milo Yiannopoulos (@Nero) on Twitter," Twitter, July 3, 2014, https://web.archive.org/web/20140703054545/https:// twitter.com/Nero.

85 a glowing writeup: Milo [Yiannopoulos], "Political Correctness Makes Race and Genetics Taboo in the West, Which Is Why China Is Winning," *Breitbart*, May 19, 2014, https://www.breitbart.com/europe/2014/05/19 /science-and-racism-book/

85 posted a screed to his blog: thezoepost, "Why Does This Exist?" WordPress, September 12, 2014, https://thezoepost.wordpress.com/.

87 doxed women and "swatted" them: Hern, "Gamergate Hits New Low with Attempts to Send Swat Teams to Critics | Gamergate | The Guardian," *Guardian*, January 13, 2015, https://www.theguardian.com/technology/2015 /jan/13/gamergate-hits-new-low-with-attempts-to-send-swat-teams-to -critics.

87 "sided with activists": Milo [Yiannopoulos], "Feminist Bullies Tearing the Video Game Industry Apart," *Breitbart*, September 1, 2014, https://www .breitbart.com/europe/2014/09/01/lying-greedy-promiscuous-feminist -bullies-are-tearing-the-video-game-industry-apart/.

87 Gamergate pushers contended: WoodysGamertag, "PKA 383 w Metokur— Metokur Discovers Wings, Drunk PKA Recap," YouTube video, 4:07:12, April 21, 2018, https://www.youtube.com/watch?v=QQBHw MAUcoU.

88 "No one is smarter than the internet": Dave Smith, "Gabe Newell's Advice in 2013 Still Rings True: 'Nobody Is Smarter than the Internet,'" *Business Insider*, November 28, 2017, https://www.businessinsider.com/valve-ceo -gabe-newells-advice-to-businesses-still-rings-true-today-2017-11.

88 "Gamers Are Dead," one headline read: "Gamers Are Dead," GamerGate Wiki, September 25, 2020, https://ggwiki.deepfreeze.it/index.php?title =Gamers_Are_Dead.

89 the highest-grossing entertainment industry: Wallace Witkowski, "Videogames Are a Bigger Industry than Movies and North American Sports Combined, Thanks to the Pandemic—MarketWatch," *MarketWatch*, January 2, 2021, https://www.marketwatch.com/story/videogames-are-a -bigger-industry-than-sports-and-movies-combined-thanks-to-the -pandemic-11608654990.

89 filed a similar suit: Staff and agencies, "Columbine Parents Sue Entertainment Companies," *Guardian*, April 24, 2001, https://www.theguardian.com /technology/2001/apr/24/internetnews1.

90 "simulated ethnicity": Kom Kunyosying and Carter Soles, "Postmodern Geekdom as Simulated Ethnicity," Jump Cut: A Review of Contemporary Media, accessed February 7, 2022, https://www.ejumpcut.org/archive/jc54 .2012/SolesKunyoGeedom/.

91 *Tropes vs. Women in Video Games*: Feminist Frequency, *Tropes vs. Women in Video Games*, season 1, YouTube, March 7, 2013, https://www.youtube .com/playlist?list=PLn4ob_5_ttEaA_vc8F3fjzE62esf9yP61.

91 the manosphere: "Manosphere," RationalWiki, July 13, 2021, https:// rationalwiki.org/wiki/Manosphere.

91 "masculinity crisis": Gurmeet Kanwal, "The Masculinity Crisis, Male Malaise, and the Challenge of Becoming a Good Man," *Psychology Today*, June 18, 2011, https://www.psychologytoday.com/us/blog/psychoanalysis -30/201106/the-masculinity-crisis-male-malaise-and-the-challenge -becoming-good; and Laurie Penny, "We Need to Talk about Masculinity," *Guardian*, May 16, 2013, https://www.theguardian.com/commentisfree /2013/may/16/masculinity-crisis-men.

91 "The End of Men": Hanna Rosin, "The End of Men," *Atlantic*, March 27, 2017, https://www.theatlantic.com/magazine/archive/2010/07/the-end-of -men/308135/.

92 "what Alex from *A Clockwork Orange* might call 'ultraviolence'": Emma Jane, "Systemic Misogyny Exposed: Translating Rapeglish from the Manosphere with a Random Rape Threat Generator," *International Journal of Cultural Studies* 21, no. 1 (November 2, 2017), https://doi.org/10.1177 /1367877917734042.

92 Many of these sites and forums: Manoel Horta Ribeiro et al., "The Evolution of the Manosphere across the Web," ResearchGate, January 21, 2020, https://www.researchgate.net/publication/338737324_The_Evolution_of _the_Manosphere_Across_the_Web.

92 hikikomori: Allie Conti, "When 'Going Outside Is Prison': The World of American Hikikomori," *Intelligencer*, February 17, 2019, https://nymag.com /intelligencer/2019/02/the-world-of-american-hikikomori.html.

92 involuntary celibates: Zack Beauchamp, "The Rise of Incels: How a Support Group for the Dateless Became a Violent Internet Subculture," *Vox*, April 23, 2019, https://www.vox.com/the-highlight/2019/4/16/18287446 /incel-definition-reddit.

93 "in a pseudo-academic, seemingly respectable bubble": "Male Supremacy," Southern Poverty Law Center, accessed February 9, 2022, https://www .splcenter.org/fighting-hate/extremist-files/ideology/male-supremacy.

93   manosphere blog *Château Heartiste*: "About," *Château Heartiste*, blog, February 6, 2017, https://archive.is/Ur7vz.

93   "The Sixteen Commandments of Poon": "The Sixteen Commandments of Poon," *Château Heartiste*, blog, December 13, 2014, http://archive.is/bAlCY.

93   r/TheRedPill: Aja Romano, "Reddit's TheRedPill, Notoriously Misogynist, Was Founded by a New Hampshire State Legislator," *Vox*, April 28, 2017, https://www.vox.com/culture/2017/4/28/15434770/red-pill-founded-by-robert-fisher-new-hampshire.

93   "discussion of sexual strategy": "Elliot Rodger: How Misogynist Killer Became 'Incel Hero,'" *BBC News*, April 26, 1928, https://www.bbc.com/news/world-us-canada-43892189.

94   defending antifeminist ideas: Abby Ohlheiser and Ben Terris, "How Mike Cernovich's Influence Moved from the Internet Fringes to the White House," *Washington Post*, April 7, 2017, https://www.washingtonpost.com/news/the-intersect/wp/2017/04/07/how-mike-cernovichs-influence-moved-from-the-internet-fringes-to-the-white-house/.

94   Cernovich had been arrested for rape: Andrew Marantz, "Trolls for Trump," *New Yorker*, October 24, 2016, http://www.newyorker.com/magazine/2016/10/31/trolls-for-trump.

94   "date rape doesn't exist": Mike Cernovich, "Why 'Date Rape' Is Harmful Concept for Men and Women," Danger and Play, October 12, 2016, http://archive.is/wysgr.

95   "people know me by Jim": Milo [Yiannopoulos], "What is #GamerGate?," Radio Nero, September 22, 2014, https://web.archive.org/web/2019031 9093709/https://ggwiki.deepfreeze.it/index.php?title=Radio_Nero

95   "To some he's a Jerry Springer of the internet age": "Mister Metokur," Encyclopedia Dramatica, September 20, 2020, https://web.archive.org/web/20210227215245/https://encyclopediadramatica.wiki/index.php/Mister_Metokur.

96   coordinate direct harassment of Quinn and dox her: "**** BEGIN LOGGING AT Mon Aug 18 17:21:25 2014," puu.sh, September 6, 2014, http://puu.sh/b0AEC/f072f259b6.txt.

96   hashtagged the whole mess #Gamergate: Adam Baldwin (@AdamBaldwin), "#GamerGate: Pt. 1: Https://M.Youtube.Com/Watch?V=C5-51PfwI3M . . . Pt. 2: Https://Www.Youtube.Com/Watch?V=pKmy5OKg6lo . . . ," Twitter, August 28, 2014, http://archive.ph/OyJrl.

96 He shared Breitbart's distaste for Hollywood liberals: "Adam Baldwin," RationalWiki, February 5, 2022, https://rationalwiki.org/wiki/Adam _Baldwin.

96 "Guys its happening": Anonymous, "/Pol/—Politically Incorrect » Thread #34787623," 4chan, August 27, 2014, http://archive.4plebs.org/pol/thread /34787623/#34803699.

96 "How deep": Anonymous, "/Pol/—Politically Incorrect » Thread #34787 623," 4chan, August 27, 2014, http://archive.4plebs.org/pol/thread/34787623.

97 an invincible god of the internet: WoodysGamertag, "PKA 383 w Metokur."

97 Metokur: James Habermann, "METOKUR," METOKUR, November 26, 2014, http://archive.is/hhnjH.

97 *School Shooter North American Tour 2012*: u/redakdal, "I Was a Former Target of Habermann's 'Metokur.Org' Website Here Is Some of the Lore," Reddit, May 9, 2019, www.reddit.com/r/MisterMetokur/comments/bmmral /i_was_a_former_target_of_habermanns_metokurorg/.

97 drew the attention of the FBI: "*School Shooter: North American Tour 2012* Pulled from Host Site," *HuffPost*, December 6, 2017, https://www.huffpost .com/entry/school-shooter-north-american-tour-2012_n_840641.

97 "I kind of like to know who runs the show": Internet Aristocrat Archive, "Tumblrisms: Ep. 4—White Privilege," YouTube video, 21:31, February 17, 2017, https://www.youtube.com/watch?v=gtQN4ViL4JI.

97 "For two years before gamergate became a thing": WoodysGamertag, "PKA 383 w Metokur."

97 "You might say, Jim you're an asshole": Internet Aristocrat Archive, "Wake Up," YouTube video, 12:03, February 17, 2017, https://www.youtube.com /watch?v=-ly30apkJzc.

99 "Tumblr is a blizzard": McFarvo, "[Mirror] [Compilation] Tumblrisms— Internet Aristocrat Aka Mister Metokur," YouTube video, 2:16:19, April 21, 2015, https://www.youtube.com/watch?v=LUZkFCRzIUI.

100 Sommers went on to be spokesperson: Rubin Report, "Feminism, Free Speech, & Gamergate | Christina Hoff Sommers | WOMEN | Rubin Report," YouTube video, 1:00:41, November 27, 2015, https://www.youtube .com/watch?v=2RNaspc5Ep4; and Planet Telex, "MSNBC—#Gamergate Interview with Christina Hoff Sommers (Oct 28 2014)," YouTube video, 6:12, October 28, 2014, https://www.youtube.com/watch?v=d4NEQm5 lUqM.

101 "Being the first artist to meme": Brenton Blanchet, "Peace, Love, and Based God," Complex, Feb. 11, 21, https://www.complex.com/pigeons-and-planes/lil-b-interview-based-god.

102 describing Zimmerman as "so based": Anonymous, "/Pol/—Politically Incorrect » Thread #23593674," 4chan, November 29, 2013, http://archive.4plebs.org/pol/thread/23593674/#23594291.

102 Yiannopoulos's first Gamergate story: Milo [Yiannopoulos], "Feminist Bullies Tearing the Video Game Industry Apart," Breitbart, September 1, 2014, https://www.breitbart.com/europe/2014/09/01/lying-greedy-promiscuous-feminist-bullies-are-tearing-the-video-game-industry-apart/.

102 "consumer movement that rejects sloppy standards in video games": Rubin Report, "Gamergate, Feminism, Atheism, Gay Rights | Milo Yiannopoulos | POLITICS | Rubin Report," YouTube video, 1:10:06, October 9, 2015, https://www.youtube.com/watch?v=1FvADt-mJ_0.

102 "This is about ritually humiliating": Sargon of Akkad, "A Conversation with Milo Yiannopoulos about #GamerGate," YouTube video, 2:26:35, April 18, 2015, https://www.youtube.com/watch?v=DzK7VqGfGSs.

103 a smoking gun: Milo [Yiannopoulos], "Exposed: The Secret Mailing List of the Gaming Journalism Elite," Breitbart, September 17, 2014, https://www.breitbart.com/europe/2014/09/17/Exposed-the-secret-mailing-list-of-the-gaming-journalism-elite/.

103 Yiannopoulos stayed on the beat for a year: Milo [Yiannopoulos], "I've Been Playing Video Games for Nearly a Year: Here's What I've Learned," Breitbart, July 16, 2015, https://www.breitbart.com/entertainment/2015/07/16/ive-been-playing-video-games-for-nearly-a-year-heres-what-ive-learned/.

103 "The current generation of social justice warriors": WoodysGamertag, "PKA 264 w/ Milo Yiannopoulos."

103 "favorite website on the internet": WoodysGamertag, "PKA 264 w/ Milo Yiannopoulos."

104 "truffle pigs": Joseph Bernstein, "Top Conservative Writer Is A Group Effort, Sources Say," BuzzFeed News, March 31, 2016, https://www.buzzfeednews.com/article/josephbernstein/top-conservative-writer-is-a-group-effort-sources-say.

104 "What we do—something quite rare in journalism these days": Channel 4 News, "Milo Yiannopoulos' Fiery Interview with Channel 4 News," YouTube video, 5:43, November 18, 2016, https://www.youtube.com/watch?v=2_vDke_nQvU.

104 "Big Milo": Milo Yiannopoulos, "Milo on the Gavin McInnes Show Talking SJWs, #Gamergate, and Free Speech," YouTube video, November 2, 2015, https://web.archive.org/web/20151103060601/https://www.youtube.com/watch?v=7sQ5OWIgFUE.

105 most enduring meme of Gamergate: J. The Perverted Summoner, "Social Justice Warrior," Know Your Meme, February 7, 2022, https://knowyourmeme.com/memes/social-justice-warrior.

106 In his goodbye to Gamergate: Gladium Spiritus, "Internet Aristocrat's Final Message to Gamergate," YouTube video, 5:03, November 29, 2014, https://www.youtube.com/watch?v=lfhseUDFI04.

106 "Gaming is going to die": McFarvo, "[Mirror] [Compilation] Tumblrisms—Internet Aristocrat Aka Mister Metokur," YouTube video, 2:16:19, April 21, 2015, https://www.youtube.com/watch?v=LUZkFCRzIUI.

CHAPTER 4: TROLL IN CHIEF

109 "we will make America great again": C-SPAN, "Donald Trump Presidential Campaign Announcement Full Speech (C-SPAN)," YouTube video, 47:08, June 16, 2015, https://www.youtube.com/watch?v=apjNfkysjbM.

109 "a president and an amusement park": Maane Khatchatourian, "[VIDEO] Donald Trump's Bid for President Mocked on Latenight—Variety," *Variety*, June 17, 2015, https://variety.com/2015/tv/news/latenight-mocks-donald-trump-president-video-1201522074/.

109 White House Correspondents' Dinner: Roxanne Roberts, "I Sat Next to Donald Trump at the Infamous 2011 White House Correspondents' Dinner," *Washington Post*, April 28, 2016, https://www.washingtonpost.com/lifestyle/style/i-sat-next-to-donald-trump-at-the-infamous-2011-white-house-correspondents-dinner/2016/04/27/5cf46b74-0bea-11e6-8ab8-9ad050f76d7d_story.html.

109 "I think that is the night he resolves to run for president.": Patrice Taddonio, "WATCH: Inside the Night President Obama Took On Donald Trump," PBS *Frontline*, September 22, 2016, https://www.pbs.org/wgbh/frontline/article/watch-inside-the-night-president-obama-took-on-donald-trump/.

110 trying to stop Native Americans from operating casinos: Joseph Tanfani, "Trump Was Once So Involved in Trying to Block an Indian Casino That He Secretly Approved Attack Ads," *Los Angeles Times*, June 30, 2016,

https://www.latimes.com/politics/la-na-pol-trump-anti-indian-campaign
-20160630-snap-story.html.

110 Trump met Cohn in 1973: Ken Auletta, "Don't Mess with Roy Cohn, the Man Who Made Donald Trump," *Esquire*, July 13, 2016, https://www.esquire.com/news-politics/a46616/dont-mess-with-roy-cohn/.

110 Trump was the last person Cohn called before he died: Marcus Baram, "Eavesdropping on Roy Cohn and Donald Trump," *New Yorker*, April 14, 2017, http://www.newyorker.com/news/news-desk/eavesdropping-on-roy-cohn-and-donald-trump.

110 the dandy Roger Stone: Ian Shearn, "Roger Stone: The Ultimate Dirty Trickster, Formed by Watergate and Tempered in New Jersey," *NJ Spotlight News*, July 13, 2020, https://www.njspotlightnews.org/2020/07/roger-stone-the-ultimate-dirty-trickster-formed-by-watergate-and-tempered-in-new-jersey/.

110 Trump had become a frequent guest: Jane Mayer, "The Making of the Fox News White House," *New Yorker*, March 11, 2019, https://www.newyorker.com/magazine/2019/03/11/the-making-of-the-fox-news-white-house.

110 Brooks Brothers riot: Michael Miller, "2000 Florida Recount: How the 'Brooks Brothers Riot' Killed the Bush-Gore Recount in Miami," *Washington Post*, November 15, 2018, https://www.washingtonpost.com/history/2018/11/15/its-insanity-how-brooks-brothers-riot-killed-recount-miami/.

111 friends with the Clintons: Maureen Dowd, "When Hillary and Donald Were Friends," *New York Times*, November 2, 2016, https://www.nytimes.com/2016/11/06/magazine/when-hillary-and-donald-were-friends.html.

111 "One thing I've learned about the press": Donald J. Trump and Tony Schwartz, *Trump: The Art of the Deal* (New York: Random House, 1987).

112 Most papers of record: Alexander Burns, "Donald Trump, Pushing Someone Rich, Offers Himself," *New York Times*, June 16, 2015, https://www.nytimes.com/2015/06/17/us/politics/donald-trump-runs-for-president-this-time-for-real-he-says.html; and Susan Page, "This Time, Donald Trump Says He's Running," *USA Today*, June 17, 2015, https://www.usatoday.com/story/news/politics/elections/2015/06/16/donald-trump-announcement-president/28782433/.

112 The mainstream media and establishment: Margaret Sullivan, "The Media Didn't Want to Believe Trump Could Win. So They Looked the Other Way," *Washington Post*, November 9, 2016, https://www.washingtonpost.com/lifestyle/style/the-media-didnt-want-to-believe-trump-could

-win-so-they-looked-the-other-way/2016/11/09/d2ea1436-a623-11e6
-8042-f4d111c862d1_story.html; and David Folkenflik, "How the Media
Failed in Covering Donald Trump," NPR, May 5, 2016, https://www.npr
.org/2016/05/05/476944825/how-the-media-failed-in-covering-donald
-trump.

112 "The moment I found out Trump could tweet": Ben Shreckinger, "'Oh,
No': The Day Trump Learned to Tweet," *Politico*, December 20, 2018,
https://www.politico.com/story/2018/12/20/oh-no-the-day-trump-learned
-to-tweet-1070789.

113 a Trump tweet for everything: Michal Kranz, "9 Tweets That Prove That
There Really Is an Old Trump Tweet for Everything," *Business Insider*,
October 15, 2017, https://www.businessinsider.com/9-trump-tweets-for
-everything-obama-hurricane-north-korea-2017-10.

113 original family name, Drumpf: Kim LaCapria, "Was Donald Trump's
Family Surname Once 'Drumpf'?," *Snopes*, February 29, 2016, https://www
.snopes.com/fact-check/donald-drumpf/.

114 mansion apartment in Trump Tower: Annie Georgia Greenberg, "Peek
inside Melania Trump's World (and Penthouse!)," *Refinery29*, January 3,
2012, https://www.refinery29.com/en-us/melania-trump-interview-pictures.

114 "virtual spokesperson for the 'birther' movement": John Sides, Michael
Tesler, and Lynn Vavreck, *Identity Crisis: The 2016 Presidential Campaign
and the Battle for the Meaning of America* (Princeton, NJ: Princeton
University Press, 2018), 5.

114 "our greatest strength": "Diversity of Humanity Is Our Greatest
Strength,'" United Nations Department of Economic and Social Affairs,
December 15, 2016, press release, https://www.un.org/development
/desa/en/news/population/global-forum-migration-development.html

115 "What if [Obama] is so outside our comprehension": Robert Costa,
"Gingrich: Obama's 'Kenyan, Anti-Colonial' Worldview," National Review
Online, September 11, 2010, https://archive.is/66fQI.

116 *Citizen Cohn*: Nicholas von Hoffman, *Citizen Cohn: The Life and Times of
Roy Cohn* (New York: Doubleday, 1988).

117 "Who Else Here / Pumped for Trump/?": Anonymous, "/Pol/—Politically
Incorrect » Thread #46711086," 4chan, June 19, 2015, http://archive.4plebs
.org/pol/thread/46711086/#46711086.

118 "It's like Lex Luthor is running for president": Anonymous, "/Pol/—
Politically Incorrect » Thread #46711086," 4chan, June 19, 2015, http://
archive.4plebs.org/pol/thread/46711086/#q46711178.

119 first Pepe-style Trump meme: Anonymous, "/Pol/—Politically Incorrect »
Thread #47721164," 4chan, July 8, 2015, http://archive.4plebs.org/pol
/thread/47959055/#47959055.

120 Trump smirking as a family of Mexican immigrants weeps: Anonymous,
"/Pol/—Politically Incorrect » Thread #48574126," 4chan, July 25, 2015,
https://archive.4plebs.org/pol/thread/48574126/#48574126.

120 "Lovable, mega-rich windbag Donald Trump is trolling the Establishment":
Milo [Yiannopoulos], "Donald Trump, King of Trolling His Critics,
Should Be the Internet's Choice for President," *Breitbart*, July 19, 2015,
https://www.breitbart.com/politics/2015/06/19/donald-trump-king-of
-trolling-his-critics-should-be-the-internets-choice-for-president/

121 "younger staffers would regularly pass around memes": Ben Shreckinger,
"World War Meme," *Politico*, March/April 2017, https://www.politico.com
/magazine/story/2017/03/memes-4chan-trump-supporters-trolls-internet
-214856/.

122 They called it The_Donald: Jason Koebler, "How r/The_donald Became
a Melting Pot of Frustration and Hate," *Vice*, July 12, 2016, https://www
.vice.com/en/article/53d5xb/what-is-rthedonald-donald-trump-subreddit.

122 Reportedly, Reddit engineers: Abby Ohlseiser, "Trump's Meme Brigade
Took Over Reddit. Now Reddit Is Trying to Stop Them," *Washington Post*,
June 17, 2016, https://www.washingtonpost.com/news/the-intersect/wp
/2016/06/17/trumps-meme-brigade-took-over-reddit-now-reddit-is
-trying-to-stop-them/.

124 "Donald Trump vs. the Republican Establishment" and following headlines: M. J. Lee, "Donald Trump vs. the Republican Establishment," *CNN*,
October 26, 2015, https://www.cnn.com/2015/10/26/politics/donald-trump
-republican-establishment/index.html; Tracey Jan and Annie Linskey,
"Republican Groups Aim to Bring Down Donald Trump," *Boston Globe*,
November 24, 2015, https://www.bostonglobe.com/news/politics/2015/11
/24/gop-establishment-fears-donald-trump-could-permanently-tarnish
-republican-party-image/EbCIEyJlbD1xF74eXe1LfP/story.html; Leigh
Ann Caldwell, "These Republican Leaders Say Trump Should Not Be
President," *NBC News*, October 25, 2016, https://www.nbcnews.com
/politics/2016-election/donald-trump-widely-condemned-republican
-leaders-legislators-n662446; and Chris Cillizza, "Why No One Should
Take Donald Trump Seriously, in One Very Simple Chart," *Washington
Post*, June 17, 2015, https://www.washingtonpost.com/news/the-fix/wp/2015

/06/17/why-no-one-should-take-donald-trump-seriously-in-1-very -simple-chart/.

125 "The cuckservative is, in habit of mind": "Literal Cuckservatives," *Château Heartiste*, July 23, 2015, https://heartiste.org/2015/07/23/literal -cuckservatives/.

125 Conservatives on sites like the Daily Caller and the blog *RedState*: Matt Lewis, "What's Behind The 'Cuckservative' Slur?," Daily Caller, July 28, 2015, http://archive.is/SSiQJ; and Erick Erickson, "'Cuckservative' Is a Racist Slur and an Attack on Evangelical Christians," *RedState*, July 29, 2015, https://redstate.com/erick/2015/07/29/cuckservative-is-a-racist-slur -and-an-attack-on-evangelical-christians-n53528.

126 "It's a byword for beta male or coward": Milo [Yiannopoulos], "'Cuckservative' Is a Gloriously Effective Insult," *Breitbart*, July 28, 2015, https://www.breitbart.com/politics/2015/07/28/cuckservative-is-a -gloriously-effective-insult-that-should-not-be-slurred-demonised-or -ridiculed/.

126 "If the media openly embraces white guilt": Anonymous, "/Pol/—Politically Incorrect » Thread #52479345," 4chan, September 25, 2015, http://archive .4plebs.org/pol/thread/52479345/#52480454.

126 only four in ten Americans: Rebecca Riffkin, "Americans' Trust in Media Remains at Historical Low," Gallup, September 28, 2015, https://news .gallup.com/poll/185927/americans-trust-media-remains-historical-low .aspx.

126 Stone up and quit the campaign in August: Ben Schreckinger, "Trump Prepares to Bolster Depleted Staff," *Politico*, August 10, 2015, https://www .politico.com/story/2015/08/donald-trump-fox-truce-121234.

128 his quintessential political slogan: Karen Tumulty, "How Donald Trump Came Up with 'Make America Great Again,'" *Washington Post*, January 18, 2019, https://www.washingtonpost.com/politics/how-donald-trump-came -up-with-make-america-great-again/2017/01/17/fb6acf5e-dbf7-11e6-ad42 -f3375f271c9c_story.html,

128 filed the trademark: "Trademark Status & Document Retrieval," U.S. Patent and Trademark Office, July 14, 2015, https://tsdr.uspto.gov/ #caseNumber=85783371&caseType=SERIAL_NO&searchType=status Search.

129 "Trump's Campaign Hat": Ashley Parker, "Trump's Campaign Hat Becomes an Ironic Summer Accessory," *New York Times*, September 11,

2015, https://www.nytimes.com/2015/09/13/fashion/trumps-campaign-hat
-becomes-an-ironic-summer-accessory.html.

129 #MAGA made a great hashtag: "#MAGA, Make America Great Again,"
#MoveMe: A Guide to Social Movements & Social Media, April 5, 2020,
https://moveme.berkeley.edu/project/maga/.

129 unseating #BlackLivesMatter: Monica Anderson et al., "2. An Analysis of
#BlackLivesMatter and Other Twitter Hashtags Related to Political or
Social Issues," Pew Research Center, July 11, 2018, http:/www.pewinternet
.org/2018/07/11/an-analysis-of-blacklivesmatter-and-other-twitter-hash
tags-related-to-political-or-social-issues.

129 dubbed the "Trump Train": Claudia Flores-Saviaga, Brian Keegan, and
Saiph Savage, *Mobilizing the Trump Train: Understanding Collective Action
in a Political Trolling Community*, June 1, 2018, https://arxiv.org/pdf/1806
.00429.pdf.

130 Ann Coulter jumped on: Kevin MacDonald, "Donald Trump's
Breakthrough Statement on Immigration," *Occidental Observer*, August 17,
2015, https://www.theoccidentalobserver.net/2015/08/17/donald-trumps
-breakthrough-statement-on-immigration/.

130 "I said if a Republican acted like me": Marantz, "Trolls for Trump," *New
Yorker*, October 31, 2016, https://www.newyorker.com/magazine/2016/10
/31/trolls-for-trump.

130 He jumped into the cuckservative campaign for the clout: "What Is a
Cuckservative?," Crime & Federalism, July 25, 2015, https://www
.crimeandfederalism.com/2015/07/what-is-a-cuckservative.html.

132 "damn good for CBS": Paul Bond, "Leslie Moonves on Donald Trump: 'It
May Not Be Good for America, but It's Damn Good for CBS,'" *Hollywood
Reporter*, February 29, 2016, https://www.hollywoodreporter.com/news
/general-news/leslie-moonves-donald-trump-may-871464/.

133 refused to disavow the KKK's David Duke: Melissa Chan, "Donald Trump
Refuses to Condemn KKK, Disavow Endorsement," *Time*, February 28,
2016, https://time.com/4240268/donald-trump-kkk-david-duke/.

133 "What do you have to lose?": Associated Press, "Trump to Black Voters:
What Do You Have to Lose?," YouTube video, 1:40, August 19, 2016,
https://www.youtube.com/watch?v=t-jasg-_E5M.

134 by creating Stop the Steal: *Ohio Democratic Party v. Ohio Republican Party,
Donald J. Trump for President, Inc., Roger J. Stone, Jr., and Stop the Steal Inc.*,
No. 1:16-cv-02645 (United States District Court for the Northern
District of Ohio, October 30, 2016).

135 derail Sanders's campaign: Aaron Blake, "Here Are the Latest, Most Damaging Things in the DNC's Leaked Emails," *Washington Post*, July 27, 2016, https://www.washingtonpost.com/news/the-fix/wp/2016/07/24/here -are-the-latest-most-damaging-things-in-the-dncs-leaked-emails/.

135 "control the party's finances": Jeff Stein, "Donna Brazile's Bombshell About the DNC and Hillary Clinton, Explained," *Vox*, November 2, 2017, https://www.vox.com/policy-and-politics/2017/11/2/16599036/donna -brazile-hillary-clinton-sanders.

135 Bernie Bros: Robinson Meyer, "Here Comes the Berniebro," *Atlantic*, October 17, 2015, https://www.theatlantic.com/politics/archive/2015/10 /here-comes-the-berniebro-bernie-sanders/411070/.

136 Sanders racked up some unexpected wins: Wilson Andrews, Kitty Bennett, and Alicia Parlapiano, "2016 Delegate Count and Primary Results," *New York Times*, July 5, 2016, https://www.nytimes.com/interactive/2016/us /elections/primary-calendar-and-results.

136 Twelve percent of Sanders's fans: Jeff Stein, "The Bernie Voters Who Defected to Trump, Explained by a Political Scientist," *Vox*, August 24, 2017, https://www.vox.com/policy-and-politics/2017/8/24/16194086/bernie -trump-voters-study.

136 low enthusiasm: Reuters, "Why Hillary Clinton's Supporters Aren't Advertising," *Fortune*, September 26, 2016, https://fortune.com/2016/09/26 /hillary-clinton-support-democrats/; Clare Foran, "The Curse of Hillary Clinton's Ambition," *The Atlantic*, September 17, 2016, https://www .theatlantic.com/politics/archive/2016/09/clinton-trust-sexism/500489/.

137 pop-up courses on memeology: Milo Yiannopoulos, "Pizza Party Ben Gives A Lesson On Memeology," YouTube video, October 18, 2016, https://web.archive.org/web/20161019100859/https://www.youtube.com /watch?v=Eq7vY4dSOek.

138 RNC loyalty pledge: M. J. Lee and Chris Moody, "Donald Trump Signs RNC Loyalty Pledge," *CNN*, September 3, 2015, https://www.cnn.com /2015/09/03/politics/donald-trump-2016-rnc-pledge-meeting/index .html.

138 the platform of the alt-right: Sarah Posner, "How Steve Bannon Created an Online Haven for White Nationalists," *Mother Jones*, August 22, 2016, https://www.motherjones.com/politics/2016/08/stephen-bannon-donald -trump-alt-right-breitbart-news/.

139 "It's been one big, bourbon-fueled": David Weigel, "The 'Alt Right' Finds a Home inside the Republican Convention," *Washington Post*, July 21, 2016,

https://www.washingtonpost.com/politics/the-alt-right-finds-a-home
-inside-the-republican-convention/2016/07/21/5890518e-4f8c-11e6-aa14
-e0c1087f7583_story.html.

140 Trump held a news conference: "Road to the White House 2016: Donald
Trump News Conference," *C-SPAN*, 57:46, July 27, 2016, https://www.c
-span.org/video/?413263-1/donald-trump-urges-russia-find-hillary
-clinton-emails-criticizes-record-tpp.

140 The press pounced on the call to action: Ashley Parker and David E.
Sanger, "Donald Trump Calls on Russia to Find Hillary Clinton's Missing
Emails," *New York Times*, July 27, 2016, https://www.nytimes.com/2016
/07/28/us/politics/donald-trump-russia-clinton-emails.html; Jose DelReal,
"Trump Launches Flurry of Attacks, Asks Russia to Hack Clinton's
Emails," *Washington Post*, July 27, 2016, https://www.washingtonpost.com
/news/post-politics/wp/2016/07/27/trump-launches-flurry-of-attacks
-asks-russia-to-hack-clintons-emails/; and Beth Reinhard and Damian
Paletta, "Donald Trump Invites Russia to Find Missing Hillary Clinton
Emails," *Wall Street Journal*, July 27, 2016, https://www.wsj.com/articles
/donald-trump-invites-russia-to-find-missing-hillary-clinton-emails
-1469638557.

141 "In the background of this entire race": Drew FitzGerald and Shelby
Holliday, "Mueller Investigators Probe Roger Stone Conference Calls,"
Wall Street Journal, October 30, 2018, https://www.wsj.com/articles/mueller
-investigators-probe-roger-stone-conference-calls-1540899120.

141 the company Cambridge Analytica: Matthew Rosenberg, Nicholas
Confessore, and Carole Cadwalladr, "How Trump Consultants Exploited
the Facebook Data of Millions," *New York Times*, March 17, 2018, https://
www.nytimes.com/2018/03/17/us/politics/cambridge-analytica-trump
-campaign.html.

141 a person from Cambridge Analytica: "Steve Bannon, Roger Stone, and
the Ongoing Investigation into Cambridge Analytica," emptywheel, May
24, 2021, https://www.emptywheel.net/2021/05/24/steve-bannon-roger
-stone-and-the-ongoing-investigation-into-cambridge-analytica/?print
=print.

142 live-posting the event to /pol/: Cassandra Fairbanks, "4Chan Poster
Gloriously Interrupts Clinton Alt-Right Speech," *We Are Change*, August 25,
2016, https://wearechange.org/4chan-poster-gloriously-interrupts-clinton
-alt-right-speech/.

143 "basket of deplorables": Domenico Montanaro, "Hillary Clinton's 'Basket Of Deplorables,' in Full Context of This Ugly Campaign," NPR, September 10, 2016, https://www.npr.org/2016/09/10/493427601/hillary-clintons-basket-of-deplorables-in-full-context-of-this-ugly-campaign.

143 On September 11, Roger Stone tweeted: Phil Owen, "David Duke, Roger Stone Turn Clinton's 'Deplorables' Comment Into 'Expendables' Memes (Photos)," *Wrap*, September 11, 2016, https://www.thewrap.com/david-duke-roger-stone-turn-clintons-deplorables-comment-into-expendables-memes-photos/.

143 "Delete your account": Hillary Clinton (@HillaryClinton), "Delete Your Account. Https://T.Co/Oa92sncRQY," Twitter, June 9, 2016, https://twitter.com/HillaryClinton/status/740973710593654784.

144 "Bureau of Memetic Warfare": Erin Gallagher, "The Bureau of Memetic Warfare—September 2015 (CW)," Medium, October 1, 2018, https://erin-gallagher.medium.com/the-bureau-of-memetic-warfare-september-2015-6243d58dc07d.

145 she was very sick: Jeva Lange, "How a Meme Made Hillary Clinton's Health a Campaign Issue," *The Week*, October 24, 2016, https://theweek.com/speedreads/657182/how-meme-made-hillary-clintons-health-campaign-issue.

145 playing on rumors seeded by Jones: Jay Bookman, "The 'Dying Hillary' Meme Is This Year's Version of Birtherism," *Atlanta Journal-Constitution*, August 22, 2016, https://www.ajc.com/blog/jay-bookman/the-dying-hillary-meme-this-year-version-birtherism/ZgbejKCiPX58lDGXDNXSmI/; and Paul Joseph Watson: Ben Collins, "'Is Hillary Dying' Hoax Started by Pal of Alex Jones," *Daily Beast*, August 9, 2016, https://www.thedailybeast.com/articles/2016/08/09/is-hillary-dying-hoax-started-by-pal-of-alex-jones.

145 "Hillary's Clinton's Health Scare: 9 Unanswered Questions": Alex Seitz-Wald et al., "Hillary Clinton's Health Scare: 9 Unanswered Questions," *NBC News*, September 12, 2016, https://www.nbcnews.com/politics/2016-election/hillary-clinton-s-health-scare-9-unanswered-questions-n646551.

145 John Podesta's private emails: Julia Ioffe, "The Secret Correspondence Between Donald Trump Jr. and WikiLeaks," *Atlantic*, November 13, 2017, https://www.theatlantic.com/politics/archive/2017/11/the-secret-correspondence-between-donald-trump-jr-and-wikileaks/545738/

146 T-shirts that read "Trump can grab my pussy!": "Trump Can Grab My Pussy T-Shirts," Redbubble, accessed February 8, 2022, https://www.redbubble.com/shop/trump+can+grab+my+pussy+t-shirts.

147 "I've switched teams": Abby Phillip (@abbydphillip), "John Podesta's Twitter Account Appears to Be Compromised Https://T.Co/8QpBu4V4fZ," Twitter, October 12, 2016, https://twitter.com/abbydphillip/status/786355121059926017.

147 political commentator Donna Brazile: Hadas Gold, "New Email Shows Brazile May Have Had Exact Wording of Proposed Town Hall Question before CNN," *Politico*, October 12, 2016, https://www.politico.com/blogs/on-media/2016/10/roland-martin-cnn-email-donna-brazile-wikileaks-229673.

147 "Four of the Juiciest Leaked Podesta Emails": Eliza Collins, "Four of the Juiciest Leaked Podesta Emails," *USA Today*, October 13, 2016, https://www.usatoday.com/story/news/politics/onpolitics/2016/10/13/four-juiciest-leaked-podesta-emails/92014368/.

148 WikiLeaks' official Twitter account posted: WikiLeaks (@wikileaks), "The Podestas' 'Spirit Cooking' Dinner? It's Not What You Think. It's Blood, Sperm and Breastmilk. But Mostly Blood. Http://Wearechange.Org/Spirit-Cooking-Disturbing-Podesta-Email-yet-Warning-Graphic-Content/ Https://T.Co/I43KiiraDh," Twitter, November 4, 2016, https://twitter.com/wikileaks/status/794450623404113920.

149 #DraftOurDaughters: "People Are Falling for the Draft Our Daughters Meme," 247Sports, October 28, 2016, https://247sports.com/college/kansas/board/103734/Contents/people-are-falling-for-the-draft-our-daughters-meme-71892478/; and Kim LaCapria, "Hillary Clinton and #DraftOur Daughters," *Snopes*, October 28, 2016, https://www.snopes.com/fact-check/hillary-clinton-and-draftourdaughters/.

149 #DrunkHillary: Abby Ohlheiser, "What's behind the 'Drunk Hillary' Meme That's Taking over the Trump Internet," *Washington Post*, November 3, 2016, https://www.washingtonpost.com/news/the-intersect/wp/2016/11/03/whats-behind-the-drunk-hillary-meme-thats-taking-over-the-trump-internet/.

149 Clinton Body Count: "Clinton Body Count," RationalWiki, November 19, 2021, https://rationalwiki.org/wiki/Clinton_body_count.

149 attorney named Linda D. Thompson: Linda Thompson, "The Clinton Body Count: Coincidence or the Kiss of Death?," First Principles Archive,

1993, https://www.fpparchive.org/media/documents/war_on_terrorism/The %20Clinton%20Body%20Count%3B%20Coincidence%20or%20the%20 Kiss%20of%20Death_Linda%20D.%20Thompson_1993_AEN%20News .pdf.

150   "What Bill did was stupid!": Donald J. Trump (@realdonaldtrump), "It Is Impossible for the FBI Not to Recommend Criminal Charges against Hillary Clinton. What She Did Was Wrong! What Bill Did Was Stupid!," Twitter, July 2, 2016, https://web.archive.org/web/20210107011645/https: /twitter.com/realDonaldTrump/status/749341789102960640.

150   no charges against Clinton: Camila Domonoske, "FBI Recommends No Charges for Hillary Clinton in Email Server Case," NPR, July 5, 2016, https://www.npr.org/sections/thetwo-way/2016/07/05/484785586/fbi -recommends-no-charges-for-hillary-clinton-in-email-server-case.

150   "mass arrest of the cabal": Anonymous, "/Pol/—Politically Incorrect » Thread #80526934," 4chan, July 10, 2016, https://archive.4plebs.org/pol /thread/80526934/#80540596.

150   "The lesson you should take": Anonymous, "/Pol/—Politically Incorrect » Thread #80632307," 4chan, July 11, 2016, http://archive.4plebs.org/pol /thread/80632307/#80632760.

150   The Seth Rich–Clinton connection theories spread: Philip Bump, "Don't Blame the Seth Rich Conspiracy on Russians. Blame Americans," *Washington Post*, July 9, 2019, https://www.washingtonpost.com/politics /2019/07/09/dont-blame-seth-rich-conspiracy-russians-blame-americans/.

151   Victor Thorn: "Sunrise, Sunset: Five Leading Extremists Dead in 2016," Southern Poverty Law Center, February 15, 2017, https://www.splcenter .org/fighting-hate/intelligence-report/2017/sunrise-sunset-five-leading -extremists-dead-2016.

151   "investigate Hillary Clinton Crimes": Carrie Johnson, "Trump Wants a Special Prosecutor for Clinton. But They Can Be Political Weapons, Too," NPR, September 1, 2016, https://www.npr.org/2016/09/01/492266302 /trump-wants-a-special-prosecutor-for-clinton-but-they-can-be-political -weapons-t.

151   stood a chance: Nolan D. McCaskill, "Trump Tells Wisconsin: Victory Was a Surprise," *Politico*, December 13, 2016, https://www.politico.com/ story/2016/12/donald-trump-wisconsin-232605.

151   "poll-watchers": John Kruzel, "Controversial Pro-Trump Group Warns Members to Avoid Election Day Meddling," *ABC News*, November 7, 2016,

https://abcnews.go.com/Politics/controversial-pro-trump-group-warns
-members-avoid-election/story?id=43372037.

152 "Meme magic is real": OhSnapYouGotServed, "DONALD J. TRUMP
DECLARED THE WINNER!," Reddit, November 9, 2016, https://
wayback.archive-it.org/org-89/20161116013309/https:/www.reddit
.com/r/The_Donald/comments/5bzjv5/donald_j_trump_declared_the
_winner/.

152 "Like [Andrew] Jackson's populism": Michael Wolff, "Ringside With Steve
Bannon at Trump Tower as the President-Elect's Strategist Plots 'An
Entirely New Political Movement' (Exclusive)," *Hollywood Reporter*,
November 18, 2016, https://www.hollywoodreporter.com/news/general
-news/steve-bannon-trump-tower-interview-trumps-strategist-plots-new
-political-movement-948747/.

153 "GOD BLESS WIKILEAKS": Matthew Rozsa, "'The Trolls Won':
Donald Trump Supporters, Including Milo Yiannopoulos and Chuck C.
Johnson, Gloat about Presidential Win," *Salon*, November 9, 2016,
https://www.salon.com/2016/11/09/the-trolls-won-donald-trump
-supporters-including-milo-yiannopoulos-and-chuck-c-johnson-gloat
-about-presidential-win/.

154 "Crying Iowan": Kyle Munson, "How This 'Crying Liberal' Iowan
Became a Worldwide Meme for Those Gloating over Trump's Win,"
Des Moines Register, January 14, 2017, https://www.desmoinesregister
.com/story/news/local/columnists/kyle-munson/2017/01/11/how-crying
-liberal-iowan-became-worldwide-meme-gloating-over-trumps-win/9625
2908/

155 "American progressives should be thanking their lucky stars": Ben
Schreckinger, "At Trump's Victory Party, Hints of Vengeance to Come,"
Politico, November 9, 2016, https://www.politico.com/story/2016/11/trump
-vengeance-victory-speech-2016-231084.

CHAPTER 5: HE WILL NOT DIVIDE US

157 "An American Tragedy": David Remnick, "An American Tragedy," *New
Yorker*, November 9, 2016, http://www.newyorker.com/news/news-desk/an
-american-tragedy-2.

157 It began with a Facebook post: Perry Stein, "The Woman Who Started the
Women's March with a Facebook Post Reflects: 'It Was Mind-Boggling,'"

Washington Post, January 31, 2017, https://www.washingtonpost.com/news /local/wp/2017/01/31/the-woman-who-started-the-womens-march-with-a -facebook-post-reflects-it-was-mind-boggling/.

158 pointed their fingers at Russia: Tom Hamburger, Rosalind S. Helderman, and Michael Birnbaum, "Inside Trump's Financial Ties to Russia and His Unusual Flattery of Vladimir Putin," *Washington Post*, June 17, 2016, https://www.washingtonpost.com/politics/inside-trumps-financial-ties -to-russia-and-his-unusual-flattery-of-vladimir-putin/2016/06/17/dbdcaac8 -31a6-11e6-8ff7-7b6c1998b7a0_story.html.

158 "Donald Trump is not an outlier": David Remnick, "Obama Reckons with a Trump Presidency," *New Yorker*, November 18, 2016, https://www .newyorker.com/magazine/2016/11/28/obama-reckons-with-a-trump -presidency.

158 "the epidemic of malicious fake news": Heidi Przybyla, "Hillary Clinton Cites 'Fake News' as Urgent Threat to Democracy," *USA Today*, December 8, 2016, https://www.usatoday.com/story/news/politics/onpolitics /2016/12/08/hillary-clinton-cites-fake-news-urgent-threat-democracy /95161136/.

158 "one of the greatest of all terms I've come up with": Brandon Carter, "Trump: 'One of the Greatest Terms I've Come up with Is "Fake,"'" *Hill*, October 8, 2017, https://thehill.com/homenews/administration/354445 -trump-one-of-the-greatest-terms-ive-come-up-with-is-fake.

158 "completely false content": Andrew Beaujon, "Trump Claims He Invented the Term 'Fake News'—Here's an Interview With the Guy Who Actually Helped Popularize It," *Washingtonian*, October 2, 2019, https://www.washingtonian.com/2019/10/02/trump-claims-he-invented -the-term-fake-news-an-interview-with-the-guy-who-actually-helped -popularize-it/.

158 Trump's first clear public use of the phrase "fake news": Donald J. Trump (@realdonaldtrump), "Reports by @CNN that I will be working on The Apprentice during my Presidency, even part time, are ridiculous & untrue— FAKE NEWS!," Twitter, December 10, 2016, accessed via Trump Twitter Archive.

159 Russian interference: Jeremy Diamond, "Russian Hacking and the 2016 Election: What You Need to Know," *CNN*, December 16, 2016, https://www .cnn.com/2016/12/12/politics/russian-hack-donald-trump-2016-election /index.html.

159 began to question the team: Jonathan Chait, "Donald Trump Building Team of Racists," *Intelligencer*, November 8, 2016, https://nymag.com /intelligencer/2016/11/donald-trump-building-team-of-racists.html.

160 "digital soldiers" speech: Rayne, "Michael Flynn's 'Revolution,'" empty-wheel, March 31, 2018, https://www.emptywheel.net/2018/03/30/michael -flynns-revolution/.

160 Flynn and his son had fought alongside these soldiers: Andrew Kaczynski and Nathan McDermott, "Michael Flynn's Son and Chief of Staff Pushed Conspiracy Theories, Obscene Memes Online," *CNN*, November 17, 2016, https://www.cnn.com/2016/11/17/politics/kfile-michael-flynn-social -media/index.html.

161 critical of Trump's message: Anonymous, "/Pol/—Politically Incorrect » Thread #98582664," 4chan, November 14, 2016, https://archive.4plebs.org /pol/thread/98582664/#98582664.

161 "really make America White Again." Andrew Anglin, "Yes, Trump Really Can Make America White Again—With or Without Cucked Congress," Daily Stormer, November 14, 2016, https://web.archive.org/web/2020100 4234047/https://dailystormer.su/yes-trump-really-can-make-america -white-again-with-or-without-cucked-congress/.

162 "Hail Trump, hail our people, hail victory!": *Atlantic*, "'Hail Trump!': Richard Spencer Speech Excerpts," YouTube video, 3:07, November 21, 2016, https://www.youtube.com/watch?v=106-bi3jlxk.

163 Heilgate: "4plebs » Global Search » Searching for Posts That Contain 'Heilgate' and in Ascending Order," 4chan, January 15, 2017, http://archive .4plebs.org/_/search/text/heilgate/order/asc/.

163 sold tickets on a sliding scale: Laila Kearney, "Trump Fans' 'Deploraball' Party Shows Rift in Alt-Right Movement," Reuters, December 29, 2016, https://www.reuters.com/article/us-usa-trump-deploraball/trump-fans -deploraball-party-shows-rift-in-alt-right-movement-idUSKBN14I1Y4.

163 "It all boils down to freedom of speech": Red Ice TV, "Baked Alaska—Oy Vey Banned from Deploraball," altCensored, January 11, 2017, https:// altcensored.com/watch?v=mO5MgST8xUk.

164 doxed the Right Stuff hosts: Jason Wilson, "Activists Claim to Unveil Leader of 'alt-Right' Website the Right Stuff," *Guardian*, January 17, 2017, https://www.theguardian.com/world/2017/jan/17/right-stuff-alt-right-site -mike-enoch-revealed.

165 "is morbidly obese": Matthew Sheffield, "The Alt-Right Eats Its Own: Neo-Nazi Podcaster 'Mike Enoch' Quits after Doxxers Reveal His Wife

Is Jewish," *Salon*, January 16, 2017, https://www.salon.com/2017/01/16/cat
-fight-on-the-alt-right-neo-nazi-podcaster-mike-enoch-quits-after
-doxxers-reveal-his-wife-is-jewish/.

165 Deploraball was held at the National Press Club: Natalie Andrews, "Before
the Inauguration Day Galas, a 'Deploraball,'" *Wall Street Journal*,
January 19, 2017, https://www.wsj.com/articles/before-the-inauguration
-day-galas-a-deploraball-1484848514.

166 Marantz attended the celebration for the *New Yorker*: Andrew Marantz,
"Trump Supporters at the DeploraBall," *New Yorker*, January 29, 2017,
https://www.newyorker.com/magazine/2017/02/06/trump-supporters-at
-the-deploraball.

166 Clapton would later walk this back in interviews: Tom Sykes, "Eric Clapton
Apologizes for Racist Past: 'I Sabotaged Everything'," *Daily Beast*,
January 12, 2018, https://www.thedailybeast.com/eric-clapton-apologizes
-for-racist-past-i-sabotaged-everything.

168 "What now?": Issie Lapowsky, "At the DeploraBall, Trump's Online Army
Wonders: What Now?" *Wired*, January 20, 2017, https://www.wired.com
/2017/01/deploraball-trumps-online-army-wonders-now/.

169 "There has been a lot of talk": Sarah Jaffe, "Trump Interruption: A
Conversation with Legba Carrefour," *Baffler*, January 19, 2017, https://
thebaffler.com/latest/interviews-for-resistance-carrefour.

169 some self-described anti-fascists threw objects: Newsy, "Protesters Smash
Windows at Trump Inauguration," YouTube video, 0:41, January 20, 2017,
https://www.youtube.com/watch?v=lVQ7LB03V-U.

169 More than two hundred arrests: Emily Shugerman, "J20 Protests: Justice
Department Drops Charges Against 129 People Involved in Trump
Inauguration Day Demonstrations," *Independent*, January 18, 2018, https://
content.jwplatform.com/previews/LcoVeDOm-9ygSIn9G.

169 Spencer told his fans: Richard B. Spencer (@RichardBSpencer), "The
Assault on Me," Periscope, January 20, 2017, https://www.pscp.tv
/RichardBSpencer/1YpJkqQoVEwKj.

170 "best of" lists: Jordan Darville, "The Best Memes of Neo-Nazi Richard
Spencer Getting Punched to Music," *Fader*, January 23, 2017, https://www
.thefader.com/2017/01/23/richard-spencer-punched-to-music-memes.

171 tweeted the hashtag #Resist: Alex Seitz-Wald, "The Anti-Trump
'Resistance' Turns a Year Old—and Grows Up," *NBC News*, January 19,
2018, https://www.nbcnews.com/storyline/2018-state-of-the-union-address
/anti-trump-resistance-turns-year-old-grows-n838821.

171 Twitter filled with jokes: Madison Malone Kircher, "Reliving the Inauguration Through Its Best and Funniest Tweets," *Intelligencer*, January 20, 2017, https://web.archive.org/web/20181116095919/https:/nymag.com/intelligencer/2017/01/best-funniest-trump-inauguration-tweets.html.

173 "Some members of the media": Hillary Crawford, "Sean Spicer Became a Meme in No Time," *Bustle*, January 22, 2017, https://www.bustle.com/p/13-sean-spicer-memes-that-put-his-absurd-inaugural-crowd-claims-in-their-place-32162.

173 "There's been a lot of talk": *CBS News*, "White House Press Secretary Sean Spicer Slams Media," YouTube video, 11:45, January 21, 2017, https://www.youtube.com/watch?v=yfcKvAWJbLo.

173 "Don't be so overly dramatic about it, Chuck": Meet the Press (@MeetThePress), "'Alternative Facts Are Not Facts. They Are Falsehoods,' Chuck Todd Tells Pres. Trump's Counselor Kellyanne Conway This Morning. WATCH: Https://T.Co/A0005dQ13r," Twitter, January 22, 2017, https://twitter.com/MeetThePress/status/823184384559878144.

173 Anti-Trump social media posts were heavily reported: "US Election 2016: Celebrities React to Donald Trump Victory," *BBC News*, November 9, 2016, https://www.bbc.com/news/entertainment-arts-37921426.

174 Jaden Smith kicked it off: TheCreator, "Jaden Smith—He Will Not Divide Us," YouTube video, 3:18, January 22, 2017, https://www.youtube.com/watch?v=iiYFKpZPRAg.

175 a masked figure approached the camera: I'm a fish, "Hewillnotdivide.Us Meets /Pol/—Highlights, Day 2 Part 1," YouTube video, 5:40, January 21, 2017, https://www.youtube.com/watch?v=g8HZVFzU7xI.

175 "Shadilay": GuAgIsOrAb, "Shadilay," Know Your Meme, June 3, 2021, https://knowyourmeme.com/memes/shadilay.

176 "Fourteen eighty-eight!": "Hewillnotdivide.Us Meets /Pol/—Highlights, Day 3 Part 2," YouTube video, 22:26, January 23, 2017, https://www.youtube.com/watch?v=7ghWluiDblk.

177 "Hitler did nothing wrong": jambi14, "Mustache Man vs. (((Shia Lebeouf)))," YouTube video, 1:27, January 23, 2017, https://www.youtube.com/watch?v=AMhPwDyj_Bw.

177 Stachebro: Tekajin, "Stachebro Joins the #HWNDU Scene /Pol/," YouTube video, 8:44, January 24, 2017, https://www.youtube.com/watch?v=gTIb-rD7qOg.

177 Well-known internet troll Brittany Venti: Autumn Able, "Brittany Venti," Know Your Meme, November 14, 2021, https://knowyourmeme.com/memes/people/brittany-venti.

177 banned from Twitch: F64_Rx, "BrittanyVenti Raided by 4Chan Then Banned," YouTube video, 54:38, June 13, 2015, https://www.youtube.com /watch?v=ypwVBV_h3po.

177 taking her cues from /pol/: Madcast Media Network, "BANNED FROM 'HE WILL NOT DIVIDE US' w/ Baked Alaska and Brittany Venti," Facebook, January 30, 2017, https://www.facebook.com/madcastmedia /videos/1330399150353208/.

177 "Sam Hyde Is the Shooter": *BuzzFeed News*, "Why 'Sam Hyde' Goes Viral After Every Mass Shooting," YouTube video, 3:11, July 2, 2019, https://www .buzzfeed.com/watch/video/86887.

177 "He can't keep getting away with this!": "Sam Hyde—He Can't Keep Getting Away With It," Know Your Meme, June 26, 2020, https:// knowyourmeme.com/photos/1866941-sam-hyde.

178 Hyde played a pickup artist: DigitalEdit, "Million Dollar Extreme Presents: World Peace—Mad at Dad? GOMAD for Chad MGTOW," Dailymotion video, 11:17, September 3, 2016, https://www.dailymotion.com/video/x4rlxmf.

179 Joe Bernstein reported on Hyde: Joseph Bernstein, "The Alt-Right Has Its Very Own TV Show on Adult Swim," *BuzzFeed News*, August 25, 2016, https://www.buzzfeednews.com/article/josephbernstein/the-alt-right-has -its-own-comedy-tv-show-on-a-time-warner-ne.

179 "Heebs will not divide us": alexsimo11, "Sam Hyde—Heebs Will Not Divide Us," YouTube, January 29, 2017, https://www.youtube.com/watch ?v=LeWuYiQ97qQ.

179 Hyde got into an altercation: suicidemorning, "Sam Hyde at #HWNDU Queens Bullshit PART TWO—1.28.2017 ##MDE @ FREENODE," YouTube video, 9:57, January 31, 2017, https://www.youtube.com/watch ?v=FB4C7ko_T2c.

180 Gionet came in a red MAGA hat: H Drone, "Baked Alaska's Message at He Will Not Divide Us," YouTube video, 11:41, January 31, 2017, https:// www.youtube.com/watch?v=tedb8brgDyw.

180 February 4 with Emily Youcis: Josh Bruhn, "Milk Man, Nathan Damigo and Emily Youcis on He Will Not Divide Us 02/04/2017," YouTube video, 11:50, February 4, 2017, https://www.youtube.com/watch?v=u_pgYOVnFJ4.

180 after video surfaced of her at Spencer's Heilgate incident: Will Bunch, "Well-Known Phillies Vendor in D.C. White-Nationalism Fracas," *Philadelphia Inquirer*, November 20, 2016, https://www.inquirer.com/philly /blogs/attytood/Well-known-Phillies-vendor-in-DC-white-nationalism -fracas.html.

180 "Shia LeBeouf, you will not replace us": Josh Bruhn, "Milk Man."

180 TRS podcast host Mike Enoch: alexsimo11, "Mike Enoch—Video 1," YouTube video, 0:40, January 29, 2017, https://www.youtube.com/watch ?v=xlqtnff1vIQ.

181 The anons even attempted to light it on fire: H Drone, "Drone Attack on HWNDU Flag: France," YouTube video, 6:22, October 24, 2017, https://www.youtube.com/watch?v=FvnWkeS6NOE.

183 "violence on innocent people": Rebecca Savransky, "Trump Threatens Funding Cut if UC Berkeley 'Does Not Allow Free Speech,'" *Hill*, February 2, 2017, https://thehill.com/homenews/administration/317494 -trump-threatens-no-federal-funds-if-uc-berkeley-does-not-allow-free.

183 Yiannopoulos joined *Tucker Carlson Tonight*: Fox News, "Milo: Media Legitimizes Violence on Conservatives," YouTube video, 15:38, February 2, 2017, https://www.youtube.com/watch?v=moNe7-sK8i8.

CHAPTER 6: UNITE THE RIGHT

185 "trivial fights": James Poniewozik, "President Trump Changes His Tone, If Not His Tune," *New York Times*, March 1, 2017, https://www.nytimes .com/2017/03/01/arts/television/president-trump-changes-his-tone-if-not -his-tune.html.

185 Executive Order 13767: "Border Security and Immigration Enforcement Improvements," *Federal Register: The Daily Journal of the United States Government*, January 30, 2017, https://www.federalregister.gov/documents /2017/01/30/2017-02095/border-security-and-immigration-enforcement -improvements.

185 February 2016 rally in Tampa: Conservative, "Trump Says 'The Wall Just Got TEN FEET HIGHER!' In Tampa, FL (2-12-16)," YouTube video, 0:39, February 13, 2016, https://www.youtube.com/watch?v=4ud3i DCZ_MA.

186 "radical Islam": Ryan Teague Beckwith, "Read Donald Trump's Speech on the Orlando Shooting," *Time*, June 13, 2016, https://time.com/4367120 /orlando-shooting-donald-trump-transcript/.

186 "A lot of people are saying": Nancy Rosenblum and Russell Muirhead, *A Lot of People Are Saying: The New Conspiracism and the Assault on Democracy* (Princeton, NJ: Princeton University Press, 2019).

186 92 percent turnover: Kathryn Dunn Tenpas, "Tracking Turnover in the Trump Administration," Brookings Institution, January 2021, https://www .brookings.edu/research/tracking-turnover-in-the-trump-administration/.

186 Flynn was forced to resign on February 13: Maggie Haberman et al., "Michael Flynn Resigns as National Security Adviser," *New York Times*, February 13, 2017, https://www.nytimes.com/2017/02/13/us/politics/donald -trump-national-security-adviser-michael-flynn.html.

186 he tweeted on March 31: Donald Trump, "Mike Flynn should ask for immunity in that this is a witch hunt (excuse for big election loss), by media & Dems, of historic proportion," Twitter, March 31, 2017, accessed on the Trump Twitter Archive V2 February 10, 2022, https://www.thetrumparchive .com/?searchbox=%22Mike+Flynn+should+ask+for+immunity%22.

187 "Nothing found. This is McCarthyism!": "Trump Wire-Tapping Claims 'Simply False'—Obama Spokesman," *BBC News*, March 4, 2017, https://www.bbc.com/news/world-us-canada-39168149.

187 sparked diplomatic tensions: Krishnadev Calamur, "Are Trump's Tweets Presidential?," *Atlantic*, December 19, 2017, https://www.theatlantic.com /video/index/513773/are-trumps-tweets-presidential/.

187 Paris Agreement: Michael D. Shear, "Trump Will Withdraw U.S. From Paris Climate Agreement," *New York Times*, June 1, 2017, https://www .nytimes.com/2017/06/01/climate/trump-paris-climate-agreement.html.

188 In late February, 2017: Oliver Darcy, "Behind the Anonymous Twitter Account That Took Down Milo Yiannopoulos," *Business Insider*, February 23, 2017, https://www.businessinsider.com/milo-yiannopoulos-reagan-battalion -anonymous-twitter-2017-2.

188 His former tour manager Gionet: Will Yates, "How Milo's Downfall Split the Alt-Right," *BBC News*, February 22, 2017, https://www.bbc.com/news /blogs-trending-39045458.

189 negative attention on CNN: Brian Stetler, "Donald Trump Attacks CNN in Tweetstorm," *CNN*, August 1, 2016, https://money.cnn.com/2016/08/01 /media/donald-trump-attacking-cnn/index.html.

190 early meme war threads: Anonymous, "/Pol/—Politically Incorrect » Thread #119553475," 4chan, April 4, 2017, https://archive.4plebs.org/pol /thread/119553475/#q119553475.

190 "Battle of the Billionaires": WWE, "Mr. McMahon and Donald Trump's Battle of the Billionaires Contract Signing," YouTube video, 22:06, December 8, 2013, https://www.youtube.com/watch?v=vVeVcV BW_CE.

190 asking his followers to identify the creator: Brian Stelter (@brianstelter), "The Anti-CNN Video Trump Tweeted Showed up on a Reddit Thread 4 Days Ago . . . Https://Reddit.Com/r/The_Donald/Comments/6jy5xo

/Trump_takes_down_fake_news_colorized_2017/," Twitter, July 2, 2017, https://twitter.com/brianstelter/status/881506511586902021.

190 "What a time to be alive with President @realDonaldTrump": Ricky Vaughn (@RickyVaughn_II), "What a Time to Be Alive with President @realDonaldTrump, God-Emperor of the Meme-Lords. #MAGA #Fraud NewsCNN #FNN Https://T.Co/Lh2g76wPOM," Twitter, July 2, 2017, https://web.archive.org/web/20170702170716if_/https:/twitter.com/Ricky Vaughn_II/status/881526821795135489.

190 "Hilarious reinforcement of FNN": Donald Trump Jr. (@DonaldJ TrumpJr), "CNN & Dems Calling Trump Assassination Play 'Artistic Expression' but WWF Joke Meme Is 'a Call for Violence'? Hilarious Reinforcement of FNN," Twitter, July 3, 2017, https://web.archive.org /web/20170707011008/https:/twitter.com/DonaldJTrumpJr/status/8818 52900770795520.

190 HanAssholeSolo was initially delighted: "Wow!! I Never Expected My Meme to Be Retweeted by the God Emporer Himself!!!" Reddit, July 2, 2017, http://archive.is/rkKQw.

191 "discovered HanAssholeSolo's identity": Andrew Kaczynski (@KFILE), "Here's Our Story on 'HanAssholeSolo' Posted by the Anti-CNN GIF Trump for the User Who Claimed Credit," Twitter, July 5, 2017, https://web .archive.org/web/20170706024636if_/https:/twitter.com/KFILE/status /882410031005802500.

191 WikiLeaks condemned the media spectacle: WikiLeaks (@wikileaks), "CNN Extorts Amateur Satirist Who Made Video Tweeted by Trump: If You Make Fun of Us Again We Will Harm You Http://Archive.Is/O7izm #selection-1233.0-1233.73 Https://T.Co/D3IvHdKUqX," Twitter, July 5, 2017, https://twitter.com/wikileaks/status/882422267166195713.

191 tweeted Mike Cernovich: Mike Cernovich, @cernovich, "How brave of CNN, a multi-billion dollar corporation, to go after a private citizen," July 4, 2017, https://archive.fo/aokVc#selection-3649.0-3649.84.

191 Posobiec jumped into the gathering storm: Jack Posobiec, @JackPosobiec, "The geniuses at CNN thought it would be a good idea to pick a fight with the American people on the 4th of July #CNNBlackmail," July 4, 2017, https://web.archive.org/web/20180808190044/https://twitter.com /jackposobiec/status/882445019830943744

191 "If you try to mock the mainstream media,": Crt, "Mister Metokur—CNN Dangerous and Fake 2017-07-04," YouTube, January 10, 2022 https://www .youtube.com/watch?v=f6t_rqFSciU

191 "Did CNN declare war on us?": Anonymous, "/Pol/—Politically Incorrect »
Thread #132426598," 4chan, July 4, 2017, https://archive.4plebs.org/pol
/thread/132426598/#q132426598.

192 "WE'RE GOING TO WAR /POL/": Anonymous, "/Pol/—Politically
Incorrect » Thread #132434649," 4chan, July 5, 2017, https://archive.4plebs
.org/pol/thread/132434649/#q132434649.

192 originated with Jack Posobiec: "Jackposobiec_tweet.Png," Southern
Poverty Law Center, July 4, 2017, https://www.splcenter.org/file/14943.

192 A rumor spread on the chans: Donald Trump Jr. (@DonaldJTrumpJr), "So
I Guess They Weren't Effective Threatening the Admin so They Go after
& Bully a 15 y/o? Seems in Line w Their 'Standards' #CNNBlackmail
Https://T.Co/U8YmNnLonj," Twitter, July 5, 2017, https://twitter.com
/DonaldJTrumpJr/status/882572743648169984.

192 "Any CNN employee": weev, "CNN Blackmails Teen Shitposter, They
Must Be Made to Taste Their Own Medicine," Daily Stormer, July 5,
2017, https://archive.ph/P4ECa.

193 Stephen Miller, an anti-immigration radical: Josh Harkinson, "Meet the
White Nationalist Trying to Ride the Trump Train to Lasting Power,"
Mother Jones, October 27, 2016, https://www.motherjones.com/politics
/2016/10/richard-spencer-trump-alt-right-white-nationalist/.

193 Richard Spencer moved to Washington, D.C.: Rosie Gray, "An Alt-Right
Leader Sets Up Shop in Northern Virginia," Atlantic, January 12, 2017,
https://www.theatlantic.com/politics/archive/2017/01/a-one-stop-shop
-for-the-alt-right/512921/.

194 courtesy of Mother Jones: Mother Jones (@MotherJones), "Meet the Dapper
White Nationalist Who Wins Even If Trump Loses Http://Ow.Ly
/MBCm305FoPW Https://T.Co/2SoYqi2bC8," Twitter, October 30, 2016,
https://twitter.com/MotherJones/status/792735410539655168.

194 Rally for Free Speech: News2Share, "LIVE—FREE SPEECH RALLY
FACES COUNTERPROTEST: Richard Spencer, Baked Alaska, and
Augustus Invictus Join Other Right-Wing Figures for a 'Freedom of
Speech Rally' on the National Mall. N2S Producers Ford Fischer and
Alejandro Alvarez Are There," Facebook, June 25, 2017, https://www
.facebook.com/N2Sreports/videos/1440631889378029/.

195 The other speakers were not so subtle: "Feuding Rallies in DC Reveal Far-
Right Groups' Different Priorities," Anti-Defamation League, June 27,
2017, https://www.adl.org/blog/feuding-rallies-in-dc-reveal-far-right-groups
-different-priorities.

195 Spencer suggested Stone bailed: Gideon Resnick, "Alt-Right Boss Attacks Trump's 'Repulsive and Creepy' Fanboys," *Daily Beast*, June 25, 2017, https://www.thedailybeast.com/alt-right-boss-attacks-trumps-repulsive -and-creepy-fanboys.

196 towered over the park: Editorial Board, "A Protest in Virginia with Echoes of the Klan," *New York Times*, May 17, 2017, https:/www.nytimes.com /2017/05/17/opinion/confederate-monument-protest-virginia.html.

198 first version of this remixed meme: "Message from @Bad Company," Discord Leaks, June 28, 2017, https://discordleaks.unicornriot.ninja /discord/view/192184?q=.

198 "Commander Davis (TWP)": Maura Mazurowski, "White Nationalist Recruitment Posts Stir Controversy on Campus," *Commonwealth Times*, August 29, 2016, https://web.archive.org/web/20170810034842/http:/www .commonwealthtimes.org/2016/08/29/white-nationalist-recruitment -posts-stir-controversy-campus.

199 inclusion of Kekistan: Don and YF, "Kekistan," Know Your Meme, December 12, 2021, https://knowyourmeme.com/memes/kekistan.

199 designed as a way to recognize one another: Anonymous, "/Pol/—Politically Incorrect » Thread #107424321," 4chan, January 16, 2017, http://archive .4plebs.org/pol/thread/107424321/#107425777.

200 "The core of marketing is aesthetic": Andrew Anglin, "PSA: When the Alt-Right Hits the Street, You Wanna Be Ready," Daily Stormer, August 9, 2017, https://web.archive.org/web/20170814125405/https:/www.dailystormer .com/psa-when-the-internet-becomes-real-life-and-the-alt-right-hits-the -street-you-wanna-be-ready/.

200 the ACLU deployed resources to defend the UTR rally's location: Joseph Goldstein, "After Backing Alt-Right in Charlottesville, A.C.L.U. Wrestles with Its Role," *New York Times*, August 17, 2017, https://www.nytimes.com /2017/08/17/nyregion/aclu-free-speech-rights-charlottesville-skokie-rally .html.

201 instructions for the rally: "Operation Unite the Right Charlottesville 2.0," Unicorn Riot, August 10, 2017, https://unicornriot.ninja/wp-content/ uploads/2017/08/OpOrd3_General.pdf.

201 a speech about white genocide: Chris Schiano, "White Supremacist Mob Carrying Torches Attacks Anti-Racist Protesters in Charlottesville," Unicorn Riot, August 12, 2017, https://unicornriot.ninja/2017/white-su premacist-mob-carrying-torches-attacks-anti-racist-protesters-charlot tesville/.

201 "our people are being torn down": "Fight and One Arrest as Protesters with Torches March Through UVA," News2Share, August 11, 2017, https://news2share.com/start/2017/08/11/fight-one-arrest-protesters-tor ches-march-uva/.

201 "Jews will not replace us": "Unite the Right Pre Game Torch March," YouTube video, August 11, 2017, http://archive.org/details/UniteTheRigh tPreGameTorchMarch.

203 *Vice* profiled Chris Cantwell as he arrived: Vice News, "Charlottesville: Race and Terror—VICE News Tonight (HBO)," *Vice News*, August 14, 2017, https://www.youtube.com/watch?v=P54sPoNlngg.

204 "We're going to fulfill the promises of Donald Trump": Sheryl Gay Stolberg and Brian M. Rosenthal, "Man Charged After White Nationalist Rally in Charlottesville Ends in Deadly Violence," *New York Times*, August 12, 2017, https://www.nytimes.com/2017/08/12/us/charlottesville-protest-white -nationalist.html.

204 James Fields: Jonathan M. Katz and Farah Stockman, "James Fields Guilty of First-Degree Murder in Death of Heather Heyer," *New York Times*, December 7, 2018, https://www.nytimes.com/2018/12/07/us/james-fields -trial-charlottesville-verdict.html.

205 statement from First Lady Melania Trump: Melania Trump 45 Archived (@FLOTUS45), "Our Country Encourages Freedom of Speech, but Let's Communicate w/o Hate in Our Hearts. No Good Comes from Violence. #Charlottesville," Twitter, August 12, 2017, https://twitter.com/FLOTUS45 /status/896409989568507906.

205 "on many sides": Angie Drobnic Holan, "PolitiFact—In Context: President Donald Trump's Statement on 'Many Sides' in Charlottesville, Va.," *PolitiFact*, August 14, 2017, https://www.politifact.com/article/2017/aug/14 /context-president-donald-trumps-saturday-statement/.

205 even The_Donald backtracked: Ashley Feinberg, "The Alt-Right Can't Disown Charlottesville," *Wired*, August 13, 2017, https://www.wired.com /story/alt-right-charlottesville-reddit-4chan/.

206 "very fine people on both sides": Angie Drobnic Holan, "In Context: Donald Trump's 'Very Fine People on Both Sides' Remarks (Transcript)," *PolitiFact*, April 26, 2019, https://www.politifact.com/article/2019/apr/26 /context-trumps-very-fine-people-both-sides-remarks/.

207 "The Trump presidency that we fought for": Peter Boyer, "Bannon: 'The Trump Presidency That We Fought For, and Won, Is Over,'" *Weekly Standard*, August 18, 2017, https://web.archive.org/web/20170820012910

/https:/www.weeklystandard.com/bannon-the-trump-presidency-that
-we-fought-for-and-won-is-over./article/2009355.

207 Roberta Kaplan: Mattie Kahn, "Two Years After Charlottesville, These
Women Are Taking the Alt-Right to Court," *Glamour*, October 7, 2019,
https://www.glamour.com/story/charlottesville-lawsuit-robbie-kaplan
-karen-dunn-amy-spitalnick.

207 "driving vehicles into protesters": Laura Adkins, "Roberta Kaplan Is
Crushing White Supremacists in Court—and She Wants America to Start
Taking Them More Seriously," *Jewish Telegraphic Agency*, January 21, 2021,
https://www.jta.org/2021/01/21/opinion/roberta-kaplan-is-crushing
-white-supremacists-in-court-and-she-wants-america-to-start-taking
-them-more-seriously.

207 "irreverent banter": George Joseph, "White Supremacists Joked About
Using Cars to Run Over Opponents Before Charlottesville," *ProPublica*,
August 28, 2017, https://www.propublica.org/article/white-supremacists
-joked-about-using-cars-to-run-over-opponents-before-charlottesville.

208 it is called deplatforming: Joan Donovan, "Navigating the Tech Stack:
When, Where and How Should We Moderate Content?" Centre for
International Governance Innovation, October 28, 2019, https://www
.cigionline.org/articles/navigating-tech-stack-when-where-and-how-should
-we-moderate-content/.

209 declared a state of emergency: Laurel Wamsley, "Florida's Governor
Declares State of Emergency Ahead of Richard Spencer Speech," NPR,
October 17, 2017, https://www.npr.org/sections/thetwo-way/2017/10/17
/558294630/floridas-governor-declares-state-of-emergency-ahead-of
-richard-spencer-speech.

209 firing shots at counterprotesters: Eric Levenson, "Police: 3 Men Made Nazi
Salutes, Shot at Protesters after Richard Spencer Event," *CNN*, October 21,
2017, https://www.cnn.com/2017/10/20/us/richard-spencer-florida-speech
-arrest-shooting/index.html.

210 anonymity and trolling served them best: Anonymous, "/Pol/—Politically
Incorrect » Thread #147543871," 4chan, November 1, 2017, https://archive
.4plebs.org/pol/thread/147543871/#147543871.

211 "trying to turn IOTBW into another Charlottesville": Anonymous,
"/Pol/—Politically Incorrect » Thread #148537296," 4chan, November 8,
2017, https://archive.4plebs.org/pol/thread/148537296/#148538342.

211 #MerchantRight: Right Wing Demystified, "Milo Under Fire from Anti-
Semitic Alt-Right for Selling 'It's Okay to Be White' T-Shirts," Medium,
November 5, 2017, https://medium.com/@rightdemystified/milo-under

-fire-from-anti-semitic-alt-right-for-selling-its-okay-to-be-white-t-shirts
-efc4a038b0d2.

CHAPTER 7: JOKER POLITICS

212 immediately started streaming: Liberum Arbitrium, "Nick Fuentes Before Unite The Right *Esoteric*," BitChute, September 19, 2020 https://www .bitchute.com/video/ZTvrRpDfR6T1/

213 drop red pills on stream: RexMode, "InfoWars Redpilled By the Alt Right at Unite the Right," BitChute, July 19, 2018, https://www.bitchute.com /video/vnmtOWkzEoGU/.

214 "A tidal wave of white identity is coming": Nicholas Fuentes, "Wow—What an Incredible Rally Here in Charlottesville. We Took Mace, Pepper Spray, Feces, They Sent in the National Guard, Counter Protesters, and Had the Governor Declare a State of Emergency—All to Silence Us. They Know the Stakes. You Can Call Us Racists, White Supremacists, Nazis, & Bigots. You Can Disavow Us on Social Media from Your Cushy Campus Reform Job. But You Will Not Replace Us. The Rootless Transnational Elite Knows That a Tidal Wave of White Identity Is Coming. And They Know That Once the Word Gets out, They Will Not Be Able to Stop Us. The Fire Rises!," Facebook, August 12, 2017, http://archive.is/tyXaB.

214 told the AP in a video interview: AP Archive, "Student Gets Death Threats after Virginia Rally," YouTube video, 3:12, August 23, 2017, https://www .youtube.com/watch?v=ftVtlOTfh18.

214 "The fix is in, it was a setup": Liberum Arbitrium, "NICK FUENTES AFTER UNITE THE RIGHT *ESOTERIC*," BitChute, September 19, 2020, https://www.bitchute.com/video/rhqEhH0NCbgc/.

215 *Nicholas J. Fuentes Show*: Nick Fuentes, Colin Bailey, and J. P. Remijas, *The Nicholas J. Fuentes Show*, IMDb, November 5, 2015, https://www.imdb.com /title/tt11898054/.

215 quickly became red-pilled: Nick Fuentes and Will Nardi, "DACA Demolition Debate Feat. Will Nardi," IMDb, September 13, 2017, https://www.imdb.com/title/tt8394412/.

215 "Donald Trump is the George Washington of this century": Nicholas Fuentes, "The Ascendency of the Madman," September 12, 2016, https://web .archive.org/web/20161110041330/http://www.nicholasjfuentes.com /home/archives/09-2016

215 "to hell with the democratic process": Nicholas Fuentes, "America Needs Trump More Than Democracy," Nicholas J. Fuentes, October 30, 2016,

https://web.archive.org/web/20170421075224/http://www.nicholasj fuentes.com/home/america-needs-trump-more-than-democracy

215 BU student roundup: Angel Cardamone et al., "YouSpeak: Who I'll Be Voting For," *BU Today*, October 31, 2016, https://www.bu.edu/articles/2016 /presidential-election-voter-psyche/.

216 "Are we living through the rapture": Liberum Arbitrium, "Nick Fuentes on Election Night 2016," BitChute, September 18, 2020, https://www .bitchute.com/video/tnJdFKhl12GO/.

216 "next rising star in the Republican party": Will Nardi, "My Strange College Rivalry with an Alt-Righter," *Vice*, April 2, 2018, https://www.vice.com/en /article/d3wkvj/college-conservativism-and-the-alt-right.

216 dream debate: Right Side Broadcasting Network, "Live: America First with Nicholas J. Fuentes Friday 3/10/17," YouTube video, 1:48:12, March 10, 2017, https://www.youtube.com/watch?v=Lydm5Q5SVnU.

217 "Time to kill the globalists": Media Matters Staff, "Right Side Broadcasting, the 'Unofficial Version of Trump TV,' Forced to Apologize for Contributor's Call to 'Kill the Globalists' at CNN," *Media Matters for America*, April 24, 2017, https:/www.mediamatters.org/cnn/right-side-broad casting-unofficial-version-trump-tv-forced-apologize-contributors-call -kill.

218 proved himself a ruthless debater: Destiny, "Debating Lauren Southern, NoBS, Fuentes, RM and More," YouTube video, 3:12:55, November 6, 2017, https://www.youtube.com/watch?v=igvA7LP6IA8.

218 "Fatter, More Racist Pepe the Frog": Aaron Mak, "The Far Right's New Toad Mascot Is a Fatter, More Racist Pepe the Frog," *Slate*, December 4, 2017, https://slate.com/technology/2017/12/groyper-the-far-right-s-new -meme-is-a-more-racist-version-of-pepe-the-frog.html.

219 "This dude and his legion of incel followers": "Nicholas J. Fuentes / America First / 'Nick the Knife'—Catboi Aficionado, Latinx White Nationalist, Manlet, Trump Dickrider, Age of Consent Abolitionist, Taliban Simp, Seething Incel," Kiwi Farms, January 6, 2020, https://kiwifarms.net /threads/nicholas-j-fuentes-america-first-nick-the-knife.64977/.

219 Jim named them "Internet Bloodsports": Xyllon's Archive, "Mister Metokur | Internet Bloodsports," YouTube video, August 27, 2019, https: //web.archive.org/web/20200418044621/https://www.youtube.com/watch ?v=ioy2Xhk1LGo; and callmeshirley, "Internet Bloodsports," Know Your Meme, May 11, 2021, https://knowyourmeme.com/memes/internet-blood sports.

219 "thot war": Anonymous, "/Pol/—Politically Incorrect » Thread #152323877," 4chan, December 7, 2017, http://archive.4plebs.org/pol/thread/152323877 /#152323877.

220 shared them on stream in December: NickFuentesArchives, "Nick Fuentes Reacts to His 23andMe Results," BitChute, 6:50, May 7, 2021, https://www .bitchute.com/video/tMQSOCfPbBbQ/.

220 "pedophile CIA LARPer": Groyper Nationalist, "Killstream: Nick Fuentes on Richard Spencer, Baked Alaska, and the Groyper Wars," YouTube, November 9, 2019, https://www.youtube.com/watch?v=_HYVAY7oe-E.

221 "pushing alt-right ideas through better propaganda": Luke O'Brien, "Trump's Most Influential White Nationalist Troll Is a Middlebury Grad Who Lives in Manhattan," *HuffPost*, April 5, 2018, https://www.huffpost .com/entry/trump-white-nationalist-troll-ricky-vaughn_n_5ac53167e4b0 9ef3b2432627.

221 "clearly couldn't keep a lid on it": Michael Edison Hayden, "The Alt-Right's First Real Political Candidate Went Too Far Right—Even for Many White Nationalists," *Newsweek*, March 14, 2018, https://www.newsweek.com/alt -rights-first-real-political-candidate-went-too-far-right-even-many-white -843664.

221 "Knife nation, raise your knives": Silent Aristocracy, "Nick the Knife Disavows Paul Nehlen," YouTube video, 3:59, April 5, 2018, https://www .youtube.com/watch?v=UmFueRntlic.

221 infighting and optics debate came to a head: Jane Coaston, "The Alt-Right Is Debating Whether to Try to Look Less like Nazis," *Vox*, August 10, 2018, https://www.vox.com/2018/8/10/17670996/alt-right-unite-the-right-nazis -charlottesville.

221 "lay low": Andrew Anglin, "Official Daily Stormer Position: Don't Go to 'Unite the Right 2'—We Disavow," Daily Caller, August 5, 2018, http:// archive.is/Qx85B.

221 "Seriously, don't go to the UTR": Anonymous, "/Pol/—Politically Incorrect » Thread #181865195," 4chan, August 10, 2018, https://archive .4plebs.org/pol/thread/181865195/#181867516.

221 "Even CIASpencer is telling people not go to UTR 2.0": Anonymous, "/Pol/—Politically Incorrect » Thread #181818426," 4chan, August 10, 2018, https://archive.4plebs.org/pol/thread/181818426/#181822335.

222 "wigger nationalists": Ben Lorber, "America First Is Inevitable," *Political Research Associates*, January 15, 2021, https://politicalresearch.org/2021/01/15 /america-first-inevitable; and Deus_Vult1488 et al., "Wignat," Urban

Dictionary, March 3, 2021, https://www.urbandictionary.com/define.php ?term=Wignat.

222 lone-wolf attack: Campbell Robertson et al., "11 Killed in Synagogue Massacre; Suspect Charged with 29 Counts," *New York Times*, Oct. 27, 2018, https://www.nytimes.com/2018/10/27/us/active-shooter-pittsburgh-syna gogue-shooting.html.

222 "Screw your optics": Kevin Roose, "On Gab, an Extremist-Friendly Site, Pittsburgh Shooting Suspect Aired His Hatred in Full," *New York Times*, October 28, 2018, https://www.nytimes.com/2018/10/28/us/gab-robert -bowers-pittsburgh-synagogue-shootings.html.

223 eighty-seven-page PDF: Brenton Tarrant, "The Great Replacement," accessed February 9, 2022, https://img-prod.ilfoglio.it/userUpload/The _Great_Replacementconvertito.pdf.

225 donated $1,700: Kelly Weill, "New Zealand Shooting Suspect Brenton Tarrant Donated to 'Identitarians,' 21st Century Fascist Movement," *Daily Beast*, March 27, 2019, https://www.thedailybeast.com/new-zealand -shooting-suspect-brenton-tarrant-donated-to-identitarians-21st-century -fascist-movement.

225 decades of anti-Muslim sentiment: Nathan Lean, *The Islamophobia Industry: How the Right Manufactures Hatred of Muslims* (London: Pluto Press, 2017).

225 September 2018: Feldman, "Tucker Carlson Slammed for Asking 'How Precisely Is Diversity Our Strength?,'" *Mediaite*, September 8, 2018, https://www.mediaite.com/tv/tucker-carlson-slammed-for-asking-how -precisely-is-diversity-our-strength/.

226 "clown world": Jared Holt, "White Nationalists Adopt Clowns as Their Next Racist Symbol (Yes, Seriously)," Right Wing Watch, April 4, 2019, https://www.rightwingwatch.org/post/white-nationalists-adopt-clowns -as-their-next-racist-symbol-yes-seriously/.

227 "Yang Gang": Samuel Argyle, "A Democratic Presidential Candidate's Curious Alt-Right Fandom," *Outline*, March 18, 2019, https://theoutline .com/post/7214/andrew-yang-campaign-alt-right.

228 hype and controversy: David Sims, "Untangling the Controversy Over the New 'Joker' Movie," *Atlantic*, October 3, 2019, https://www.theatlantic .com/entertainment/archive/2019/10/joker-movie-controversy/599326/.

228 "Why So Socialist" signs: Matt Jaffe, "Political Radar: Biden's Florida Rally Disrupted by Protesters," *ABC News*, November 2, 2008, https://web .archive.org/web/20081207002330/http:/blogs.abcnews.com/politicalradar /2008/11/bidens-florida.html.

229 Joker Obama: Mark Milian, "Obama Joker Artist Unmasked: A Fellow Chicagoan," *Los Angeles Times*, August 17, 2009, https://latimesblogs.latimes.com/washington/2009/08/obama-joker-artist.html.

229 "The American right's first successful use of street art": Ben Walters, "Why the Obama as Joker poster leaves a bad taste in the mouth," *Guardian*, August 5, 2009, https://www.theguardian.com/film/filmblog/2009/aug/05/obama-as-joker-poster.

229 August 30, 2009: Danielle Wong, " 'Freedom Lover' behind 'Obama Joker' Posters," *Toronto Star*, August 30, 2009, sec. GTA, https://www.thestar.com/news/gta/2009/08/30/freedom_lover_behind_obama_joker_posters.html; and Spitefinished, "Obama Is the Joker—Aka Barry Soetoro—Aka Alex Jones 1 of 3," Dailymotion video, 9:00, June 9, 2015, https://www.dailymotion.com/video/x2t8mna.

229 "it's hilarious to me": Spiro Kass, "LT Alumnus Steals Spotlight with Political Activism," *LION Online*, September 21, 2017, https://www.lionnewspaper.com/news/2017/09/21/lt-alumnus-steals-spotlight-with-political-activism/.

230 Gang Weed: Don, "Gang Weed," Know Your Meme, May 7, 2021, https://knowyourmeme.com/memes/sites/gang-weed; and Brian Feldman, "Once You Understand 'Gang Weed,' You'll Understand Everything," *Intelligencer*, August 2, 2018, https://nymag.com/intelligencer/2018/08/once-you-understand-gang-weed-youll-understand-everything.html.

231 reactionaries like Fuentes: Nick Fuentes, "Gamers Rise Up," IMDb, August 28, 2018, https://www.imdb.com/title/tt8913004/.

231 "We live in a society": Bill Wilson, "Make Joaquin Phoenix Say 'We Live in a Society' in the New Joker Film," Change.org, September 25, 2018, https://www.change.org/p/warner-brothers-make-joaquin-phoenix-say-we-live-in-a-society-in-the-new-joker-film.

232 proximity to the alt-right: Brendan Joel Kelley, "Turning Point USA's Blooming Romance with the Alt-Right," Southern Poverty Law Center, February 16, 2018, https://www.splcenter.org/hatewatch/2018/02/16/turning-point-usas-blooming-romance-alt-right.

233 Beginning on October 7: Mark Hernandez, "Conservative Activist Charlie Kirk Kicks off Culture War Tour at UNR, Attracts Protests," *Nevada Independent*, October 8, 2019, https://thenevadaindependent.com/article/conservative-activist-charlie-kirk-kicks-off-culture-war-tour-at-unr-attracts-protests.

233 went so far as to fire: "Turning Point USA," Anti-Defamation League, accessed February 9, 2022, https://www.adl.org/resources/backgrounders/turning-point-usa.

234 "debate me" style: Donna Zuckerberg, "The Problems with Online 'Debate Me' Culture," *Washington Post*, August 29, 2019, https://www.washingtonpost .com/outlook/whats-wrong-with-online-debate-me-culture/2019/08/29 /c0ec8aa2-c9ca-11e9-8067-196d9f17af68_story.html.

234 "an America First perspective": Couch Pimps Troll Team, "Charlie Kirk Calls USS Liberty Attacks A 'Conspiracy' + Embarrasses Himself," YouTube video, 1:28, October 23, 2019, https://www.youtube.com/watch ?v=Qo2lc2C8Azk.

234 founded the American Identity Movement: "American Identity Movement (AIM)," Anti-Defamation League, accessed February 9, 2022, https://www .adl.org/education/references/hate-symbols/american-identity-move ment-aim.

235 chat logs and real identities were leaked: Chris Schiano and Freddy Martinez, "Neo-Nazi Hipsters Identity Evropa Exposed In Discord Chat Leak," Unicorn Riot, March 6, 2019, https://unicornriot.ninja/2019/neo -nazi-hipsters-identity-evropa-exposed-in-discord-chat-leak/.

235 called upon AIM to join the Groypers: The Red Elephants Vincent James, "Charlie Kirk Security PHYSICALLY REMOVED Nick Fuentes at Politicon 2019," altCensored, October 28, 2019, https://altCensored.com /watch?v=GiUeCcpTUvM.

235 "How does homosexual sex help": Darren C G, "Culture War—Real Conservatives," YouTube video, 4:45, November 3, 2019, https://www .youtube.com/watch?v=2OsQ8gyAZiU.

235 Halloween podcast: McSpencer Group, "Groyper Nation Takes on the Culture War and the Rise and Fall . . . And Rise? of Paleoconservatives," *Radix Journal*, October 31, 2019, https://podcastaddict.com/episode/856 26153

235 "I'm not a left-wing person": Nick the Knife, "Nick Fuentes vs Ronny Cameron," AltCensored, Nov 1, 2019, https://www.altcensored.com/watch ?v=B43_xEmHi00.

236 "What you're seeing here is a fringe": Marty ScorchedEarthse, "Groyper War: Dan Crenshaw Groyped Hard at UT Austin Q&A," YouTube video, 7:20, November 7, 2019, https://www.youtube.com/watch?v=djBU9 BUDZY0.

236 On November 8: Leily Rezvani and Emma Talley, "Conservative Commentator Ben Shapiro Blasts Alt-Right, Radical Left, Identity Politics in MemAud Lecture," *Stanford Daily*, November 8, 2019, https://stanford daily.com/2019/11/08/conservative-commentator-ben-shapiro-blasts-alt -right-radical-left-identity-politics-in-memaud-lecture/.

236 Ben Shapiro gave a long speech: Nick the Knife, "Nick Fuentes reacts to Ben Shapiro Stanford Speech," AltCensored, November 8, 2019, https://altcensored.com/watch?v=fyugppKsHhU.

236 Fuentes reacted on his YouTube video livestream: Meto Fembot Clips, "Entire Nick Fuentes Reaction to Ben Shapiro—America First After Hours," YouTube video, 1:58:04, November 8, 2019, https://www.youtube.com/watch?v=E4IaiKJdJQw.

236 "shabbos goy race traitor": Jared Holt, "Anti-Semitic Outburst Cut From White Nationalist Nick Fuentes' Podcast on El Paso Shooting," Right Wing Watch, August 7, 2019, https://www.rightwingwatch.org/post/anti-semitic-outburst-cut-from-white-nationalist-nick-fuentes-podcast-on-el-paso-shooting/.

237 "It's because people hijack it": Groyper Nationalist, "Triggered Donald Trump Jr. Featuring Charlie Kirk Turning Point USA at UCLA November 10 2019," YouTube video, 35:00, November 10, 2019, https://www.youtube.com/watch?v=gtFduLsWRyU.

237 Trump Jr. only found out later: Ben Collins, "Pro-Trump Conservatives Are Getting Trolled in Real Life by a Far-Right Group," NBC News, November 12, 2019, https://www.nbcnews.com/tech/tech-news/pro-trump-conservatives-are-getting-trolled-real-life-far-right-n1080986.

237 tweeting support for Fuentes: Mister AntiBully (@MisterAntiBully), "Audience: We Want to Ask Questions TPUSA: Have Sex Incel This Will End Well. Pic.Twitter.Com/DrXlVyjIsk," Twitter, November 10, 2019, http://archive.is/eYKHo.

237 He made a video: Full-Blast Forever, "Mister Metokur: Nick Fuentes vs The World," YouTube video, 1:39:57, October 31, 2019, https://www.youtube.com/watch?v=LdZsxDsNjmk.

237 Yiannopoulos took notice too: Jack, "Milo Yiannopoulos Interviews Nicholas J Fuentes," BitTube, December 26, 2019, https://bittube.tv/post/465ed757-6a52-456a-a4f5-b7091e097afa.

238 crashed the annual TPUSA conference: Andy Ngo, "Nick Fuentes Is Asked About Kassy Dillon," YouTube video, 1:40, December 21, 2019, https://www.youtube.com/watch?v=zzIowpw35Y4; and Zachary Petrizzo, "Nick Fuentes Trying to Bicker with Ben Shapiro Riles Up the Internet (Updated)," Daily Dot, May 19, 2021, https://www.dailydot.com/debug/ben-shapiro-nick-fuentes/.

238 "Destroy the GOP": Christo Aivalis, "Trump Supporters and Nick Fuentes Chant 'DESTROY THE GOP' at Trump DC Rally," YouTube video, 7:22, December 12, 2020, https://www.youtube.com/watch?v=eNlCXsDwLQo.

CHAPTER 8: THESE PEOPLE ARE SICK

239 suspicion at the time: Julian Borger, "Donald Trump Expected to Abandon Iran Nuclear Deal Next Week," *Guardian*, October 6, 2017, https://www.theguardian.com/world/2017/oct/06/calm-before-the-storm-trump-set-to-walk-away-from-iran-nuclear-deal.

240 "You guys know what this represents?": "President Trump Photo Opportunity with Military Commanders," *C-SPAN*, 1:03, October 5, 2017, https://www.c-span.org/video/?435220-101/president-hints-calm-storm-dinner-military-commanders; Jennifer Calfas, "President Trump Warns of 'the Calm Before the Storm' During Military Meeting," *Time*, October 5, 2017, https://time.com/4971738/donald-trump-calm-before-the-storm-military-white-house/; and Jill Colvin, "With No Elaboration, Trump Talks of 'Calm before the Storm,'" *CTV News*, October 6, 2017, https://www.ctvnews.ca/world/with-no-elaboration-trump-talks-of-calm-before-the-storm-1.3621648.

241 "NORTH KOREA???": Anonymous, "/Pol/—Politically Incorrect » Thread #144204668," 4chan, October 5, 2017, http://archive.4plebs.org/pol/thread/144204668/#144204668.

241 *New York Times* broke allegations: Jodi Kantor and Megan Twohey, "Harvey Weinstein Paid Off Sexual Harassment Accusers for Decades," *New York Times*, October 5, 2017, https://www.nytimes.com/2017/10/05/us/harvey-weinstein-harassment-allegations.html.

241 "HRC extradition already in motion": Anonymous, "/Pol/—Politically Incorrect » Thread #146981635," 4chan, October 28, 2017, https://archive.4plebs.org/pol/thread/146981635/#q147012719.

241 "Hillary Clinton will be arrested": Anonymous, "/Pol/—Politically Incorrect » Thread #146981635," 4chan, October 28, 2017, https://archive.4plebs.org/pol/thread/146981635/#147005381.

242 give or take about a dozen "lost drops": The Q Origins Project, "How Q's 'Lost Drops' Undermine the QAnon Myth," Bellingcat, April 22, 2021, https://www.bellingcat.com/news/rest-of-world/2021/04/22/how-qs-lost-drops-undermine-the-qanon-myth/

242 not some Beltway insider like they insinuated: Abigail W. Xavier, Robert Amour and the Q Origins Project, "Where in the World is Q? Clues from Image Metadata," Bellingcat, May 10, 2021, https://www.bellingcat.com/news/rest-of-world/2021/05/10/where-in-the-world-is-q-clues-from-image-metadata/

244 treatise on the subject of global governance: H. G. Wells, *The New World Order* (London: Secker & Warburg, 1940), https://gutenberg.net.au/ebooks04/0400671h.html.

245 historic speech to the UN: "Gorbachev at the United Nations," *C-SPAN*, 1:35:15, December 7, 1988, https://www.c-span.org/video/?5292-1/gorbachev-united-nations.

245 "a new world order, where diverse nations are drawn together": "Address Before a Joint Session of the Congress on the State of the Union," George H. W. Bush Presidential Library and Museum, January 19, 1991, https://bush41library.tamu.edu/archives/public-papers/2656.

245 Q directly mentioned the New World Order: "Intel Drop #140," Q Alerts, November 11, 2017, https://qalerts.app/?n=140.

247 "An Empire has been slowly rising": Daniel de Leon, "Imperium in Imperio," *New York Daily People*, June 4, 1903, transcribed by Robert Bills, uploaded to the Marxists Internet Archive December 2006, https://www.marxists.org/archive/deleon/pdf/1903/jun04_1903.pdf.

247 "potential for the disastrous rise of misplaced power": "President Dwight Eisenhower Farewell Address," *C-SPAN*, 16:02, October 16, 2010, https://www.c-span.org/video/?15026-1/president-dwight-eisenhower-farewell-address.

247 "the deep state": Ryan Gingeras, "How the Deep State Came to America: A History," War on the Rocks, February 4, 2019, https://warontherocks.com/2019/02/how-the-deep-state-came-to-america-a-history/.

247 interviewed Scott about the deep state: Infowars.com and GCNLive.com, "Alex Jones Radio Show—March 30 2010," Internet Archive, March 30, 2010, http://archive.org/details/AlexJonesRadioShow-March302010.

248 "there is another government concealed": Mike Lofgren, "Essay: Anatomy of the Deep State," BillMoyers.com, February 21, 2014, https://billmoyers.com/2014/02/21/anatomy-of-the-deep-state/.

248 mass of leaks: Amanda Taub and Max Fisher, "As Leaks Multiply, Fears of a 'Deep State' in America," *New York Times*, February 17, 2017, https://www.nytimes.com/2017/02/16/world/americas/deep-state-leaks-trump.html.

248 convinced the right: Alana Abramson, "President Trump's Allies Keep Talking About the 'Deep State.' What's That?," *Time*, March 8, 2017, http://time.com/4692178/donald-trump-deep-state-breitbart-barack-obama/.

248 tweeted the phrase for the first time: Brendan Brown, "Search on Trump Twitter Archive for 'Deep State,'" Trump Twitter Archive V2, September 14, 2020, //www.thetrumparchive.com.

248 throughout his presidency: Becca Clemons, Molly Roberys, and Courtney Kan, "The Trump Administration, in Its Own Words," *Washington Post*, February 20, 2018, https://web.archive.org/web/20180220014139/https:/www.washingtonpost.com/graphics/2018/opinions/the-year-in-trump-quotes/.

248 Q used the meme: "Drop Search Results: Deep State," Q Alerts, September 30, 2020, https://qalerts.app/?q=deep+state&sortasc=1.

248 allegations of the Trump campaign colluding with Russia: Editorial Board, "Trump's Shadowy Money Trail," *New York Times*, May 9, 2018, https://www.nytimes.com/2018/05/09/opinion/trumps-shadowy-money-trail.html.

248 "Trump vs. the 'Deep State'": Evan Osnos, "Trump vs. the 'Deep State,'" *New Yorker*, May 14, 2018, https://www.newyorker.com/magazine/2018/05/21/trump-vs-the-deep-state.

249 Flynn resigned: "Michael Flynn: Timeline of His Rise, Fall and Guilty Plea," 2/14/17, *NBC News*, accessed February 9, 2022, https://www.nbcnews.com/news/us-news/mike-flynn-timeline-his-rise-fall-russia-call-n720671; and Maggie Haberman et al., "Michael Flynn Resigns as National Security Adviser," *New York Times*, February 13, 2017, https://www.nytimes.com/2017/02/13/us/politics/donald-trump-national-security-adviser-michael-flynn.html.

250 later filed to trademark the name: Candace Rondeaux, "The Digital General: How Trump Ally Michael Flynn Nurtured—and Profited From—the QAnon Conspiracy Theory," *The Intercept*, June 27, 2021, https://theintercept.com/2021/06/27/qanon-michael-flynn-digital-soldiers/.

250 first message about Flynn: "Intel Drop #14," Q Alerts, October 31, 2017, https://qalerts.app/?n=14.

250 "focus on Flynn": "Intel Drop #36," Q Alerts, November 2, 2017, https://qalerts.app/?n=36.

250 Flynn pleaded guilty: Tucker Higgins and Dan Mangan, "Michael Flynn, Trump's Ex-National Security Adviser, Pleads Guilty to Lying to the FBI; Now Cooperating with Russia Probe," *CNBC*, December 1, 2017, https://www.cnbc.com/2017/12/01/court-schedules-plea-hearing-for-flynn-at-1030-am-et.html.

250 "It is a shame": Donald J. Trump (@realdonaldtrump), "I Had to Fire General Flynn Because He Lied to the Vice President and the FBI. He Has Pled Guilty to Those Lies. It Is a Shame Because His Actions during the

Transition Were Lawful. There Was Nothing to Hide!," Twitter, December 2, 2017, https://web.archive.org/web/20190624012514/https:/twitter.com/realDonaldTrump/status/937007006526959618.

250 "Who knows where the bodies are buried?": "Intel Drop #260," Q Alerts, December 5, 2017, https://qalerts.app/?n=260.

251 "Disinfo is necessary": "Drop Search Results: Disinfo Is Necessary," Q Alerts, November 7, 2018, https://qalerts.app/?q=disinfo+is+necessary.

251 Open-source intelligence: Nihad A. Hassan and Rami Hijazi, "Open Source Intelligence Methods and Tools: A Practical Guide to Online Intelligence," WorldCat, 2018, https://www.books24x7.com/marc.asp?bookid=142755.

251 collective digital sleuthing: P. M. Krafft and Joan Donovan, "Disinformation by Design: The Use of Evidence Collages and Platform Filtering in a Media Manipulation Campaign," *Political Communication* 37, no. 2 (March 3, 2020): 194–214, https://doi.org/10.1080/10584609.2019.1686094.

252 dissenting opinions: Anonymous, "/Pol/—Politically Incorrect » Thread #147505376," 4chan, November 1, 2017, http://archive.4plebs.org/pol/thread/147505376/#147505376.

254 she was in Zuccotti Park: Jan Jekielek, "'This Is a Precipice'—Tracy Beanz on the 2020 Election, Information Warfare, and Draining the Swamp," *NTD*, 41:17, December 26, 2020, https://www.ntd.com/this-is-a-precipice-tracy-beanz-on-the-2020-election-information-warfare-and-draining-the-swamp_545386.html.

255 Q used a phrase: Anonymous, "/Pol/—Politically Incorrect » Thread #147970787," 4chan, November 4, 2017, https://archive.4plebs.org/pol/thread/147970787/#147975558.

255 "We've become a whore house": Anonymous, "/Pol/—Politically Incorrect » Thread #149079020," 4chan, November 12, 2017, http://archive.4plebs.org/pol/thread/149079020/#149079925.

255 Brennan later vigorously disavowed Watkins: Chris Francescani, "The Men Behind QAnon," ABC News, September 22, 2020, https://abcnews.go.com/Politics/men-qanon/story?id=73046374.

256 Trump retweeted the first: Alex Kaplan, "Trump Has Repeatedly Amplified QAnon Twitter Accounts. The FBI Has Linked the Conspiracy Theory to Domestic Terror," *Media Matters for America*, January 11, 2021, https://www.mediamatters.org/twitter/fbi-calls-qanon-domestic-terror-threat-trump-has-amplified-qanon-supporters-twitter-more-20.

256 "Who is Q?": Kelly Weill, "Roseanne Keeps Promoting QAnon, the Pro-Trump Conspiracy Theory That Makes Pizzagate Look Tame," *Daily Beast*, June 19, 2018, https://www.thedailybeast.com/roseanne-keeps-promoting-qanon-the-pro-trump-conspiracy-theory-that-makes-pizzagate-look-tame.

256 "We joked about it for years": 8chan (8ch.net) (@infinitechan), "We Joked about It for years, but #QAnon Is Making It a Reality: Boomers! On Your Imageboard. Https://T.Co/SG6ovnich2," Twitter, January 7, 2018, https://twitter.com/infinitechan/status/950118385517408256.

256 "Where we go one, we go all": "Intel Drop #513," Q Alerts, January 8, 2018, https://qalerts.app/?n=513.

257 "The Storm is upon us": The Hagmann Report, "Dr. Jerome Corsi—Analysis of Recent Q-Anon Postings—The Hagmann Report," BitChute, 24:17, January 9, 2018, https://www.bitchute.com/video/Dn-nsXSFkls/.

257 "irrefutable proof" that Q was real: Kyle Mantyala, "Jerome Corsi Has Uncovered Irrefutable Proof of the Authenticity of 'QAnon,'" Right Wing Watch, January 11, 2018, https://www.rightwingwatch.org/post/jerome-corsi-has-uncovered-irrefutable-proof-of-the-authenticity-of-qanon/.

257 "Look familiar? Note the desk": "Intel Drop #481," Q Alerts, January 6, 2018, https://qalerts.app/?n=481.

258 banned Tracy Diaz's Q subreddit: Andrew Wyrich, "Reddit Bans Far-Right r/CBTS_stream Subreddit Over Content Violation," *Daily Dot*, May 21, 2021, https://www.dailydot.com/debug/reddit-bans-r-cbts_stream/.

258 "Some are building a big following": "Intel Drop #1295," Q Alerts, April 29, 2018, https://qalerts.app/?n=1295.

258 "completely compromised": Kyle Mantyala, "Stick a Fork in QAnon: Alex Jones and Jerome Corsi Claim That QAnon Has Been 'Completely Compromised,'" Right Wing Watch, May 11, 2018, https://www.rightwingwatch.org/post/stick-a-fork-in-qanon-alex-jones-and-jerome-corsi-claim-that-qanon-has-been-completely-compromised/.

259 *Time* named Q: Time Staff, "25 Most Influential People on the Internet in 2018," *Time*, June 30, 2018, http://archive.is/1592u.

259 QAnon adherents showed up at Trump's Tampa rally: Justin Bank, Liam Stack, and Daniel Victor, "From 2018: Explaining QAnon, the Internet Conspiracy Theory That Showed Up at a Trump Rally," *New York Times*, August 1, 2018, https://www.nytimes.com/2018/08/01/us/politics/what-is-qanon.html.

259 Sanders was questioned: "Sarah Huckabee Sanders on 'QAnon' Conspiracy Theory," *CBS News*, 1:09, January 2, 2018, https://www.cbsnews.com/video/sarah-huckabee-sanders-on-qanon-conspiracy-theory/.

259 The_Donald banned QAnon discussion: Ben Collins and Brandy Zadrozny, "The Far Right Is Struggling to Contain Qanon after Giving It Life," *NBC News*, August 10, 2018, https://www.nbcnews.com/tech/tech-news/far-right-struggling-contain-qanon-after-giving-it-life-n899741.

259 Reddit banned it in early September: David Covucci, "Reddit Bans Popular QAnon Forum Great Awakening," *Daily Dot*, May 21, 2021, https://www.dailydot.com/debug/reddit-bans-qanon-forum-great-awakening/.

259 Mueller concluded his investigation: Sharon LaFraniere, "Mueller, in First Comments on Russia Inquiry, Declines to Clear Trump," *New York Times*, May 29, 2019, https://www.nytimes.com/2019/05/29/us/politics/mueller-special-counsel.html.

260 several QAnon accounts: Alex Kaplan, "Trump Has Repeatedly Amplified QAnon Twitter Accounts." *Media Matters for America*, August 1, 2019, https://www.mediamatters.org/twitter/fbi-calls-qanon-domestic-terror-threat-trump-has-amplified-qanon-supporters-twitter-more-20

261 "My #QAnon conspiracy conspiracy": Richard Spencer (@RichardBSpencer), "It's Doubtful That Mainstream, FOX-Level 'Conservatives' Will Embrace Q. But They Won't Denounce Him Either. The Phenomenon Serves Their Purposes, and They Will Put Forth a Slightly Less Wacky Version of the Q Narrative," Twitter, August 3, 2018, https://twitter.com/RichardBSpencer/status/1025184493705940992.

262 tone-deaf tweet: MATT DRUDGE (@DRUDGE), "Harvey Weinsten [*sic*] Complicated. Spent Magical Evening with Him at Soho House London Talking Movie Music. Others Always Said He Was Pure Monster," Twitter, October 6, 2017, http://archive.is/QF8sN.

262 Disney fired director: Brooke Barnes, "Disney Fires 'Guardians of the Galaxy' Director over Offensive Tweets," *New York Times*, July 20, 2018, https://www.nytimes.com/2018/07/20/business/media/james-gunn-fired-offensive-tweets.html

262 "The Harvey Weinstein case showed us": Itay Hod, "Mike Cernovich, Who Got James Gunn Fired Over Rape Tweets, Has History of Rape Tweets," *The Wrap*, July 24, 2018, https://www.thewrap.com/mike-cernovich-who-got-james-gunn-fired-over-rape-tweets-has-history-of-rape-tweets/

263   became a hero to the QAnon community: Will Sommer, "QAnon's Newest Hero Is D-List 'Vanderpump Rules' Star Isaac Kappy," *Daily Beast*, August 6, 2018, https://www.thedailybeast.com/qanons-newest-hero-is-a-d-list-vanderpump-rules-star.

263   On August 2: Helen Holmes, "Isaac Kappy, Who Appeared on 'Vanderpump Rules,' Is a Conspiracy Theory Shill," *Observer*, August 6, 2018: https://observer.com/2018/08/isaac-kappy-infowars-guest-qanon-supporter/.

264   "Everything has meaning": "Drop Search Results: Chester," Q Alerts, December 9, 2017, https://qalerts.app/?q=chester.

264   "Wow, what a baby": EJ Dickson, "Meet the Parents of 'QBaby', Star of the Trump Rally and New QAnon Mascot," *Rolling Stone*, July 18, 2019, https://www.rollingstone.com/culture/culture-news/qbaby-qanon-conspiracy-theory-trump-rally-860526/.

265   "While removing 8chan from our network takes heat off of us": Matthew Prince, "Terminating Service for 8chan," Cloudflare Blog, August 4, 2019, https://blog.cloudflare.com/terminating-service-for-8chan/.

266   Jeffrey Epstein died in his prison cell: William K. Rashbaum, Benjamin Weiser, and Michael Gold, "Jeffrey Epstein Dead in Suicide at Jail, Spurring Inquiries," *New York Times*, August 10, 2019, https://www.nytimes.com/2019/08/10/nyregion/jeffrey-epstein-suicide.html.

267   Trump supporter Paul Gosar: Jim Small, "Gosar Hides Twitter Message: 'Epstein Didn't Kill Himself,'" *Arizona Mirror*, November 13, 2019, https://www.azmirror.com/blog/gosar-hides-twitter-message-epstein-didnt-kill-himself/.

268   "I watched this Q phenomenon start": Banned.Video, "Alex Jones To Reveal The Founders Of Q," BitChute, 33:42, April 1, 2020, https://www.bitchute.com/video/BdJuy3fXLeKh/.

CHAPTER 9: FUCK AROUND AND FIND OUT

270   first anime-style Corona-Chan mascot: Autumn Able, "Corona-Chan," Know Your Meme, January 10, 2022, https://knowyourmeme.com/memes/corona-chan.

270   "Corona-Chan spreads love": Anonymous, "/Pol/—Politically Incorrect » Thread #240362042," 4chan, January 21, 2020, https://archive.4plebs.org/pol/thread/240362042/.

270   "It's fake": Anonymous, "/Pol/—Politically Incorrect » Thread #240468830," 4chan, January 22, 2020, http://archive.4plebs.org/pol/thread/240468830/#240468830.

272 Dylan Louis Monroe and his Deep State Mapping Project: "Covid Map,"
       Great Awakening Report, May 29, 2020, https://greatawakeningreport.com
       /covid-map/.

272 veteran right-wing tastemakers like Jim: Mister Metokur, "Great Wu Flu,"
       YouTube Video, January 24, 2020, accessed via https://odysee.com/@
       MisterMetokurArchive:7/The-Great-Wu-Flu_MIRROR:9. Martin Rooke,
       "Alternative Media Framing of COVID-19 Risks," *Current Sociology*,
       May 28, 2021, https://journals.sagepub.com/doi/full/10.1177/001139212
       11006115.

275 "You know, I don't know if this is coronavirus": *Fox & Friends*, "Donald
       Trump Jr.: Democrats Hoping for Coronavirus Disaster Is 'New Level of
       Sickness'," Fox News, February 28, 2020, https://video.foxnews.com/v
       /6136865482001#sp=show-clips.

275 Jared Kushner reportedly axed: Katherine Eban, "How Jared Kushner's
       Secret Testing Plan 'Went Poof into Thin Air,'" *Vanity Fair*, July 30, 2020,
       https://www.vanityfair.com/news/2020/07/how-jared-kushners-secret
       -testing-plan-went-poof-into-thin-air.

276 "Chinese Virus": Katie Rogers, Lara Jakes, and Ana Swanson, "Trump
       Defends Using 'Chinese Virus' Label, Ignoring Growing Criticism," *New
       York Times*, March 18, 2020, https://www.nytimes.com/2020/03/18/us
       /politics/china-virus.html.

276 anon on /pol/ had first posted: Anonymous, "/Pol/—Politically Incorrect »
       Thread #240802092," 4chan, January 25, 2020, http://archive.4plebs.org
       /pol/thread/240802092/#240803758.

276 tweeted on March 9, 2020: Charlie Kirk (@charliekirk11), "Why Is No One
       Talking about Punishing the Chinese Governemnt for the ChinaVirus?
       They Are Destablizing the World Economy Because of Their Lies, Deceit,
       and Unsanitary Conditions. They Need to Pay a Very Steep Price for What
       They Are Doing to Our Country Make China Pay!" Twitter, March 9,
       2020, https://twitter.com/charliekirk11/status/1237076555014098945.

276 next day he tweeted: Charlie Kirk (@charliekirk11), "Now, More than Ever,
       We Need the Wall With China Virus Spreading across the Globe, the US
       Stands a Chance If We Can Control of Our Borders President Trump Is
       Making It Happen I Explain Why This Matters & SO MUCH MORE!
       Subscribe—Https://Apple.Co/3355T5b Https://T.Co/97bN8Ll5bX," Twitter,
       March 10, 2020, https://twitter.com/charliekirk11/status/1237306970429
       775872.

277 Senator Tom Cotton and House minority leader Kevin McCarthy: Yulin
       Hswen et al., "Association of '#Covid19' Versus '#Chinesevirus' with

Anti-Asian Sentiments on Twitter: March 9–23, 2020," *American Journal of Public Health* 111, no. 5 (May 2021): 956–64, https://doi.org/10.2105/AJPH.2021.306154; and Kimmy Yan, "Trump Tweets about Coronavirus Using Term 'Chinese Virus,'" *NBC News*, March 16, 2020, https://www.nbcnews.com/news/asian-america/trump-tweets-about-coronavirus-using-term-chinese-virus-n1161161.

277 Bannon linked up with him: Rosalind Helderman, Josh Dawsey, and Matt Zapotosky, "How Former Trump Adviser Steve Bannon Joined Forces with a Chinese Billionaire Who Has Divided the President's Allies," *Washington Post*, September 13, 2020, https://www.washingtonpost.com/politics/steve-bannon-guo-wengui/2020/09/13/8b43cd06-e964-11ea-bc79-834454439a44_story.html.

277 Bannon signed a $1 million deal: Jonathan Swan and Erica Pandey, "Exclusive: Steve Bannon's $1 Million Deal Linked to a Chinese Billionaire," *Axios*, October 29, 2019, https://www.axios.com/steve-bannon-contract-chinese-billionaire-guo-media-fa6bc244-6d7a-4a53-9f03-1296d4fae5aa.html.

277 "We got elected on Drain the Swamp": Michael Lewis, "Has Anyone Seen the President?," *Bloomberg*, February 9, 2018, https://www.bloomberg.com/opinion/articles/2018-02-09/has-anyone-seen-the-president.

278 "'flood the zone'": "Flood the Zone," Wiktionary, November 13, 2020, https://en.wiktionary.org/w/index.php?title=flood_the_zone&oldid=61100644.

279 "Himalaya movement": Melanie Smith, Erin McAweeney, and Léa Ronzaud, *The COVID-19 "Infodemic,"* Graphika, April 2020, https://public-assets.graphika.com/reports/Graphika_Report_Covid19_Infodemic.pdf.

279 disinformation engine throughout 2020: Jeanne Whalen, Craig Timberg, and Eva Dou, "Chinese Businessman with Links to Steve Bannon Is Driving Force for a Sprawling Disinformation Network, Researchers Say," *Washington Post*, May 17, 2021, https://www.washingtonpost.com/technology/2021/05/17/guo-wengui-disinformation-steve-bannon/.

279 spreading medical misinformation: Ariel Bogle and Iris Zhao, "Anti-Beijing Group with Links to Steve Bannon Spreading COVID-19 Misinformation in Australia," ABC News Australia, October 8, 2020, https://www.abc.net.au/news/science/2020-10-09/anti-beijing-group-with-links-to-steve-bannon-misinformation/12735638.

279 #CCPvirus: Jennifer Zeng (@jenniferatntd), "Somewhere in #Wuhan, People Moving Body Secretly as 'Zero New Cases' Has Become a Political

Task, and Communities Dare Not Break the 'Zero New Cases' Record, so They Arrange to Have the Body Moved at Midnight. #CCPVirus #COVID2019 #Coronavirus #CoronavirusPandemic Https://T.Co /L2doNCTT1A," Twitter, April 7, 2020, https://twitter.com/jenniferatntd /status/1247522839147597825.

279 "trying to interrupt the United State elections": Echo Hui and Hagar Cohen, "They Once Peddled Misinformation for Guo Wengui and Steve Bannon. Now They're Speaking Out," ABC News Australia, October 31, 2020, https://www.abc.net.au/news/2020-11-01/behind-the-scenes-of-the -guo-and-bannon-led-propaganda-machine/12830824.

279 consistent 87 percent: Amina Dunn, "Trump's Approval Ratings so Far Are Unusually Stable—and Deeply Partisan," Pew Research Center, August 24, 2020, https://www.pewresearch.org/fact-tank/2020/08/24/trumps-approval -ratings-so-far-are-unusually-stable-and-deeply-partisan/.

280 death toll was being exaggerated: Jon Henley and Niamh McIntyre, "Survey Uncovers Widespread Belief in 'Dangerous' Covid Conspiracy Theories," *Guardian*, October 26, 2020, https://www.theguardian.com /world/2020/oct/26/survey-uncovers-widespread-belief-dangerous-covid -conspiracy-theories.

280 global internet use: "Digital Around the World," DataReportal—Global Digital Insights, January 2022, https://datareportal.com/global-digital -overview.

282 "Fuck Around Find Out": WXYZ-TV Channel 7 Detroit, "20-1013 Fox, et al. Preliminary Hearing—E-Filed," Scribd, October 14, 2020, https:// www.scribd.com/document/480091222/20-1013-Fox-Et-Al-Preliminary -Hearing-E-filed.

283 wearing it on T-shirts: 1776.com, "PROUD BOYS FF FAFO $30.00— $40.00," sold by the Green Dragon, September 30, 2020, accessed February 9, 2022, https://web.archive.org/web/20210126184256/https://1776.shop/pro duct/ff-fafo/.

283 FAFO adorned an unofficial antifa flag: deathschemist BLACK LIVES MATTER (@deathschemist1), "@stolenvalorcop @BigMeanInternet on the Contrary, the Left Is Starting to Realise Just How Powerful It Really Is. the Alligator's Mouth Is Open. Https://T.Co/Kly2k7l6gw," Twitter, June 9, 2020, https://twitter.com/deathschemist1/status/1270474837 920800769.

283 Meshawn Maddock: David D. Kirkpatrick and Mike McIntire, "'Its Own Domestic Army': How the G.O.P. Allied Itself with Militants," *New York*

Times, February 9, 2021, https://www.nytimes.com/2021/02/08/us/militias-republicans-michigan.html.

284 "well over a thousand": Austin Kellerman (@AustinKellerman), "MUST SEE: Hundreds of People Protesting Stay-at-Home Restrictions Outside the Michigan Capitol. Michigan Ranks #7 among US States with More than 40k #coronavirus Cases. @WOODTV's @LeonHendrix Reports for #NexstarNation's Newsfeed Now. #COVID19 Https://T.Co/FwzP2oJGtb," Twitter, April 30, 2020, https://twitter.com/AustinKellerman/status/1255885103898734593.

284 Two young girls: Resist Programming (@RzstProgramming), "At That Michigan Reopen Rally Today, Two Girls Danced. One Danced as a Minstrel with an Obama Mask on. The Other with a Trump Mask. This Has a 'Birth of a Nation' Black Politician Scene Vibe to It. Https://T.Co/8F6KqmbOT8," Twitter, April 30, 2020, https://twitter.com/RzstProgramming/status/1255996307929477122; and Read The Dispossessed by Ursula K. LeGuin (@JoshuaPotash), "This Happened Today at the 'Liberate' Nonsense in Michigan. Almost Feels like It's Not Just about the Stay Home Order. Https://T.Co/KpMXSjnAod," Twitter, April 30, 2020, https://twitter.com/JoshuaPotash/status/125593844909 87004673.

284 "My private security": Benny (@bennyjohnson), "My Private Security: Https://T.Co/CQJ3O8NViN," Twitter, April 30, 2020, https://twitter.com/bennyjohnson/status/1255888636744253440.

284 "loomed": Kathleen Gray, "In Michigan, a Dress Rehearsal for the Chaos at the Capitol on Wednesday," *New York Times*, January 9, 2021, https://www.nytimes.com/2021/01/09/us/politics/michigan-state-capitol.html.

284 hundreds crowded: Leon Hendrix (@LeonHendrix), "Inside the Michigan Capitol Right Now. Https://T.Co/Wu08AXRUM4," Twitter, April 30, 2020, https://twitter.com/LeonHendrix/status/1255914659435200512.

284 video from the lobby: NowThis (@nowthisnews), "Anti-Lockdown Protesters, Some Carrying Firearms, Demonstrated inside the Michigan State Capitol Thursday as Lawmakers Debated Statewide Lockdown Extensions Https://T.Co/CR8mHWrWqd," Twitter, April 30, 2020, https://twitter.com/nowthisnews/status/1255973450914488320.

285 Pastel QAnon: Kaitlyn Tiffany, "The Women Making Conspiracy Theories Beautiful," *Atlantic*, August 18, 2020, https://www.theatlantic.com/technology/archive/2020/08/how-instagram-aesthetics-repackage-qanon/615364/.

288 *Fall of the Cabal*: Interstellar Times, "THE FALL OF THE CABAL: THE END OF THE WORLD AS WE KNOW IT [2020]," Bitchute, March 22, 2020, https://www.bitchute.com/video/MYHTpUW9KAXQ/.

289 mobilizing in the streets: Steve Scauzillo, "Rally to 'Save the Children' from Human Traffickers Held in Upland," *Daily Bulletin*, July 31, 2020, https://www.dailybulletin.com/2020/07/31/rally-to-save-the-children -from-human-traffickers-held-in-upland/.

289 "Has anyone else noticed": Small Town Timbo (@TJPatriot1), "@God FamilyJesus @MrBOTUS_520 @Qanon76 @ToddBurgun @Returnofthe Gedi @T_Hammer_1776 @X22Report Has Anyone Else Noticed What's Going on with Your Normies Friends on Facebook Etc? People Who Have No Idea Who or What Q Is Are Sharing #SaveTheChildren Memes and Dark to Light Related Info. We Are Watching the #GreatAwakening in Real Time," Twitter, July 31, 2020, https://twitter.com/TJPatriot1/status /1289280053256130561.

289 "Child Lives Matter": RDM Team, "Child Lives Matter Protest," *Real Deal Media*, August 12, 2020, https://web.archive.org/web/202 00812161836/https:/realdealmedia.com/2020/07/31/child-lives-matter -protest/.

290 When George Floyd: New York Times Staff, "How George Floyd Died, and What Happened Next," *New York Times*, Nov 5, 2020, https://www .nytimes.com/article/george-floyd.html.

290 majority of BLM protests were entirely peaceful: Sanya Mansoor, "93% of Black Lives Matter Protests Have Been Peaceful: Report," *Time*, September 5, 2020, https://time.com/5886348/report-peaceful -protests/.

291 Proud Boys, along with other groups: Kelly Weill, "The Far Right Is Stirring Up Violence at Seattle's Capitol Hill Autonomous Zone," *Daily Beast*, June 16, 2020, https://www.thedailybeast.com/seattle-capitol-hill -autonomous-zone-visited-by-violent-proud-boys.

291 "riot porn": Joan Donovan, "How an Overload of Riot Porn Is Driving Conflict in the Streets," *MIT Technology Review*, September 3, 2020, https://www.technologyreview.com/2020/09/03/1007931/riot-porn-right -wing-vigilante-propaganda-social-media/.

291 designate antifa a terrorist organization: Maggie Haberman and Charlie Savage, "Trump, Lacking Clear Authority, Says U.S. Will Declare Antifa a Terrorist Group," *New York Times*, May 31, 2020, https://www.nytimes .com/2020/05/31/us/politics/trump-antifa-terrorist-group.html.

291 perpetuated by fake Twitter accounts: Brandy Zadrozny and Ben Collins, "Antifa Rumors Spread on Local Social Media with No Evidence," *NBC News*, June 2, 2020, https://www.nbcnews.com/tech/tech-news/antifa-rumors -spread-local-social-media-no-evidence-n1222486.

292 "When the looting starts, the shooting starts": Davey Alba, Kate Conger, and Raymond Zhong, "Twitter Adds Warnings to Trump and White House Tweets, Fueling Tensions," *New York Times*, May 29, 2020, https:// www.nytimes.com/2020/05/29/technology/trump-twitter-minneapolis -george-floyd.html.

295 pundits surmised: Justine Coleman, "Democrats More Likely than Republicans to Mail in Ballots Early: Poll," *The Hill*, September 15, 2020, https://thehill.com/homenews/campaign/516521-democrats-more-likely -to-mail-in-ballots-early-than-republicans-poll.

296 Biden's double-digit lead in the polls: Grace Sparks, "CNN Poll of Polls: Biden Maintains Double-Digit Lead over Trump Nationally, with Coronavirus a Top Issue," *CNN*, July 20, 2020, https://www.cnn.com/2020 /07/20/politics/poll-of-polls-july-trump-biden-coronavirus/index.html.

296 TikTok claimed: Taylor Lorenz, Kellen Browning, and Sheera Frenkel, "TikTok Teens and K-Pop Stans Say They Sank Trump Rally," *New York Times*, June 21, 2020, https://www.nytimes.com/2020/06/21/style/tiktok -trump-rally-tulsa.html.

296 "Trump Staffers Blame Themselves": Oma Seddiq, "'We Killed Herman Cain': Trump Staffers Say They Blame Themselves for Cain's COVID-19 Death after He Attended Tulsa Rally," *Business Insider*, November 11, 2021, https://www.businessinsider.com/trump-staffers-blame-themselves-for -herman-cains-covid-19-death-book-2021-11.

296 Trump Trains: Joel Rose, "As Pro-Trump Caravans Hit Roads Across U.S., Organizers Are Upbeat Despite Tensions," NPR, September 24, 2020, https://www.npr.org/2020/09/24/916497045/as-pro-trump-caravans-hit -roads-across-u-s-organizers-are-upbeat-despite-tension.

296 Trump Boat Parade: Bryan Pietsch and Aimee Ortiz, "At Least 4 Boats Sink During 'Trump Boat Parade' in Texas, Officials Say," *New York Times*, September 5, 2020, https://www.nytimes.com/2020/09/05/us/Texas-boat -parade-trump.html.

297 "I feel very badly": Alan Feuer, William K. Rashbaum, and Maggie Haberman, "Steve Bannon Is Charged with Fraud in We Build the Wall Campaign," *New York Times*, August 20, 2020, https://www.nytimes.com /2020/08/20/nyregion/steve-bannon-arrested-indicted.html.

297 released on a $5 million bail bond: Victoria Bekiempis, "Steve Bannon Pleads Not Guilty to Fraud after Arrest on Luxury Yacht," *Guardian*, August 20, 2020, https://www.theguardian.com/us-news/2020/aug/20/steve -bannon-arrested-charged-fraud-we-build-the-wall.

298 "We have the hard drive": Rachel Olding, "Steve Bannon Boasted on Dutch TV Weeks Ago That He Had Hunter Biden's Hard Drive," *Daily Beast*, October 16, 2020, https://www.thedailybeast.com/steve-bannon-boasted -on-dutch-tv-weeks-ago-that-he-had-hunter-bidens-hard-drive.

298 "Proud Boys," Trump said: Sheera Frenkel and Annie Karni, "Proud Boys Celebrate Trump's 'Stand by' Remark About Them at the Debate," *New York Times*, September 30, 2020, https://www.nytimes.com/2020/09 /29/us/trump-proud-boys-biden.html.

298 gave Hunter Biden's laptop to the *Wall Street Journal*: Ben Smith, "Trump Had One Last Story to Sell. The Wall Street Journal Wouldn't Buy It," *New York Times*, October 25, 2020, https://www.nytimes.com/2020/10/25 /business/media/hunter-biden-wall-street-journal-trump.html.

298 Hunter Biden's nudes: "GNEWS Homepage," *GNEWS*, October 25, 2020, http://archive.is/jWp9v.

298 "number one propagandist for Guo Wengui": Hui and Cohen, "They Once Peddled Misinformation for Guo Wengui and Steve Bannon."

299 "There has been zero mention": Anonymous, "/Pol/—Politically Incorrect » Thread #284786496," 4chan, October 26, 2020, http://archive.4plebs.org /pol/thread/284786496/#284870715.

299 "/pol/ sure loves to click": Anonymous, "/Pol/—Politically Incorrect » Thread #285154313," 4chan, October 27, 2020, http://archive.4plebs.org /pol/thread/285154313/#285176795.

300 "Less Hunter Biden dick pics": Anonymous, "/Pol/—Politically Incorrect » Thread #287822528," 4chan, November 5, 2020, http://archive.4plebs.org /pol/thread/287822528/#287823720.

300 tweeted dozens: Brendan Brown, "Search on Trump Twitter Archive Nov 2-3, 2020," Trump Twitter Archive V2, Accessed March 11, 2022, https:// www.thetrumparchive.com/?dates=%5B%222020-11-02%22%2C%22202 0-11-03%22%5D&results=1

301 Fox News became: Sarah Ellison, "Trump Campaign Was Livid When Fox News Called Arizona for Biden, and Tensions Boiled over On-Air," *Washington Post*, November 4, 2020, https://www.washingtonpost.com /lifestyle/style/fox-news-election-night-arizona/2020/11/04/194f9968 -1e71-11eb-90dd-abd0f7086a91_story.html.

CHAPTER 10: STOP THE STEAL

303 "So we're going to walk down Pennsylvania Avenue": CNN, "Read: Former President Donald Trump's January 6 speech," *CNN*, https://www .cnn.com/2021/02/08/politics/trump-january-6-speech-transcript/index .html.

304 At one point he entered an office in the building: Michael Balsamo, "Far-Right Personality 'Baked Alaska' Arrested in Riot Probe," Associated Press, January 16, 2021, https://apnews.com/article/joe-biden-donald-trump -capitol-siege-alaska-crime-6666c735165a19a6ee019e412235bd8d.

306 Gionet included: Aja Romano, "Baked Alaska's Clout-Chasing Spiral into White Supremacy Is an Internet Morality Tale," Vox, January 17, 2021, https://www.vox.com/22235691/baked-alaska-tim-gionet-arrest-capitol -riot-alt-right-buzzfeed.

307 "Stop the Steal," a memetic phrase: Rosie Gray, "Trump Ally Roger Stone Says He's Planning 'Days Of Rage' at the Convention," *BuzzFeed News*, April 1, 2016, https://www.buzzfeednews.com/article/rosiegray/trump-ally -roger-stone-says-hes-planning-days-of-rage-at-the.

308 led Facebook to terminate several of his pages: Elizabeth Dwoskin, "Facebook Takes down a Widespread Network of Pages Tied to Stephen Bannon for Pushing Misinformation," *Washington Post*, November 9, 2020, https://www.washingtonpost.com/technology/2020/11/09/facebook-steve -bannon-misinformation/.

308 "We're Not Gonna Take It": "Intel Drop #4953," Q Alerts, December 8, 2020, https://qalerts.app/?n=4953.

309 "11:00 A.M.," Trump tweeted: Natasha Jokic, "Trump's Four Seasons Total Landscaping Conference Twitter Reactions," BuzzFeed, November 8, 2020, https://www.buzzfeed.com/natashajokic1/four-seasons-landscaping -tweets.

309 reporter Jim Acosta tweeted: Tia Landry (@tia_ms17), "My Favorite of the Four Seasons Total Landscaping Moments Https://T.Co/SBn6fyIjw9," Twitter, November 7, 2020, https://twitter.com/tia_ms17/status/1325104 921566453760.

310 "release the Kraken": andcallmeshirley, "Release the Kraken!," Know Your Meme, November 2, 2021, https://knowyourmeme.com/memes/release-the -kraken.

310 "It's gonna be biblical": Newsmax TV, "Sidney Powell: It Will Be BIBLICAL," YouTube video, 20:40, November 21, 2020, https://www .youtube.com/watch?v=Y68pEknYyCM.

310 according to fact checkers: Amy Sherman and Miriam Valverde, "Joe Biden Is Right That More Than 60 of Trump's Election Lawsuits Lacked Merit," PolitiFact, January 8, 2021, https://www.politifact.com/factchecks/2021/jan/08/joe-biden/joe-biden-right-more-60-trumps-election-lawsuits-l/.

310 "fantastical": Alison Durkee, "'Kraken' Sanctions Hearing: Lin Wood Blames Sidney Powell in Attempt to Evade Punishment as Judge Expresses Skepticism," *Forbes*, July 12, 2021, https://www.forbes.com/sites/alisondurkee/2021/07/12/kraken-sanctions-hearing-lin-wood-blames-sidney-powell-in-attempt-to-evade-punishment-as-judge-expresses-skepticism/.

311 Women for America First: Brian Schwartz, "Pro-Trump Dark Money Groups Organized the Rally That Led to Deadly Capitol Hill Riot," CNBC, April 9, 2021, https://www.cnbc.com/2021/01/09/pro-trump-dark-money-groups-organized-the-rally-that-led-to-deadly-capitol-hill-riot.html.

311 on sites like Reddit replacement TheDonald.win: Ryan Goodman and Justin Hendrix, "The Absence of 'The Donald'," Just Security, December 6, 2021, https://www.justsecurity.org/79446/the-absence-of-the-donald/.

311 a garage's three-hour limit: Faine Greenwood (@faineg), "The Fascists Totally Are Going to Take over DC but First They Need to Find Parking. (3 Hours Is Enough to Execute a Coup, Right?) Https://T.Co/1QmCK HONcG," Twitter, January 6, 2021, https://twitter.com/faineg/status/1346815005359013888.

312 Bannon posted to a Stop the Steal Facebook page: David Gilbert, "Steve Bannon Urged Facebook Followers to 'Take Action' on Eve of Capitol Riot," *Vice*, January 15, 2021, https://www.vice.com/en/article/n7vqgb/steve-bannon-urged-facebook-followers-to-take-action-on-eve-of-capitol-riot.

312 *War Room* podcast: Dan Evon, "Did Bannon Say 'All Hell Is Going to Break Loose' Before Capitol Attack?" *Snopes*, July 29, 2021, https://www.snopes.com/fact-check/bannon-hell-capitol-attack/.

312 "Tomorrow is a great day": Jan 6th Protest and Save America March, "Alex Jones Lays Out What Really Happened at the US Capitol," Banned.Video, January 7, 2021, https://futurenews.news/watch?id=5ff74f7d1669d333f2b28be4.

313 some of whom witnessed: Rachel Levy, Dan Frosch, and Sadie Gurman, "Capitol Riot Warnings Weren't Acted On as System Failed," *Wall Street Journal*, February 8, 2021, https://www.wsj.com/articles/capitol-riot-warnings-werent-acted-on-as-system-failed-11612787596?mod=article_inline.

313 "Let's take the fucking Capitol!": Georgia Wells, Rebecca Ballhaus, and Keach Hagey, "Proud Boys, Seizing Trump's Call to Washington, Helped

Lead Capitol Attack," *Wall Street Journal*, January 17, 2021, https://www .wsj.com/articles/proud-boys-seizing-trumps-call-to-washington-helped -lead-capitol-attack-11610911596.

313 Tarrio had told them this was their D-day: Sadie Gurman and Aruna Viswanatha, "Prosecutors Report Evidence of Advance Coordination in Capitol Riots," *Wall Street Journal*, January 15, 2021, https://www.wsj.com /articles/federal-agencies-congress-launch-reviews-into-handling-of -capitol-riots-11610738140?mod=article_inline.

314 Members of the Oath Keepers, Proud Boys, and other militia groups: Dmitriy Khavin, Haley Willis, Evan Hill, Natalie Reneau, Drew Jordan, Cora Engelbrecht, Christiaan Triebert, Stella Cooper, Malachy Browne and David Botti, "Day of Rage: How Trump Supporters Took the US Capitol," *New York Times*, June 30, 2021, https://www.nytimes.com/video /us/politics/100000007606996/capitol-riot-trump-supporters.html.

315 "Not gonna lie. . . . .aside from my kids, this was, indeed, the best day of my life": Rebecca Cohen, "A Texas Sheriff's Lieutenant Who Called the Capitol Riot One of the Best Days of Her Life Has Been Fired," *Insider*, December 28, 2021 https://www.insider.com/texas-sheriffs-lieutenant-at -capitol-riot-fired-2021-12.

315 fired for her participation: Rebecca Cohen, "A Texas Sheriff's Lieutenant Who Called the Capitol Riot One of the Best Days of Her Life Has Been Fired," MSN, December 28, 2021, https://www.msn.com/en-us/news/crime /a-texas-sheriffs-lieutenant-who-called-the-capitol-riot-one-of-the-best -days-of-her-life-has-been-fired/ar-AASdixv.

315 frantically texting: Tom Dreisbach and David Folkenflik, "The Texts Fox Hosts Sent during the Jan. 6 Riot Don't Match How Fox Covered It on Air," NPR, December 15, 2021, https://www.npr.org/2021/12/15/1064 614645/the-texts-fox-hosts-sent-during-the-jan-6-riot-dont-match-how -fox-covered-it-on-.

316 deleted more than seventy thousand QAnon-related accounts: Kate Conger, "Twitter, in Widening Crackdown, Removes Over 70,000 QAnon Accounts," *New York Times*, January 20, 2021, https://www.nytimes.com /2021/01/11/technology/twitter-removes-70000-qanon-accounts.html.

316 YouTube promised: Jennifer Elias, "YouTube Video Says It Will Move More Quickly to Suspend Channels Posting Videos Claiming Widespread Voter Fraud," CNBC, January 7, 2021, https://www.cnbc.com/2021/01/07 /youtube-says-it-will-suspend-channels-claiming-widespread-voter-fraud .html.

316   Mike Lindell, Lin Wood, Sidney Powell, 8kun administrator Ron Watkins: Roger Stone, and Steve Bannon, "Twitter Bans Michael Flynn, Sidney Powell in QAnon Account Purge," NBC News, January 8, 2021, https://www.nbcnews.com/tech/tech-news/twitter-bans-michael-flynn-sidney-powell-qanon-account-purge-n1253550.

316   "It breaks my heart": Matthew Brown and William Cummings, "Republicans' Opinions of Trump's Role in Capitol Riots Softened between Jan. 6 and Acquittal Vote," USA Today, February 15, 2021, https://www.usatoday.com/story/news/politics/2021/02/15/evlolving-republican-attitudes-trump-role-capitol-riot/6740345002/.

317   Laura Ingraham suggested: Meg Anderson, "Antifa Didn't Storm the Capitol. Just Ask the Rioters," NPR, March 2, 2021, https://www.npr.org/2021/03/02/972564176/antifa-didnt-storm-the-capitol-just-ask-the-rioters.

317   On January 13: Seung Min Kim and Paul Kane, "McConnell Breaks with Trump, Says He'll Consider Convicting Him in Senate Trial," Washington Post, January 14, 2021, https://www.washingtonpost.com/politics/mcconnell-trump-impeach-senate-riot/2021/01/13/e4dab8d8-55c6-11eb-a817-e5e7f8a406d6_story.html.

317   half of Republicans polled: Zachary Petrizzo, "Half of Republicans Think Jan. 6 Siege Was Peaceful or Staged by Antifa, New Poll Finds | Salon.Com," Salon, April 6, 2021, https://www.salon.com/2021/04/06/half-of-republicans-think-jan-6-siege-was-peaceful-or-staged-by-antifa-new-poll-finds/.

318   carrying a Thin Blue Line flag: Associated Press, "Jan. 6 Committee: DC Metro Officer Saw Law Enforcement Support Flag amid Riots," USA Today, July 27, 2021, https://www.usatoday.com/videos/news/politics/2021/07/27/officer-describes-seeing-thin-blue-line-flag-amid-jan-6-riot/5387278001/.

318   using the pole of a Thin Blue Line flag: Travis Gettys, "New Video Shows Trump Supporters Assaulting Officer Michael Fanone Beneath 'Blue Lives Matter' Flag," Raw Story, October 20, 2021, https://www.rawstory.com/michael-fanone-capitol-2655328214/.

318   warned that he could destroy America: John McNeill, "How Fascist Is Donald Trump? There's Actually a Formula for That," Washington Post, October 21, 2016, https://www.washingtonpost.com/posteverything/wp/2016/10/21/how-fascist-is-donald-trump-theres-actually-a-formula-for-that/; Dylan Matthews, "This Is How the American System of Government Will Die," Vox, March 3, 2015, https://www.vox.com/2015/3/3/8120965

/american-government-problems; Andrew Sullivan, "America and the Abyss," Intelligencer, November 3, 2016, https://nymag.com/intelligencer /2016/11/andrew-sullivan-trump-america-and-the-abyss.html; and Jamelle Bouie, "Donald Trump Is a Fascist," *Slate*, November 25, 2015, https://slate .com/news-and-politics/2015/11/donald-trump-is-a-fascist-it-is-the -political-label-that-best-describes-the-gop-front-runner.html.

318 warning Americans that the United States could be next: Phoebe Neidl, "Masha Gessen: A Russian's Perspective on Trump's Autocratic Impulses," *Rolling Stone*, August 31, 2017, https://www.rollingstone.com/politics /politics-features/masha-gessen-a-russians-perspective-on-trumps -autocratic-impulses-128037/; Yascha Mounk, "Yes, American Democracy Could Break Down," *Politico*, October 22, 2016, http://politi.co/2zUV1tZ.

318 checks and balances: Zachary Karabell, "Why Trump Can't Become a Dictator," *Politico*, June 21, 2016, https://www.politico.com/magazine/story /2016/06/2016-donald-trump-dictator-fascist-checks-and-balances-us -politics-government-213978/; Jon Michaels, "Op-Ed: The Founders Anticipated Trump. We Can Handle This," *Los Angeles Times*, November 11, 2016, https://www.latimes.com/opinion/op-ed/la-oe-michaels-checks -balances-trump-20161111-story.html.

320 "Is this America?" It was the same question: PBS NewsHour, "WATCH: Asked About Racist Abuse on Jan. 6, Officer Dunn Says, 'I Guess It Is America,'" YouTube video, 4:18, July 27, 2021, https://www.youtube.com /watch?v=RnrpwQ_gzP8.

323 hundreds of treaties: Vine Deloria, *Behind the Trail of Broken Treaties: An Indian Declaration of Independence* (Austin: University of Texas Press, 2010).

323 redefine the meaning of Native American: Kim TallBear, *Native American DNA: Tribal Belonging and the False Promise of Genetic Science* (Minneapolis: University of Minnesota Press, 2013).

325 "The message is self-generated": Manuel Castells, *Communication Power* (New York: Oxford University Press, 2009).

329 shaped how they reach new audiences: Joan Donovan, Becca Lewis, and Brian Friedberg, "Parallel Ports: Sociotechnical Change from the Alt-Right to Alt-Tech," in *Post-Digital Cultures of the Far Right*, ed. Maik Fielitz and Nick Thurston (New York: Columbia University Press, 2019), 49–65, https:// mediarep.org/bitstream/handle/doc/13283/Post_Digital_Cultures_49-65 _Donovan_ea_Parallel_Ports_.pdf.

329 Whitney Phillips and Ryan Milner: Whitney Phillips and Ryan Milner, *You Are Here: A Field Guide for Navigating Polarized Speech, Conspiracy Theories, and our Polluted Media Landscape* (Cambridge, MA: MIT Press, 2021).

330 calling them out: Joan Donovan and Ahmed Khan, "Big Tech Was Allowed to Spread Misinformation Unchecked. Will Biden Hold Them Accountable?," *Guardian*, January 27, 2021, sec. Technology, https://www.theguardian.com/technology/commentisfree/2021/jan/27/qanon-facebook-google-twitter-misinformation-big-tech.

330 among these powerful elites: Dylan Byers and Ben Collins, "Trump Hosted Zuckerberg for Undisclosed Dinner at the White House in October," *NBC News*, November 20, 2019, https://www.nbcnews.com/tech/tech-news/trump-hosted-zuckerberg-undisclosed-dinner-white-house-october-n1087986.

330 Change the Terms: "Reducing Hate Online," Change the Terms, July 20, 2021, https://www.changetheterms.org/.

330 Stop Hate for Profit: "Stop Hate for Profit," Color of Change, June 19, 2020, https://colorofchange.org/stop-hate-for-profit/.

331 the freest speech will benefit only: Joan Donovan, "How Trump Put Himself in Charge of Twitter's Decency Standards," *Washington Post*, July 19, 2019, https://www.washingtonpost.com/outlook/2019/07/19/how-trump-put-himself-charge-twitters-decency-standards/.

EPILOGUE

334 charged with conspiracy: *United States of America v Thomas Caldwell et. al.* (United States District Court for the District of Columbia, May 26, 2021).

334 subpoenaed to testify: "Select Committee Subpoenas Nicholas J. Fuentes & Patrick Casey," Select Committee to Investigate the January 6th Attack on the United States Capitol, January 19, 2022, https://january6th.house.gov/news/press-releases/select-committee-subpoenas-nicholas-j-fuentes-patrick-casey.

335 arrested on January 15: Aja Romano, "Baked Alaska, Alt-Right Troll Arrested for the Capitol Riot, Explained," *Vox*, January 17, 2021, https://www.vox.com/22235691/baked-alaska-tim-gionet-arrest-capitol-riot-alt-right-buzzfeed.

335 charged with violent and disorderly conduct: Michael Kunzelman, "'Baked Alaska,' Far-Right Troll Charged in Capitol Riots, Avoids House Arrest,"

Alaska Public Media, June 7, 2021, https://www.alaskapublic.org/2021/06/06/baked-alaska-far-right-troll-charged-in-capitol-riots-avoids-house-arrest/.

336 "We will treat them fairly": "Trump Says He Would Pardon Jan. 6 Rioters If He Runs and Wins," Reuters, January 29, 2022, https://www.reuters.com/world/us/trump-says-he-would-pardon-jan-6-rioters-if-he-runs-wins-2022-01-30/.

IMAGE CREDITS

INTRODUCTION

p. 1   inhauscreative via Getty Images.

p. 6   Andrew Caballero-Reynolds via Getty Images.

p. 15 Unknown, *Meme War Veteran*, February 20, 2017, meme, Imgur, https://imgur.com/GCf3Uvk.

CHAPTER 1: WE ARE THE 99 PERCENT

p. 23 David Shankbone, *Day 36 Occupy Wall Street October 21 2011 Shankbone 46*, October 21, 2011, photograph, Creative Commons, https://commons.wikimedia.org/wiki/File:Day_36_Occupy_Wall_Street_October_21_2011_Shankbone_46.JPG, CC BY 3.0 https://creativecommons.org/licenses/by/3.0/deed.en.

p. 27 Dbking (David), *Tea Party Protest Sign During the Taxpayer March on Washington*, September 12, 2009, photograph, Creative Commons, https://commons.wikimedia.org/wiki/File:Day_36_Occupy_Wall_Street_October_21_2011_Shankbone_46.JPG CC BY 4.0 https://creativecommons.org/licenses/by/4.0/.

p. 31 Ilias Bartolini, *We Are the 99%*, October 16, 2011, photograph, Flickr, https://www.flickr.com/photos/45538835@N05/6247188828, CC BY 4.0 https://creativecommons.org/licenses/by/4.0/.

p. 32 Adbusters Media Foundation, *What is Our One Demand, Adbusters America #97—Post Anarchism*, July 2011, pages 50–51, accessed via Internet Archive https://archive.org/details/adbusters-56-were-back/Adbusters%20%2397%20-%20Post%20Anarchism/.

p. 38 Unknown, *Ron Paul Revolution*, January 20, 2008 (upload date), meme, Wikimedia, https://commons.wikimedia.org/wiki/File:Ron_Paul_revolution.jpg.

p. 39 Roger Sayles, *Granny Warrior's Ron Paul Bus—Lake Jackson, TX*, February 2012, photograph, Flickr, https://www.flickr.com/photos/serfs-up/8494845512/, CC BY-ND 4.0 https://creativecommons.org/licenses/by-nd/4.0/.

p. 42   Unknown, *It's Happening*, January 2012, meme, 4chan, accessed via Know Your Meme, https://knowyourmeme.com/photos/242631-doom -paul-its-happening.

p. 43   Unknown, *Doom Paul / It's Happening—Image #543,992*, May 2013, meme, accessed via Know Your Meme, https://knowyourmeme.com/photos /543992-doom-paul-its-happening.

CHAPTER 2: A SAFE SPACE FOR HATE

p. 49   Dylann Roof, title unknown, date unknown, photograph, The Last Rhodesian, accessed via Internet Archive https://archive.org/details/Dy lannRoofPhotoCollectionFromWebSiteLastRhodesian.com/.

p. 52   A W Mann, title unknown, date unknown, illustration, accessed at Resist .com via Internet Archive, https://web.archive.org/web/20041128124506 /http://www.resist.com/CARTOON%20GALLERY/KIKES/jews _image15.jpg.

p. 54   Unknown, title unknown, November 26, 2016 (upload date), meme, Imgur, https://imgur.com/LGWMntK.

p. 55   Unknown, *Population of /pol/*, December 2015 (upload date), meme, Imgur, https://imgur.com/Tkk7FCu.

p. 56   Andrew Anglin, *The Daily Stormer Logo and Banner*, September 7, 2016, graphic, accessed via Wikimedia, https://commons.wikimedia.org/wiki /File:Daily_Stormer_logo.png.

p. 59   Unknown, *Change, Hope—Hang, Rope*, date unknown, meme, accessed via FunnyJunk https://funnyjunk.com/Change+hope+hang+rope/funny -pictures/5380752/.

p. 68   Unknown, *Black and White IQ Distribution*, circa 2014, infographic, accessed via https://i.4pcdn.org/pol/1435886197172.jpg.

CHAPTER 3: GAMERS RISE UP

p. 78   Unknown, *Supreme Gentleman*, May 24, 2014, meme, Imgur, https://imgur .com/Zoo9JEY.

p. 82   Unknown, *We All Know That Feel*, circa 2011, meme, accessed via Esquilo .io, https://esquilo.io/png/i-know-that-feel-bro-png-picture.

p. 83   LeWeb14, *Milo Yiannopoulos, Founder & Editor-in-Chief, The Kernel @ LeWeb London 2012 Central Hall Westminster-1883*, Creative Commons.

p. 86   Unknown, title unknown (variation of Gamergate logo), September 2, 2014, meme, 4chan, accessed via Internet Archive, https://web.archive.org/web /20140903171832/http://archive.moe/v/thread/261310162/#q261312315, https://usergallery.gamer-info.com/17679/cf3bf64134155da2a7aa214ad5 900430.jpg.

p. 98   Antifemcomics, *Inside the Feminist Mind*, circa 2015, meme, Twitter, accessed via https://web.elastic.org/~fche/mirrors/antifemcomics/.

p. 105   Unknown, *I Am a Social Justice Warrior,* July 5, 2014, meme, 4chan, accessed via Know Your Meme, https://knowyourmeme.com/photos/788452-2014 -tumblr-4chan-raids.

CHAPTER 4: TROLL IN CHIEF

p. 108   SOPA Images via Getty Images.

p. 113   Unknown, *Trump the Bankrupt Millionaire,* circa August 2016, meme, accessed via Know Your Meme, https://knowyourmeme.com/photos /1154171-donald-trump.

p. 118   Unknown, *Smug Frog,* circa 2011, meme, accessed via Know Your meme, https://knowyourmeme.com/memes/smug-frog.

p. 119   Unknown, title unknown (God Emperor Trump), circa 2015, meme, accessed via 4plebs, http://archive.4plebs.org/pol/thread/55116222/#q55116698.

p. 120   Unknown, title unknown (Trump Border Pepe), circa July 2015, meme, 4chan, accessed via 4plebs, http://archive.4plebs.org/pol/thread/48506166 /#48507382.

p. 128   Unknown, title unknown (MAGA Flag Wojak), circa March 2016, meme, 4chan, accessed via 4plebs, http://archive.4plebs.org/pol/thread/65842019 /#65842603.

p. 134   Donald Trump [@realdonaldtrump], *Meme of Ted Cruz (Liar Liar),* Instagram, March 26, 2016, https://www.instagram.com/p/BDEHPEgmhRv/.

p. 144   Donald Trump Jr [@donaldtrumpjr], *The Deplorables,* Instagram, September 10, 2016, https://www.instagram.com/p/BKMtdN5Bam5/.

p. 146   Unknown, title unknown (Grab'em By the Pussy), circa October 2016, meme, accessed via Stripers Online, https://www.stripersonline.com /surftalk/topic/807843-biden-proves-foot-is-ok-by-bending-his-knee /#comment-15554681

p. 153   Unknown, *me irl* (Pepe White House), meme, imgur, November 9, 2016, https://imgur.com/awYyp5C.

p. 154   Unknown, *Liberal Stages of Life,* meme, circa November 2016, https://pbs .twimg.com/media/CzBsa4zUoAAtMa_.jpg.

CHAPTER 5: HE WILL NOT DIVIDE US

p. 156   Win McNamee / Staff via Getty Images.

p. 171   sjjr, *If You're Decent and You Know It, Punch a Nazi,* January 27, 2017, Imgur, https://imgur.com/gallery/zXB4W.

p. 172   Unknown, title unknown, (Trump inauguration), circa January 2017, meme, accessed via Starecat, https://starecat.com/to-be-fair-inauguration-obama -2009-trump-2017-white-empty-area-is-ku-klux-klan/.

p. 174   Shia LaBeouf [@thecampaignbook], *He Will Not Divide Us,* January 20, 2017, photograph, Twitter, https://twitter.com/thecampaignbook/status /822443598771785732.

p. 176 Unknown, *Museum of Kek*, uploaded January 21, 2017, Imgur, photograph, https://imgur.com/r/4chan/3V1tP.

p. 178 Million Dollar Extreme, *Sam Hyde with Rifle*, October 21, 2016, video still, accessed via Wikimedia, https://commons.wikimedia.org/wiki /File:Sam_Hyde.jpg, CC BY 3.0 https://creativecommons.org/licenses/by /3.0/deed.en.

CHAPTER 6: UNITE THE RIGHT

p. 184 Unknown, title unknown (Meme War Veteran Pepe), circa January 2017, meme, 4chan, accessed via 4plebs, http://archive.4plebs.org/pol/thread /106415262/#106419854.

p. 189 Bill Pugliano / Stringer via Getty Images.

p. 192 Unknown, title unknown (CNN Blackmail), circa July 2017, meme, accessed via Twitter, https://twitter.com/CustardPancake/status/88255560 6732636160.

p. 197 Jason Kessler [@maddimension], *Unite the Right*, flyer, Discord, accessed via Unicorn Riot Discord leaks, https://discordleaks.unicornriot.ninja /discord/view/224938#msg.

p. 198 Fox Tx, *Join or Die*, June 28, 2017, flyer, Discord, accessed via Unicorn Riot Discord Leaks, https://discordleaks.unicornriot.ninja/discord/ view/200517#msg.

p. 199 NurPhoto via Getty Images.

p. 205 Unknown, title unknown (Here Comes a New Challenger), circa September 2017, meme, 4chan, accessed via 4plebs, http://archive .4plebs.org/pol/thread/141977366/#q141982348.

p. 210 Unknown, title unknown (IOTBW Pepe), November 2011, Imgur, meme, accessed via https://i.4pcdn.org/pol/1603073923227.png.

CHAPTER 7: JOKER POLITICS

p. 212 Unknown, *America First with Nicholas J Fuentes*, circa 2017, collage, accessed via https://m.media-amazon.com/images/M/MV5BMWMw OWYoNDEtMThiMCooYmNlLTliODItZDI4MWVlMTQzN TcoXkEyXkFqcGdeQXVyMzEzMzcyMjU@._V1_.jpg.

p. 219 Unknown, *When Did Everything Get So Cozy*, circa 2017, meme, accessed via https://i.4pcdn.org/pol/1512549094834.png.

p. 223 Unknown, title unknown (Saint Tarrant), circa March 2019, meme, accessed via https://i.4pcdn.org/pol/1552944496614.jpg.

p. 227 Unknown, title unknown (Clown World), circa 2019, meme, accessed via https://torako.wakarimasen.moe/file/torako/biz/image/1600/68/160068 1076861.jpg.

p. 229 Unknown, title unknown (Obama Socialism Joker), circa 2009, poster, accessed via https://www.pngkey.com/download/u2e6t4e6q80oi1i1_dont -know-who-to-attribute-the-original-links/.

p. 230 Unknown, *Be careful with what you wished for*, April 10, 2015, meme, 9gag, accessed via Internet Archive, https://web.archive.org/web/20150414071913/https://9gag.com/gag/aXpWo46.

p. 231 Unknown, title unknown (Joker Groyper), circa 2019, meme, accessed via 4plebs http://archive.4plebs.org/pol/thread/232225100/#232231754.

p. 233 Yankee (marv mode) [@nervousamerican], *Walking Groyper*, July 14, 2019, meme, Twitter, https://twitter.com/nervousamerican/status/11505289 47517644801.

CHAPTER 8: THESE PEOPLE ARE SICK

p. 239 VoxDawg, *Q Gadsden*, July 3, 2018, meme, Imgur, https://imgur.com/t/wwg1wga/7IDaxG6.

p. 240 Unknown, title unknown (Until You Wake Up, We Will Fight For You), circa 2019, accessed via Neon Revolt, https://www.neonrevolt.com/wp-content/uploads/2019/12/f102690bf1a9b37ce61c3f534ddoa06 46fc6e4501ae8978a3a6b6c4b57ef4277_compressed.jpg?w=640.

p. 246 MyFortis via Getty Images.

p. 249 Maga_Patriot, *General Flynn I Digital Army*, circa 2019, meme, Imgflip, https://imgflip.com/i/2mb5t2.

p. 260 Unknown, title unknown (Trump Q), November 6, 2019, meme, Imgur, https://imgur.com/KeJ2Bws.

p. 265 Zach Gibson / Stringer via Getty Images.

CHAPTER 9: FUCK AROUND AND FIND OUT

p. 269 Mark Makela/Stringer via Getty Images

p. 271 Unknown, *I Love You Ebola Chan*, August 7, 2014, meme, 4chan, accessed via Know Your Meme, https://knowyourmeme.com/memes/ebola-chan.

p. 271 Unknown, *Corona Chan*, January 22, 2020, meme, 4chan, accessed via 4plebs, http://archive.4plebs.org/pol/thread/240435037/#240436890.

p. 273 Unknown, title unknown (Hazmat Apu), January 2020, meme, 4chan, accessed via 4plebs, http://archive.4plebs.org/pol/chunk/240849756/#240850161.

p. 275 Unknown, title unknown (Covid Deaths Meme), circa Spring 2020, infographic, accessed via Twitter, https://twitter.com/Voice_OfReality/status/1261854218975096832.

p. 278 Don Emmert via Getty Images.

p. 283 Deathschemist [@deathschemist1] *Fuck Around and Find Out*, June 9, 2020, meme, Twitter, https://twitter.com/deathschemist1/status/12704748379 20800769.

p. 294 Unknown, title unknown (Apu Kyle), circa August 2020, meme, 4chan, accessed via 4plebs, http://archive.4plebs.org/pol/thread/274667663/#274670673.

p. 299 Unknown, title unknown (Dick Pic War), circa November 2020, meme, 4chan, accessed via https://i.4pcdn.org/pol/1598496026771.jpg.

p. 302 Unknown, title unknown (Maga Copium), circa November 2020, meme, Twitter, accessed via https://pbs.twimg.com/media/Emg5AAlXIAEpPeV .jpg.

CHAPTER 10: STOP THE STEAL

p. 303 Baked Alaska, *Trump Rally DC*, January 6, 2021, screenshot, DLive, accessed via Bitchute, https://www.bitchute.com/video/EZ2EhdN2klAe/.

p. 305 Robert Nickelsberg via Getty Images.

p. 308 NurPhoto via Getty Images.

p. 313 Robert Nickelsberg via Getty Images.

p. 328 Robyn Beck via Getty Images.

INDEX

Note: Page numbers in *italics* indicate images.

A NOTE ON THE AUTHORS

Joan Donovan, PhD, is the research director of Harvard Kennedy School's Shorenstein Center and one of the world's foremost experts on media and disinformation. **Emily Dreyfuss** is a journalist who covers the intersection of society and technology; her writing has appeared in *Wired*, the *Atlantic*, and the *New York Times*, among other publications. **Brian Friedberg** is an ethnographer at Harvard Kennedy School who researches far-right and political communities online and has published definitive QAnon explainers in *Wired* and the *Hill*. Together, the authors work on Harvard Kennedy School's Technology and Social Change Research Project.